An Introductory Dictionary of Lacanian Psychoanalysis

Jacques Lacan is arguably the most original and influential psychoanalytic thinker since Freud. His ideas have revolutionised the clinical practice of psychoanalysis and continue to have a major impact in fields as diverse as film studies, literary criticism, feminist theory and philosophy. Lacan's writings are notorious for their complexity and idiosyncratic style and *An Introductory Dictionary of Lacanian Psychoanalysis* will be invaluable for reading in every discipline where his influence is felt.

Detailed definitions are provided for over two hundred Lacanian terms. Attention is given both to Lacan's use of common psychoanalytic terms and how his own terminology developed through the various stages of his teaching. Taking full account of the clinical basis of Lacan's work, the dictionary details the historical and institutional background to Lacanian ideas. Each major concept is traced back to its origins in the work of Freud, Saussure, Hegel and others.

An Introductory Dictionary of Lacanian Psychoanalysis provides a unique source of reference for psychoanalysts in training and in practice. Placing Lacan's ideas in their clinical context, the dictionary is also an ideal companion for readers in other disciplines.

Dylan Evans trained as a Lacanian psychoanalyst in Buenos Aires, London and Paris. He is a Lecturer in Psychoanalytic Studies at the University of Brunel and is in private practice in London.

An Introductory Dictionary of Lacanian Psychoanalysis

Dylan Evans

London and New York

First published 1996
by Routledge
11 New Fetter Lane, London EC4P 4EE

Simultaneously published in the USA and Canada
by Routledge
29 West 35th Street, New York, NY 10001

Typeset in Times by J&L Composition Ltd, Filey, North Yorkshire
Printed and bound in Great Britain by
TJ Press (Padstow) Ltd, Padstow, Cornwall

British Library Cataloguing in Publication Data
A catalogue record for this book is available from the British Library

Library of Congress Cataloguing in Publication Data
A catalogue record for this book has been requested

ISBN 0–415–13522–2
      0–415–13523–0 (pbk)

Contents

List of figures

Preface

My discourse proceeds in the following way: each term is sustained only in its topological relation with the others.

Jacques Lacan (S11, 89)

Psychoanalytic theories are languages in which to discuss psychoanalytic treatment. Today there are many such languages, each with its own particular lexis and syntax. The fact that these languages use many of the same terms, inherited from Freud, can create the impression that they are in fact all dialects of the same language. Such an impression is, however, misleading. Each psychoanalytic theory articulates these terms in a unique way, as well as introducing new terms of its own, and is thus a unique language, ultimately untranslatable. One of the most important psychoanalytic languages in use today is that developed by the French psychoanalyst, Jacques Lacan (1901–81). This dictionary is an attempt to explore and elucidate this language, which has often been accused of being infuriatingly obscure and sometimes of constituting a totally incomprehensible 'psychotic' system. This obscurity has even been seen as a deliberate attempt to ensure that Lacanian discourse remains the exclusive property of a small intellectual elite, and to protect it from external criticism. If this is the case, then this dictionary is a move in the other direction, an attempt to open Lacanian discourse up to wider scrutiny and critical engagement.

The dictionary is an ideal way of exploring a language since it has the same structure as a language; it is a synchronic system in which the terms have no positive existence, since they are each defined by their mutual differences; it is a closed, self-referential structure in which meaning is nowhere fully present but always delayed in continual metonymy; it defines each term by reference to other terms and thus denies the novice reader any point of entry (and, to refer to a Lacanian formula, if there is no point of entry, there can be no sexual relationship).

Many others have perceived the value of the dictionary as a tool for exploring psychoanalytic theory. The most famous example is the classic dictionary of psychoanalysis by Laplanche and Pontalis (1967). There is also the short dictionary by Rycroft (1968) which is extremely readable. In addition to these two dictionaries which concentrate mainly on Freud, there are also dictionaries of Kleinian psychoanalysis (Hinshelwood, 1989), of Jungian psychoanalysis (Samuels *et al.*, 1986), and of psychoanalysis and feminism (Wright, 1992).

A dictionary of Lacanian psychoanalysis is conspicuous by its absence from the above list. It is not that no such dictionary has yet been written; there are, in fact, a number of dictionaries in French that deal extensively with Lacanian terms (Chemama, 1993; Kauftman, 1994), and even a humorous Lacanian dictionary (Saint-Drôme, 1994). However, none of these has yet been translated, and thus the anglophone student of Lacan has been left without a useful tool of reference. The dictionaries by Laplanche and Pontalis (1967) and by Wright (1992) include articles on some Lacanian terms, but not many. A few English-language publications have included glossaries which provide a key to a number of Lacanian terms (e.g. Sheridan, 1977; Roustang, 1986), but these too include only a few terms, with extremely brief remarks attached to each. The present work will therefore go some way towards filling an obvious gap in reference material in psychoanalysis.

While many have seen the value of the dictionary as a tool for exploring psychoanalytic languages, not so many have been fully aware of the dangers involved. One important danger is that, by emphasising the synchronic structure of language, the dictionary can obscure the diachronic dimension. All languages, including those which are otherwise known as psychoanalytic theories, are in a continual state of flux, since they change with use. By overlooking this dimension, the dictionary can create the erroneous impression that languages are fixed unchanging entities.

This dictionary attempts to avoid this danger by incorporating etymological information wherever appropriate and by giving some indication of how Lacan's discourse evolved over the course of his teaching. Lacan's engagement with psychoanalytic theory spans fifty years, and it is hardly surprising that his discourse underwent important changes during this time. However, these changes are not always well understood. Broadly speaking, there are two main ways of misrepresenting them. On the one hand, some commentators present the development of Lacan's thought in terms of dramatic and sudden 'epistemological breaks'; 1953, for example, is sometimes presented as the moment of a radically new 'linguistic turn' in Lacan's work. On the other hand, some writers go to the other extreme and present Lacan's work as a single unfolding narrative with no changes of direction, as if all the concepts existed from the beginning.

In discussing how the various terms in Lacan's discourse undergo semantic shifts during the course of his work, I have tried to avoid both of these errors. By showing how the changes are often gradual and hesitant, I hope to problematise the simplistic narratives of epistemological breaks. One important point that such narratives ignore is that whenever Lacan's terms acquire new meanings, they never lose their older ones; his theoretical vocabulary advances by means of accretion rather than mutation. On the other hand, by pointing out the changes and semantic shifts, I hope to counter the illusion that all of Lacan's concepts are always already there (an illusion which Lacan himself condemns; Lacan, 1966c: 67). In this way it should be possible to appreciate both the elements that remain constant in Lacan's teaching and those that shift and evolve.

The dictionary contains entries for over two hundred terms used by Lacan in the course of his work. Many more terms could have been included, and the main criterion for selecting these terms rather than others is one of frequency. The reader will therefore find entries for such terms as 'symbolic', 'neurosis', and other such terms which figure prominently in Lacan's work, but not to other terms such as 'holophrase', which Lacan only discusses on three or four occasions.

In addition to terms frequently employed by Lacan, a few other terms have been included which Lacan employs infrequently or not at all. In this group are terms which serve to provide a historical and theoretical context for Lacan's own terms (e.g. 'Kleinian psychoanalysis'), and terms which bring together an important set of related themes in his work which would otherwise be distributed among disparate entries (e.g. 'sexual difference').

Besides the criteria of frequency and contextual information, the selection of terms has also, inevitably, been governed by my own particular way of reading Lacan. Another writer, with a different reading of Lacan, would undoubtedly have made a different selection of terms. I do not pretend that the reading implicit in my selection of terms is the only or the best reading of Lacan. It is one reading of Lacan among many, as partial and selective as any other.

The partiality and limitations of this dictionary concern not only the matter of the selection of terms, but also the matter of sources. Thus the dictionary is not based on the complete works of Lacan, which have not yet been published in their entirety, but only on a selection of his works (mainly the published works, plus a few unpublished ones). This almost exclusive reliance on published material means that there are inevitably gaps in the dictionary. However, as Lacan himself points out, 'the condition of any reading is, of course, that it impose limits on itself' (S20, 62).

The aim has not been, therefore, to present a work of the same breadth and detail as the classic dictionary by Laplanche and Pontalis, but merely to present a broad outline of the most salient terms in Lacanian discourse; hence the adjective 'introductory' in the title. At a future date it may be possible to produce a more comprehensive and detailed edition of this dictionary based on Lacan's complete works, but the current absence of any English-language dictionary of Lacanian thought is perhaps sufficient justification for publishing the work in its present incomplete and rudimentary state. This dictionary may thus be thought of as a resistance, in the way Lacan defined resistance, as 'the present state of an interpretation' (S2, 228).

Another self-imposed limitation has been the decision to restrict references to secondary sources to a minimum. Thus the reader will find few allusions to Lacan's commentators and intellectual heirs. To exclude references to the work of present-day Lacanian analysts is not such a grave omission as it might seem, since this work has consisted almost entirely of *commentaries* on Lacan rather than of radically original developments (the work of Jacques-Alain Miller is a notable exception). Such a scenario is completely different to that of Klein's thought, which has been developed in very original ways by such followers as Paula Heimann, Wilfred Bion, Donald Meltzer and others.

However, to exclude references to the work of Lacan's more radical critics, such as Jacques Derrida, Hélène Cixous and Luce Irigaray, or to those who have applied his work in the fields of literary criticism and film theory, may seem a more glaring omission. There are two main reasons for this omission. Firstly, it is often forgotten in the English-speaking world that Lacan's work is first and foremost aimed at providing analysts with help in conducting analytic treatment. By excluding references to the applications of Lacan's work in literary criticism, film studies and feminist theory I hope to emphasise this point and thus to counter the neglect of Lacan's clinical basis by his English-speaking readers. Secondly, I also want to encourage the reader to engage directly with Lacan himself, on Lacan's own terms, without prejudicing the debate for or against him by reference to his admirers or to his critics. However, there are some exceptions to this rule of omission, when the debate around a particular term has seemed to be so important that it would be misleading to omit all reference to it (e.g. 'phallus', 'gaze').

My decision to stress the clinical basis of Lacan's work is not aimed at excluding non-analysts from engaging with Lacan. On the contrary; the dictionary is aimed not only at psychoanalysts, but also at readers approaching Lacan's work from other disciplines. Lacan himself actively encouraged debate between psychoanalysts and philosophers, linguists, mathematicians, anthropologists and others, and today there is growing interest in Lacanian psychoanalysis in many other areas, especially in film studies, feminist theory and literary criticism. For those with backgrounds in these disciplines the difficulties involved in reading Lacan can be especially great precisely due to their unfamiliarity with the dynamics of psychoanalytic treatment. By stressing the clinical basis of Lacan's work, I hope to situate the terms in their proper context and thus make them clearer to readers who are not psychoanalysts. It is my belief that this is important even for those readers who wish to use Lacan's work in other areas such as cultural theory.

Another problem for readers approaching Lacan's work from non-psychoanalytic backgrounds may be their unfamiliarity with the Freudian tradition in which Lacan worked. This dictionary addresses this issue by presenting, in many cases, a short summary of the way Freud used the term, before outlining the specifically Lacanian usage. Because of their brevity, these summaries run the risk of oversimplifying complex concepts, and will undoubtedly strike those more familiar with Freud's work as somewhat rudimentary. Nevertheless, it is hoped that they will be helpful to those readers unversed in Freud.

Given the wide range of readers at whom this dictionary is aimed, one problem has been to decide the level of complexity at which to pitch the entries. The solution attempted here has been to pitch different entries at different levels. There is thus a basic core of entries pitched at a low level of complexity, some of which present the most fundamental terms in Lacan's discourse (e.g. 'psychoanalysis', 'mirror stage', 'language'), while others sketch the historical context in which these terms evolved (e.g. Freud (return to), 'International Psycho-Analytical Association', 'school', 'seminar', 'ego-psychology'). These entries then refer the reader to more complex terms, which are pitched at a higher level and which the beginner should not hope to grasp immediately. This will I hope allow the reader to find some kind of direction in navigating through the dictionary. However, the dictionary is not an 'introduction to Lacan'; there are already plenty of introductory works on Lacan available in English (e.g. Benvenuto and Kennedy, 1986; Bowie, 1991; Grosz, 1990; Lemaire, 1970; Sarup, 1992), including some excellent ones (e.g. Žižek, 1991; Leader, 1995). The dictionary is, rather, an *introductory reference book*, a guide which the reader may refer back to in order to answer a specific question or to follow up a particular line of enquiry. It is not meant to be a substitute for reading Lacan, but a companion to such reading. For this reason copious page references have been provided throughout the dictionary, the intention being to allow the reader to go back to the text and place the references in context.

Another problem concerns the issue of translation. Different translators have used different words to render Lacan's terminology into English. For example Alan Sheridan and John Forrester render Lacan's opposition between *sens* and *signification* as 'meaning' and 'signification', whereas Stuart Schneiderman prefers 'sense' and 'meaning' respectively. Anthony Wilden renders *parole* as 'word', whereas Sheridan prefers 'speech'. In all cases, I have followed Sheridan's usage, on the grounds that it is his translations of Lacan's *Écrits* and *The Seminar, Book XI, The Four Fundamental Concepts of Psychoanalysis* that are still the main texts for readers of Lacan in English. In order to avoid possible confusion, the French terms used by Lacan are also given along with the English translations. I have also followed Sheridan's practice of leaving certain terms untranslated (e.g. *jouissance*), again on the grounds that this has become established practice in anglophone Lacanian discourse (although I personally agree with Forrester's criticisms of such a practice; see Forrester, 1990: 99–101).

The one issue on which I differ from Sheridan is my decision to leave his algebraic symbols in their original form. For example I have left the symbols A and *a* as they are, rather than translating them as O and *o* as Sheridan does. Not only is this common practice in translating Lacan into other languages (such as Spanish and Portuguese), but Lacan himself preferred his 'little letters' to remain untranslated. Furthermore, as has become clear at the various international conferences of Lacanian psychoanalysis, it is very useful for analysts with different mother-tongues to have some basic symbols in common which can facilitate their discussions of Lacan.

With respect to the English words used to translate Freud's German terms, I have generally adopted those used by James Strachey in the *Standard Edition*, with the exception (now common practice) of rendering *Trieb* as 'drive' rather than 'instinct'.

Another, more fundamental problem is the paradox involved in the very act of writing a dictionary of Lacanian terms. Dictionaries usually attempt to pin down the meaning(s) of each term and eradicate ambiguity. The whole thrust of Lacan's discourse, however, subverts any such attempt to halt the continual slippage of the signified under the signifier. His style, notorious for its difficulty and complexity, was, argues Derrida, deliberately constructed 'so as to check almost permanently any access to an isolatable content, to an unequivocal, determinable meaning beyond writing' (Derrida, 1975: 420). To attempt to provide 'adequate definitions' for Lacan's terms would therefore be completely at odds with Lacan's work, as Alan Sheridan remarks in his translator's note to *Écrits* (Sheridan, 1977: vii). In Sheridan's short glossary of Lacanian terms, which appears in the same translator's note, he points out that Lacan himself preferred that certain terms be left without any comment at all, 'on the grounds that any comment would prejudice its effective operation' (Sheridan, 1977: vii). In these cases, Lacan prefers to leave 'the reader to develop an appreciation of the concepts in the course of their use' (Sheridan, 1977: xi).

On the basis of these comments it would seem that, contrary to my initial statements about a dictionary being an ideal way to explore Lacan's work, nothing could be further from the spirit of that work than to enclose it in a dictionary. Perhaps this is true. It is certainly true that no one ever learned a language by reading a dictionary. However, I have not tried to provide 'adequate definitions' for each term, but simply to evoke some of their complexity, to show something of the way they shift during the course of Lacan's work, and to provide some indication of the overall architecture of Lacan's discourse. As the entries are arranged in alphabetical order, instead of being ordered according to a particular construction, readers can start wherever they wish, and then refer back to Lacan's texts and/or follow the cross-references to other terms in the dictionary. In this way, each reader will find their own way through the dictionary, as each one, as Lacan himself would have said, is led by their desire to know.

Dylan Evans
London, June 1995

The format of the dictionary

Except when a word is always used in the same language (e.g. *objet petit a, aphanisis*), the heading for each entry is in English. Where appropriate, the English term is followed immediately by the French original in brackets.

The use of the masculine personal pronoun should not be taken to imply an exclusive reference to the male sex.

Cross-references to other entries in the dictionary are indicated by small capitals.

Page references are to the English translations where these exist, and to the French originals in the case of works for which no English translation has yet been published. In the case of the most commonly cited works, the following abbreviations have been used:

E   Jacques Lacan, *Écrits. A Selection*, trans. Alan Sheridan, London: Tavistock Publications, 1977 (see Appendix).

Ec   Jacques Lacan, *Écrits*, Paris: Seuil, 1966 (see Appendix).

S1   Jacques Lacan, *The Seminar. Book I. Freud's Papers on Technique, 1953–54*, trans. with notes by John Forrester, New York: Norton; Cambridge: Cambridge University Press, 1988.

S2   Jacques Lacan, *The Seminar. Book II. The Ego in Freud's Theory and in the Technique of Psychoanalysis, 1954–55*, trans. Sylvana Tomaselli, notes by John Forrester, New York: Norton; Cambridge: Cambridge University Press, 1988.

S3   Jacques Lacan, *The Seminar. Book III. The Psychoses, 1955–56*, trans. Russell Grigg, notes by Russell Grigg, London: Routledge, 1993.

S4   Jacques Lacan, *Le Séminaire. Livre IV. La relation d'objet, 1956–57*, ed. Jacques-Alain Miller, Paris: Seuil, 1994.

S7   Jacques Lacan, *The Seminar. Book VII. The Ethics of Psychoanalysis, 1959–60*, trans. Dennis Porter, notes by Dennis Porter, London: Routledge, 1992.

S8   Jacques Lacan, *Le Séminaire. Livre VIII. Le transfert, 1960–61*, ed. Jacques-Alain Miller, Paris: Seuil, 1991.

S11 Jacques Lacan, *The Seminar. Book XI. The Four Fundamental*

Concepts of Psychoanalysis, 1964, trans. Alan Sheridan, London: Hogarth Press and Institute of Psycho-Analysis, 1977.

S17 Jacques Lacan, *Le Séminaire. Livre XVII. L'envers de la psychanalyse, 1969–70*, ed. Jacques-Alain Miller, Paris: Seuil, 1991.

S20 Jacques Lacan, *Le Séminaire. Livre XX. Encore, 1972–73*, ed. Jacques-Alain Miller, Paris: Seuil, 1975.

SE Sigmund Freud, *Standard Edition of the Complete Psychological Works of Sigmund Freud* (24 volumes), translated and edited by James Strachey in collaboration with Anna Freud, assisted by Alix Strachey and Alan Tyson, London: Hogarth Press and the Institute of Psycho-Analysis; New York: Norton, 1953–74.

Acknowledgements

Acknowledgements are due to Cambridge University Press and to Norton for permission to quote from and reproduce a figure from *The Seminar. Book I. Freud's Papers on Technique, 1953–54* (trans. John Forrester, with notes by John Forrester, Cambridge University Press, 1987) and to quote from *The Seminar. Book II. The Ego in Freud's Theory and in the Technique of Psychoanalysis, 1954–55* (trans. Sylvana Tomaselli, notes by John Forrester, Cambridge University Press, 1988).

Acknowledgements are due to Norton for permission to quote and reproduce figures from the following publications, all by Jacques Lacan: *Écrits: A Selection* (trans. Alan Sheridan, New York: Norton, 1977); *Écrits* (Paris: Seuil, 1966); *Le Séminaire. Livre IV. La relation d'objet* (ed. Jacques-Alain Miller, Paris: Seuil, 1994); *Le Séminaire. Livre XVII. L'envers de la psychanalyse* (ed. Jacques-Alain Miller, Paris: Seuil, 1991); *Le Séminaire. Livre XX. Encore* (ed. Jacques-Alain Miller, Paris: Seuil, 1975).

My thanks go to all those who have helped in various ways in the production of this dictionary. Julia Borossa, Christine Bousfield, Vincent Dachy, Alison Hall, Eric Harper, Michele Julien, Michael Kennedy, Richard Klein, Darian Leader, David Macey, Alan Rowan, Gerry Sullivan, Fernando S. Teixeira Filho and Luke Thurston all read parts of the typescript and suggested some improvements, as did an anonymous Routledge reader. Needlesss to say, the responsibility for any errors is entirely mine. I am especially grateful to Luke Thurston for writing the article on *sinthome*. Edwina Welham and Patricia Stankiewicz at Routledge supervised the transition from typescript to printed volume.

It remains only to thank my partner, Marcela Olmedo, for her patient support during the writing of this dictionary, and for her help with the artwork.

Chronology

Below is a brief chronology which lists some of the major events in Lacan's life. This chronology has been compiled on the basis of the information provided by Bowie (1991: 204–13), Macey (1988: ch. 7) and, above all, Roudinesco (1986, 1993). Those who are interested in more detailed information are advised to consult these three sources, as well as Forrester (1990: ch. 6), Miller (1981), and Turkle (1978). For more anecdotal accounts see Clément (1981) and Schneiderman (1983).

1901   Jacques-Marie Émile Lacan born on 13 April in Paris, the first child of Alfred Lacan and Émilie Baudry.

1903   Birth of Madeleine, Lacan's sister (25 December).

1908   Birth of Marc-François, Lacan's brother (25 December).

1910   Freud founds the International Psycho-Analytical Association (IPA).

1919   Lacan finishes his secondary education at the Collège Stanislas.

1921   Lacan is discharged from military service because of thinness. In the following years he studies medicine in Paris.

1926   Lacan's first collaborative publication appears in the *Revue Neurologique*. The Société Psychanalytique de Paris (SPP) is founded.

1927   Lacan begins his clinical training in psychiatry.

1928   Lacan studies under Gaëtan Gatian de Clérambault at the special infirmary for the insane attached to the Police Préfecture.

1929   Lacan's brother, Marc-François, joins the Benedictines.

1930   Lacan publishes his first non-collaborative article in *Annales Médico-Psychologiques*.

1931   Lacan becomes increasingly interested in surrealism and meets Salvador Dalí.

1932   Lacan publishes his doctoral dissertation (*On paranoiac psychosis in its relations to the personality*) and sends a copy to Freud. Freud acknowledges receipt by postcard.

1933 Two articles by Lacan are published in the surrealist journal *Minotaure*. Alexandre Kojève begins lecturing on Hegel's *Phenomenology of Spirit* at the École des Hautes Études. Lacan attends these lectures regularly over the following years.

1934 Lacan, who is already in analysis with Rudolph Loewenstein, joins the SPP as a candidate member. He marries Marie-Louise Blondin in January, who gives birth to their first child, Caroline, the same month.

1935 Marc-François Lacan is ordained priest.

1936 Lacan presents his paper on the mirror stage to the fourteenth congress of the IPA at Marienbad on 3 August. He sets up private practice as a psychoanalyst.

1938 Lacan becomes a full member of the SPP, and his article on the family is published in the *Encyclopédie Française*. After Hitler's annexation of Austria, Freud leaves Vienna to settle in London; on his way to London he passes through Paris, but Lacan decides not to attend the small gathering organised in Freud's honour.

1939 Thibaut, the second child of Lacan and Marie-Louise, is born in August. On 23 September Freud dies in London at the age of eighty-three. After Hitler's invasion of France the SPP ceases to function. During the war Lacan works at a military hospital in Paris.

1940 Sibylle, third child of Lacan and Marie-Louise, is born in August.

1941 Sylvia Bataille, estranged wife of Georges Bataille, gives birth to Judith. Though Judith is Lacan's daughter, she receives the surname Bataille because Lacan is still married to Marie-Louise. Marie-Louise now requests a divorce.

1945 After the liberation of France, the SPP recommences meetings. Lacan travels to England where he spends five weeks studying the situation of psychiatry during the war years. His separation from Marie-Louise is formally announced.

1947 Lacan publishes a report on his visit to England.

1949 Lacan presents another paper on the mirror stage to the sixteenth IPA congress in Zurich on 17 July.

1951 Lacan begins giving weekly seminars in Sylvia Bataille's apartment at 3 rue de Lille. At this time, Lacan is vice-president of the SPP. In response to Lacan's practice of using sessions of variable duration, the SPP's commission on instruction demands that he regularise his practice. Lacan promises to do so, but continues to vary the time of the sessions.

1953   Lacan marries Sylvia Bataille and becomes president of the SPP. In June Daniel Lagache, Juliette Favez-Boutonier and Françoise Dolto resign from the SPP to found the Société Française de Psychanalyse (SFP). Soon after, Lacan resigns from the SPP and joins the SFP. Lacan opens the inaugural meeting of the SFP on the 8 July, where he delivers a lecture on 'the symbolic, the imaginary and the real'. He is informed by letter that his membership of the IPA has lapsed as a result of his resignation from the SPP. In September Lacan attends the sixteenth Conference of Psychoanalysts of the Romance Languages in Rome; the paper he writes for the occasion ('The function and field of speech and language in psychoanalysis') is too long to be read aloud and is distributed to participants instead. In November Lacan begins his first public seminar in the Hôpital Sainte-Anne. These seminars, which will continue for twenty-seven years, soon become the principal platform for Lacan's teaching.

1954   The IPA refuses the SFP's request for affiliation. Heinz Hartmann intimates in a letter to Daniel Lagache that Lacan's presence in the SFP is the main reason for this refusal.

1956   The SFP renews its request for IPA affiliation, which is again refused. Lacan again appears to be the main sticking-point.

1959   The SFP again renews its request for IPA affiliation. This time the IPA sets up a committee to evaluate the SFP's application.

1961   The IPA committee arrives in Paris to interview members of the SFP and produces a report. On consideration of this report, the IPA rejects the SFP's application for affiliation as a member society and grants it instead 'study-group' status pending further investigation.

1963   The IPA committee conducts more interviews with SFP members and produces another report in which it recommends that the SFP be granted affiliation as a member society on condition that Lacan and two other analysts be removed from the list of training analysts. The report also stipulates that Lacan's training activity should be banned for ever, and that trainee analysts should be prevented from attending his seminar. Lacan will later refer to this as his 'excommunication'. Lacan then resigns from the SFP.

1964   In January Lacan moves his public seminar to the École Normale Supérieure, and in June he founds his own organisation, the École Freudienne de Paris (EFP).

1965   The SFP is dissolved.

1966   A selection of Lacan's collected papers are published under the title *Écrits*. Lacan delivers a paper to a conference at Johns Hopkins University, Baltimore.

1967   Lacan proposes that the EFP adopt a new procedure called 'the pass', in which members can testify to the end of their analysis.

1968   Lacan voices his sympathy with the student protests in May. A department of psychology is set up by Lacan's followers at the University of Vincennes (Paris VIII) and opens its doors in December amid continuing student demonstrations.

1969   Lacan's public seminar transfers to the Faculté de Droit.

1973   An edited transcript of Lacan's seminar of 1964 (*The Four Fundamental Concepts of Psychoanalysis*) is brought out by Éditions du Seuil; this is the first of Lacan's seminars to be published.

1975   Lacan visits the United States, where he lectures at Yale University and the Massachusetts Institute of Technology and meets Noam Chomsky.

1980   After furious internal disputes within the EFP, it is dissolved by Lacan, who creates in its stead the Cause freudienne. He attends an international conference of Lacanian analysts in Caracas.

1981   The Cause freudienne is dissolved and the École de la Cause freudienne is created to replace it. Lacan dies in Paris on 9 September at the age of eighty.

An Introductory Dictionary of Lacanian Psychoanalysis

absence (*absence*) The symbolic order is characterised by the fundamental binary opposition between absence and presence (S4, 67–8).

In the symbolic order 'nothing exists except upon an assumed foundation of
absence' (Ec, 392). This is a basic difference between the symbolic and the
real; 'There is no absence in the real. There is only absence if you suggest that
there may be a presence there where there isn't one' (S2, 313) (see PRIVATION).

As Roman Jakobson showed with his analysis of phonemes, all linguistic
phenomena may be entirely characterised in terms of the presence or absence
of certain 'distinctive features'. Lacan sees the game of *fort!/da!*, which Freud
describes in *Beyond the Pleasure Principle* (Freud, 1920g), as a primitive
phonemic opposition representing the child's entry into the symbolic order.
The two sounds made by the child, O/A, are 'a pair of sounds modulated on
presence and absence' (E, 65), and these sounds are related 'to the presence
and absence of persons and things' (E, 109, n. 46).

Lacan notes that the word is 'a presence made of absence' (E, 65) because (i)
the symbol is used in the absence of the thing and (ii) signifiers only exist
insofar as they are opposed to other signifiers.

Because of the mutual implication of absence and presence in the symbolic
order, absence can be said to have an equally positive existence in the
symbolic as presence. This is what allows Lacan to say that 'the nothing'
(*le rien*) is in itself an object (a partial object) (S4, 184–5).

It is around the presence and absence of the PHALLUS that sexual difference is
symbolically apprehended by the child.

act (*acte*) Lacan draws a distinction between mere 'behaviour', which all
animals engage in, and 'acts', which are symbolic and which can only be
ascribed to human subjects (S11, 50). A fundamental quality of an act is that
the actor can be held responsible for it; the concept of the act is thus an ethical
concept (see ETHICS).

However, the psychoanalytic concept of responsibility is very different from
the legal concept. This is because the concept of responsibility is linked with
the whole question of intentionality, which is complicated in psychoanalysis
by the discovery that, in addition to his conscious plans, the subject also has
unconscious intentions. Hence someone may well commit an act which he
claims was unintentional, but which analysis reveals to be the expression of an
unconscious desire. Freud called these acts 'parapraxes', or 'bungled actions'
(Fr. *acte manqué*); they are 'bungled', however, only from the point of view of
the conscious intention, since they are successful in expressing an unconscious
desire (see Freud, 1901b). Whereas in law, a subject cannot be found guilty of
murder (for example) unless it can be proved that the act was intentional, in
psychoanalytic treatment the subject is faced with the ethical duty of assuming

responsibility even for the *unconscious* desires expressed in his actions (see BEAUTIFUL SOUL). He must recognise even apparently accidental actions as true acts which express an intention, albeit unconscious, and assume this intention as his own. Neither ACTING OUT nor a PASSAGE TO THE ACT are true acts, since the subject does not assume responsibility for his desire in these actions.

The ethics of psychoanalysis also enjoin the *analyst* to assume responsibility for his acts, i.e. his interventions in the treatment. The analyst must be guided in these interventions by an appropriate desire, which Lacan calls the desire of the analyst. An intervention can only be called a true psychoanalytic act when it succeeds in expressing the desire of the analyst – that is, when it helps the analysand to move towards the end of analysis. Lacan dedicates a year of his seminar to discussing further the nature of the psychoanalytic act (Lacan, 1967–8).

A bungled action is, as has been stated, succesful from the point of view of the unconscious. Nevertheless, this success is only partial because the unconscious desire is expressed in a distorted form. It follows that, when it is fully and consciously assumed, 'suicide is the only completely succesful act' (Lacan, 1973a: 66–7), since it then expresses completely an intention which is both conscious and unconscious, the conscious assumption of the unconscious death drive (on the other hand, a sudden impulsive suicide attempt is not a true act, but probably a passage to the act). The death drive is thus closely connected with the ethical domain in Lacan's thought (see the example of Empedocles, E, 104, and Lacan's discussion of *Antigone* in S7, ch. 21).

acting out   'Acting out' is the term which is used in the *Standard Edition* to translate the German term *Agieren* used by Freud. Lacan, following a tradition in psychoanalytic writing, uses this term in English.

One of the most important themes running throughout Freud's work is the opposition between repeating and remembering. These are, so to speak, 'contrasting ways of bringing the past into the present' (Laplanche and Pontalis, 1967: 4). If past events are repressed from memory, they return by expressing themselves in actions; when the subject does not remember the past, therefore, he is condemned to repeat it by acting it out. Conversely, psychoanalytic treatment aims to break the cycle of repetition by helping the patient to remember.

Although an element of repetition can be found in almost every human action, the term 'acting out' is usually reserved for those actions which display 'an impulsive aspect relatively out of harmony with the subject's usual motivational patterns' and which are therefore 'fairly easy to isolate from the overall trends of his activity' (Laplanche and Pontalis, 1967: 4). The subject himself fails to understand his motives for the action.

From a Lacanian perspective, this basic definition of acting out is true but incomplete; it ignores the dimension of the Other. Thus while Lacan maintains that acting out results from a failure to recollect the past, he emphasises the intersubjective dimension of recollection. In other words, recollection does not merely involve recalling something to consciousness, but also communicating this to an Other by means of speech. Hence acting out results when recollection is made impossible by the refusal of the Other to listen. When the Other has become 'deaf', the subject cannot convey a message to him in words, and is forced to express the message in actions. The acting out is thus a ciphered message which the subject addresses to an Other, although the subject himself is neither conscious of the content of this message nor even aware that his actions express a message. It is the Other who is entrusted with deciphering the message; yet it is impossible for him to do so.

In order to illustrate his remarks on acting out, Lacan refers to the case of the young homosexual woman treated by Freud (Freud, 1920a). Freud reports that the young woman made a point of appearing in the company of the woman she loved in the busiest streets of Vienna, especially in the streets near her father's place of business. Lacan argues that this was an acting out because it was a message which the young woman was addressing to her father who would not listen to her (Lacan, 1962–3: seminar of 23 January 1963).

In the example of the young homosexual woman, the acting out occurred before she began a course of psychoanalytic treatment with Freud. Such acting out can be considered as 'transference without analysis', or 'wild transference' (Lacan, 1962–3: seminar of 23 January 1963). However, most analysts argue that 'when it occurs in the course of analysis – whether during the actual session or not – acting out should be understood in its relationship to the transference' (Laplanche and Pontalis, 1967: 4). Freud stated that it is a basic principle of psychoanalytic treatment to 'force as much as possible into the channel of memory and to allow as little as possible to emerge as repetition' (Freud, 1920g: SE XVIII, 19). Therefore when an analysand acts out an unconscious wish aroused during a recent analytic session outside the consulting room this must be seen as a resistance to the treatment. However, since every resistance to analysis is a resistance of the analyst himself (E, 235), when acting out occurs during the treatment it is often due to a mistake made by the analyst. The analyst's mistake is usually to offer an inappropriate interpretation which reveals a momentary 'deafness' to the speech of the analysand. As an illustration of this, Lacan refers to a case history described by the ego-psychologist Ernst Kris (Kris, 1951). Lacan argues that the interpretation given by Kris was accurate at one level, but did not go to the heart of the matter, and thus provoked an acting out: after the session, the analysand went to eat some 'fresh brains' at a nearby restaurant. This action, states Lacan, was a ciphered message addressed to the analyst, indicating that the interpretation had failed to touch on the most essential aspect of the patient's symptom (Lacan, 1962–3: seminar of 23 January 1963; see also E, 238–9 and S1, 59–61).

Lacan dedicates several classes of his 1962–3 seminar to establishing a distinction between acting out and the PASSAGE TO THE ACT.

adaptation (*adaptation*)   The concept of adaptation is a biological concept (see BIOLOGY); organisms are supposed to be driven to adapt themselves to fit the environment. Adaptation implies a harmonious relation between the *Innenwelt* (inner world) and *Umwelt* (surrounding world).

EGO-PSYCHOLOGY applies this biological concept to psychoanalysis, explaining neurotic symptoms in terms of maladaptive behaviour (such as applying archaic defence mechanisms in contexts where they are no longer appropriate), and arguing that the aim of psychoanalytic treatment is to help the patient adapt to reality.

From his early work in the 1930s on, Lacan opposes any attempt to explain human phenomena in terms of adaptation (see Lacan, 1938: 24; Ec, 158; Ec, 171–2). This forms a constant theme in Lacan's work; in 1955, for example, he states that 'the dimension discovered by analysis is the opposite of anything which progresses through adaptation' (S2, 86). He takes this view for several reasons:

1. The stress on the adaptive function of the ego misses the ego's alienating function and is based on a simplistic and unproblematic view of 'reality'. Reality is not a simple, objective thing to which the ego must adapt, but is itself a product of the ego's fictional misrepresentations and projections. Therefore 'it is not a question of adapting to it [reality], but of showing it [the ego] that it is only too well adapted, since it assists in the construction of that very reality' (E, 236). The task of psychoanalysis is rather to subvert the illusory sense of adaptation, since this blocks access to the unconscious.

2. To set adaptation as the aim of the treatment is to turn the analyst into the arbiter of the patient's adaptation. The analyst's own 'relation to reality thus goes without saying' (E, 230); it is automatically assumed that the analyst is better adapted than the patient. This inevitably turns psychoanalysis into the exercise of power, in which the analyst forces his own particular view of reality onto the patient; this is not psychoanalysis but SUGGESTION.

3. The idea of harmony between the organism and its environment, implicit in the concept of adaptation, is inapplicable to human beings because man's inscription in the symbolic order de-naturalises him and means that 'in man the imaginary relation [to nature] has deviated'. Whereas 'all animal machines are strictly riveted to the conditions of the external environment' (S2, 322), in the human being there is 'a certain biological gap' (S2, 323; see GAP). Any attempt to regain harmony with nature overlooks the essentially excessive drive potential summed up in the death drive. Human beings are essentially maladaptive.

Lacan argues that the stress put by ego-psychology on the adaptation of the patient to reality reduces psychoanalysis to an instrument of social control and conformity. He sees this as a complete betrayal of psychoanalysis, which he regards as an essentially subversive practice.

Lacan regards it as significant that the adaptation theme was developed by the European psychoanalysts who had emigrated to the USA in the late 1930s;

these analysts felt not only that they had to adapt to life in the USA, but also that they had to adapt psychoanalysis to American tastes (E, 115).

affect (*affect*)   In Freud's work, the term 'affect' stands in opposition to the term 'idea'. The opposition between the affective and the intellectual is one of the oldest themes in philosophy, and made its way into Freud's vocabulary via German psychology.

For Lacan, however, the opposition between the affective and the intellectual is not valid in the psychoanalytic field. 'This opposition is one of the most contrary to analytic experience and most unenlightening when it comes to understanding it' (S1, 274).

Thus, in response to those who accuse Lacan of being over-intellectual and of neglecting the role of affect, it can be pointed out that this criticism is based on what Lacan saw as a false opposition (Lacan also argued that criticisms of being over-intellectual were often merely excuses for sloppy thinking – see E, 171). Psychoanalytic treatment is based on the symbolic order, which transcends the opposition between affect and intellect. On the one hand, psychoanalytic experience 'is not that of an affective smoochy-woochy' (S1, 55). On the other hand, nor is psychoanalytic treatment an intellectual affair; 'we are not dealing here with an intellectual dimension' (S1, 274). The Lacanian psychoanalyst must thus be aware of the ways in which both 'affective smoochy-woochy' and intellectualisation can be resistances to analysis, imaginary lures of the ego. Anxiety is the only affect that is not deceptive.

Lacan is opposed to those analysts who have taken the affective realm as primary, for the affective is not a separate realm opposed to the intellectual: 'The affective is not like a special density which would escape an intellectual accounting. It is not to be found in a mythical beyond of the production of the symbol which would precede the discursive formulation' (S1, 57). However, he rejects accusations of neglecting the role of affect, pointing to the fact that a whole year of the seminar is dedicated precisely to discussing anxiety (Lacan, 1973a: 38).

Lacan does not propose a general theory of affects, but only touches on them insofar as they impinge on psychoanalytic treatment. He insists on the relationship of affect to the symbolic order; affect means that the subject is affected by his relation with the Other. He argues that affects are not signifiers but signals (S7, 102–3), and emphasises Freud's position that repression does not bear upon the affect (which can only be transformed or displaced) but upon the ideational representative (which is, in Lacan's terms, the signifier) (Ec, 714).

Lacan's comments on the concept of affect have important implications in clinical practice. Firstly, all the concepts in psychoanalysis which have traditionally been conceived in terms of affects, such as the transference, must be rethought in terms of their symbolic structure, if the analyst is to direct the treatment correctly.

Secondly, the affects are lures which can deceive the analyst, and hence the analyst must be wary of being tricked by his own affects. This does not mean that the analyst must disregard his own feelings for the patient, but simply that he must know how to make adequate use of them (see COUNTERTRANSFERENCE).

Finally, it follows that the aim of psychoanalytic treatment is not the reliving of past experiences, nor the abreaction of affect, but the articulation in speech of the truth about desire.

Another term in Lacan's discourse, related to but distinct from 'affect', is the term 'passion'. Lacan speaks of the 'three fundamental passions': love, hate and ignorance (S1, 271); this is a reference to Buddhist thought (E, 94). These passions are not imaginary phenomena, but located at the junctions between the three orders.

aggressivity (*agressivité*)   Aggressivity is one of the central issues that Lacan deals with in his papers in the period 1936 to the early 1950s. The first point that should be noted is that Lacan draws a distinction between aggressivity and aggression, in that the latter refers only to violent acts whereas the former is a fundamental relation which underlies not only such acts but many other phenomena also (see S1, 177). Thus aggressivity is just as present, Lacan argues, in apparently loving acts as in violent ones; it 'underlies the activity of the philanthropist, the idealist, the pedagogue, and even the reformer' (E, 7). In taking this stance, Lacan is simply restating Freud's concept of ambivalence (the interdependence of love and hate), which Lacan regards as one of the fundamental discoveries of psychoanalysis.

Lacan situates aggressivity in the dual relation between the ego and the counterpart. In the MIRROR STAGE, the infant sees its reflection in the mirror as a wholeness, in contrast with the uncoordination in the real body: this contrast is experienced as an aggressive tension between the specular image and the real body, since the wholeness of the image seems to threaten the body with disintegration and fragmentation (see FRAGMENTED BODY).

The consequent identification with the specular image thus implies an ambivalent relation with the counterpart, involving both eroticism and aggression. This 'erotic aggression' continues as a fundamental ambivalence underlying all future forms of identification, and is an essential characteristic of narcissism. Narcissism can thus easily veer from extreme self-love to the opposite extreme of 'narcissistic suicidal aggression' (*agression suicidaire narcissique*) (Ec, 187).

By linking aggressivity to the imaginary order of eros, Lacan seems to diverge significantly from Freud, since Freud sees aggressivity as an outward manifestation of the death drive (which is, in Lacanian terms, situated not in the imaginary but in the symbolic order). Aggressivity is also related by Lacan to the Hegelian concept of the fight to the death, which is a stage in the dialectic of the master and the slave.

Lacan argues that it is important to bring the analysand's aggressivity into play early in the treatment by causing it to emerge as negative transference.

This aggressivity directed towards the analyst then becomes 'the initial knot of the analytic drama' (E, 14). This phase of the treatment is very important since if the aggressivity is handled correctly by the analyst, it will be accompanied by 'a marked decrease in the patient's deepest resistances' (Lacan, 1951b: 13).

algebra (*algèbre*)   Algebra is a branch of MATHEMATICS which reduces the solution of problems to manipulations of symbolic expressions. Lacan begins to use algebraic symbols in his work in 1955 (see SCHEMA L), in an attempt to formalise psychoanalysis. Three main reasons lie behind this attempt at formalisation:

1. Formalisation is necessary for psychoanalysis to acquire scientific status (see SCIENCE). Just as Claude Lévi-Strauss uses quasi-mathematical formulae in an attempt to set anthropology on a more scientific footing, Lacan attempts to do the same for psychoanalysis.

2. Formalisation can provide a core of psychoanalytic theory which can be transmitted integrally even to those who have never experienced psychoanalytic treatment. The formulae thus become an essential aspect of the training of psychoanalysts which take their place alongside the training analysis as a medium for the transmission of psychoanalytic knowledge.

3. Formalisation of psychoanalytic theory in terms of algebraic symbols is a means of preventing intuitive understanding, which Lacan regards as an imaginary lure which hinders access to the symbolic. Rather than being understood in an intuitive way, the algebraic symbols are to be used, manipulated and read in various different ways (see E, 313).

Most English translations of Lacan also translate the algebraic symbols which appear in his work. For example, Alan Sheridan, in his translation of *Écrits*, renders the symbol A (for *Autre*) as O (for Other). However, Lacan was opposed to such a practice, as Sheridan himself points out (Sheridan, 1977: xi). In this dictionary, in line with Lacan's own preference, the algebraic symbols are left as they are in the original French texts.

The algebraic symbols used by Lacan, which appear principally in the MATHEMES, SCHEMA L and the GRAPH OF DESIRE, are listed below, together with their most common meaning. However, it is important to remember that the symbols do not always refer to the same concept throughout Lacan's work, but are used in different ways as his work develops. The most important example of such a shift in meaning is the use of the symbol *a*, which is used in radically different ways in the 1950s and in the 1960s. However, even other symbols which are relatively stable in meaning are occasionally used in very different ways; for example, *s* nearly always designates the signified, but is used in one algorithm to denote the subject supposed to know (see Lacan, 1967). Therefore some caution should be exercised when referring to the following list of equivalences.

ALGEBRA

A	=	the big Other
A̶	=	the barred Other
a	=	(see *objet petit a*)
a'	=	(see *objet petit a*)
S	=	1. (before 1957) the subject
		2. (from 1957 on) the signifier
		3. (in the schemas of Sade) the raw subject of pleasure
$\bar{S}$	=	the barred subject
S_1	=	the master signifier
S_2	=	the signifying chain/knowledge
s	=	the signified (in the Saussurean algorithm)
S(A̶)	=	the signifier of a lack in the Other
s(A)	=	the signification of the Other (the message/symptom)
D	=	demand
d	=	desire
m	=	the ego (*moi*)
i	=	the specular image (schema R)
i(a)	=	1. the specular image (graph of desire)
		2. the ideal ego (optical model)
I	=	the ego-ideal (schema R)
I(A)	=	the ego-ideal (graph of desire)
Π	=	the real phallus
Φ	=	the symbolic phallus [upper-case phi]
φ	=	the imaginary phallus [lower-case phi]
(−φ)	=	castration [minus phi]
S	=	the symbolic order (schema R)
R	=	the field of reality (schema R)
I	=	the imaginary order (schema R)
P	=	the symbolic father/Name-of-the-Father
p	=	the imaginary father
M	=	the symbolic mother
J	=	*jouissance*
Jφ	=	phallic *jouissance*
JA	=	the *jouissance* of the other
E	=	the statement
e	=	the enunciation
V	=	the will to enjoy (*volonté de jouissance*)

The typographical details and diacritics are extremely important in Lacanian algebra. The difference between upper- and lower-case symbols, the difference between italicised and non-italicised symbols, the use of the apostrophe, the minus sign, and subscripts; all these details play their part in the algebraic system. For example the upper-case letters usually refer to the symbolic order, whereas the lower-case letters usually refer to the imaginary. The use of the bar is also important, and varies even within the same formula.

alienation (*aliénation*)   The term 'alienation' does not constitute part of Freud's theoretical vocabulary. In Lacan's work the term implies both psychiatric and philosophical references:

● **Psychiatry**   French psychiatry in the nineteenth century (e.g. Pinel) conceived of mental illness as *aliénation mentale*, and a common term in French for 'madman' is *aliéné* (a term which Lacan himself uses; Ec, 154).

● **Philosophy**   The term 'alienation' is the usual translation for the German term *Entfremdung* which features in the philosophy of Hegel and Marx. However, the Lacanian concept of alienation differs greatly from the ways that the term is employed in the Hegelian and Marxist tradition (as Jacques-Alain Miller points out; S11, 215). For Lacan, alienation is not an accident that befalls the subject and which can be transcended, but an essential constitutive feature of the subject. The subject is fundamentally SPLIT, alienated from himself, and there is no escape from this division, no possibility of 'wholeness' or synthesis.

Alienation is an inevitable consequence of the process by which the ego is constituted by identification with the counterpart: 'the initial synthesis of the ego is essentially an alter ego, it is alienated' (S3, 39). In Rimbaud's words, 'I is an other' (E, 23). Thus alienation belongs to the imaginary order: 'Alienation is constitutive of the imaginary order. Alienation is the imaginary as such' (S3, 146). Although alienation is an essential characteristic of all subjectivity, psychosis represents a more extreme form of alienation.

Lacan coined the term EXTIMACY to designate the nature of this alienation, in which alterity inhabits the innermost core of the subject. Lacan devotes the whole of chapter 16 of *The Seminar, Book XI, The Four Fundamental Concepts of Psychoanalysis* (1964a) to a discussion of alienation and the related concept of separation.

analysand/psychoanalysand (*analysant/psychanalysant*)
Before 1967, Lacan refers to the one who is 'in' psychoanalytic treatment as the 'patient' (Fr. *patient*) or the 'subject', or uses the technical term *(psych)analysé*. However, in 1967 Lacan introduces the term *(psych)analysant*, based on the English term '(psycho)analysand' (Lacan, 1967: 18). Lacan prefers this term because, being derived from the gerund, it indicates that the one who lies on the couch is the one who does most of the work. This contrasts with the old term *(psych)analysé* which, being derived from the passive participle, suggests either a less active participation in the analytic process, or that the analytic process has finished. In Lacan's view, the analysand is not 'analysed' by the analyst; it is the analysand who analyses, and the task of the analyst is to help him to analyse well.

anxiety (*angoisse*)   Anxiety has long been recognised in psychiatry as one of the most common symptoms of mental disorder. Psychiatric descriptions of anxiety generally refer to both mental phenomena (apprehension, worry) and bodily phenomena (breathlessnes, palpitations, muscle tension, fatigue, dizziness, sweating and tremor). Psychiatrists also distinguish between generalised anxiety states, when 'free-floating anxiety' is present most of the time, and 'panic attacks', which are 'intermittent episodes of acute anxiety' (Hughes, 1981: 48–9).

The German term employed by Freud (*Angst*) can have the psychiatric sense described above, but is by no means an exclusively technical term, being also in common use in ordinary speech. Freud developed two theories of anxiety during the course of his work. From 1884 to 1925 he argued that neurotic anxiety is simply a transformation of sexual libido that has not been adequately discharged. In 1926, however, he abandoned this theory and argued instead that anxiety was a reaction to a 'traumatic situation' – an experience of HELPLESSNESS in the face of an accumulation of excitation that cannot be discharged. Traumatic situations are precipitated by 'situations of danger' such as birth, loss of the mother as object, loss of the object's love and, above all, castration. Freud distinguishes between 'automatic anxiety', when the anxiety arises directly as a result of a traumatic situation, and 'anxiety as signal', when the anxiety is actively reproduced by the ego as a warning of an anticipated situation of danger.

Lacan, in his pre-war writings, relates anxiety primarily to the threat of fragmentation with which the subject is confronted in the mirror stage (see FRAGMENTED BODY). It is only long after the mirror stage, he argues, that these fantasies of bodily dismemberment coalesce around the penis, giving rise to castration anxiety (Lacan, 1938: 44). He also links anxiety with the fear of being engulfed by the devouring mother. This theme (with its distinctly Kleinian tone) remains an important aspect of Lacan's account of anxiety thereafter, and marks an apparent difference between Lacan and Freud: whereas Freud posits that one of the causes of anxiety is separation from the mother, Lacan argues that it is precisely a lack of such separation which induces anxiety.

After 1953, Lacan comes increasingly to articulate anxiety with his concept of the real, a traumatic element which remains external to symbolisation, and hence which lacks any possible mediation. This real is 'the essential object which isn't an object any longer, but this something faced with which all words cease and all categories fail, the object of anxiety *par excellence*' (S2, 164).

As well as linking anxiety with the real, Lacan also locates it in the imaginary order and contrasts it with guilt, which he situates in the symbolic (Lacan, 1956b: 272–3). 'Anxiety, as we know, is always connected with a loss . . . with a two-sided relation on the point of fading away to be superseded by something else, something which the patient cannot face without vertigo' (Lacan, 1956b: 273).

In the seminar of 1956–7 Lacan goes on to develop his theory of anxiety further, in the context of his discussion of PHOBIA. Lacan argues that anxiety is the radical danger which the subject attempts to avoid at all costs, and that the various subjective formations encountered in psychoanalysis, from phobias to fetishism, are protections against anxiety (S4, 23). Anxiety is thus present in all neurotic structures, but is especially evident in phobia (E, 321). Even a phobia is preferable to anxiety (S4, 345); a phobia at least replaces anxiety (which is terrible precisely because it is not focused on a particular object but revolves around an absence) with fear (which is focused on a particular object and thus may be symbolically worked-through) (S4, 243–6).

In his analysis of the case of Little Hans (Freud, 1909b), Lacan argues that anxiety arises at that moment when the subject is poised between the imaginary preoedipal triangle and the Oedipal quaternary. It is at this junction that Hans's real penis makes itself felt in infantile masturbation; anxiety is produced because he can now measure the difference between that for which he is loved by the mother (his position as imaginary phallus) and that which he really has to give (his insignificant real organ) (S4, 243). Anxiety is this point where the subject is suspended between a moment where he no longer knows where he is and a future where he will never again be able to refind himself (S4, 226). Hans would have been saved from this anxiety by the castrating intervention of the real father, but this does not happen; the father fails to intervene to separate Hans from the mother, and thus Hans develops a phobia as a substitute for this intervention. Once again, what emerges from Lacan's account of Little Hans is that it is not separation from the mother which gives rise to anxiety, but failure to separate from her (S4, 319). Consequently, castration, far from being the principal source of anxiety, is actually what saves the subject from anxiety.

In the seminar of 1960–1 Lacan stresses the relationship of anxiety to desire; anxiety is a way of sustaining desire when the object is missing and, conversely, desire is a remedy for anxiety, something easier to bear than anxiety itself (S8, 430). He also argues that the source of anxiety is not always internal to the subject, but can often come from another, just as it is transmitted from one animal to another in a herd; 'if anxiety is a signal, it means it can come from another' (S8, 427). This is why the analyst must not allow his own anxiety to interfere with the treatment, a requirement which he is only able to meet because he maintains a desire of his own, the desire of the analyst (S8, 430).

In the seminar of 1962–3, entitled simply 'Anxiety', Lacan argues that anxiety is an affect, not an emotion, and furthermore that it is the only affect which is beyond all doubt, which is not deceptive (see also S11, 41). Whereas Freud distinguished between fear (which is focused on a specific object) and anxiety (which is not), Lacan now argues that anxiety is not without an object (*n'est pas sans objet*); it simply involves a different kind of object, an object which cannot be symbolised in the same way as all other objects. This object is *objet petit a*, the object-cause of desire, and anxiety appears when something appears in the place of this object. Anxiety arises when the subject is confronted by the desire of the Other and does not know what object he is for that desire.

It is also in this seminar that Lacan links anxiety to the concept of lack. All desire arises from lack, and anxiety arises when this lack is itself lacking; anxiety is the lack of a lack. Anxiety is not the absence of the breast, but its enveloping presence; it is the possibility of its absence which is, in fact, that which saves us from anxiety. Acting out and passage to the act are last defences against anxiety.

Anxiety is also linked to the mirror stage. Even in the usually comforting experience of seeing one's reflection in the mirror there can occur a moment when the specular image is modified and suddenly seems strange to us. In this way, Lacan links anxiety to Freud's concept of the uncanny (Freud, 1919h).

Whereas the seminar of 1962–3 is largely concerned with Freud's second theory of anxiety (anxiety as signal), in the seminar of 1974–5 Lacan appears to return to the first Freudian theory of anxiety (anxiety as transformed libido). Thus he comments that anxiety is that which exists in the interior of the body when the body is overcome with phallic *jouissance* (Lacan, 1974–5: seminar of 17 December 1974).

aphanisis   The literal meaning of this Greek term is 'disappearance'. It was first introduced into psychoanalysis by Ernest Jones, who uses it to mean 'the disappearance of sexual desire' (Jones, 1927). For Jones, the fear of *aphanisis* exists in both sexes, giving rise to the castration complex in boys and to penis envy in girls.

Lacan takes up Jones's term, but modifies it substantially. For Lacan, *aphanisis* does not mean the disappearance of desire, but the disappearance of the subject (see S11, 208). The *aphanisis* of the subject is the fading of the subject, the fundamental division of the subject (see SPLIT) which institutes the dialectic of desire (see S11, 221). Far from the disappearance of desire being the object of fear, it is precisely what the neurotic aims at; the neurotic attempts to shield himself from his desire, to put it aside (S8, 271).

Lacan also uses another term, 'fading', in a way that makes it synonymous with the term *aphanisis*. Fading (a term which Lacan uses directly in English) refers to the disappearance of the subject in the process of alienation. The term is used by Lacan when describing the MATHEMES of the drive and of fantasy: the subject 'fades' or 'disappears' in the face of demand and in the face of the object, as is shown by the fact that the subject is barred in these mathemes.

art (*art*)   Freud valued art as one of humanity's great cultural institutions, and dedicated many papers to discussing both the process of artistic creation in general and certain works of art in particular. He explained artistic creation by reference to the concept of SUBLIMATION, a process in which sexual libido is redirected towards non-sexual aims. Freud also dedicated a number of papers to analysing particular works of art, especially works of literature, which he argued could be useful to psychoanalysis in two main ways. Firstly, these works often express in poetic form truths about the psyche, which implies that creative writers can intuit directly the truths which psychoanalysts only discover later by more laborious means. Secondly, Freud also argued that a close psychoanalytic reading of works of literature could uncover elements of the author's psyche. While most of Freud's papers on particular works of art concern works of literature, he did not entirely neglect other art forms; for example he devoted one paper to discussing Michelangelo's statue of Moses (Freud, 1914b).

Lacan's works also abound in discussions of particular works of art. Like Freud, Lacan devotes most of his attention to works of literature of all genres: prose (e.g. the discussion of *The Purloined Letter* by Edgar Allan Poe in S2, ch. 16, and Lacan, 1955a), drama (e.g. the discussions of Shakespeare's *Hamlet* in Lacan, 1958–9, and of Sophocles' *Antigone* in S7, chs 19–21) and poetry (e.g. the discussion of *Booz endormi* by Victor Hugo in S3, 218–25; S4, 377–8; E, 156–8; S8, 158–9). However, Lacan also discusses the visual arts, devoting several lectures in his 1964 seminar to discussing painting, particularly anamorphotic art (S11, chs 7–9, where he discusses Holbein's *The Ambassadors*; see also S7, 139–42).

There are, nevertheless, significant differences between the ways in which Freud and Lacan approach works of art. Though Lacan does speak about sublimation, unlike Freud he does not believe that it is possible or even desirable for psychoanalysts to say anything about the psychology of the artist on the basis of an examination of a work of art (see his critical remarks on 'psychobiography'; Ec, 740–1). Just because the most fundamental complex (Oedipus) in psychoanalytic theory is taken from a literary work, Lacan says, does not mean that psychoanalysis has anything to say about Sophocles (Lacan, 1971: 3).

Lacan's exclusion of the artist from his discussions of works of art means that his readings of literary texts are not concerned to reconstruct the author's intentions. In his suspension of the question of authorial intent, Lacan is not merely aligning himself with the structuralist movement (after all, authorial intent had been bracketed by New Criticism long before the structuralists appeared on the scene), but is rather illustrating the way in which the analyst should proceed when listening to and interpreting the discourse of the analysand. The analyst must, in other words, treat the analysand's discourse as a text:

> You must start from the text, start by treating it, as Freud does and as he recommends, as Holy Writ. The author, the scribe, is only a pen-pusher, and

he comes second. . . . Similarly, when it comes to our patients, please give more attention to the text than to the psychology of the author – the entire orientation of my teaching is that.

(S2, 153)

Lacan's discussions of literary texts are thus not exercises in literary criticism for its own sake, but performances designed to give his audience an idea of how they are to read the unconscious of their patients. This method of reading is similar to those employed by formalism and structuralism; the signified is neglected in favour of the signifier, content is bracketed in favour of formal structures (although Jacques Derrida has argued that Lacan does not in fact follow his own method; see Derrida, 1975).

Besides serving as models of a method of reading, which Lacan recommends analysts to follow when reading the discourse of their patients, Lacan's discussions of literary texts also aim to extract certain elements which serve as metaphors to illustrate some of his most important ideas. For example, in his reading of Poe's *The Purloined Letter*, Lacan points to the circulating LETTER as a metaphor for the determinative power of the signifier.

A new branch of so-called 'psychoanalytic literary criticism' now claims to be inspired by Lacan's approach to literary texts (e.g. Muller and Richardson, 1988, and Wright, 1984; other works dealing with Lacan and cultural theory are Davis, 1983; Felman, 1987; MacCannell, 1986). However, while such projects are interesting in their own right, they do not usually approach literature in the same way as Lacan. That is, while psychoanalytic literary criticism aims to say something about the texts studied, both aspects of Lacan's approach (to illustrate a mode of analytic interpretation, and to illustrate psychoanalytic concepts) are concerned not with saying something about the texts themselves, but merely with using the texts to say something about psychoanalysis. This is perhaps the most important difference between Lacan's approach to works of art and Freud's. Whereas some of Freud's works are often taken to imply that psychoanalysis is a metadiscourse, a master narrative providing a general hermeneutic key that can unlock the hitherto unsolved secrets of literary works, it is impossible to read Lacan as making any such claims. For Lacan, while psychoanalysis might be able to learn something about literature, or use literary works to illustrate certain of its methods and concepts, it is doubtful whether literary criticism can learn anything from psychoanalysis. Hence Lacan rejects the idea that a literary criticism which makes use of psychoanalytic concepts could be called 'applied psychoanalysis', since '[p]sychoanalysis is only applied, in the proper sense of the term, as a treatment, and thus to a subject who speaks and listens' (Ec, 747).

autonomous ego   The term 'autonomous ego' was coined by the proponents of EGO-PSYCHOLOGY. According to the proponents of ego-psychology, the EGO becomes autonomous by achieving a harmonious balance between its primitive drives and the dictates of reality. The autonomous ego is thus synomymous with 'the strong ego', 'the well-adapted ego', 'the healthy ego'. Psychoanalysis was conceived of by the proponents of ego-psychology as the process of helping the analysand's ego to become autonomous: this was supposed to be achieved by the identification of the analysand with the strong ego of the analyst.

Lacan is very critical of the concept of the autonomous ego (see E, 306–7). He argues that the ego is not free but determined by the symbolic order. The autonomy of the ego is simply a narcissistic illusion of mastery. It is the symbolic order, and not the ego, which enjoys autonomy.

B

bar (*barre*) The term 'bar' first appears in Lacan's work in 1957, where it is introduced in the context of a discussion of Saussure's concept of the SIGN (E, 149). In this context, the bar is the line that separates the signifier from the signified in the Saussurean algorithm (see Figure 18), and stands for the resistance inherent in signification which is only crossed in metaphor. Lacan takes pleasure in the fact that, in French, *barre* is an anagram of *arbre* (tree), since it is precisely with a tree that Saussure illustrates his own concept of the sign (E, 154).

Not long after the 1957 paper in which the term first appears, in the seminar of 1957–8, Lacan goes on to use the bar to strike through his algebraic symbols S and A in a manner reminiscent of Heidegger's practice of crossing out the word 'being' (see Heidegger, 1956). The bar is used to strike through the S to produce, $, the 'barred subject'. The bar here represents the division of the subject by language, the SPLIT. Thus whereas before 1957 S designates the subject (e.g. in schema L), from 1957 on S designates the signifier and $ designates the (divided) subject. The bar is also used to strike through the A (the big Other) to produce the algebraic notation for the 'barred Other', Ⱥ. However, Lacan continues to use both signs in his algebra (e.g. in the graph of desire). The barred Other is the Other insofar as it is castrated, incomplete, marked by a lack, as opposed to the complete, consistent, uncastrated Other, an un-barred A, which does not exist.

In 1973 the bar is used to strike through the definite article *la* whenever it precedes the noun *femme* (woman), as in Lacan's famous phrase *la femme n'existe pas* ('woman does not exist'). The definite article in French indicates universality, and by crossing it out Lacan illustrates his thesis that femininity is resistant to all forms of generalisation (see S20, 68).

In addition to these functions, the bar can also be interpreted as the symbolic phallus (which itself is never barred), as the symbol of negation in the

15

formulae of sexuation (see SEXUAL DIFFERENCE), and as the *trait unaire* (see IDENTIFICATION).

beautiful soul (*belle âme*)

The beautiful soul (Ger. *schöne Seele*) is a stage in the dialectic of self–consciousness which Hegel describes in the *Phenomenology of Spirit* (Hegel, 1807). The beautiful soul projects its own disorder onto the world and attempts to cure this disorder by imposing 'the law of the heart' on everyone else. For Lacan, the beautiful soul is a perfect metaphor for the ego; 'the ego of modern man . . . has taken on its form in the dialectical impasse of the *belle âme* who does not recognise his very own *raison d'être* in the disorder that he denounces in the world' (E, 70). In a more extreme way, the beautiful soul also illustrates the structure of paranoiac misrecognition (see *MÉCONNAISSANCE*) (Ec, 172–3).

The concept of the beautiful soul illustrates the way that neurotics often deny their own responsibility for what is going on around them (see ACT). The ethics of psychoanalysis enjoin analysands to recognise their own part in their sufferings. Thus when Dora complains about being treated as an object of exchange by the men around her, Freud's first intervention is to confront her with her own complicity in this exchange (Ec, 218–19; see Freud, 1905e).

being (*être*)

Lacan's use of the term 'being' introduces a metaphysical note to his discourse that distinguishes it from most other schools of psychoanalytic theory, which refuse to engage with their metaphysical and philosophical foundations (see E, 228). Lacan argues that it is necessary for psychoanalysts to engage with such concerns, for when the analyst intervenes his action 'goes to the heart of [the analysand's] being', and this also affects his own being, since he cannot 'remain alone outside the field of play' (E, 228). Hence 'it is certainly in the relation to being that the analyst has to find his operating level' (E, 252). Lacan also argues that during the course of the treatment the analyst is subjected to a progressive loss of being (Fr. *désêtre*), as he is gradually reduced to being a mere object for the analysand.

Lacan's discussion of being is clearly influenced by the ideas of Martin Heidegger (see Heidegger, 1927). Being belongs to the symbolic order, since it is 'the relation to the Other in which being finds its status' (E, 251). This relation, like the Other itself, is marked by a lack (*manque*), and the subject is constituted by this lack of being (*manque-à-être*), which gives rise to desire, a want-to-be (*manque-à-être*); desire is thus essentially a desire for being.

Whenever Lacan opposes being to EXISTENCE, it is with existence in the real, which contrasts with the symbolic function of being. Something may thus *be* without *existing*, when it is constructed from speech but finds no correlate in the real (e.g. the complete Other). Conversely, something may *exist* without *being*, such as the 'ineffable, stupid existence' of the subject, which cannot be completely reduced to a signifying articulation (E, 194).

Lacan coins the neologism *parlêtre* from the verbal noun *être* (being) and the verb *parler* (to speak) to emphasise his point that being is constituted in and through language. A human being is above all a speaking being.

Bejahung

In his 'Reply to Jean Hyppolite's commentary on Freud's *Negation*' (Lacan, 1954b), Lacan describes a primordial act of affirmation which is logically prior to any act of NEGATION. Lacan uses Freud's German term, *Bejahung* (affirmation) to denote this primordial affirmation (Ec, 387; see Freud, 1925h). Whereas negation concerns what Freud called 'the judgement of existence', *Bejahung* denotes something more fundamental, namely the primordial act of symbolisation itself, the inclusion of something in the symbolic universe. Only after a thing has been symbolised (at the level of *Bejahung*) can the value of existence be attributed to it or not (negation).

Lacan posits a basic alternative between *Bejahung* and the psychotic mechanism he later calls FORECLOSURE; the former designates a primordial inclusion of something in the symbolic, whereas foreclosure is a primordial refusal to include something (the Name-of-the-Father) in the symbolic (S3, 82).

biology (*biologie*)

Freud's work is full of references to biology. Freud regarded biology as a model of scientific rigour on which to base the new science of psychoanalysis. Lacan, however, is strongly opposed to any attempt to construct psychoanalysis upon a biological model, arguing that the direct application of biological (or ethological/psychological) concepts (such as ADAPTATION) to psychoanalysis will inevitably be misleading and will obliterate the essential distinction between NATURE and culture. Such biologising explanations of human behaviour ignore, according to Lacan, the primacy of the symbolic order in human existence. Lacan sees this 'biologism' in the work of those psychoanalysts who have confused desire with need, and drives with instincts, concepts which he insists on distinguishing.

These arguments are evident from the very earliest of Lacan's psychoanalytic writings. In his 1938 work on the family, for example, he rejects any attempt to explain family structures on the basis of purely biological data, and argues that human psychology is regulated by complexes rather than by instincts (Lacan, 1938: 23–4).

Lacan argues that his refusal of biological reductionism is not a contradiction of Freud but a return to the essence of Freud's work. When Freud used biological models, he did so simply because biology was at that time a model of scientific rigour in general, and because the conjectural sciences had not then achieved the same degree of rigour. Freud certainly did not confuse psychoanalysis with biology or any other exact science, and when he borrowed concepts from biology (such as the concept of the drive) he reworked them in such a radical way that they become totally new concepts. For example, the concept of the death instinct 'is not a question of biology' (E,

102). Lacan expresses his point with a paradox: 'Freudian biology has nothing to do with biology' (S2, 75).

Lacan, like Freud, uses concepts borrowed from biology (e.g. imago, dehiscence), and then reworks them in an entirely symbolic framework. Perhaps the most significant example of this is Lacan's concept of the PHALLUS, which he conceives as a signifier and not as a bodily organ. Thus while Freud conceives of the castration complex and sexual difference in terms of the presence and absence of the penis, Lacan theorises them in non-biological, non-anatomical terms (the presence and absence of the phallus). This has been one of the main attractions of Lacanian theory for certain feminist writers who have seen it as a way of constructing a non-essentialist account of gendered subjectivity.

However, while Lacan consistently rejects all forms of biological reductionism, he also rejects the culturalist position which completely ignores the relevance of biology (Ec, 723). If 'biologising' is understood correctly (that is, not as the reduction of psychic phenomena to crude biological determination, but as discerning the precise way in which biological data impact on the psychical field), then Lacan is all in favour of biologising thought (Ec, 723). The clearest examples of this are Lacan's appeals to examples from animal ethology to demonstrate the power of images to act as releasing mechanisms; hence Lacan's references to pigeons and locusts in his account of the mirror stage (E, 3), and to crustaceans in his account of mimicry (S11, 99) (see GESTALT).

Thus in his account of sexual difference, Lacan follows Freud's rejection of the false dichotomy between 'anatomy or convention' (Freud, 1933a: SE XXII, 114). Lacan's concern is not to privilege either term but to show how both interact in complex ways in the process of assuming a sexual position.

Borromean knot (*noeud borroméen*)

References to knots can be found in Lacan's work as early as the 1950s (e.g. E, 281), but it is not until the early 1970s that Lacan begins to examine knots from the point of view of their topological properties. The study of knot theory marks an important development in Lacan's TOPOLOGY; from the study of surfaces (the moebius strip, the torus, etc.) Lacan moves to the much more complex area of the topology of knots. Topology is increasingly seen as a radically non-metaphorical way of exploring the symbolic order and its interactions with the real and the imaginary; rather than simply *representing* structure, topology *is* that structure. In this late period of his work, one kind of knot comes to interest Lacan more than any other: the Borromean knot.

The Borromean knot (shown in Figure 1), so called because the figure is found on the coat of arms of the Borromeo family, is a group of three rings which are linked in such a way that if any one of them is severed, all three become separated (S20, 112). Strictly speaking, it would be more appropriate to refer to this figure as a chain rather than a knot, since it involves the

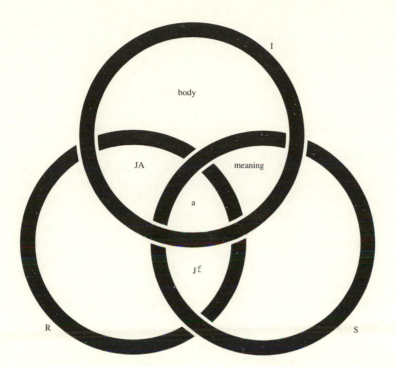

Figure 1 The Borromean knot

interconnection of several different threads, whereas a knot is formed by a single thread. Although a minimum of three threads or rings are required to form a Borromean chain, there is no maximum number; the chain may be extended indefinitely by adding further rings, while still preserving its Borromean quality (i.e. if any of the rings is cut, the whole chain falls apart).

Lacan first takes up the Borromean knot in the seminar of 1972–3, but his most detailed discussion of the knot comes in the seminar of 1974–5. It is in this seminar that Lacan uses the Borromean knot as, among other things, a way of illustrating the interdependence of the three orders of the real, the symbolic and the imaginary, as a way of exploring what it is that these three orders have in common. Each ring represents one of the three orders, and thus certain elements can be located at intersections of these rings.

In the seminar of 1975–6, Lacan goes on to describe psychosis as the unravelling of the Borromean knot, and proposes that in some cases this is prevented by the addition of a fourth ring, the SINTHOME, which holds the other three together.

C

captation (*captation*)   The French substantive *captation* is a neologism coined by the French psychoanalysts Édouard Pichon and Odile Codet, from the verb *capter* (which Forrester translates as 'to captate', reviving an obsolete English verb in a quasi-technical sense – see S1, 146 and note). It was adopted by Lacan in 1948 to refer to the imaginary effects of the SPECULAR IMAGE (see E, 18), and occurs regularly in his work from this point on. The double sense of the French term nicely indicates the ambiguous nature of the power of the specular image. On the one hand, it has the sense of 'captivation', thus expressing the fascinating, seductive power of the image. On the other hand, the term also conveys the idea of 'capture', which evokes the more sinister power of the image to imprison the subject in a disabling fixation.

cartel (*cartel*)   The cartel is the basic working unit on which Lacan based his SCHOOL of psychoanalysis, the *École Freudienne de Psychanalyse* (EFP), and most Lacanian associations continue to organise work in cartels today.

The cartel is essentially a study group consisting of three to five people (though Lacan considers four the optimum number), plus a supervisor (known as a 'plus-one'; Fr. *plus-un*) who moderates the group's work. A cartel is created when a group of people decide to work together on a particular aspect of psychoanalytic theory which is of interest to them, and it is then registered in the school's list of cartels. Although participation in cartels plays an important part in the training (*formation*) of Lacanian analysts, membership of cartels is not restricted to members of the school. Indeed, Lacan welcomed the exchange of ideas between analysts and those from other disciplines, and saw the cartel as one structure which would serve to encourage this exchange.

By organising research work around a small-scale unit like the cartel, Lacan hoped to avoid the effects of massification which he regarded as partly to blame for the sterility of the International Psycho-Analytical Association (IPA).

castration complex (*complexe de castration*)   Freud first described the castration complex in 1908, arguing that the child, on discovering the anatomical difference between the sexes (the presence or absence of the penis), makes the assumption that this difference is due to the female's penis having been cut off (Freud, 1908c). The castration complex is thus the moment when one infantile theory (everyone has a penis) is replaced by a new one (females have been castrated). The consequences of this new infantile theory are different in the boy and in the girl. The boy fears that his own penis will be cut off by the father (castration anxiety), while the girl sees herself as already castrated (by the mother) and attempts to deny this or to compensate for it by seeking a child as a substitute for the penis (penis envy).

The castration complex affects both sexes because its appearance is closely linked with the phallic phase, a moment of psychosexual development when the child, whether boy or girl, knows only one genital organ – the male one. This phase is also known as the infantile genital organisation because it is the first moment when the partial drives are unified under the primacy of the genital organs. It thus anticipates the genital organisation proper which arises at puberty, when the subject is aware of both the male and the female sexual organs (see Freud, 1923e).

Freud argued that the castration complex is closely linked to the OEDIPUS COMPLEX, but that its role in the Oedipus complex is different for the boy and the girl. In the case of the boy, the castration complex is the point of exit from the Oedipus complex, its terminal crisis; because of his fear of castration (often aroused by a threat) the boy renounces his desire for the mother and thus enters the latency period. In the case of the girl, the castration complex is the point of entry into the Oedipus complex; it is her resentment of the mother, whom she blames for depriving her of the penis, that causes her to redirect her libidinal desires away from the mother and onto the father. Because of this difference, in the case of the girl the Oedipus complex has no definitive terminal crisis comparable to the boy's (Freud, 1924d).

Freud came to see the castration complex as a universal phenomenon, one which is rooted in a basic 'rejection of femininity' (*Ablehnung der Weiblichkeit*). It is encountered in every subject, and represents the ultimate limit beyond which psychoanalytic treatment cannot go (Freud, 1937c).

Lacan, who talks more often about 'castration' than 'the castration complex', does not discuss the castration complex very much in his early work. He dedicates a few paragraphs to it in his article on the family, where he follows Freud in stating that castration is first and foremost a fantasy of the mutilation of the penis. Lacan links this fantasy with a whole series of fantasies of bodily dismemberment which originate in the image of the fragmented body; this image is contemporary with the mirror stage (six to eighteen months), and it is only much later that these fantasies of dismemberment coalesce around the specific fantasy of castration (Lacan, 1938: 44).

It is not until the mid-1950s that the castration complex comes to play a prominent role in Lacan's teaching, primarily in the seminar of 1956–7. It is in this seminar that Lacan identifies castration as one of three forms of 'lack of object', the others being frustration and privation (see LACK). Unlike frustration (which is an imaginary lack of a real object) and privation (which is a real lack of a symbolic object), castration is defined by Lacan as a symbolic lack of an imaginary object; castration does not bear on the penis as a real organ, but on the imaginary PHALLUS (S4, 219). Lacan's account of the castration complex is thus raised out of the dimension of simple biology or anatomy: 'It is insoluble by any reduction to biological givens' (E, 282).

Following Freud, Lacan argues that the castration complex is the pivot on which the whole Oedipus complex turns (S4, 216). However, whereas Freud argues that these two complexes are articulated differently in boys and girls, Lacan argues that the castration complex always denotes the final moment of the Oedipus complex in both sexes. Lacan divides the Oedipus complex into three 'times' (Lacan, 1957–8: seminar of 22 January 1958). In the first time, the child perceives that the mother desires something beyond the child himself – namely, the imaginary phallus – and then tries to be the phallus for the mother (see PREOEDIPAL PHASE). In the second time, the imaginary father intervenes to deprive the mother of her object by promulgating the incest taboo; properly speaking, this is not castration but privation. Castration is only realised in the third and final time, which represents the 'dissolution' of the Oedipus complex. It is then that the real father intervenes by showing that he really posesses the phallus, in such a way that the child is forced to abandon his attempts to be the phallus (S4, 208–9, 227).

From this account of the Oedipus complex, it is clear that Lacan uses the term 'castration' to refer to two different operations:

● **Castration of the mother** In the first time of the Oedipus complex, 'the mother is considered, by both sexes, as possessing the phallus, as the phallic mother' (E, 282). By promulgating the incest taboo in the second time, the imaginary father is seen to deprive her of this phallus. Lacan argues that properly speaking, this is not castration but privation. However, Lacan himself often uses these terms interchangeably, speaking both of the privation of the mother and of her castration.

● **Castration of the subject** This is castration proper, in the sense of being a symbolic act which bears on an imaginary object. Whereas the castration/ privation of the mother which comes about in the second time of the Oedipus complex negates the verb 'to have' (the mother does not *have* the phallus), the castration of the subject in the third time of the Oedipus complex negates the verb 'to be' (the subject must renounce his attempts to *be* the phallus for the mother). In renouncing his attempts to be the object of the mother's desire, the subject gives up a certain *jouissance* which is never regained despite all attempts to do so; 'Castration means that *jouissance* must be refused so that it can be reached on the inverted ladder (*l'échelle renversée*) of the Law of desire' (E, 324). This applies equally to boys and girls: this 'relationship to the phallus . . . is established without regard to the anatomical difference of the sexes' (E, 282).

On a more fundamental level, the term castration may also refer not to an 'operation' (the result of an intervention by the imaginary or real father) but to a state of lack which already exists in the mother prior to the subject's birth. This lack is evident in her own desire, which the subject perceives as a desire for the imaginary phallus. That is, the subject realises at a very early stage that the mother is not complete and self-sufficient in herself, nor fully satisfied with her child (the subject himself), but desires something else. This is the subject's first perception that the Other is not complete but lacking.

Both forms of castration (of the mother and of the subject) present the subject with a choice: to accept castration or to deny it. Lacan argues that it is only by accepting (or 'assuming') castration that the subject can reach a degree of psychic normality. In other words, the assumption of castration has a 'normalising effect'. This normalising effect is to be understood in terms of both psychopathology (clinical structures and symptoms) and sexual identity.

• **Castration and clinical structures** It is the refusal of castration that lies at the root of all psychopathological structures. However, since it is impossible to accept castration entirely, a completely 'normal' position is never achieved. The closest to such a position is the neurotic structure, but even here the subject still defends himself against the lack in the Other by repressing awareness of castration. This prevents the neurotic from fully assuming his desire, since 'it is the assumption of castration that creates the lack upon which desire is instituted' (Ec, 852). A more radical defence against castration than repression is disavowal, which is at the root of the perverse structure. The psychotic takes the most extreme path of all; he completely repudiates castration, as if it had never existed (S1, 53). This repudiation of symbolic castration leads to the return of castration in the real, such as in the form of hallucinations of dismemberment (as in the case of the Wolf Man; see S1, 58–9) or even self-mutilation of the real genital organs.

• **Castration and sexual identity** It is only by assuming castration (in both senses) that the subject can take up a sexual position as a man or a woman (see SEXUAL DIFFERENCE). The different modalities of refusing castration find expression in the various forms of perversion.

cause (*cause*) The concept of causality forms an important thread that runs throughout Lacan's entire œuvre. It first appears in the context of the question of the cause of psychosis, which is a central concern of Lacan's doctoral thesis (Lacan, 1932). Lacan returns to this question in 1946, where the cause of madness becomes the very essence of all psychical causality. In the 1946 paper he reiterates his earlier view that a specifically psychical cause is needed to explain psychosis; however, he also questions the possibility of defining 'psychical' in terms of a simple opposition to the concept of matter, and this leads him, in 1955, to dispense with the simplistic notion of 'psychogenesis' (S3, 7).

In the 1950s Lacan begins to address the very concept of causality itself, arguing that it is to be situated on the border between the symbolic and the real; it implies 'a mediation between the chain of symbols and the real' (S2, 192). He argues that the concept of causality, which underpins all science, is itself a non-scientific concept; 'the very notion of cause . . . is established on the basis of an original wager' (S2, 192).

In the seminar of 1962–3, Lacan argues that the true meaning of causality should be looked for in the phenomenon of anxiety, for anxiety is the cause of doubt. He then links this with the concept of OBJET PETIT A, which is now defined as the *cause* of desire, rather than that towards which desire tends.

In 1964, Lacan uses Aristotle's typology of causes to illustrate the difference between the symbolic and the real (see CHANCE).

Lacan returns to the subject of causality in his 1965–6 seminar, where he distinguishes between magic, religion, science and psychoanalysis on the basis to their relationship to truth as cause (see Lacan, 1965a).

Lacan also plays on the ambiguity of the term, since besides being 'that which provokes an effect', a cause is also 'that for which one fights, that which one defends'. Lacan clearly sees himself as fighting for 'the Freudian cause' (the name he gave to the school he founded in 1980), although this fight can only be won when one realises that the cause of the unconscious is always 'a lost cause' (S11, 128).

chance (*chance*)   Freud has often been accused of a crude determinism, since no slip or blunder, no matter how apparently insignificant, is ever ascribed to chance. Indeed, Freud wrote, 'I believe in external (real) chance, it is true, but not in internal (psychical) accidental events' (Freud, 1901: 257).

Lacan expresses the same belief in his own terms: chance, in the sense of pure contingency, only exists in the real. In the symbolic order, there is no such thing as pure chance.

In the seminar of 1964, Lacan uses Aristotle's distinction between two kinds of chance to illustrate this distinction between the real and the symbolic. In the second book of the *Physics*, where the concept of causality (see CAUSE) is discussed, Aristotle explores the role of chance and fortune in causality. He distinguishes between two types of chance: *automaton*, which refers to chance events in the world at large, and *tyche*, which designates chance insofar as it affects agents who are capable of moral action.

Lacan redefines *automaton* as 'the network of signifiers', thus locating it in the symbolic order. The term thus comes to designate those phenomena which seem to be chance but which are in truth the insistence of the signifier in determining the subject. *Automaton* is not truly arbitrary: only the real is truly arbitrary, since 'the real is beyond the *automaton*' (S11, 59).

The real is aligned with *tyche*, which Lacan redefines as 'the encounter with the real'. *Tyche* thus refers to the incursion of the real into the symbolic order: unlike the *automaton*, which is the structure of the symbolic order which determines the subject, *tyche* is purely arbitrary, beyond the determinations of the symbolic order. It is a knock on the door that interrupts a dream, and on a more painful level it is trauma. The traumatic event is the encounter with the real, extrinsic to signification.

code (*code*) Lacan borrows the term 'code' from Roman Jakobson's theory of communication. Jakobson presents his opposition 'code vs message' as an equivalent of Saussure's *langue* vs *parole*. However, Lacan draws an important distinction between the concepts of LANGUAGE and code (see E, 84). Codes are the province of animal communication, not of intersubjective communication. Whereas the elements of a language are SIGNIFIERS, the elements of a code are indices (see INDEX). The fundamental difference is that there is a fixed bi-univocal (one-to-one) relationship between an index and its referent, whereas there is no such relationship between a signifier and a referent or between a signifier and a signified. Because of the bi-univocal relation of indices and referents, codes lack what Lacan regards as the fundamental feature of human languages: the potential for ambiguity and equivocation (see Lacan, 1973b).

Lacan is not always consistent in maintaining this opposition between code and language. In the seminar of 1958–9, for example, when presenting the elementary cell of the graph of desire, he designates one point as the code, which he also designates as the place of the Other and the battery of signifiers. In this case, it is clear that the term 'code' is being used in the same sense as the term 'language', namely, to designate the set of signifiers available to the subject.

cogito Lacan's works abound in references to the famous phrase by Descartes, *cogito ergo sum* ('I think, therefore I am' – see Descartes, 1637: 54). This phrase (which Lacan often refers to simply as 'the *cogito*') comes to stand, in Lacan's work, for Descartes's entire philosophy. Lacan's attitude to Cartesianism is extremely complex, and only a few of the most important points can be summarised here.

1. On one level, the *cogito* comes to stand for the modern western concept of the EGO, based as it is on the notions of the self-sufficiency and self-transparency of CONSCIOUSNESS, and the autonomy of the ego (see E, 6). Although Lacan does not believe that the modern western concept of the ego was invented by Descartes or by any other individual, he argues that it was born in the same era in which Descartes was writing (the mid-sixteenth to the early seventeenth century), and is particularly clearly expressed by Descartes (see S2, 6–7). Thus, although this concept of the ego seems so natural and eternal to western man today, it is in fact a relatively recent cultural construct; its eternal-natural appearance is in fact an illusion produced by retroaction (S2, 4–5).

Lacan argues that the experience of psychoanalytic treatment 'is an experience that leads us to oppose any philosophy directly issuing from the *Cogito*' (E, 1; see S2, 4). Freud's discovery of the unconscious subverts the Cartesian concept of subjectivity because it disputes the Cartesian equation subject = ego = consciousness. One of Lacan's main criticisms of ego-psychology and object-relations theory is that these schools betrayed Freud's discovery by returning to the pre-Freudian concept of the subject as an autonomous ego (S2, 11).

2. On another level, Lacan's views can be seen not only as a subversion of the *cogito*, but also as an extension of it, for the *cogito* not only encapsulates the false equation subject = ego = consciousness which Lacan opposes, but also focuses attention on the concept of the SUBJECT, which Lacan wishes to retain. Thus the *cogito* contains within itself the seeds of its own subversion, by putting forward a concept of subjectivity which undermines the modern concept of the ego. This concept of subjectivity refers to what Lacan calls 'the subject of science': a subject who is denied all intuitive access to knowledge and is thus left with reason as the only path to knowledge (Ec, 831; see Ec, 858).

By opposing the subject to the ego, Lacan proposes that the subject of the Cartesian *cogito* is in fact one and the same as the subject of the unconscious. Psychoanalysis can thus operate with a Cartesian method, advancing from doubt to certainty, with the crucial difference that it does not start from the statement 'I think' but from the affirmation 'it thinks' (*ça pense*) (S11, 35–6). Lacan rewrites Descartes's phrase in various ways, such as 'I think where I am not, therefore I am where I do not think' (E, 166). Lacan also uses the *cogito* to distinguish between the subject of the statement and the subject of the ENUNCIATION (see S11, 138–42; see S17, 180–4).

communication (*communication*)   Most theories of communication offered by modern linguistics are characterised by two important features. Firstly, they usually involve a reference to the category of intentionality, which is conceived of as coterminous with consciousness (e.g. Blakemore, 1992: 33). Secondly, they represent communication as a simple process in which a message is sent by one person (the addresser) to another (the addressee) (e.g. Jakobson, 1960: 21).

However, both these features are put into question by the specific experience of communication in psychoanalytic treatment. Firstly, SPEECH is revealed to possess an intentionality that goes beyond conscious purpose. Secondly, the speaker's message is seen to be not merely directed at another but also at himself; 'in human speech the sender is always a receiver at the same time' (S3, 24). Putting these two points together, it can be said that the part of the speaker's message which is addressed to himself is the unconscious intention behind the message. When speaking to the analyst, the analysand is also addressing a message to himself, but is not aware of this. The task of the analyst is to enable the analysand to hear the message he is unconsciously addressing to himself; by interpreting the analysand's words, the analyst permits the analysand's message to return to him in its true, unconscious dimension. Hence Lacan defines analytic communication as the act whereby 'the sender receives his own message from the receiver in an inverted form' (Ec, 41).

complex (*complexe*)   The term 'complex' occupies an important place in Lacan's work before 1950, where it is closely related to the IMAGO. Whereas the imago designates an imaginary stereotype relating to one person, the complex is a whole constellation of interacting imagos; it is the internalisation of the subject's earliest social structures (i.e. the relationships between the various actors in his family environment). A complex involves multiple identifications with all the interacting imagos, and thus provides a script according to which the subject is led 'to play out, as the sole actor, the drama of conflicts' between the members of his family (Ec, 90).

In his pre-war work, Lacan argues that it is because human psychology is based on the complexes, which are entirely cultural products, rather than on natural INSTINCTS, that human behaviour cannot be explained by reference to biological givens. Nevertheless, while drawing this explicit contrast between complexes and instincts, Lacan also recognises that complexes may be compared to instincts in that they make up for the instinctual inadequacy (*insuffisance vitale*) of the human infant, and argues that the complexes are propped on biological functions such as weaning (Lacan, 1938: 32–3).

In 1938 Lacan identifies three 'family complexes', each of which is the trace of a 'psychical crisis' which accompanies a 'life crisis'. The first of these complexes is the weaning complex (*complexe du sevrage*). Taking up the idea of a 'trauma of weaning', first developed by René Laforgue in the 1920s, Lacan argues that no matter how late weaning occurs, it is always perceived by the infant as coming too early.

> Whether traumatic or not, weaning leaves in the human psyche a permanent trace of the biological relation which it interrupts. This life crisis is in effect accompanied by a psychical crisis, without doubt the first whose solution has a dialectical structure.
>
> (Lacan, 1938: 27)

After the weaning complex comes the intrusion complex (*complexe de l'intrusion*), which represents the experience that the child has when he realises that he has siblings. The child must then cope with the fact that he is no longer the exclusive object of his parents' attention. The third and final family complex is the OEDIPUS COMPLEX.

After their appearance in the 1938 paper, the terms 'weaning complex' and 'intrusion complex' disappear almost completely from Lacan's work (there is a brief reference to them in 1950, but little else; Ec, 141). However, the Oedipus complex remains a fundamental reference point throughout, and this is complemented by a growing interest, from 1956 on, in the CASTRATION COMPLEX.

consciousness (*conscience*)   In the so-called 'topographical model', Freud isolates consciousness as one of the parts of the psyche, along with the UNCONSCIOUS and the preconscious. Lacan finds Freud's remarks on consciousness far weaker than his formulations on the unconscious; 'while he [Freud] can give a coherent, balanced account of the majority of other parts of the psychic apparatus, when it's a question of consciousness, he always encounters mutually contradictory conditions' (S2, 117). According to Lacan, Freud's problems with discussing consciousness return again and again to haunt his theory: 'The difficulties which this system of consciousness raises reappear at each level of Freud's theorising' (S2, 117). In particular, Lacan rejects the apparent attempts in Freud's work to link the consciousness-perception system to the EGO, unless this link is carefully theorised. If there is a link between the ego and consciousness, it is in terms of a lure; the illusion of a fully self-transparent consciousness is subverted by the whole psychoanalytic experience (see COGITO). 'Consciousness in man is by essence a polar tension between an *ego* alienated from the subject and a perception which fundamentally escapes it, a pure *percipi*' (S2, 177).

In 1954 Lacan gives 'a materialist definition of the phenomenon of consciousness' (S2, 40–52). However, matter is not to be confused with nature; Lacan argues that consciousness does not evolve from the natural order; it is radically discontinuous, and its origin is more akin to creation than to evolution (S7, 213–14; 223).

In the 1960s Lacan rethinks the illusion of a self-consciousness (*Selbstbewußtsein*) fully present to itself in terms of his concept of the SUBJECT SUPPOSED TO KNOW.

counterpart (*semblable*)   The term 'counterpart' plays an important part in Lacan's work from the 1930s on, and designates other people in whom the subject perceives a likeness to himself (principally a visual likeness). The counterpart plays an important part in the intrusion complex and in the MIRROR STAGE (which are themselves closely interrelated).

The intrusion complex is one of the three 'family complexes' which Lacan discusses in his 1938 article on the family, and arises when the child first realises that he has siblings, that other subjects *like him* participate in the family structure. The emphasis here is on likeness; the child identifies with his siblings on the basis of the recognition of bodily similarity (which depends, of course, on their being a relatively small age difference between the subject and his siblings). It is this identification that gives rise to the 'imago of the counterpart' (Lacan, 1938: 35–9).

The imago of the counterpart is interchangeable with the image of the subject's own body, the SPECULAR IMAGE with which the subject identifies in the mirror stage, leading to the formation of the ego. This interchangeability is evident in such phenomena as TRANSITIVISM, and illustrates the way that the subject constitutes his objects on the basis of his ego. The image of another person's body can only be identified with insofar as it is perceived as similar to one's own body, and conversely the counterpart is only recognised as a separate, identifiable ego by projecting one's own ego onto him.

In 1955 Lacan introduces a distinction between 'the big Other' and 'the little other' (or 'the imaginary other'), reserving the latter term for the counterpart and/or specular image. The counterpart is the little other because it is not truly other at all; it is not the radical alterity represented by the Other, but the other insofar as he is similar to the ego (hence the interchangeability of *a* and *a'* in schema L).

countertransference (*contre-transfert*) Freud coined the term 'countertransference' to designate the analyst's 'unconscious feelings' towards the patient. Although Freud only used the term very rarely, it became much more widely used in psychoanalytic theory after his death. In particular, analysts soon divided over the role allotted to countertransference in discussions of technique. On the one hand, many analysts argued that countertransference manifestations were the result of incompletely analysed elements in the analyst, and that such manifestations should therefore be reduced to a minimum by a more complete training analysis. On the other hand, some analysts from the Kleinian school, beginning with Paula Heimann, argued that the analyst should be guided in his interpretations by his own countertransference reactions, taking his own feelings as an indicator of the patient's state of mind (Heimann, 1950). Whereas the former group regarded countertransference as an obstacle to analysis, the latter group regarded it as a useful tool.

In the 1950s, Lacan presents countertransference as a RESISTANCE, an obstacle which hinders the progress of psychoanalytic treatment. Like all resistances to treatment, countertransference is ultimately a resistance of the analyst. Thus Lacan defines countertransference as 'the sum of the prejudices, passions, perplexities, and even the insufficient information of the analyst at a certain moment of the dialectical process' of the treatment (Ec, 225).

Lacan refers to two of Freud's case studies to illustrate what he means. In 1951, he refers to the Dora case (Freud, 1905e), and argues that Freud's countertransference was rooted in his belief that heterosexuality is natural rather than normative, and in his identification with Herr K. Lacan argues that it was these two factors which caused Freud to handle the treatment badly and provoke the 'negative transference' which led to Dora breaking off the treatment (Lacan, 1951a).

In 1957 Lacan presents a similar analysis of Freud's treatment of the young homosexual woman (Freud, 1920a). He argues that when Freud interpreted the woman's dream as expressing a wish to deceive him, he was focusing on the imaginary dimension of the woman's transference rather than on the symbolic dimension (S4, 135). That is, Freud interpreted the dream as something directed at him personally, rather than as something directed at the Other.

Lacan argues that Freud did this because he found the woman attractive and because he identified with the woman's father (S4, 106–9). Once again, Freud's countertransference brought the treatment to a premature end, though this time it was Freud who decided to terminate it.

The preceding examples might seem to suggest that Lacan aligns himself with those analysts who argue that the training analysis should give the analyst the capacity to transcend all affective reactions to the patient. However, Lacan absolutely rejects this point of view, which he dismisses as a 'stoical ideal' (S8, 219). The training analysis does not put the analyst beyond passion, and to believe that it does would be to believe that all the passions stem from the unconscious, an idea which Lacan rejects. If anything, the better analysed the analyst is, the more likely he is to be frankly in love with, or be quite repulsed by, the analysand (S8, 220). If, then, the analyst does not act on the basis of these feelings, it is not because his training analysis has drained away his passions, but because it has given him a desire which is even stronger than those passions, a desire which Lacan calls the DESIRE OF THE ANALYST (S8, 220–1).

Hence Lacan does not entirely reject Paula Heimann's position. He accepts that analysts have feelings towards their patients, and that sometimes the analyst can direct the treatment better by reflecting on these feelings. For example, if Freud had reflected a bit more on his feelings towards the young homosexual woman, he might have avoided interpreting her dream as a message addressed directly to him (S4, 108).

> No one has ever said that the analyst should never have feelings towards his patient. But he must know not only not to give into them, to keep them in their place, but also how to make adequate use of them in his technique.
>
> (S1, 32)

If countertransference is condemned by Lacan, then, it is because he defines it not in terms of affects felt by the analyst, but as the analyst's failure to use those affects appropriately.

In the 1960s Lacan becomes very critical of the term countertransference. He argues that it connotes a symmetrical relationship between the analyst and the analysand, whereas the transference is anything but a symmetrical relationship. When speaking of the analyst's position it is both misleading and unnecessary to use the term countertransference; it is sufficient to speak of the different ways in which the analyst and analysand are implicated in the transference (S8, 233). 'The transference is a phenomenon in which subject and psycho-analyst are both included. To divide it in terms of transference and counter-transference . . . is never more than a way of avoiding the essence of the matter' (S11, 231).

D

death (*mort*)   The term *death* occurs in various contexts in Lacan's work.

1. Death is constitutive of the symbolic order, because the symbol, by standing in place of the thing which it symbolises, is equivalent to the death of the thing: 'the symbol is the murder of the thing' (E, 104). Also, the 'first symbol' in human history is the tomb (E, 104). It is only by virtue of the signifier that man has access to and can conceive of his own death; 'It is in the signifier and insofar as the subject articulates a signifying chain that he comes up against the fact that he may disappear from the chain of what he is' (S7, 295). The signifier also puts the subject beyond death, because 'the signifier already considers him dead, by nature it immortalises him' (S3, 180). Death in the symbolic order is related to the death of the Father (i.e. the murder of the father of the horde in *Totem and Taboo*; Freud, 1912–13); the symbolic father is always a dead father.

2. In the seminar of 1959–60, 'The Ethics of Psychoanalysis', Lacan talks about the 'second death' (a phrase which he coins in reference to a passage from the Marquis de Sade's novel *Juliette*, in which one of the characters speaks of a 'second life', see Sade, 1797: 772, quoted in S7, 211). The first death is the physical death of the body, a death which ends one human life but which does not put an end to the cycles of corruption and regeneration. The second death is that which prevents the regeneration of the dead body, 'the point at which the very cycles of the transformations of nature are annihilated' (S7, 248). The concept of the second death is used by Lacan to formulate ideas on various themes: beauty (S7, 260; it is the function of beauty to reveal man's relationship to his own death – S7, 295); the direct relationship to being (S7, 285); and the sadistic fantasy of inflicting perpetual pain (S7, 295). The phrase 'zone between-two-deaths' (*l'espace de l'entre-deux-morts*), which was originally coined by one of Lacan's students (see S7, 320), is taken up by Lacan to designate 'the zone in which tragedy is played out' (S8, 120).

3. Death plays an important role in the philosophical systems of Hegel and Heidegger, and Lacan draws on both of these in his theorisation of the role of death in psychoanalysis. From Hegel (via Kojève), Lacan takes the idea that death is both constitutive of man's freedom and 'the absolute Master' (Kojève, 1947: 21). Death plays a crucial part in the Hegelian dialectic of the MASTER and the slave where it is intimately linked with desire, since the master only affirms himself for others by means of a desire for death (E, 105). From Heidegger, Lacan takes the idea that human existence only takes on meaning by virtue of the finite limit set by death, so that the human subject is properly a 'being-for-death'; this corresponds to Lacan's view that the analysand should come, via the analytic process, to assume his own mortality (E, 104–5).

4. In his comparison between psychoanalytic treatment and the game of bridge, Lacan describes the analyst as playing the position of the 'dummy' (in

French, *le mort*; literally, 'the dead person'). 'The analyst intervenes concretely in the dialectic of analysis by pretending that he is dead . . . he makes death present' (E, 140). The analyst 'cadaverises' himself (*se corpsifiat*).

5. The question which constitutes the structure of OBSESSIONAL NEUROSIS concerns death; it is the question 'Am I dead or alive?' (S3, 179–80).

death drive (*pulsion de mort*)   Although intimations of the concept of the death drive (*Todestrieb*) can be found early on in Freud's work, it was only in *Beyond the Pleasure Principle* (1920g) that the concept was fully articulated. In this work Freud established a fundamental opposition between life drives (eros), conceived of as a tendency towards cohesion and unity, and the death drives, which operate in the opposite direction, undoing connections and destroying things. However, the life drives and the death drives are never found in a pure state, but always mixed/fused together in differing proportions. Indeed, Freud argued that were it not for this fusion with erotism, the death drive would elude our perception, since in itself it is silent (Freud, 1930a: SE, XXI, 120).

The concept of the death drive was one of the most controversial concepts introduced by Freud, and many of his disciples rejected it (regarding it as mere poetry or as an unjustifiable incursion into metaphysics), but Freud continued to reaffirm the concept for the rest of his life. Of the non-Lacanian schools of psychoanalytic theory, only Kleinian psychoanalysis takes the concept seriously.

Lacan follows Freud in reaffirming the concept of the death drive as central to psychoanalysis: 'to ignore the death instinct in his [Freud's] doctrine is to misunderstand that doctrine entirely' (E, 301).

In Lacan's first remarks on the death drive, in 1938, he describes it as a nostalgia for a lost harmony, a desire to return to the preoedipal fusion with the mother's breast, the loss of which is marked on the psyche in the weaning complex (Lacan, 1938: 35). In 1946 he links the death drive to the suicidal tendency of narcissism (Ec, 186). By linking the death drive with the preoedipal phase and with narcissism, these early remarks would place the death drive in what Lacan later comes to call the imaginary order.

However, when Lacan begins to develop his concept of the three orders of imaginary, symbolic and real, in the 1950s, he does not situate the death drive in the imaginary but in the symbolic. In the seminar of 1954–5, for example, he argues that the death drive is simply the fundamental tendency of the symbolic order to produce REPETITION; 'The death instinct is only the mask of the symbolic order' (S2, 326). This shift also marks a difference with Freud, for whom the death drive was closely bound up with biology, representing the fundamental tendency of every living thing to return to an inorganic state. By situating the death drive firmly in the symbolic, Lacan articulates it with culture rather than nature; he states that the death drive 'is not a question of biology' (E, 102), and must be distinguished from the biological instinct to return to the inanimate (S7, 211–12).

Another difference between Lacan's concept of the death drive and Freud's emerges in 1964. Freud opposed the death drive to the sexual drives, but now Lacan argues that the death drive is not a separate drive, but is in fact an aspect of every DRIVE. 'The distinction between the life drive and the death drive is true in as much as it manifests two aspects of the drive' (S11, 257). Hence Lacan writes that 'every drive is virtually a death drive' (Ec, 848), because (i) every drive pursues its own extinction, (ii) every drive involves the subject in repetition, and (iii) every drive is an attempt to go beyond the pleasure principle, to the realm of excess JOUISSANCE where enjoyment is experienced as suffering.

defence (*défense*) From his earliest works, Freud situated the concept of defence at the heart of his theory of neurosis. Defence refers to the reaction of the ego to certain interior stimuli which the ego perceives as dangerous. Although Freud later came to argue that there were different 'mechanisms of defence' in addition to REPRESSION (see Freud, 1926d), he makes it clear that repression is unique in the sense that it is constitutive of the unconscious. Anna Freud attempted to classify some of these mechanisms in her book *The Ego and the Mechanisms of Defence* (1936).

Lacan is very critical of the way in which Anna Freud and ego-psychology interpret the concept of defence. He argues that they confuse the concept of defence with the concept of RESISTANCE (Ec, 335). For this reason, Lacan urges caution when discussing the concept of defence, and prefers not to centre his concept of psychoanalytic treatment around it. When he does discuss defence, he opposes it to resistance; whereas resistances are transitory imaginary responses to intrusions of the symbolic and are on the side of the object, defences are more permanent symbolic structures of subjectivity (which Lacan usually calls FANTASY rather than defence). This way of distinguishing between resistance and defence is quite different from that of other schools of psychoanalysis, which, if they have distinguished between defence and resistance at all, have generally tended to regard defences as transitory phenomena and resistances as more stable.

The opposition between desire and defence is, for Lacan, a dialectical one. Thus he argues in 1960 that, like the neurotic, the pervert 'defends himself in his desire', since 'desire is a defence (*défense*), a prohibition (*défense*) against going beyond a certain limit in *jouissance*' (E, 322). In 1964 he goes on to argue: 'To desire involves a defensive phase that makes it identical with not wanting to desire' (S11, 235).

delusion (*délire*) Delusions are usually defined in psychiatry as firmly held, incorrigible false beliefs, inconsistent with the information available and with the beliefs of the subject's social group (see American Psychiatric

Association, 1987: 395; Hughes, 1981: 206). Delusions are the central clinical feature of PARANOIA, and can range from single ideas to complex networks of beliefs (called *delusional systems*).

In Lacanian terms, the paranoiac lacks the NAME-OF-THE-FATHER, and the delusion is the paranoiac's attempt to fill the hole left in his symbolic universe by the absence of this primordial signifier. Thus the delusion is not the 'illness' of paranoia itself; it is, on the contrary, the paranoiac's attempt to heal himself, to pull himself out of the breakdown of the symbolic universe by means of a substitute formation. As Freud commented in his work on Schreber, 'What we take to be the pathological production, the delusional formation, is in reality the attempt at recovery, the reconstruction' (Freud, 1911c: SE XII, 71).

Lacan insists on the significance of the delusion and stresses the importance of attending closely to the psychotic patient's own account of his delusion. The delusion is a form of discourse, and must therefore be understood as 'a field of signification that has organised a certain signifier' (S3, 121). For this reason all delusional phenomena are 'clarified in reference to the functions and structure of speech' (S3, 310).

The paranoid delusional construction may take many forms. One common form, the 'delusion of persecution', revolves around the Other of the Other, a hidden subject who pulls the strings of the big Other (the symbolic order), and who controls our thoughts, conspires against us, watches us, etc.

demand (*demande*)

demand (*demande*) The French terms *demander* and *demande* lack the connotations of imperativeness and urgency conveyed by the English word 'demand', and are perhaps closer to the English words 'ask for' and 'request'. However, all English translations of Lacan use the term 'demand' in order to maintain consistency.

Although the term 'demand' only begins to figure prominently in Lacan's work from 1958 on, related themes are already present in the 1956–7 seminar. It is in this seminar that Lacan discusses the call (*l'appel*), the baby's cry to the mother (S4, 182). Lacan argues that this cry (*cri*) is not merely an instinctual signal but 'is inserted in a synchronic world of cries organised in a symbolic system' (S4, 188). In other words, the infant's screams become organised in a linguistic structure long before the child is capable of articulating recognisable words.

It is the symbolic nature of the infant's screams which forms the kernel of Lacan's concept of demand, which Lacan introduces in 1958 in the context of his distinction between NEED, demand and DESIRE. Lacan argues that since the infant is incapable of performing the specific actions that would satisfy its biological needs, it must articulate those needs in vocal form (demands) so that another (the mother) will perform the specific action instead. The primary example of such a biological need is hunger, which the child articulates in a scream (a demand) so that the mother will feed it.

However, because the object which satisfies the child's need is provided by another, it takes on the added significance of being a proof of the Other's love. Accordingly demand too acquires a double function: in addition to articulating a need, it also becomes a demand for love. And just as the symbolic function of the object as a proof of love overshadows its real function as that which satisfies a need, so too the symbolic dimension of demand (as a demand for love) eclipses its real function (as an articulation of need). It is this double function which gives birth to desire, since while the needs which demand articulates may be satisfied, the craving for love is unconditional and insatiable, and hence persists as a leftover even after the needs have been satisfied; this leftover constitutes desire.

Demand is thus intimately linked to the human subject's initial HELPLESSNESS. By forcing the analysand to express himself entirely in speech, the psychoanalytic situation puts him back in the position of the helpless infant, thus encouraging REGRESSION.

> Through the mediation of the demand, the whole past opens up right down to early infancy. The subject has never done anything other than demand, he could not have survived otherwise, and we just follow on from there.
>
> (E, 254)

However, while the speech of the analysand is itself already a demand (for a reply), this demand is underpinned by deeper demands (to be cured, to be revealed to himself, to become an analyst) (E, 254). The question of how the analyst engages with these demands is crucial. Certainly the analyst does not attempt to gratify the analysand's demands, but nor is it simply a question of frustrating them (see FRUSTRATION).

In 1961, Lacan rethinks the various stages of libidinal organisation as forms of demand. The oral stage is constituted by a demand to be fed, which is a demand made by the subject. In the anal stage, on the other hand, it is not a question of the subject's demand, but the demand of the Other (the parent who disciplines the child in potty-training) (S8, 238–46, 269). In both of these pregenital stages the satisfaction of demand eclipses desire; only in the genital stage does desire come to be fully constituted (S8, 270).

desire (*désir*)   Lacan's term, *désir*, is the term used in the French translations of Freud to translate Freud's term *Wunsch*, which is translated as 'wish' by Strachey in the *Standard Edition*. Hence English translators of Lacan are faced with a dilemma; should they translate *désir* by 'wish', which is closer to Freud's *Wunsch*, or should they translate it as 'desire', which is closer to the French term, but which lacks the allusion to Freud? All of Lacan's English translators have opted for the latter, since the English term 'desire' conveys, like the French term, the implication of a continuous force, which is essential to Lacan's concept. The English term also carries with it the same allusions to Hegel's *Begierde* as are carried by the French term, and thus retains the philosophical nuances which are so essential to Lacan's concept of *désir* and which make it 'a category far wider and more abstract than any employed by Freud himself' (Macey, 1995: 80).

If there is any one concept which can claim to be the very centre of Lacan's thought, it is the concept of desire. Lacan follows Spinoza in arguing that 'desire is the essence of man' (S11, 275; see Spinoza, 1677: 128); desire is simultaneously the heart of human existence, and the central concern of psychoanalysis. However, when Lacan talks about desire, it is not any kind of desire he is referring to, but always unconscious desire. This is not because Lacan sees conscious desire as unimportant, but simply because it is unconscious desire that forms the central concern of psychoanalysis. Unconscious desire is entirely sexual; 'the motives of the unconscious are limited . . . to sexual desire . . . The other great generic desire, that of hunger, is not represented' (E, 142).

The aim of psychoanalytic treatment is to lead the analysand to recognise the truth about his desire. However, it is only possible to recognise one's desire when it is articulated in speech: 'It is only once it is formulated, named in the presence of the other, that desire, whatever it is, is recognised in the full sense of the term' (S1, 183).

Hence in psychoanalysis 'what's important is to teach the subject to name, to articulate, to bring this desire into existence' (S2, 228). However, it is not a question of seeking a new means of expression for a given desire, for this would imply a expressionist theory of language. On the contrary, by articulating desire in speech, the analysand brings it into existence:

> That the subject should come to recognise and to name his desire; that is the efficacious action of analysis. But it isn't a question of recognising something which would be entirely given. . . . In naming it, the subject creates, brings forth, a new presence in the world.
>
> (S2, 228–9)

However, there is a limit to how far desire can be articulated in speech because of a fundamental 'incompatibility between desire and speech' (E, 275); it is this incompatibility which explains the irreducibility of the unconscious (i.e. the fact that the unconscious is not that which *is not known*, but that which *cannot be known*). Although the truth about desire is present to some degree in all speech, speech can never articulate the *whole* truth about desire; whenever speech attempts to articulate desire, there is always a leftover, a surplus, which exceeds speech.

One of Lacan's most important criticisms of the psychoanalytic theories of his day was that they tended to confuse the concept of desire with the related concepts of DEMAND and NEED. In opposition to this tendency, Lacan insists on distinguishing between these three concepts. This distinction begins to emerge in his work in 1957 (see S4, 100–1, 125), but only crystallises in 1958 (Lacan, 1958c).

Need is a purely biological INSTINCT, an appetite which emerges according to the requirements of the organism and which abates completely (even if only temporarily) when satisfied. The human subject, being born in a state of helplessness, is unable to satisfy its own needs, and hence depends on the Other to help it satisfy them. In order to get the Other's help, the infant must express its needs vocally; need must be articulated in demand. The primitive demands of the infant may only be inarticulate screams, but they serve to bring the Other to minister to the infant's needs. However, the presence of the Other soon acquires an importance in itself, an importance that goes beyond the satisfaction of need, since this presence symbolises the Other's love. Hence demand soon takes on a double function, serving both as an articulation of need and as a demand for love. However, whereas the Other can provide the objects which the subject requires to satisfy his needs, the Other cannot provide that unconditional love which the subject craves. Hence even after the needs which were articulated in demand have been satisfied, the other aspect of demand, the craving for love, remains unsatisfied, and this leftover is desire. 'Desire is neither the appetite for satisfaction, nor the demand for love, but the difference that results from the subtraction of the first from the second' (E, 287).

Desire is thus the surplus produced by the articulation of need in demand; 'Desire begins to take shape in the margin in which demand becomes separated from need' (E, 311). Unlike a need, which can be satisfied and which then ceases to motivate the subject until another need arises, desire can never be satisfied; it is constant in its pressure, and eternal. The realisation of desire does not consist in being 'fulfilled', but in the reproduction of desire as such.

Lacan's distinction between need and desire, which lifts the concept of desire completely out of the realm of biology, is strongly reminiscent of Kojève's distinction between animal and human desire; desire is shown to be distinctively human when it is directed either toward another desire, or to an object which is 'perfectly useless from the biological point of view' (Kojève, 1947: 6).

It is important to distinguish between desire and the drives. Although they both belong to the field of the Other (as opposed to love), desire is one whereas the drives are many. In other words, the drives are the particular (partial) manifestations of a single force called desire (although there may also be desires which are not manifested in the drives: see S11, 243). There is only one object of desire, OBJET PETIT A, and this is represented by a variety of partial objects in different partial drives. The OBJET PETIT A is not the object towards which desire tends, but the cause of desire. Desire is not a relation to an object, but a relation to a LACK.

One of Lacan's most oft-repeated formulas is: 'man's desire is the desire of the Other' (S11, 235). This can be understood in many complementary ways, of which the following are the most important.

1. Desire is essentially 'desire of the Other's desire', which means both

desire to be the object of another's desire, and desire for recognition by another. Lacan takes this idea from Hegel, via Kojève, who states:

> Desire is human only if the one desires, not the body, but the Desire of the other . . . that is to say, if he wants to be 'desired' or 'loved', or, rather, 'recognised' in his human value. . . . In other words, all human, anthropogenetic Desire . . . is, finally, a function of the desire for 'recognition'.
>
> (Kojève, 1947: 6)

Kojève goes on to argue (still following Hegel) that in order to achieve the desired recognition, the subject must risk his own life in a struggle for pure prestige (see MASTER). That desire is essentially desire to be the object of another's desire is clearly illustrated in the first 'time' of the Oedipus complex, when the subject desires to be the phallus for the mother.

2. It is *qua* Other that the subject desires (E, 312): that is, the subject desires from the point of view of another. The effect of this is that 'the object of man's desire . . . is essentially an object desired by someone else' (Lacan, 1951b: 12). What makes an object desirable is not any intrinsic quality of the thing in itself but simply the fact that it is desired by another. The desire of the Other is thus what makes objects equivalent and exchangeable; this 'tends to diminish the special significance of any one particular object, but at the same time it brings into view the existence of objects without number' (Lacan, 1951b: 12).

This idea too is taken from Kojève's reading of Hegel; Kojève argues that 'Desire directed toward a natural object is human only to the extent that it is "mediated" by the Desire of another directed towards the same object: it is human to desire what others desire, because they desire it' (Kojève, 1947: 6). The reason for this goes back to the former point about human desire being desire for recognition; by desiring that which another desires, I can make the other recognise my right to possess that object, and thus make the other recognise my superiority over him (Kojève, 1947: 40).

This universal feature of desire is especially evident in hysteria; the hysteric is one who sustains another person's desire, converts another's desire into her own (e.g. Dora desires Frau K because she identifies with Herr K, thus appropriating his perceived desire; S4, 138; see Freud, 1905e). Hence what is important in the analysis of a hysteric is not to find out the object of her desire but to discover the place from which she desires (the subject with whom she identifies).

3. Desire is desire *for* the Other (playing on the ambiguity of the French preposition *de*). The fundamental desire is the incestuous desire for the mother, the primordial Other (S7, 67).

4. Desire is always 'the desire for something else' (E, 167), since it is impossible to desire what one already has. The object of desire is continually deferred, which is why desire is a METONYMY (E, 175).

5. Desire emerges originally in the field of the Other; i.e. in the unconscious.

The most important point to emerge from Lacan's phrase is that desire is a social product. Desire is not the private affair it appears to be but is always constituted in a dialectical relationship with the perceived desires of other subjects.

The first person to occupy the place of the Other is the mother, and at first the child is at the mercy of her desire. It is only when the Father articulates desire with the law by castrating the mother that the subject is freed from subjection to the whims of the mother's desire (see CASTRATION COMPLEX).

desire of the analyst (*désir de l'analyste*)   The phrase 'the desire of the analyst' is an ambiguous one that seems to oscillate in Lacan's work between two meanings:

● **A desire attributed to the analyst**   As well as attributing knowledge to the analyst, so also the analysand attributes desire to the analyst. The analyst is therefore not only a SUBJECT SUPPOSED TO KNOW but also a 'subject supposed to desire'. Thus the phrase 'the analyst's desire' does not refer the real desire in the analyst's psyche, but to the desire which the analysand attributes to him.

The task of the analyst throughout the treatment is to make it impossible for the analysand to be sure that he knows what the analyst wants from him; the analyst must make sure that his desire 'remains an x' for the analysand (S11, 274). In this way the analyst's supposed desire becomes the driving force of the analytic process, since it keeps the analysand working, trying to discover what the analyst wants from him; 'the desire of the analyst is ultimately that which operates in psychoanalysis' (Ec, 854). By presenting the analysand with an enigmatic desire, the analyst occupies the position of the Other, of whom the subject asks *Che vuoi?* ('What do you want from me?'), with the result that the subject's fundamental fantasy emerges in the transference.

● **A desire proper to the analyst**   The other sense of the phrase 'the desire of the analyst' refers to the desire which must animate the analyst in the way he directs treatment. This is easier to define negatively than positively. It is certainly not a desire for the impossible (S7, 300). Nor is it a desire to 'do good' or 'to cure'; on the contrary, it is 'a non-desire to cure' (S7, 218). It is not a desire that the analysand identify with the analyst; 'the analyst's desire . . . tends in a direction that is the exact opposite of identification' (S11, 274). Rather than identification, the analyst desires that the analysand's own unique truth emerge in the treatment, a truth that is absolutely different to that of the analyst; the analyst's desire is thus 'a desire to obtain absolute difference' (S11, 276). It is in the sense of 'a desire proper to the analyst' that Lacan wishes to locate the question of the analyst's desire at the heart of the ethics of psychoanalysis.

How is it that the analyst comes to be guided by the desire which is proper to his function? According to Lacan, this can only occur by means of a training analysis. The essential requirement, the condition *sine qua non* for becoming an analyst, is to undergo analytic treatment oneself. In the course of this treatment there will be a mutation in the economy of desire in the analyst-to-be; his desire will be restructured, reorganised (S8, 221–2). Only if this happens will he be able to function properly as an analyst.

development (*développement*) Psychoanalysis is presented by EGO-PSYCHOLOGY as a form of developmental psychology, with the emphasis placed on the temporal development of the child's sexuality. According to this interpretation, Freud shows how the child progresses through the various pregenital stages (the oral and anal stages) to maturity in the GENITAL stage.

In his early work Lacan seems to accept this developmental reading of Freud (which he labels 'geneticism'), at least in the matter of a genetic order for the three 'family complexes' (Lacan, 1938) and for ego defences (E, 5). As late as 1950 he takes seriously such genetic concepts as 'objectal fixation' and 'stagnation of development' (Ec, 148). However, in the early 1950s he begins to become extremely critical of geneticism for various reasons. Firstly, it presupposes a natural order for sexual development and takes no account of the symbolic articulation of human sexuality, thus ignoring the fundamental differences between drives and instincts. Secondly, it is based on a linear concept of time which is completely at odds with the psychoanalytic theory of TIME. Finally, it assumes that a final synthesis of sexuality is both possible and normal, whereas for Lacan no such synthesis exists. Thus, while both ego-psychology and OBJECT-RELA-TIONS THEORY propose the concept of a final stage of psychosexual development, in which the subject attains a 'mature' relation with the object, described as a genital relation, this is totally rejected by Lacan. Lacan argues that such a state of final wholeness and maturity is not possible because the subject is irremediably split, and the metonymy of desire is unstoppable. Furthermore, Lacan points out that 'the object which corresponds to an advanced stage of instinctual maturity is a rediscovered object' (S4, 15); the so-called final stage of maturity is nothing more than the encounter with the object of the first satisfactions of the child.

Lacan disputes the geneticist reading of Freud, describing it as a 'mythology of instinctual maturation' (E, 54). He argues that the various 'stages' analysed by Freud (oral, anal and genital) are not observable biological phenomena which develop naturally, such as the stages of sensoriomotor development, but 'obviously more complex structures' (E, 242). The pregenital stages are not chronologically ordered moments of a child's development, but essentially timeless structures which are projected retroactively onto the past; 'they are ordered in the retroaction of the Oedipus complex' (E, 197). Lacan thus dismisses all attempts to draw empirical evidence for the sequence of psychosexual stages by means of 'the so-called direct observation of the child' (E, 242), and places the emphasis on the reconstruction of such stages in the analysis of adults; 'It is by starting with the experience of the adult that we must grapple, retrospectively, *nachträglich*, with the supposedly original experiences' (S1, 217). In 1961, the pregenital stages are conceived by Lacan as forms of DEMAND.

The complex relationship between the chronological emergence of phenomena and the logical sequence of structures is also illustrated by reference to the question of language acquisition. On the one hand, psycholinguistics has discovered a natural order of development, in which the infant progresses through a sequence of biologically predetermined stages (babbling, followed by phoneme acquisition, then isolated words, and then sentences of increasing complexity). Lacan, however, is not interested in this chronological sequence, since it only deals with 'the emergence, properly speaking, of a phenomenon' (S1, 179). What interests Lacan is not the phenomena (external appearance) of language but the way language positions the subject in a symbolic structure. In respect of the latter, Lacan points out that 'the child already has an initial appreciation of the symbolism of language' well before he can speak, 'well before the exteriorised appearance of language' (S1, 179; see S1, 54). However, the question of how this 'initial appreciation' of the symbolic comes about is almost impossible to theorise, since it is not a question of a gradual acquisition of one signifier after another but the 'all or nothing' entry into a 'universe' of signifiers. A signifier is only a signifier by virtue of its relation to other signifiers, and so cannot be acquired in isolation. Thus the transition to the symbolic is always a question of creation *ex nihilo*, a radical discontinuity between one order and another, and never a question of a gradual evolution. The last term is particularly distasteful for Lacan, who warns his students to 'beware of that register of thought known as evolutionism' (S7, 213), and prefers to describe psychic change in terms of metaphors of creation *ex nihilo*.

Lacan's opposition to notions of development and evolution are not based on an opposition to the notion of psychic change in itself. On the contrary, Lacan insists on the historicity of the psyche, and sees the restoration of fluidity and movement to the psyche as the aim of psychoanalytic treatment. His opposition to the concept of development only reflects his suspicion of all normative models of psychic change; the subject is involved in a continual process of becoming, but this process is threatened, not aided, by imposing a fixed 'providential' model of genetic development upon it. Lacan thus argues that 'in psychoanalysis, history is a dimension different to that of development, and that it is an aberration to try to reduce the former to the latter. History only proceeds out of beat with development' (Ec, 875).

What, then, is to be made of the two great 'stages' which dominate Lacan's teaching, the mirror stage and the Oedipus complex? The mirror stage is clearly related to an event which can be located in a specific time in the life of the child (between six to eighteen months), but this event is only of interest to Lacan because it illustrates the essentially timeless structure of the dual relationship; and it is this structure that constitutes the heart of the mirror stage. (It is interesting to note that the French term *stade* can be understood in both temporal and spatial terms, as a 'stage', or as a 'stadium'). Likewise, while Freud locates the Oedipus complex at a specific age (the third to the fifth year of life), Lacan conceives of the Oedipus complex as a timeless triangular structure of subjectivity. It follows that questions of exactly *when* the ego is constituted, or *when* the child enters the Oedipus complex, which have led to so much controversy between other schools of psychoanalysis, are of little interest to Lacan. While Lacan admits that the 'ego is constituted at a specific moment in the history of the subject' (S1, 115), and that there is a moment when the Oedipus complex is formed, he is not interested in the question of exactly when those moments occur. The question of when the child makes his entry into the symbolic order is irrelevant to psychoanalysis. All that matters is that before he does so he is incapable of speech and so inaccesible to psychoanalysis, and that after he does so everything prior to that moment is transformed retroactively by the symbolic system.

dialectic (*dialectique*)   The term 'dialectic' originated with the Greeks, for whom it denoted (among other things) a discursive procedure in which an opponent in a debate is questioned in such a way as to bring out the contradictions in his discourse. This is the tactic which Plato ascribes to Socrates, who is shown as beginning most dialogues by first reducing his interlocutor to a state of confusion and helplessness. Lacan compares this to the first stage of psychoanalytic treatment, when the analyst forces the analysand to confront the contradictions and gaps in his narrative. However, just as Socrates then proceeds to draw out the truth from the confused statements of his interlocutor, so also the analyst proceeds to draw out the truth from the analysand's free associations (see S8, 140). Thus Lacan argues that 'psychoanalysis is a dialectical experience' (Ec, 216), since the analyst must engage the analysand in 'a dialectical operation' (S1, 278). It is only by means of 'an endless dialectical process' that the analyst can subvert the ego's disabling illusions of permanence and stability, in a manner identical to the Socratic Dialogue (Lacan, 1951b: 12).

Although the origin of dialectics goes back to the Greek philosophers, its dominance in modern philosophy is due to the revival of the concept in the eighteenth century by the post-Kantian idealists Fichte and Hegel, who conceived of the dialectic as a triad of thesis, antithesis and synthesis. For Hegel, the dialectic is both a method of exposition and the structure of historical progress itself. Thus in *Phenomenology of Spirit* (1807), Hegel shows how consciousness progresses towards absolute knowledge by means of a series of confrontations between opposing elements. Each confrontation is resolved by an operation called the *Aufhebung* (usually translated as 'sublation') in which a new idea (the synthesis) is born from the opposition between thesis and antithesis; the synthesis simultaneously annuls, preserves and raises this opposition to a higher level.

The particular way in which the Hegelian dialectic is appropriated by Lacan owes much to Alexandre Kojève, whose lectures on Hegel Lacan attended in Paris in the 1930s (see Kojève, 1947). Following Kojève, Lacan puts great emphasis on the particular stage of the dialectic in which the MASTER confronts the slave, and on the way that DESIRE is constituted dialectically by a relationship with the desire of the Other. Using the Dora case to illustrate his point, Lacan shows how psychoanalytic treatment progresses towards truth by a series of dialectical reversals (Lacan, 1951a). Lacan also makes use of the concept of *Aufhebung* to show how the symbolic order can simultaneously annul, preserve and raise an imaginary object (the imaginary phallus) to the status of a signifier (the symbolic phallus); the phallus then becomes 'the signifier of this *Aufhebung* itself, which it inaugurates by its disappearance' (E, 288).

However, there are also important differences between the Lacanian dialectic and the Hegelian dialectic. For Lacan, there is no such thing as a final synthesis such as is represented by Hegel's concept of absolute knowledge; the irreducibility of the unconscious represents the impossibility of any such absolute knowledge. For Lacan, then, 'the *Aufhebung* is one of those sweet dreams of philosophy' (S20, 79). This denial of a final synthesis subverts the very concept of progress itself. Thus Lacan contrasts his own version of the *Aufhebung* with that of Hegel, arguing that it replaces Hegel's idea of PROGRESS with 'the avatars of a lack' (Ec, 837).

disavowal (*déni*) Freud uses the term *Verleugnung* to denote 'a specific mode of defence which consists in the subject's refusing to recognise the reality of a traumatic perception' (Laplanche and Pontalis, 1967: 118). He introduces the term in 1923 in connection with the castration complex, the traumatic perception being the sight of the female genitalia; when children first discover the absence of the penis in the girl, they 'disavow the fact and believe that they do see a penis all the same' (Freud, 1923e: SE XIX, 143–4). Freud continues to employ the term throughout the rest of his work, linking it specifically both to psychosis and to FETISHISM. In these clinical conditions, disavowal is always accompanied by the opposite attitude (acceptance of reality), since it is 'rarely or perhaps never' possible for 'the ego's detachment from reality to be carried through completely' (Freud, 1940a: SE XXIII, 201). The coexistence in the ego of these two contradictory attitudes to reality leads to what Freud terms 'the splitting of the ego' (see SPLIT).

While Freud's use of the term is quite consistent, he does not distinguish the term rigorously from other related operations. Lacan, however, works the term into a rigorous theory, relating it and contrasting it specifically with the operations of REPRESSION and FORECLOSURE. Whereas Freud had only linked disavowal to one form of PERVERSION, Lacan makes it the fundamental operation in all forms of perversion. And whereas Freud had also linked disavowal with psychosis, Lacan limits disavowal exclusively to the structure of perversion. Disavowal is the fundamental operation in perversion, just as repression and foreclosure are the fundamental operations in neurosis and psychosis. Thus, in Lacan's account, disavowal is one way of responding to the castration of the Other; whereas the neurotic represses the realisation of castration, the pervert disavows it.

Like Freud, Lacan asserts that disavowal is always accompanied by a simultaneous acknowledgement of what is disavowed. Thus the pervert is not simply ignorant of castration; he simultaneously knows it and denies it. Whereas the term disavowal originally denotes, in Freud's work, only one side of this operation (the side of denial), for Lacan the term comes to denote both sides, the simultaneous denial and recognition of castration.

Whereas Freud relates disavowal to the perception of the absence of the penis in women, Lacan relates it to the realisation of the absence of the PHALLUS in the Other. The traumatic perception is, in Lacan's account, the realisation that the cause of desire is always a lack. It is this realisation that disavowal concerns; disavowal is the failure to accept that lack causes desire, the belief that desire is caused by a presence (e.g. the fetish).

discourse (*discours*)   Whenever Lacan uses the term 'discourse' (rather than, say, 'speech') it is in order to stress the transindividual nature of language, the fact that speech always implies another subject, an interlocutor. Thus the famous Lacanian formula, 'the unconscious is the discourse of the other' (which first appears in 1953, and later becomes 'the unconscious is the discourse of the Other') designates the unconscious as the effects on the subject of speech that is addressed to him from elsewhere; by another subject who has been forgotten, by another psychic locality (the other scene).

In 1969, Lacan begins to use the term 'discourse' in a slightly different way, though one that still carries with it the stress on INTERSUBJECTIVITY. From this point on the term designates 'a social bond, founded in language' (S20, 21). Lacan identifies four possible types of social bond, four possible articulations of the symbolic network which regulates intersubjective relations. These 'four discourses' are the discourse of the master, the discourse of the university, the discourse of the hysteric, and the discourse of the analyst. Lacan represents each of the four discourses by an algorithm: each algorithm contains the following four algebraic symbols:

S_1 = the master signifier

S_2 = knowledge (*le savoir*)

$\$$ = the subject

a = surplus enjoyment

What distinguishes the four discourses from one another is the positions of these four symbols. There are four positions in the algorithms of the four discourses, each of which is designated by a different name. The names of the four positions are shown in Figure 2; Lacan gives different names to these

$$\frac{\text{the agent}}{\text{truth}} \qquad \frac{\text{the other}}{\text{production}}$$

Figure 2   The structure of the four discourses
Source: Jacques Lacan, *Le Séminaire. Livre XX. Encore*, ed. Jacques-Alain Miller, Paris: Seuil, 1975.

positions at different points in his work, and this figure is taken from the 1972–3 seminar (S20, 21).

Each discourse is defined by writing the four algebraic symbols in a different position. The symbols always remain in the same order, so each discourse is simply the result of rotating the symbols a quarter turn. The top-left position ('the agent') is the dominant position which defines the discourse. In addition to the four symbols, each algorithm also contains an arrow going from the agent to the other. The four discourses are shown in Figure 3 (taken from S17, 31).

In 1971, Lacan proposes that the position of the agent is also the position of the SEMBLANCE. In 1972, Lacan inscribes two arrows in the formulas instead of one; one arrow (which Lacan labels 'impossibility') goes from the agent to the other, and the other arrow (which is labelled 'powerlessness') goes from production to truth (S20, 21).

The discourse of the MASTER is the basic discourse from which the other three discourses are derived. The dominant position is occupied by the master signifier (S_1), which represents the subject ($\$$) for another signifier or, more precisely, for all other signifiers (S_2); however, in this signifying operation there is always a surplus, namely, *objet petit a*. The point is that all attempts at totalisation are doomed to failure. The discourse of the master 'masks the division of the subject' (S17, 118). The discourse also illustrates clearly the structure of the dialectic of the master and the slave. The master (S_1) is the agent who puts the slave (S_2) to work; the result of this work is a surplus (a) that the master attempts to appropriate.

Discourse of the master
$$\frac{S_1 \rightarrow S_2}{\$ \qquad a}$$

Discourse of the university
$$\frac{S_2 \rightarrow a}{S_1 \qquad \$}$$

Discourse of the hysteric
$$\frac{\$ \rightarrow S_1}{a \qquad S_2}$$

Discourse of the analyst
$$\frac{a \rightarrow \$}{S_2 \qquad S_1}$$

Figure 3   The four discourses
Source: Jacques Lacan, *Le Séminaire. Livre XVII. L'envers de la psychanalyse*, ed. Jacques-Alain Miller, Paris: Seuil, 1975.

The discourse of the university is produced by a quarter turn of the discourse of the master (anticlockwise). The dominant position is occupied by knowledge (*savoir*). This illustrates the fact that behind all attempts to impart an apparently 'neutral' knowledge to the other can always be located an attempt at mastery (mastery of knowledge, and domination of the other to whom this knowledge is imparted). The discourse of the university represents the hegemony of knowledge, particularly visible in modernity in the form of the hegemony of science.

The discourse of the hysteric is also produced by a quarter turn of the discourse of the master, but in a clockwise direction. It is not simply 'that which is uttered by a hysteric', but a certain kind of social bond in which any subject may be inscribed. The dominant position is occupied by the divided subject, the symptom. This discourse is that which points the way towards knowledge (S17, 23). Psychoanalytic treatment involves 'the structural introduction of the discourse of the hysteric by means of artificial conditions'; in other words, the analyst 'hystericises' the patient's discourse (S17, 35).

The discourse of the analyst is produced by a quarter turn of the discourse of the hysteric (in the same way as Freud developed psychoanalysis by giving an interpretative turn to the discourse of his hysterical patients). The position of the agent, which is the position occupied by the analyst in the treatment, is occupied by *objet petit a*; this illustrates the fact that the analyst must, in the course of the treatment, become the cause of the analysand's desire (S17, 41). The fact that this discourse is the inverse of the discourse of the master emphasises that, for Lacan, psychoanalysis is an essentially subversive practice which undermines all attempts at domination and mastery. (For further information on the four discourses, see Bracher *et al.*, 1994.)

drive (*pulsion*) Freud's concept of the drive (*Trieb*) lies at the heart of his theory of sexuality. For Freud, the distinctive feature of human sexuality, as opposed to the sexual life of other animals, is that it is not regulated by any INSTINCT (a concept which implies a relatively fixed and innate relationship to an object) but by the drives, which differ from instincts in that they are extremely variable, and develop in ways which are contingent on the life history of the subject.

Lacan insists on maintaining the Freudian distinction between *Trieb* ('drive') and *Instinkt* ('instinct'), and criticises James Strachey for obliterating this distinction by translating both terms as 'instinct' in the *Standard Edition* (E, 301). Whereas 'instinct' denotes a mythical pre-linguistic NEED, the drive is completely removed from the realm of BIOLOGY. The drives differ from biological needs in that they can never be satisfied, and do not aim at an object but rather circle perpetually round it. Lacan argues that the purpose of the drive (*Triebziel*) is not to reach a *goal* (a final destination) but to follow its *aim* (the way itself), which is to circle round the object (S11, 168). Thus the real purpose of the drive is not some mythical goal of full satisfaction, but to return to its circular path, and the real source of enjoyment is the repetitive movement of this closed circuit.

Lacan reminds his readers that Freud defined the drive as a montage composed of four discontinuous elements: the pressure, the end, the object and the source. The drive cannot therefore be conceived of as 'some ultimate given, something archaic, primordial' (S11, 162); it is a thoroughly cultural and symbolic construct. Lacan thus empties the concept of the drive of the lingering references in Freud's work to energetics and hydraulics.

Lacan incorporates the four elements of the drive in his theory of the drive's 'circuit'. In this circuit, the drive originates in an erogenous zone, circles round the object, and then returns to the erogenous zone. This circuit is structured by the three grammatical voices

1 The active voice (e.g. to see)
2 The reflexive voice (e.g. to see oneself)
3 The passive voice (e.g. to be seen)

The first of these two times (active and reflexive voices) are autoerotic: they lack a subject. Only in the third time (the passive voice), when the drive completes its circuit, does 'a new subject' appear (which is to say that before this time, there was no subject: see S11, 178). Although the third time is the passive voice, the drive is always essentially active, which is why Lacan writes the third time not as 'to be seen' but as 'to make oneself be seen'. Even supposedly 'passive' phases of the drive such as masochism involve activity (S11, 200). The circuit of the drive is the only way for the subject to transgress the pleasure principle.

Freud argued that sexuality is composed of a number of partial drives (Ger. *Partieltrieb*) such as the oral drive and the anal drive, each specified by a different source (a different erotogenic zone). At first these component drives function anarchically and independently (viz. the 'polymorphous perversity' of children), but in puberty they become organised and fused together under the primacy of the genital organs (Freud, 1905d). Lacan emphasises the partial nature of all drives, but differs from Freud on two points.

1. Lacan rejects the idea that the partial drives can ever attain any complete organisation or fusion, arguing that the primacy of the genital zone, if achieved, is always a highly precarious affair. He thus challenges the notion, put forward by some psychoanalysts after Freud, of a genital drive in which the partial drives are completely integrated in a harmonious fashion.

2. Lacan argues that the drives are partial, not in the sense that they are parts of a whole (a 'genital drive'), but in the sense that they only represent sexuality partially; they do not represent the reproductive function of sexuality but only the dimension of enjoyment (S11, 204).

Lacan identifies four partial drives: the oral drive, the anal drive, the scopic

	PARTIAL DRIVE	EROGENOUS ZONE	PARTIAL OBJECT	VERB
D	Oral drive	Lips	Breast	To suck
	Anal drive	Anus	Faeces	To shit
d	Scopic drive	Eyes	Gaze	To see
	Invocatory drive	Ears	Voice	To hear

Figure 4   Table of partial drives

drive, and the invocatory drive. Each of these drives is specified by a different partial object and a different erogenous zone, as shown in Figure 4.

The first two drives relate to demand, whereas the second pair relate to desire.

In 1957, in the context of the graph of desire, Lacan proposes the formula ($\mathcal{S} \Diamond D$) as the MATHEME for the drive. This formula is to be read: the barred subject in relation to demand, the fading of the subject before the insistence of a demand that persists without any conscious intention to sustain it.

Throughout the various reformulations of drive-theory in Freud's work, one constant feature is a basic dualism. At first this dualism was conceived in terms of an opposition between the sexual drives (*Sexualtriebe*) on the one hand, and the ego-drives (*Ichtriebe*) or drives of self-preservation (*Selbsterhaltungstriebe*) on the other. This opposition was problematised by Freud's growing realisation, in the period 1914–20, that the ego-drives are themselves sexual. He was thus led to reconceptualise the dualism of the drives in terms of an opposition between the life drives (*Lebenstriebe*) and the death drives (*Todestriebe*).

Lacan argues that it is important to retain Freud's dualism, and rejects the monism of Jung, who argued that all psychic forces could be reduced to one single concept of psychic energy (S1, 118–20). However, Lacan prefers to reconceptualise this dualism in terms of an opposition between the symbolic and the imaginary, and not in terms of an opposition between different kinds of drives. Thus, for Lacan, all drives are sexual drives, and every drive is a DEATH DRIVE since every drive is excessive, repetitive, and ultimately destructive (Ec, 848).

The drives are closely related to DESIRE; both originate in the field of the subject, as opposed to the genital drive, which (if it exists) finds its form on the side of the Other (S11, 189). However, the drive is not merely another name for desire: they are the partial aspects in which desire is realised. Desire is one and undivided, whereas the drives are partial manifestations of desire.

dual relation (*relation duelle*) Duality and dual relations are essential characteristics of the imaginary order. The paradigmatic dual relation is the relation between the EGO and the SPECULAR IMAGE (*a* and *a'*) which Lacan analyses in his concept of the MIRROR STAGE. The dual relation is always characterised by illusions of similarity, symmetry and reciprocity.

In contrast to the duality of the imaginary order, the symbolic order is characterised by triads. In the symbolic order all relations involve not two but three terms; the third term is the big Other, which mediates all imaginary dual relations. The illusion of reciprocity in the imaginary dual relationship contrasts with the symbolic, which is the realm of 'absolute non-reciprocity' (Ec, 774). The Oedipus complex is the paradigmatic triangular structure, since the Father is introduced into the dual relation between mother and child as a third term. The Oedipal passage from a dual relation to a triangular structure is none other than the passage from the imaginary to the symbolic order. Indeed, the very concept of structure itself involves a minimum of three terms; 'there are always three terms in the structure' (S1, 218).

The opposition between imaginary dyads and symbolic triads is complicated by Lacan's discussion of the 'imaginary triad' (E, 197; S4, 29). The imaginary triad is Lacan's attempt to theorise the PREOEDIPAL STAGE in terms other than those of a merely dual relationship, and refers to the moment preceding the Oedipus complex, when a third element (the imaginary phallus) circulates between the mother and infant. When the father intervenes in the Oedipus complex he can therefore be seen either as a third element (between mother and child) or as a fourth element (in addition to mother, child and phallus). It is for this reason that Lacan writes that in the Oedipus complex 'it is not a question of a father–mother–child triangle, but of a triangle (father)–phallus–mother–child' (S3, 319).

One of Lacan's most frequent criticisms of the psychoanalytic theory of his day is that it constantly fails to theorise the role of the symbolic, and thus reduces the psychoanalytic encounter to an imaginary dual relationship between analyst and analysand. Lacan argues that this error lies behind a whole series of misunderstandings in psychoanalytic theory (see E, 246). In particular, it reduces analytic treatment to an ego-to-ego encounter which, because of the aggressivity inherent in all imaginary dual relations, often degenerates into a 'fight to the death' between analyst and analysand, a power struggle in which they are 'at daggers drawn' (see MASTER).

Against such a misconception, Lacan insists on the function of the symbolic in the analytic process, which introduces the Other as the third term in the analytic encounter. 'It is within a three- rather than two-term relation that we have to formulate the analytic experience' (S1, 11). Rather than seeing the treatment as a power struggle in which the analyst must overcome the patient's resistance, which is not psychoanalysis but suggestion, the analyst must realise that both he and the patient are equally subjected to the power of a third term: language itself.

Lacan's rejection of duality can also be seen in his rejection of all dualistic schemes of thought in favour of triadic schemes; 'all two-sided relationships are always stamped with the style of the imaginary' (Lacan, 1956b: 274). For example instead of the traditional binary opposition between what is real and what is imaginary, Lacan proposes a tripartite model of real, imaginary and symbolic. Other such triadic schemes are the three clinical structures of neurosis, psychosis and perversion; the three formations of the ego (ego-ideal, ideal ego and superego); the triad nature–culture–society; etc. However, as if to counteract this trend, Lacan also emphasised the importance of schemes involving four elements (see QUATERNARY).

E

ego (*moi*)   From very early on in his work, Lacan plays on the fact that the German term which Freud uses (*Ich*) can be translated into French by two words: *moi* (the usual term which French psychoanalysts use for Freud's *Ich*) and *je*. This had first been pointed out by the French grammarian, Édouard Pichon (see Roudinesco, 1986: 301). Thus, for example, in his paper on the mirror stage, Lacan oscillates between the two terms (Lacan, 1949). While it is difficult to discern any systematic distinction between the two terms in this paper, it is clear that they are not simply used interchangeably, and in 1956 he is still groping for a way to distinguish clearly between them (S3, 261). It was the publication of Jakobson's paper on shifters in 1957 that allowed Lacan to theorise the distinction more clearly; thus, in 1960, Lacan refers to the *je* as a SHIFTER, which designates but does not signify the subject of the enunciation (E, 298). Most English translations make Lacan's usage clear by rendering *moi* as 'ego' and *je* as 'I'.

When Lacan uses the Latin term *ego* (the term used to translate Freud's *Ich* in the *Standard Edition*), he uses it in the same sense as the term *moi*, but also means it to imply a more direct reference to Anglo-American schools of psychoanalysis, especially EGO-PSYCHOLOGY.

Freud's use of the term *Ich* (ego) is extremely complex and went through many developments throughout the course of his work before coming to denote one of the three agencies of the so-called 'structural model' (the others being the id and the superego). Despite the complexity of Freud's formulations on the ego, Lacan discerns two main approaches to the ego in Freud's work, and points out that they are apparently contradictory. On the one hand, in the context of the theory of narcissism, 'the ego takes sides against the object', whereas on the other hand, in the context of the so-called 'structural model', 'the ego takes sides with the object' (Lacan, 1951b: 11). The former approach places the ego firmly in the libidinal economy and links it with the pleasure principle, whereas the latter approach links the ego to the perception-consciousness system and opposes it to the pleasure principle. Lacan claims too that the apparent contradiction between these two accounts 'disappears when we free ourselves from a naive conception of the reality-principle' (Lacan, 1951b: 11; see REALITY PRINCIPLE). Thus the reality that the ego mediates with, in the latter account, is in fact made out of the pleasure principle which the ego represents in the former account. However, it is arguable whether this argument really resolves the contradiction or whether it does not, in effect, simply privilege the former account at the expense of the latter (see S20, 53, where the ego is said to grow 'in the flowerpot of the pleasure principle').

Lacan argues that Freud's discovery of the unconscious removed the ego from the central position to which western philosophy, at least since Descartes, had traditionally assigned it. Lacan also argues that the proponents of ego-psychology betrayed Freud's radical discovery by relocating the ego as the centre of the subject (see AUTONOMOUS EGO). In opposition to this school of thought, Lacan maintains that the ego is not at the centre, that the ego is in fact an object.

The ego is a construction which is formed by identification with the specular image in the MIRROR STAGE. It is thus the place where the subject becomes alienated from himself, transforming himself into the counterpart. This alienation on which the ego is based is structurally similar to paranoia, which is why Lacan writes that the ego has a paranoiac structure (E, 20). The ego is thus an imaginary formation, as opposed to the SUBJECT, which is a product of the symbolic (see E, 128). Indeed, the ego is precisely a *méconnaissance* of the symbolic order, the seat of resistance. The ego is structured like a symptom: 'The ego is structured exactly like a symptom. At the heart of the subject, it is only a privileged symptom, the human symptom *par excellence*, the mental illness of man' (S1, 16).

Lacan is therefore totally opposed to the idea, current in ego-psychology, that the aim of psychoanalytic treatment is to strengthen the ego. Since the ego is 'the seat of illlusions' (S1, 62), to increase its strength would only succeed in increasing the subject's alienation. The ego is also the source of resistance to psychoanalytic treatment, and thus to strengthen it would only increase those resistances. Because of its imaginary fixity, the ego is resistant to all subjective growth and change, and to the dialectical movement of desire. By undermining the fixity of the ego, psychoanalytic treatment aims to restore the dialectic of desire and reinitiate the coming-into-being of the subject.

Lacan is opposed to the ego-psychology view which takes the ego of the analysand to be the ally of the analyst in the treatment. He also rejects the view that the aim of psychoanalytic treatment is to promote the ADAPTATION of the ego to reality.

ego-ideal (*idéal du moi*)   In Freud's writings it is difficult to discern any systematic distinction between the three related terms 'ego-ideal' (*Ich-ideal*), 'ideal ego' (*Ideal Ich*), and superego (*Über-Ich*), although neither are the terms simply used interchangeably. Lacan, however, argues that these three 'formations of the ego' are each quite distinct concepts which must not be confused with one another.

In his pre-war writings Lacan is mainly concerned to establish a distinction between the ego-ideal and the superego, and does not refer to the ideal ego. Although both the ego-ideal and the SUPEREGO are linked with the decline of the Oedipus complex, and both are products of identification with the father, Lacan argues that they represent different aspects of the father's dual role. The superego is an unconscious agency whose function is to repress sexual desire for the mother, whereas the ego-ideal exerts a conscious pressure towards sublimation and provides the coordinates which enable the subject to take up a sexual position as a man or woman (Lacan, 1938: 59–62).

In his post-war writings Lacan pays more attention to distinguishing the ego-ideal from the ideal ego (Fr. *moi idéal*. Note: at one point, in 1949, Lacan uses the term *je-idéal* to render Freud's *Ideal-Ich* [E, 2]; however, he soon abandons this practice and for the rest of his work uses the term *moi idéal*.). Thus in the 1953–4 seminar, he develops the OPTICAL MODEL to distinguish between these two formations. He argues that the ego-ideal is a symbolic introjection, whereas the ideal ego is the source of an imaginary projection (see S8, 414). The ego-ideal is the signifier operating as ideal, an internalised plan of the law, the guide governing the subject's position in the symbolic order, and hence anticipates secondary (Oedipal) identification (S1, 141) or is a product of that identification (Lacan, 1957–8). The ideal ego, on the other hand, originates in the specular image of the mirror stage; it is a promise of future synthesis towards which the ego tends, the illusion of unity on which the ego is built. The ideal ego always accompanies the ego, as an ever-present attempt to regain the omnipotence of the preoedipal dual relation. Though formed in primary identification, the ideal ego continues to play a role as the source of all secondary identifications (E, 2). The ideal ego is written *i(a)* in Lacanian algebra, and the ego ideal is written I(A).

ego-psychology (*psychologie du moi*)   Ego-psychology has been, since its development in the 1930s, the dominant school of psychoanalysis in the INTERNATIONAL PSYCHO-ANALYTICAL ASSOCATION (IPA). It draws mainly on Freud's structural model of the psyche, which was first put forward in *The Ego and the Id* (1923b). This model comprises three agencies: the id, the EGO and the superego. Since the ego plays a crucial role in mediating between the conflicting demands of the instinctual id, the moralistic superego and external reality, more attention began to be paid to its development and structure. Anna Freud's book *The Ego and the Mechanisms of Defence* (1936) was one of the first works to focus almost entirely on the ego, and the trend became firmly established in Heinz Hartmann's *Ego Psychology and the Problem of Adaptation* (1939), which is now regarded as the foundational text of ego-psychology. Ego-psychology was taken to the United States by the Austrian analysts who emigrated there in the late 1930s, and since the early 1950s it has been the dominant school of psychoanalysis not only in the United States but also in the whole of the IPA. This position of dominance has enabled ego-psychology to present itself as the inheritor of Freudian psychoanalysis in its purist form, when in fact there are radical differences between some of its tenets and Freud's work.

For much of his professional life, Lacan disputed ego-psychology's claim to be the true heir to the Freudian legacy, even though Lacan's analyst, Rudolph Loewenstein, was one of ego-psychology's founding fathers. After Lacan was expelled from the IPA in 1953, he was free to voice his criticisms of ego-psychology openly, and during the rest of his life he developed a sustained and powerful critique. Much of Lacanian theory cannot be properly understood without reference to the ideas of ego-psychology with which Lacan contrasts it. Lacan challenged all the central concepts of ego-psychology, such as the concepts of ADAPTATION and the AUTONOMOUS EGO. His criticisms of ego-psychology are often intertwined with his criticisms of the IPA which was dominated by this particular school of thought. Lacan presents both ego-psychology and the IPA as the 'antithesis' of true psychoanalysis (E, 116) and argues that both were irremediably corrupted by the culture of the United States (see FACTOR C). Lacan's powerful critique has meant that few people now accept uncritically the claims of ego-psychology to identify itself as 'classical psychoanalysis'.

end of analysis (*fin d'analyse*)   In 'Analysis Terminable and Interminable', Freud discusses the question of whether it is ever possible to conclude an analysis, or whether all analyses are necessarily incomplete (Freud, 1937c). Lacan's answer to this question is that it is indeed possible to speak of concluding an analysis. Although not all analyses are carried through to their conclusion, analytic treatment is a logical process which has an end, and Lacan designates this end-point by the term 'end of analysis'.

Given that many analyses are broken off before the end of analysis is reached, the question arises as to whether such analyses can be considered succesful or not. To answer this question it is necessary to distinguish between the end of analysis and the aim of psychoanalytic treatment. The aim of psychoanalytic treatment is to lead the analysand to articulate the truth about his desire. Any analysis, however incomplete, may be regarded as successful when it achieves this aim. The question of the end of analysis is therefore something more than whether a course of analytic treatment has or has not achieved its aim; it is a question of whether or not the treatment has reached its logical end-point.

Lacan conceives of this end-point in various ways.

1. In the early 1950s, the end of analysis is described as 'the advent of a true speech and the realisation by the subject of his history' (E, 88) (see SPEECH). 'The subject . . . begins the analysis by speaking about himself without speaking to you, or by speaking to you without speaking about himself. When he can speak to you about himself, the analysis will be over' (Ec, 373, n. 1). The end of analysis is also described as coming to terms with one's own mortality (E, 104–5).

2. In 1960, Lacan describes the end of analysis as a state of anxiety and abandonment, and compares it to the HELPLESSNESS of the human infant.

3. In 1964 he describes it as the point when the analysand has 'traversed the radical fantasy' (S11, 273) (see FANTASY).

4. In the last decade of his teaching, he describes the end of analysis as 'identification with the *sinthome*', and as 'knowing what to do with the *sinthome*' (see SINTHOME).

Common to all these formulations is the idea that the end of analysis involves a change in the subjective position of the analysand (the analysand's 'subjective destitution'), and a corresponding change in the position of the analyst (the loss of being [Fr. *désêtre*] of the analyst, the fall of the analyst from the position of the subject-supposed-to-know). At the end of the analysis, the analyst is reduced to a mere surplus, a pure *objet petit a*, the cause of the analysand's desire.

Since Lacan argues that all psychoanalysts should have experienced the process of analytic treatment from beginning to end, the end of analysis is also the passage from analysand to analyst. 'The true termination of an analysis' is therefore no more and no less than that which 'prepares you to become an analyst' (S7, 303).

In 1967, Lacan introduced the procedure of the PASS as a means of testifying to the end of one's analysis. By means of this procedure, Lacan hoped to avoid the dangers of regarding the end of analysis as a quasi-mystical, ineffable experience. Such a view is antithetical to psychoanalysis, which is all about putting things into words.

Lacan criticises those psychoanalysts who have seen the end of analysis in terms of identification with the analyst. In opposition to this view of psychoanalysis, Lacan states that the 'crossing of the plane of identification is possible' (S11, 273). Not only is it possible to go beyond identification, but it is necessary, for otherwise it is not psychoanalysis but suggestion, which is the antithesis of psychoanalysis; 'the fundamental mainspring of the analytic operation is the maintenance of the distance between the I – identification – and the *a*' (S11, 273).

Lacan also rejects the idea that the end of analysis involves the 'liquidation' of the transference (see S11, 267). The idea that the transference can be 'liquidated' is based on a misunderstanding of the nature of the transference, according to which the transference is viewed as a kind of illusion which can be transcended. Such a view is erroneous because it entirely overlooks the symbolic nature of the transference; transference is part of the essential structure of speech. Although analytic treatment involves the resolution of the particular *transference relationship* established with the analyst, transference itself still subsists after the end of analysis.

Other misconceptions of the end of analysis which Lacan rejects are: 'strengthening the ego', 'adaptation to reality' and 'happiness'. The end of analysis is not the disappearance of the symptom, nor the cure of an underlying disease (e.g. neurosis), since analysis is not essentially a therapeutic process but a search for truth, and the truth is not always beneficial (S17, 122).

enunciation (*énonciation*)   In linguistic theory in Europe, one important distinction is that between the enunciation and the statement (Fr. *énoncé*). The distinction concerns two ways of regarding linguistic production. When linguistic production is analysed in terms of abstract grammatical units (such as sentences), independent of the specific circumstances of occurrence, it is referred to as a statement. On the other hand, when linguistic production is analysed as an individual act performed by a particular speaker at a specific time/place, and in a specific situation, it is referred to as an enunciation (Ducrot and Todorov, 1972: 405–10).

Long before Lacan uses these terms, he is already making a similar distinction. In 1936, for example, he stresses that the act of speaking contains a meaning in itself, even if the words spoken are 'meaningless' (Ec, 83). Prior to any function it may have in 'conveying a message', speech is an appeal to the other. This attention to the act of speaking in itself, irrespective of the content of the utterance, anticipates Lacan's attention to the dimension of the enunciation.

When Lacan does come to use the term 'enunciation' in 1946, it is first of all to describe strange characteristics of psychotic language, with its 'duplicity of the enunciation' (Ec, 167). Later, in the 1950s, the term is used to locate the subject of the unconscious. In the graph of desire, the lower chain is the statement, which is speech in its conscious dimension, while the upper chain is 'the unconscious enunciation' (E, 316). In designating the enunciation as unconscious, Lacan affirms that the source of speech is not the ego, nor consciousness, but the unconscious; language comes from the Other, and the idea that 'I' am master of my discourse is only an illusion. The very word 'I' *(Je)* is ambiguous; as SHIFTER, it is both a signifier acting as subject of the statement, and an index which designates, but does not signify, the subject of the enunciation (E, 298). The subject is thus split between these two levels, divided in the very act of articulating the *I* that presents the illusion of unity (see S11, 139).

ethics (*éthique*)   Lacan asserts that ethical thought 'is at the centre of our work as analysts' (S7, 38), and a whole year of his seminar is devoted to discussing the articulation of ethics and psychoanalysis (Lacan, 1959–60).

Simplifying matters somewhat, it could be said that ethical problems converge in psychoanalytic treatment from two sides: the side of the analysand and the side of the analyst.

On the side of the analysand is the problem of guilt and the pathogenic nature of civilised morality. In his earlier work, Freud conceives of a basic conflict between the demands of 'civilised morality' and the essentially amoral sexual drives of the subject. When morality gains the upper hand in this conflict, and the drives are too strong to be sublimated, sexuality is either expressed in perverse forms or repressed, the latter leading to neurosis. In Freud's view, then, civilised morality is at the root of nervous illness (Freud, 1908d). Freud further developed his ideas on the pathogenic nature of morality in his theory of an unconscious sense of guilt, and in his later concept of the superego, an interior moral agency which becomes more cruel to the extent that the ego submits to its demands (Freud, 1923b).

On the side of the analyst is the problem of how to deal with the pathogenic morality and unconscious guilt of the analysand, and also with the whole range of ethical problems that may arise in psychoanalytic treatment.

These two sources of ethical problems pose different questions for the analyst:

Firstly, how is the analyst to respond to the analysand's sense of guilt? Certainly not by telling the analysand that he is not really guilty, or by attempting 'to soften, blunt or attenuate' his sense of guilt (S7, 3), or by analysing it away as a neurotic illusion. On the contrary, Lacan argues that the analyst must take the analysand's sense of guilt seriously, for at bottom whenever the analysand feels guilty it is because he has, at some point, given way on his desire. 'From an analytic point of view, the only thing of which one can be guilty is of having given ground relative to one's desire' (S7, 319). Therefore, when the analysand presents him with a sense of guilt, the analyst's task is to discover *where* the analysand has given way on his desire.

Secondly, how is the analyst to respond to the pathogenic morality which acts via the superego? Freud's views of morality as a pathogenic force might seem to imply that the analyst simply has to help the analysand free himself from moral constraints. However, while such an interpretation may find some support in Freud's earlier work (Freud, 1908d), Lacan is firmly opposed to such a view of Freud, preferring the more pessimistic Freud of *Civilization and Its Discontents* (Freud, 1930a) and stating categorically that 'Freud was in no way a progressive' (S7, 183). Psychoanalysis, then, is not simply a libertine ethos.

This seems to present the analyst with a moral dilemma. On the one hand, he cannot simply align himself with civilised morality, since this morality is pathogenic. On the other hand, nor can he simply adopt an opposing libertine approach, since this too remains within the field of morality (see S7, 3–4). The rule of neutrality may seem to offer the analyst a way out of this dilemma, but in fact it does not, for Lacan points out that there is no such thing as an ethically neutral position. The analyst cannot avoid, then, having to face ethical questions.

An ethical position is implicit in every way of directing psychoanalytic treatment, whether this is admitted or not by the analyst. The ethical position of the analyst is most clearly revealed by the way that he formulates the goal of the treatment (S7, 207). For example the formulations of ego-psychology about the adaptation of the ego to reality imply a normative ethics (S7, 302). It is in opposition to this ethical position that Lacan sets out to formulate his own analytic ethic.

The analytic ethic that Lacan formulates is an ethic which relates action to desire (see ACT). Lacan summarises it in the question 'Have you acted in conformity with the desire that is in you?' (S7, 314). He contrasts this ethic with the 'traditional ethics' (S7, 314) of Aristotle, Kant and other moral philosophers on several grounds.

Firstly, traditional ethics revolves around the the concept of the Good, proposing different 'goods' which all compete for the position of the Sovereign Good. The psychoanalytic ethic, however, sees the Good as an obstacle in the path of desire; thus in psychoanalysis 'a radical repudiation of a certain ideal of the good is necessary' (S7, 230). The psychoanalytic ethic rejects all ideals, including ideals of 'happiness' and 'health'; and the fact that ego-psychology has embraced these ideals bars it from claiming to be a form of psychoanalysis (S7, 219). The desire of the analyst cannot therefore be the desire to 'do good' or 'to cure' (S7, 218).

Secondly, traditional ethics has always tended to link the good to pleasure; moral thought has 'developed along the paths of an essentially hedonistic problematic' (S7, 221). The psychoanalytic ethic, however, cannot take such an approach because psychoanalytic experience has revealed the duplicity of pleasure; there is a limit to pleasure and, when this is transgressed, pleasure becomes pain (see JOUISSANCE).

Thirdly, traditional ethics revolves around 'the service of goods' (S7, 314) which puts work and a safe, ordered existence before questions of desire; it tells people to make their desires wait (S7, 315). The psychoanalytic ethic, on the other hand, forces the subject to confront the relation between his actions and his desire in immediacy of the present.

After his 1959–60 seminar on ethics, Lacan continues to locate ethical questions at the heart of psychoanalytic theory. He interprets the *soll* in Freud's famous phrase *Wo es war, soll Ich werden* ('Where id was, there ego shall be', Freud, 1933a: SE XXII, 80) as an ethical duty (E, 128), and argues that the status of the unconscious is not ontological but ethical (S11, 33). In the 1970s he shifts the emphasis of psychoanalytic ethics from the question of acting ('Have you *acted* in accordance with your desire?') to the question of speech; it now becomes an ethic of 'speaking well' (*l'éthique du Bien-dire*) (Lacan, 1973a: 65). However, this is more a difference of emphasis than an opposition, since for Lacan to speak well is in itself an act.

It is fundamentally an ethical position which separates psychoanalysis from SUGGESTION; psychoanalysis is based on a basic respect for the patient's right to resist domination, whereas suggestion sees such resistance as an obstacle to be crushed.

existence (*existence*) The term 'existence' is employed by Lacan in various ways (see Žižek, 1991: 136–7):

● **Existence in the symbolic** This sense of existence is to be understood in the context of Freud's discussion of the 'judgement of existence', by which the existence of an entity is affirmed prior to attributing any quality to it (see Freud, 1925h; see BEJAHUNG). Only what is integrated in the symbolic order fully 'exists' in this sense, since 'there is no such thing as a prediscursive reality' (S20, 33). It is in this sense that Lacan argues that 'woman does not exist' (Lacan, 1973a: 60); the symbolic order contains no signifier for femininity, and hence the feminine position cannot be fully symbolised.

It is important to note that, in the symbolic order, 'nothing exists except on an assumed foundation of absence. Nothing exists except insofar as it does not exist' (Ec, 392). In other words, everything that exists in the symbolic order only exists by virtue of its difference to everything else. It was Saussure who first pointed this out when he argued that in language there are no positive terms, only differences (Saussure, 1916).

● **Existence in the real** In this sense, it is only that which is impossible to symbolise that exists: the impossible Thing at the heart of the subject. 'There is in effect something radically unassimilable to the signifier. It's quite simply the subject's singular existence' (S3, 179). This is the existence of the subject of the unconscious, S, which Lacan describes as an 'ineffable, stupid existence' (E, 194).

This second sense of the term existence is exactly the opposite of existence in the first sense. Whereas existence in the first sense is synonymous with Lacan's use of the term BEING, existence in the second sense is opposed to being.

Lacan coins the neologism *ex-sistence* to express the idea that the heart of our being (*Kern unseres Wesen*) is also radically Other, strange, outside (Ec, 11); the subject is decentred, his centre is outside of himself, he is ex-centric. Lacan also speaks of the 'ex-sistence (*Entstellung*) of desire in the dream' (E, 264), since the dream cannot represent desire except by distorting it.

extimacy (*extimité*) Lacan coins the term *extimité* by applying the prefix *ex* (from *exterieur*, 'exterior') to the French word *intimité* ('intimacy'). The resulting neologism, which may be rendered 'extimacy' in English, neatly expresses the way in which psychoanalysis problematises the opposition between inside and outside, between container and contained (see S7, 139). For example, the real is just as much inside as outside, and the unconscious is not a purely interior psychic system but an intersubjective structure ('the unconscious is outside'). Again, the Other is 'something strange to me, although it is at the heart of me' (S7, 71). Furthermore, the centre of the subject is outside; the subject is ex-centric (see E, 165, 171). The structure of extimacy is perfectly expressed in the topology of the TORUS and of the MOEBIUS STRIP.

The concept of extimacy has been further developed by Jacques-Alain Miller in his seminar of 1985–6 (see the summary of this seminar and other related articles in Bracher *et al.*, 1994).

F

factor *c* (*facteur c*)   Lacan coined the term 'factor *c*' at a psychiatric congress in 1950. Factor *c* is 'the constant characteristic of any given cultural milieu' (E, 37): it is an attempt to designate that part of the symbolic order which marks the particular features of one culture as opposed to another (*c* stands for culture). Although it would be interesting to speculate on the possible applications of this concept to the interrelationship between different cultural milieux and psychoanalysis, Lacan only gives one example of the *c* factor; ahistoricism, he argues, is the *c* factor of the culture of the United States (see E, 37 and E, 115). The 'American way of life' revolves around such signifiers as 'happiness', 'adaptation', 'human relations' and 'human engineering' (E, 38). Lacan regards the *c* factor of United States culture as particularly antithetical to psychoanalysis, and sees it as largely responsible for the errors which have beset psychoanalytic theory in the USA (such as EGO-PSYCHOLOGY).

fantasy (*fantasme*)   The concept of fantasy (spelt 'phantasy' in the *Standard Edition*) is central to Freud's work. Indeed, the origin of psychoanalysis is bound up with Freud's recognition in 1897 that memories of seduction are sometimes the product of fantasy rather than traces of real sexual abuse. This crucial moment in the development of Freud's thought (which is often simplistically dubbed 'the abandonment of the seduction theory') seems to imply that fantasy is opposed to reality, a purely illusory product of the imagination which stands in the way of a correct perception of reality. However, such a view of fantasy cannot be maintained in psychoanalytic theory, since reality is not seen as an unproblematic given in which there is a single objectively correct way of perceiving, but as something which is itself discursively constructed. Therefore the change in Freud's ideas in 1897 does not imply a rejection of the veracity of all memories of sexual abuse, but the discovery of the fundamentally discursive and imaginative nature of memory; memories of past events are continually being reshaped in accordance with unconscious desires, so much so that symptoms originate not in any supposed 'objective facts' but in a complex dialectic in which fantasy plays a vital role. Freud uses the term 'fantasy', then, to denote a scene which is presented to the imagination and which stages an unconscious desire. The subject invariably plays a part in this scene, even when this is not immediately apparent. The fantasised scene may be conscious or unconscious. When unconscious, the analyst must reconstruct it on the basis of other clues (see Freud, 1919e).

While Lacan accepts Freud's formulations on the importance of fantasy and on its visual quality as a scenario which stages desire, he emphasises the protective function of fantasy. Lacan compares the fantasy SCENE to a frozen image on a cinema screen; just as the film may be stopped at a certain point in order to avoid showing a traumatic scene which follows, so also the fantasy scene is a defence which veils castration (S4, 119–20). The fantasy is thus characterised by a fixed and immobile quality.

Although 'fantasy' only emerges as a significant term in Lacan's work from 1957 on, the concept of a relatively stable mode of DEFENCE is evident earlier on (see, for example, Lacan's remark in 1951 on 'the permanent modes by which the subject constitutes his objects'; Ec, 225). This concept is at the root both of Lacan's idea of fantasy and of his notion of clinical structure; both are conceived of as a relatively stable way of defending oneself against castration, against the lack in the Other. Each clinical structure may thus be distinguished by the particular way in which it uses a fantasy scene to veil the lack in the Other. The neurotic fantasy, which Lacan formalises in the matheme ($\$ \lozenge a$), appears in the graph of desire as the subject's response to the enigmatic desire of the Other, a way of answering the question about what the Other wants from me (*Che vuoi?*) (see E, 313). The matheme is to be read: the barred subject in relation to the object. The perverse fantasy inverts this relation to the object, and is thus formalised as $a \lozenge \$$ (Ec, 774).

Although the matheme ($\$ \lozenge a$) designates the general structure of the neurotic fantasy, Lacan also provides more specific formulas for the fantasy of the hysteric and that of the obsessional neurotic (S8, 295). While the various formulas of fantasy indicate the common features of the fantasies of those who share the same clinical structure, the analyst must also attend to the unique features which characterise each patient's particular fantasmatic scenario. These unique features express the subject's particular mode of JOUISSANCE, though in a distorted way. The distortion evident in the fantasy marks it as a compromise formation; the fantasy is thus both that which enables the subject to sustain his desire (S11, 185; Ec, 780), and 'that by which the subject sustains *himself* at the level of his vanishing desire' (E, 272, emphasis added).

Lacan holds that beyond all the myriad images which appear in dreams and elsewhere there is always one 'fundamental fantasy' which is unconscious (see S8, 127). In the course of psychoanalytic treatment, the analyst reconstructs the analysand's fantasy in all its details. However, the treatment does not stop there; the analysand must go on to 'traverse the fundamental fantasy' (see S11, 273). In other words, the treatment must produce some modification of the subject's fundamental mode of defence, some alteration in his mode of *jouissance*.

Although Lacan recognises the power of the image in fantasy, he insists that this is due not to any intrinsic quality of the image in itself but to the place which it occupies in a symbolic structure; the fantasy is always 'an image set to work in a signifying structure' (E, 272). Lacan criticises the Kleinian account of fantasy for not taking this symbolic structure fully into account, and thus remaining at the level of the imaginary; 'any attempt to reduce [fantasy] to the imagination . . . is a permanent misconception' (E, 272). In the 1960s, Lacan devotes a whole year of his seminar to discussing what he calls 'the logic of fantasy' (Lacan, 1966–7), again stressing the importance of the signifying structure in fantasy.

father (*père*) From very early on in his work, Lacan lays great importance on the role of the father in psychic structure. In his 1938 article on the family, he attributes the importance of the OEDIPUS COMPLEX to the fact that it combines in the figure of the father two almost conflicting functions: the protective function and the prohibitive function. He also points to the contemporary social decline in the paternal imago (clearly visible in the images of absent fathers and humiliated fathers) as the cause of current psychopathological peculiarities (Lacan, 1938: 73). The father continues to be a constant theme of Lacan's work thereafter.

Lacan's emphasis on the importance of the father can be seen as a reaction against the tendency of Kleinian psychoanalysis and object-relations theory to place the mother–child relation at the heart of psychoanalytic theory. In opposition to this tendency, Lacan continually stresses the role of the father as a third term who, by mediating the imaginary DUAL RELATION between the MOTHER and the child, saves the child from psychosis and makes possible an entry into social existence. The father is thus more than a mere rival with whom the subject competes for the mother's love; he is the representative of the social order as such, and only by identifying with the father in the Oedipus complex can the subject gain entry into this order. The absence of the father is therefore an important factor in the aetiology of all psychopathological structures.

However, the father is not a simple concept but a complex one, one which begs the question of what exactly is meant by the term 'father'. Lacan argues that the question 'What is a father?' forms the central theme which runs throughout Freud's entire work (S4, 204–5). It is in order to answer this question that, from 1953 on, Lacan stresses the importance of distinguishing between the symbolic father, the imaginary father, and the real father:

FATHER

● **The symbolic father** The symbolic father is not a real being but a position, a function, and hence is synonymous with the term 'paternal function'. This function is none other than that of imposing the LAW and regulating desire in the Oedipus complex, of intervening in the imaginary dual relationship between mother and child to introduce a necessary 'symbolic distance' between them (S4, 161). 'The true function of the Father . . . is fundamentally to unite (and not to set in opposition) a desire and the Law' (E, 321). Although the symbolic father is not an actual subject but a position in the symbolic order, a subject may nevertheless come to occupy this position, by virtue of exercising the paternal function. Nobody can ever occupy this position completely (S4, 205, 210, 219). However, the symbolic father does not usually intervene by virtue of someone incarnating this function, but in a veiled fashion, for example by being mediated by the discourse of the mother (see S4, 276).

The symbolic father is the fundamental element in the structure of the symbolic order; what distinguishes the symbolic order of culture from the imaginary order of nature is the inscription of a line of male descendence. By structuring descendence into a series of generations, patrilineality introduces an order 'whose structure is different from the natural order' (S3, 320). The symbolic father is also the dead father, the father of the primal horde who has been murdered by his own sons (see Freud, 1912–13). The symbolic father is also referred to as the NAME-OF-THE-FATHER (S1, 259).

The presence of the imaginary phallus as a third term in the preoedipal imaginary triangle indicates that the symbolic father is already functioning at the preoedipal stage; behind the symbolic mother, there is always the symbolic father. The psychotic, however, does not even get this far; indeed, it is the absence of the symbolic father which characterises the essence of the psychotic structure (see FORECLOSURE).

● **The imaginary father** The imaginary father is an imago, the composite of all the imaginary constructs that the subject builds up in fantasy around the figure of the father. This imaginary construction often bears little relationship to the father as he is in reality (S4, 220). The imaginary father can be construed as an ideal father (S1, 156; E, 321), or the opposite, as 'the father who has fucked the kid up' (S7, 308). In the former guise, the imaginary father is the prototype of God-figures in religions, an all-powerful protector. In the latter role, the imaginary father is both the terrifying father of the primal horde who imposes the incest taboo on his sons (see Freud, 1912–13), and the agent of PRIVATION, the father whom the daughter blames for depriving her of the symbolic phallus, or its equivalent, a child (S4, 98; see Figure 7 and S7, 307). In both guises, though, whether as the ideal father or as the cruel agent of privation, the imaginary father is seen as omnipotent (S4, 275–6). Psychosis and perversion both involve, in different ways, a reduction of the symbolic father to the imaginary father.

● **The real father**   While Lacan is quite clear in defining what he means by the imaginary father and the symbolic father, his remarks on the real father are quite obscure (see, for example, S4, 220). Lacan's only unequivocal formulation is that the real father is the agent of castration, the one who performs the operation of symbolic castration (S17, 149; see Figure 7 and S7, 307). Apart from this, Lacan gives few other clues about what he means by the phrase. In 1960, he describes the real father as the one who 'effectively occupies' the mother, the 'Great Fucker' (S7, 307), and even goes on to say, in 1970, that the real father is the spermatozoon, though he immediately qualifies this statement with the remark that nobody has ever thought of himself as the son of a spermatozoon (S17, 148). On the basis of these comments, it seems possible to argue that the real father is the biological father of the subject. However, since a degree of uncertainty always surrounds the question of who the biological father really is ('"*pater semper incertus est*", while the mother is "*certissima*"'; Freud, 1909c: SE IX, 239), it would be more precise to say that the real father is the man who is *said to be* the subject's biological father. The real father is thus an effect of language, and it is in this sense that the adjective real is to be understood here: the real of language, rather than the real of biology (S17, 147–8).

The real father plays a crucial role in the Oedipus complex; it is he who intervenes in the third 'time' of the Oedipus complex as the one who castrates the child (see CASTRATION COMPLEX). This intervention saves the child from the preceding anxiety; without it, the child requires a phobic object as a symbolic substitute for the absent real father. The intervention of the real father as agent of castration is not simply equivalent to his physical presence in the family. As the case of Little Hans indicates (Freud, 1909b), the real father may be physically present and yet fail to intervene as agent of castration (S4, 212, 221). Conversely, the intervention of the real father may well be felt by the child even when the father is physically absent.

fetishism (*fétichisme*)   The term 'fetish' first came into widespread use in the eighteenth century in context of the study of 'primitive religions', in which it denoted an inanimate object of worship (an etymology which Lacan believes is important; S8, 169). In the nineteenth century, Marx borrowed the term to describe the way that, in capitalist societies, social relations assume the illusory form of relations between things ('commodity fetishism'). It was Krafft–Ebing who, in the last decade of the nineteenth century, first applied the term to sexual behaviour. He defined fetishism as a sexual PERVERSION in which sexual excitement is absolutely dependent on the presence of a specific object (the fetish). It is this definition that Freud and most other writers on sexuality have adopted since. The fetish is usually an inanimate object such as a shoe or piece of underwear.

Freud argued that fetishism (seen as an almost exclusively male perversion) originates in the child's horror of female castration. Confronted with the mother's lack of a penis, the fetishist disavows this lack and finds an object (the fetish) as a symbolic substitute for the mother's missing penis (Freud, 1927e).

In Lacan's first approach to the subject of fetishism, in 1956, he argues that fetishism is a particularly important area of study and bemoans its neglect by his contemporaries. He stresses that the equivalence between the fetish and the maternal PHALLUS can only be understood by reference to linguistic transformations, and not by reference to 'vague analogies in the visual field' such as comparisons between fur and pubic hair (Lacan, 1956b: 267). He cites Freud's analysis of the phrase '*Glanz auf der Nase*' as support for his argument (see Freud, 1927e).

In the following years, as Lacan develops his distinction between the penis and phallus, he emphasises that the fetish is a substitute for the latter, not the former. Lacan also extends the mechanism of DISAVOWAL, making it the operation constitutive of perversion itself, and not just of the fetishistic perversion. However, he retains Freud's view that fetishism is an exclusively male perversion (Ec, 734), or at least extremely rare among women (S4, 154).

In the seminar of 1956–7, Lacan elaborates an important distinction between the fetish object and the phobic object; whereas the fetish is a symbolic substitute for the mother's missing phallus, the phobic object is an imaginary substitute for symbolic castration (see PHOBIA). Like all perversions, fetishism is rooted in the preoedipal triangle of mother–child–phallus (S4, 84–5, 194). However, it is unique in that it involves both identification with mother *and* with the imaginary phallus; indeed, in fetishism, the subject oscillates between these two identifications (S4, 86, 160).

Lacan's statement, in 1958, that the penis 'takes on the value of a fetish' for heterosexual women raises a number of interesting questions (E, 290). Firstly, it reverses Freud's views on fetishism; rather than the fetish being a symbolic substitute for the real penis, the real penis may itself become a fetish by substituting the woman's absent symbolic phallus. Secondly, it undermines the claims (made by both Freud and Lacan) that fetishism is extremely rare among women; if the penis can be considered a fetish, then fetishism is clearly far more prevalent among women than among men.

foreclosure (*forclusion*)

From his doctoral dissertation in 1932 on, one of the central quests which animates Lacan's work is that of identifying a specific psychical cause for PSYCHOSIS. In the course of addressing this problem, two themes are constant.

- **The exclusion of the FATHER**   As early as 1938 Lacan relates the origin of psychosis to an exclusion of the father from the family structure, with the consequent reduction of the latter to mother–child relations (Lacan, 1938: 49). Later on in his work, when Lacan distinguishes between the real, imaginary and symbolic father, he specifies that it is the absence of the symbolic father which is linked to psychosis.

• **The Freudian concept of** *Verwerfung* Freud uses the term *Verwerfung* (translated as 'repudiation' in the *Standard Edition*) in a number of disparate ways (see Laplanche and Pontalis, 1967: 166), but Lacan focuses on one in particular: namely, the sense of a specific defence mechanism which is distinct from repression (*Verdrängung*), in which 'the ego rejects the incompatible idea together with its affect and behaves as if the idea had never occurred to the ego at all' (Freud, 1894a: SE III, 58). In 1954, basing himself on a reading of the 'Wolf Man' case history (see Freud, 1918b: SE XVII, 79–80), Lacan identifies *Verwerfung* as the specific mechanism of psychosis, in which an element is rejected outside the symbolic order just as if it had never existed (Ec, 386–7; S1, 57–9). At this time Lacan proposes various ways of translating the term *Verwerfung* into French, rendering it as *rejet, refus* (S1, 43) and *retranchement* (Ec, 386). It is not until 1956 that Lacan proposes the term *forclusion* (a term in use in the French legal system; in English, 'foreclosure') as the best way of translating *Verwerfung* into French (S3, 321). It is this term that Lacan continues to use for the rest of his work.

In 1954, when Lacan first turns to the Freudian concept of *Verwerfung* in his search for a specific mechanism for psychosis, it is not clear exactly *what* is repudiated; it can be castration that is repudiated, or speech itself (S1, 53), or 'the genital plane' (S1, 58). Lacan finds a solution to the problem at the end of 1957, when he proposes the idea that it is the NAME-OF-THE-FATHER (a fundamental signifier) that is the object of foreclosure (E, 217). In this way Lacan is able to combine in one formula both of the themes that had previously dominated his thinking on the causality of psychosis (the absence of the father and the concept of *Verwerfung*). This formula remains at the heart of Lacan's thinking on psychosis throughout the rest of his work.

When the Name-of-the-Father is foreclosed for a particular subject, it leaves a hole in the symbolic order which can never be filled; the subject can then be said to have a psychotic structure, even if he shows none of the classical signs of psychosis. Sooner or later, when the foreclosed Name-of-the-Father re-appears in the real, the subject is unable to assimilate it, and the result of this 'collision with the inassimilable signifier' (S3, 321) is the 'entry into psychosis' proper, characterised typically by the onset of HALLUCINATIONS and/or DELUSIONS.

Foreclosure is to be distinguished from other operations such as REPRESSION, NEGATION, and PROJECTION.

• **Repression** Foreclosure differs from repression in that the foreclosed element is not buried in the unconscious but expelled from the unconscious. Repression is the operation which constitutes neurosis, whereas foreclosure is the operation which constitutes psychosis.

• **Negation** Foreclosure differs from negation in that it involves no initial judgement of existence (see BEJAHUNG). Whereas negation involves the denial of some element whose existence has previously been registered, with foreclosure it is as if the foreclosed element had never existed at all.

• **Projection** Foreclosure is a specifically psychotic mechanism, whereas for Lacan projection is a purely neurotic mechanism. And whereas with projection, the direction of the process is from inside to outside, with foreclosure the foreclosed element returns from outside. Freud had noted this in *Psycho-Analytic Notes on an Autobiographical Account of a Case of Paranoia* (1911c), where he wrote of Schreber's hallucinations: 'It was incorrect to say that the perception which was suppressed internally is projected outwards; the truth is rather, as we now see, that what was abolished internally returns from without' (SE XII, 71). Lacan not only quotes this sentence of Freud's, but also rephrases it in his own terms; 'whatever is refused in the symbolic order . . . reappears in the real' (S3, 13).

In 1957 Lacan briefly links the term *Verwerfung* to the mechanism by which the superego is produced via identification with the father in the dissolution of the Oedipus complex (S4, 415). This is clearly not the psychotic mechanism of foreclosure but a normal/neurotic process.

formation (*formation*) The 'formations of the unconscious' are those phenomena in which the laws of the unconscious are most clearly visible; the joke, the dream, the SYMPTOM, and the lapsus (parapraxis). The fundamental mechanisms involved in the formations of the unconscious were referred to by Freud as the 'laws of the unconscious', condensation and displacement, which Lacan redefines as metaphor and metonymy.

The 'formation of analysts' (*formation des analystes*) means the TRAINING of psychoanalysts (see E, 144–5).

The 'formations of the ego' are the three elements related to the ego: the superego, the ideal ego, and the ego-ideal.

founding speech (*parole fondant*) The term 'founding speech' (sometimes rendered 'foundational speech') emerges in Lacan's work at the time of his growing attention to LANGUAGE in the early 1950s (see Lacan, 1953a). The point Lacan draws attention to in his use of this term is the way that SPEECH can radically transform both the speaker and the addressee in the act of utterance. Lacan's two favourite examples of this are the phrases 'You are my master/teacher [*maître*]' and 'You are my wife', which serve to position the speaker as 'pupil' and 'husband' respectively. In other words, the crucial aspect of founding speech is that it not only transforms the other but also transforms the subject (see E, 85). 'Founding speech, which envelops the subject, is everything that has constituted him, his parents, his neighbours, the whole structure of his community, and not only constituted him as symbol, but constituted him in his being' (S2, 20). Lacan refers to the same function of speech as 'elective speech' in the seminar of 1955–6 and as 'votive speech' in the seminar of 1956–7.

Lacan plays on the homophony between *tu es ma mère* ('you are my mother') and *tuer ma mère* ('to kill my mother') to illustrate the way that the founding speech addressed to the other may reveal a repressed murderous desire (E, 269).

fragmented body (*corps morcelé*) The notion of the fragmented body is one of the earliest original concepts to appear in Lacan's work, and is closely linked to the concept of the MIRROR STAGE. In the mirror stage the infant sees its reflection in the mirror as a whole/synthesis, and this perception causes, by contrast, the perception of its own body (which lacks motor coordination at this stage) as divided and fragmented. The anxiety provoked by this feeling of fragmentation fuels the identification with the specular image by which the ego is formed. However, the anticipation of a synthetic ego is henceforth constantly threatened by the memory of this sense of fragmentation, which manifests itself in 'images of castration, emasculation, mutilation, dismemberment, dislocation, evisceration, devouring, bursting open of the body' which haunt the human imagination (E, 11). These images typically appear in the analysand's dreams and associations at a particular phase in the treatment – namely, the moment when the analysand's aggressivity emerges in the negative transference. This moment is an important early sign that the treatment is progressing in the right direction, i.e. towards the disintegration of the rigid unity of the ego (Lacan, 1951b: 13).

In a more general sense, the fragmented body refers not only to images of the physical body but also to any sense of fragmentation and disunity: 'He [the subject] is originally an inchoate collection of desires – there you have the true sense of the expression *fragmented body*' (S3, 39). Any such sense of disunity threatens the illusion of synthesis which constitutes the ego.

Lacan also uses the idea of the fragmented body to explain certain typical symptoms of hysteria. When a hysterical paralysis affects a limb, it does not respect the physiological structure of the nervous system, but instead reflects the way the body is divided up by an 'imaginary anatomy'. In this way, the fragmented body is 'revealed at the organic level, in the lines of fragilization that define the anatomy of phantasy, as exhibited in the schizoid and spasmodic symptoms of hysteria' (E, 5).

Freud, return to (*Freud, retour à*) The whole of Lacan's work can only be understood within the context of the intellectual and theoretical legacy of Sigmund Freud (1856–1939), the founder of psychoanalysis. Lacan first trained as a psychoanalyst within the INTERNATIONAL PSYCHO-ANALYTICAL ASSOCIATION (IPA), the organisation founded by Freud which presented itself as the sole legitimate heir to the Freudian legacy. However, Lacan gradually

67

began to develop a radical critique of the way that most analysts in the IPA had interpreted Freud. After being expelled from the IPA in 1953, Lacan developed his polemic further, arguing that Freud's radical insights had been universally betrayed by the three major schools of psychoanalysis within the IPA: EGO-PSYCHOLOGY, KLEINIAN PSYCHOANALYSIS, and OBJECT-RELATIONS THEORY. To remedy this situation, Lacan proposed to lead a 'return to Freud', both in the sense of a renewed attention to the actual texts of Freud himself, and a return to the essence of Freud's work which had been betrayed by the IPA. Reading Freud in the original German allowed Lacan to discover elements which had been obscured by poor translation and ignored by other commentators. Thus much of Lacan's work is taken up with detailed textual commentaries on specific works by Freud, and by numerous references to the work of other analysts whose ideas Lacan refutes. To understand Lacan's work, therefore, it is necessary both to have a detailed understanding of Freud's ideas and also a grasp of the way these ideas were developed and modified by the other analysts (the 'post-Freudians') whom Lacan criticises. These ideas are the background against which Lacan develops his own 'return to Freud'.

> What such a return [to Freud] involves for me is not a return of the repressed, but rather taking the antithesis constituted by the phase in the history of the psychoanalytic movement since the death of Freud, showing what psychoanalysis is not, and seeking with you the means of revitalizing that which has continued to sustain it, even in deviation . . .
>
> (E, 116)

However, Lacan's work itself puts in question the narrative of a return to orthodoxy implicit in the expression 'return to Freud', for Lacan's way of reading Freud and his style of presentation are so original that they seem to belie his modest claims to be a mere commentator. Furthermore, while it is true that Lacan returns to the actual texts of Freud himself, it is also true that Lacan returns to specific aspects of the Freudian conceptual legacy, privileging particular concepts at the expense of others. It might be argued, then, that Lacan is no more 'faithful' to Freud's work than the post-Freudians whom he criticises for having betrayed Freud's message; like them, Lacan selects and develops certain themes in Freud's work and neglects or reinterprets others. Lacanian psychoanalysis might therefore be described as a 'post-Freudian' form of psychoanalysis, along with ego-psychology, Kleinian psychoanalysis and object-relations theory.

However, this is not the way Lacan sees his work. Lacan argues that there is a deeper logic at work in Freud's texts, a logic which endows those texts with a consistency despite the apparent contradictions. Lacan claims that his reading of Freud, and his alone, brings out this logic, and shows us that 'the different stages and changes in direction' in Freud's work 'are governed by Freud's inflexibly effective concern to maintain it in its primary rigour' (E, 116). In other words, while Lacan's reading of Freud may be as partial as any other in the sense that it privileges particular aspects of Freud's work, this is not, in Lacan's view, justification for regarding all interpretations of Freud as equally valid. Thus Lacan's declarations of loyalty and accusations of betrayal cannot be seen as a mere rhetorical strategy. Certainly, they do have a rhetorico-political function, in that presenting himself as 'more Freudian' than anyone else allowed Lacan to challenge the effective monopoly on the Freudian legacy that the IPA still enjoyed in the 1950s. However, Lacan's statements are also an explicit claim to have teased out a coherent logic in Freud's writings that no one else had perceived before.

frustration (*frustration*) The English term 'frustration' came into increasing prominence in certain branches of psychoanalytic theory in the 1950s, together with a shift in emphasis from the Oedipal triangle to the mother–child relation. In this context, frustration was generally understood as the act whereby the MOTHER denies the child the object which would satisfy one of his biological NEEDS. To frustrate a child in this way was thought by some analysts to be a major factor in the aetiology of neurosis.

'Frustration' is also the term which the *Standard Edition* uses to translate Freud's term *Versagung*. While this term is not extremely prominent in Freud's work, it does form part of his theoretical vocabulary. At a first glance, indeed, it may appear that Freud discusses frustration in the way described above. For example he certainly attributes to frustration an important place in the aetiology of symptoms, stating that 'it was a *frustration* that made the patient ill' (Freud, 1919a: SE XVII, 162). Hence when Lacan argues that the term 'frustration' is 'quite simply absent from Freud's work' (S3, 235), what he means is that the Freudian concept of *Versagung* does not correspond to the concept of frustration as described in the above paragraph. Lacan argues that those who have theorised the concept of frustration in this way have, by deviating from Freud's work, led psychoanalytic theory into a series of impasses (S4, 180). Thus in the seminar of 1956–7 he seeks a way of reformulating the concept in accordance with the logic of Freudian theory.

Lacan begins by classifying frustration as one of the three types of 'lack of object', distinct from both castration and privation (see LACK). Although he concedes that frustration is at the heart of the primary relations between mother and child (S4, 66), he argues that frustration does not concern biological needs but the DEMAND for love. This is not to say that frustration has nothing to do with a real object capable of satisfying a need (e.g. a breast, or a feeding bottle); on the contrary, such an object is certainly involved, at least at first (S4, 66). However, what is important is that the real function of this object (to satisfy a need, such as hunger) is soon completely overshadowed by its symbolic function, namely, the fact that it functions as a symbol of the mother's love (S4, 180–2). The object is thus valued more for being a symbolic gift than for its capacity to satisfy a need. As a gift, it is inscribed in the symbolic network of laws which regulate the circuit of exchanges, and thus seen as something to which the subject has a legitimate claim (S4, 101). Frustration, properly speaking, can only occur in the context of this legal order, and thus when the object which the infant demands is not provided, one can only speak of frustration when the infant senses that it has been wronged (S4, 101). In such a case, when the object is eventually provided, the sense of wrong (of broken promises, of love withheld) persists in the child, who then consoles himself for this by enjoying the sensations which follow the satisfaction of the original need. Thus, far from frustration involving the failure to satisfy a biological need, it often involves precisely the opposite; a biological need is satisfied as a vain attempt to compensate for the true frustration, which is the refusal of love.

Frustration plays an important role in psychoanalytic treatment. Freud noted that, to the extent that distressing symptoms disappear as the treatment progresses, the patient's motivation to continue the treatment tends to diminish accordingly. In order, therefore, to avoid the risk of the patient losing motivation altogether and breaking off the treatment prematurely, Freud recommended that the analyst must 're-instate [the patient's suffering] elsewhere in the form of some appreciable privation' (Freud, 1919a: SE XVII, 163). This technical advice is generally known as the rule of abstinence, and implies that the analyst must continually frustrate the patient by refusing to gratify his demands for love. In this way, 'the patient's need and longing should be allowed to persist in her, in order to serve as forces impelling her to do work and to make changes' (Freud, 1915a: SE XII, 165).

While Lacan agrees with Freud that the analyst must not gratify the analysand's demands for love, he argues that this act of frustration is not to be seen as an end in itself. Rather, frustration must be seen simply as a means to enable the signifiers of previous demands to appear. 'The analyst is he who supports the demand, not, as has been said, to frustrate the subject, but in order to allow the signifiers in which his frustration is bound up to reappear' (E, 255). The aim of the analyst is, by supporting the analysand's demands in a state of frustration, to go beyond demand and cause the analysand's desire to appear (E, 276).

Lacan differs from Freud in the way he theorises the rule of abstinence. For Freud, the rule of abstinence primarily concerned the analysand's abstinence from sexual activity; if a patient implores the analyst to make love to her, the analyst must frustrate her by refusing to do so. While Lacan agrees with this advice, he stresses that there is a much more common demand that the analyst can also frustrate – the analysand's demand for a reply. The analysand expects the analyst to follow the rules of everyday conversation. By refusing to follow these rules – remaining silent when the analysand asks a question, or taking the analysand's words in a way other than that in which they were intended – the analyst has a powerful means at his disposal for frustrating the analysand.

There is another way that the analyst frustrates the analysand which Lacan mentions in 1961. This is the analyst's refusal to give the signal of anxiety to the analysand – the absence of anxiety in the analyst at all times, even when the analysand demands that the analyst experience anxiety. Lacan suggests that this may be the most fruitful of all forms of frustration in psychoanalytic treatment (S8, 428).

G

gap (*béance*) The French term *béance* is an antiquated literary term which means a 'large hole or opening'. It is also a scientific term used in medicine to denote the opening of the larynx.

The term is used in several ways in Lacan's work. In 1946, he speaks of an 'interrogative gap' which opens up in madness, when the subject is perplexed by the phenomena which he experiences (hallucinations, etc.) (Ec, 165–6).

In the early 1950s, the term comes to refer to the fundamental rupture between man and NATURE, which is due to the fact that 'in man, the imaginary relation has deviated, in so far as that is where the gap is produced whereby death makes itself felt' (S2, 210). This gap between man and nature is evident in the mirror stage:

> One has to assume a certain biological gap in him [man], which I try to define when I talk to you about the mirror stage. . . . The human being has a special relation with his own image – a relation of gap, of alienating tension.
> (S2, 323)

The function of the imaginary is precisely to fill this gap, thus covering over the subject's division and presenting an imaginary sense of unity and wholeness.

In 1957 the term is used in the context of the relationship between the sexes; 'in the relation between man and woman . . . a gap always remains open' (S4, 374; see S4, 408). This anticipates Lacan's later remarks on the non-existence of the SEXUAL RELATIONSHIP.

In 1964, Lacan argues that 'the relation of the subject to the Other is entirely produced in a process of gap' (S11, 206), and states that the subject is constituted by a gap, since the subject is essentially divided (see SPLIT). He also argues that the concept of causality is essentially problematic because there is always a mysterious, inexplicable gap between cause and effect (S11, 21–2).

Lacan also uses the term 'dehiscence' in a way that makes it practically synonymous, in his discourse, with the term 'gap'. Dehiscence is a botanical term which designates the bursting open of mature seed-pods; Lacan uses the term to refer to the split which is constitutive of the subject: there is 'a vital dehiscence that is constitutive of man' (E, 21). This split is also the division between culture and nature which means that man's relation to the latter 'is altered by a certain dehiscence at the heart of the organism, a primordial Discord' (E, 4).

gaze (*regard*)   Lacan's first comments on the gaze appear in the first year of his seminar (Lacan, 1953–4), in reference to Jean-Paul Sartre's phenomenological analysis of 'the look' (the fact that the English translators of Sartre and Lacan have used different terms obscures the fact that both use the same term in French – *le regard*). For Sartre, the gaze is that which permits the subject to realise that the Other is also a subject; 'my fundamental connection with the Other-as-subject must be able to be referred back to my permanent possibility of *being seen* by the Other' (Sartre, 1943: 256 – emphasis in original). When the subject is surprised by the gaze of the Other, the subject is reduced to shame (Sartre, 1943: 261). Lacan does not, at this point, develop his own concept of the gaze, and seems to be in general agreement with Sartre's views on the subject (S1, 215). Lacan is especially taken with Sartre's view that the gaze does not necessarily concern the organ of sight;

> Of course what *most often* manifests a look is the convergence of two ocular globes in my direction. But the look will be given just as well on occasion when there is a rustling of branches, or the sound of a footstep followed by silence, or the slight opening of a shutter, or a light movement of a curtain.
> (Sartre, 1943: 257)

It is only in 1964, with the development of the concept of OBJET PETIT A as the cause of desire, that Lacan develops his own theory of the gaze, a theory which is quite distinct from Sartre's (Lacan, 1964a). Whereas Sartre had conflated the gaze with the act of looking, Lacan now separates the two; the gaze becomes the object of the act of looking, or, to be more precise, the object of the scopic drive. The gaze is therefore, in Lacan's account, no longer on the side of the subject; it is the gaze of the Other. And whereas Sartre had conceived of an essential reciprocity between seeing the Other and being-seen-by-him, Lacan now conceives of an antinomic relation between the gaze and the eye: the eye which looks is that of the subject, while the gaze is on the side of the object, and there is no coincidence between the two, since 'You never look at me from the place at which I see you' (S11, 103). When the subject looks at an object, the object is always already gazing back at the subject, but from a point at which the subject cannot see it. This split between the eye and the gaze is nothing other than the subjective division itself, expressed in the field of vision.

The concept of the gaze was taken up by psychoanalytic film criticism in the 1970s (e.g. Metz, 1975), especially by feminist film critics (e.g. Mulvey, 1975; Rose, 1986). However, many of these critics have conflated Lacan's concept of the gaze with the Sartrean concept of the gaze and other ideas on vision such as

Foucault's account of panopticism. Much of so-called 'Lacanian film theory' is thus the site of great conceptual confusion (see Joan Copjec, 1989). See also Jay (1993).

genital (*génital*) In the stages of psychosexual DEVELOPMENT listed by Freud, the genital stage is the last stage in the series, coming after the two pregenital stages (the oral stage and the anal stage). The genital stage first arises between the ages of three and five (the infantile genital organisation, or phallic phase) and is then interrupted by the latency period, before returning at puberty (the genital stage proper). Freud defined this stage as the final 'complete organisation' of the libido, a synthesis of the previously anarchic 'polymorphous perversity' of the pregenital stages (see Freud, 1940a: SE XXIII, 155). Because of this, the concept of 'genitality' came to represent a privileged value in psychoanalytic theory after Freud, coming to represent a stage of full psychosexual maturity (Balint's 'genital love').

Lacan rejects most psychoanalytic theory concerning the genital stage, genital love, etc., calling it an 'absurd hymn to the harmony of the genital' (E, 245). According to Lacan, there is nothing harmonious about genitality.

● **The genital stage** The stages of psychosexual development are conceived by Lacan not as natural phases of biological maturation but as forms of DEMAND which are structured retroactively (S8, 238–46). In the oral and anal stages desire is eclipsed by demand, and it is only in the genital stage that desire is fully constituted (S8, 270). Thus Lacan does follow Freud in describing the genital stage as a third moment which comes after the oral and anal stages (S8, 268). However, Lacan's discussion of this stage focuses on what Freud referred to as the *infantile* genital organisation (also known as the phallic phase); a stage when the child knows only one sexual organ (the male one) and passes through the castration complex. Thus the genital phase is only thinkable, Lacan emphasises, insofar as it is marked by the sign of castration; 'genital realisation' can only be achieved on condition that the subject first assumes his own castration (S4, 219). Furthermore, Lacan insists that even when the polymorphous perverse sexuality of the pregenital phases comes under the domination of the genital organisation, this does not mean that pregenital sexuality is abolished; 'The most archaic aspirations of the child are . . . a nucleus that is never completely resolved under some primacy of genitality' (S7, 93). He therefore rejects the concept of a final stage of synthesis; synthesis is not possible for human beings, in Lacan's view, since human subjectivity is essentially and irremediably divided.

● **The genital drive** The genital drive is not listed by Lacan as one of the partial drives. Given that Lacan argues that every drive is a partial drive, his refusal to include the genital drive among the partial drives is tantamount to questioning its existence. In 1964, Lacan makes this explicit. He writes: 'the genital drive, if it exists, is not at all articulated like the other drives' (S11,

189). Unlike the other drives, the genital drive (if it exists) 'finds its form' on the side of the Other (S11, 189). Furthermore, there is no 'genital object' that would correspond to a supposed genital drive.

● **Genital love** Lacan rejects Michael Balint's concept of 'genital love' (Balint, 1947). The term indicates a psychosexual maturity in which the two elements of sensuality and affection are completely integrated and harmonised, and in which there is thus no longer any ambivalence. Freud, however, never used the term, and Lacan rejects it as completely alien to psychoanalytic theory. For Lacan, the idea of final psychosexual maturity and synthesis implied in the term 'genital love' is an illusion which completely overlooks 'the barriers and snubs (*Erniedrigungen*) that are so common even in the most fulfilled love relation' (E, 245). There is no such thing as a post-ambivalent object relation.

The concept of genital love is closely linked to that of 'oblativity', a term used by some psychoanalysts to designate a mature form of love in which one loves the other person for what he is rather than for what he can give. Lacan is as critical of the concept of oblativity as he is of the concept of genital love, viewing it as a form of moralism and a betrayal of the analytic discovery of the part-object (S8, 173–4). He argues that the concept of oblativity has little to do with genitality and has far more in common with anal erotism. Following Freud's equation between faeces and gifts, Lacan states that the formula of oblativity – 'everything for the other' – shows that it is a fantasy of the obsessional neurotic (S8, 241).

gestalt *Gestalt* is a German word meaning an organised pattern or whole which has properties other than those of its components in isolation. The experimental study of gestalts began in 1910 with the study of certain phenomena of perception, and led to a school of thought known as 'gestalt psychology' which was based on a holistic concept of mind and body and which stressed the psychological importance of body presentation. These ideas formed the basis of Gestalt therapy as developed by Paul Goodman, Fritz Perls and Ralph Hefferline.

When Lacan refers to the gestalt, he refers specifically to one kind of organised pattern, namely the visual image of another member of the same species, which is perceived as a unified whole. Such an image is a gestalt because it has an effect which none of its component parts have in isolation; this effect is to act as a 'releasing mechanism' (Fr. *déclencheur*) which triggers certain instinctual responses, such as reproductive behaviour (S1, 121f). In other words, when an animal perceives a unified image of another member of its species, it responds in certain instinctual ways. Lacan gives many examples from ethology of such instinctual responses to images (e.g. E, 3), but his main interest is in the way the gestalt functions in human beings. For humans the body image is also a gestalt which produces instinctual responses, especially sexual ones, but the power of the image is also more than merely instinctual; it constitutes the essential captivating power of the SPECULAR IMAGE (see CAPTATION). It is by identifying with the unified gestalt of the body image that the ego is formed in the mirror stage. However, the imaginary unity of the ego is constantly threatened by fears of disintegration, which manifest themselves in images of the FRAGMENTED BODY; these images represent the opposite of the unified gestalt of the body image.

graph of desire (*graphe du désir*)   The graph of desire is a topographical representation of the structure of desire. Lacan first develops the graph of desire in *The Seminar, Book V* (Lacan, 1957–8) in order to illustrate the psychoanalytic theory of jokes (see Freud, 1905c). The graph reappears in some of the following seminars (see Lacan, 1958–9 and 1960–1), but then all but disappears from Lacan's work. The graph appears in various forms, although the most well known form of it appears in 'The subversion of the subject and the dialectic of desire' (Lacan, 1960a). In this paper, Lacan builds up the graph of desire in four stages. The first of these stages is the 'elementary cell' of the graph (Figure 5; see E, 303).

The horizontal line represents the diachronic SIGNIFYING CHAIN; the horseshoe-shaped line represents the vector of the subject's intentionality. The double intersection of these two lines illustrates the nature of retroaction: the message,

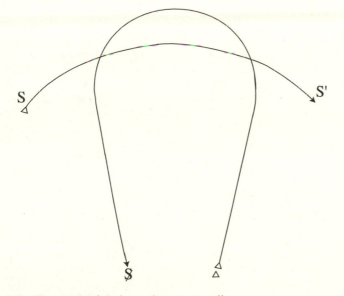

Figure 5   The graph of desire – elementary cell
Source: Jacques Lacan, *Écrits*, Paris: Seuil, 1966.

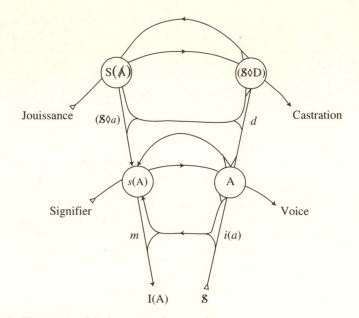

Figure 6 The graph of desire – complete graph
Source: Jacques Lacan, *Écrits*, Paris: Seuil, 1966.

at the point marked *s*(A) in the complete graph, is the POINT DE CAPITON determined retroactively by the particular punctuation given to it by the Other, A. The prelinguistic mythical subject of pure need, indicated by the triangle, must pass through the defiles of the signifier which produces the divided subject, $.

The intermediate stages of the graph of desire are not meant to show any evolution or temporal development, since the graph always exists as a whole; they are simply pedagogical devices used by Lacan in order to illustrate the structure of the complete graph (Figure 6; see E, 315 and Ec, 817).

In the complete graph there are not one but two signifying chains. The lower chain (from the signifier to the voice) is the conscious signifying chain, the level of the statement. The upper chain (from *jouissance* to castration) is the signifying chain in the unconscious, the level of the ENUNCIATION. The structure is thus duplicated: the upper part of the graph is structured exactly like the lower part.

hallucination (*hallucination*)

hallucination (*hallucination*) Hallucinations are usually defined in psychiatry as 'false perceptions', that is, perceptions which arise 'in the absence of an appropriate external stimulus' (Hughes, 1981: 208; see American Psychiatric Association, 1987: 398). Lacan finds such definitions inadequate, since they ignore the dimension of meaning and signification (Ec, 77; see E, 180). Hallucinations are a typical phenomenon of PSYCHOSIS, and are usually auditory (hearing voices), but may also be visual, somatic, tactile, olfactory, or gustatory.

Lacan argues that psychotic hallucinations are a consequence of the operation of FORECLOSURE. Foreclosure refers to the absence of the NAME-OF-THE-FATHER from the symbolic universe of the psychotic subject. A hallucination is the return of this foreclosed signifier in the dimension of the real; 'that which has not emerged into the light of the symbolic appears in the real' (Ec, 388). This is not to be confused with PROJECTION, which Lacan regards as a mechanism proper to neurosis rather than psychosis. In this distinction, Lacan follows Freud's analysis of Schreber's hallucinations; 'It was incorrect to say that the perception which suppressed internally is projected outwards; the truth is rather, as we now see, that what was abolished internally returns from without' (Freud, 1911c: SE XII, 71).

While hallucinations are most commonly associated with psychosis, there is another sense in which they play an important part in the structure of desire in all subjects. Freud argues that '[t]he first wishing seems to have been a hallucinatory cathecting of the memory of satisfaction' (Freud, 1900a: SE V, 598).

helplessness (*détresse*)

helplessness (*détresse*) The term 'helplessness' (Ger. *Hilflosigkeit*) has a specific meaning in Freud's work, where it denotes the state of the newborn baby who is incapable of carrying out the specific actions required to satisfy its own NEEDS, and so is completely dependent on other people (especially the MOTHER).

The helplessness of the human baby is grounded in its prematurity of birth, a fact which was pointed out by Freud and which Lacan takes up in his early writings. Compared to other animals such as apes, the human baby is relatively unformed when it is born, especially with respect to motor coordination. This means that it is more dependent than other animals, and for a longer time, on its parents.

Lacan follows Freud in highlighting the importance of the initial dependence of the human baby on the mother. Lacan's originality lies in the way he draws attention to 'the fact that this dependence is maintained by a world of language' (E, 309). The mother interprets the baby's cries as hunger, tiredness, loneliness, etc. and retroactively determines their meaning (see PUNC-

TUATION). The child's helplessness contrasts with the omnipotence of the mother, who can decide whether or not to satisfy the child's needs (S4, 69, 185). The recognition of this contrast engenders a depressive effect in the child (S4, 186).

Lacan also uses the concept of helplessness to illustrate the sense of abandonment and subjective destitution that the analysand feels at the END OF ANALYSIS. 'At the end of a training analysis the subject should reach and know the domain and level of the experience of absolute disarray' (S7, 304).The end of analysis is thus not conceived of by Lacan as the realisation of some blissful plenitude, but quite the contrary, as a moment when the subject comes to terms with his utter solitude. However, whereas the infant can rely on its mother's help, the analysand at the end of analysis 'can expect help from no one' (S7, 304). If this seems to present a particularly ascetic view of psychoanalytic treatment, this is exactly how Lacan wishes it to be seen; psychoanalysis is, in Lacan's words, a 'long subjective ascesis' (E, 105).

hysteria (*hystérie*)   The nosographical category of hysteria dates back to ancient Greek medicine, which conceived of it as a female disease caused by the womb wandering throughout the body (in Greek *hysteron* means womb). The term acquired an important place in psychiatry in the nineteenth century, especially in the work of Jean-Martin Charcot, under whom Freud studied in 1885–6. It was in the course of treating hysterical patients in the 1890s that Freud developed the psychoanalytical method of treatment (free association, etc.) and began to form the major concepts of psychoanalytic theory. Freud's first properly psychoanalytic case history concerns the treatment of a hysterical woman known as 'Dora' (Freud, 1905e).

The classic symptomatology of hysteria involves physical symptoms such as local paralyses, pains and anaesthesias, for which no organic cause can be found, and which are articulated around an 'imaginary anatomy' which bears no relation to the real structure of the nervous system (see Lacan, 1951b: 13). However, although Lacan does discuss the symptomatology of hysteria, linking it to the imago of the FRAGMENTED BODY (E, 5), he comes to define hysteria not as a set of symptoms but as a STRUCTURE. This means that a subject may well exhibit none of the typical bodily symptoms of hysteria and yet still be diagnosed as a hysteric by a Lacanian analyst.

Like Freud, Lacan regards hysteria as one of the two main forms of NEUROSIS, the other being OBSESSIONAL NEUROSIS. In the seminar of 1955–6 Lacan develops the idea that the structure of a neurosis is that of a question, and that what differentiates hysteria from obsessional neurosis is the nature of this question. Whereas obsessional neurosis concerns the question of the subject's existence, hysteria concerns the question of the subject's sexual position. This question may be phrased 'Am I a man or a woman?' or, more precisely, 'What is a woman?' (S3, 170–5). This is true for both male and female hysterics (S3, 178). Lacan thus reaffirms the ancient view that there is an intimate connection between hysteria and femininity. Indeed, most hysterics are women, just as most obsessional neurotics are men.

The structure of desire, as desire of the Other, is shown more clearly in hysteria than in any other clinical structure; the hysteric is precisely someone who appropriates another's desire by identifying with them. For example Dora identifies with Herr K, taking as her own the desire which she perceives him to have for Frau K (S4, 138). However, as the case of Dora also shows, the hysteric only sustains the desire of the Other on condition that she is not the object of that desire (Ec, 222); she cannot bear to be taken as the object of desire because that would revive the wound of privation (S17, 84). It is this privileged relation between the structure of desire and the structure of hysteria which explains why Lacan devotes so much attention to this clinical structure, and why he develops the idea in the 1970s that it is necessary, in psychoanalytic treatment, to 'hystericise' the analysand. Hysteria, as a clinical structure, must be distinguished from Lacan's concept of the DISCOURSE of the hysteric, which designates a particular form of social bond.

I

id (*ça*) Freud borrowed the term *das Es* (which the *Standard Edition* translates as 'the Id') from Georg Groddeck, one of the first German psychiatrists to support psychoanalysis, although as Freud also noted, Groddeck himself seems to have taken the term from Nietzsche (Freud, 1923b: SE XIX, 23, n. 3; see Nietzsche, 1886: 47). Groddeck argued that 'what we call the ego behaves essentially passively in life, and . . . we are "lived" by unknown and uncontrollable forces' (Freud, 1923b: SE XIX, 23), and used the term *das Es* to denote these forces. The term first appears in Freud's work in the early 1920s, in the context of the second model of the psyche; in this model, the psyche is divided into three agencies: the id, the EGO and the SUPEREGO. The id corresponds roughly to what Freud called the unconscious system in his first model of the psyche, but there are also important differences between these two concepts (see Laplanche and Pontalis, 1967: 197–9).

Lacan's main contribution to the theory of the id is to stress that the 'unknown and uncontrollable forces' in question are not primitive biological needs or wild instinctual forces of nature, but must be conceived of in linguistic terms:

> The *Es* with which analysis is concerned is made of the signifier which is already there in the real, the uncomprehended signifier. It is already there, but it is made of the signifier, it is not some kind of primitive and confused property relevant to some kind of pre-established harmony . . .
>
> (S4, 49)

Lacan conceives of the id as the unconscious origin of speech, the symbolic 'it' beyond the imaginary ego (the French term *ça* used by Lacan is much closer to Freud's *Es*, both being ordinary terms in everyday use, unlike the Latin *id* used in the *Standard Edition*). Thus whereas Groddeck states that 'the affirmation "I live" is only conditionally correct, it expresses only a small and superficial part of the fundamental principle "Man is lived by the It"' (Groddeck, 1923: 5), Lacan's view could be summed up in similar terms, only replacing the verb 'to live' with the verb 'to speak'; the affirmation 'I speak' is only a superficial part of the fundamental principle 'Man is spoken by it'. Hence the phrase which Lacan frequently uses when discussing the id; 'it speaks' (*le ça parle*) (e.g. S7, 206).The symbolic nature of the id, beyond the imaginary sense of self constituted by the ego, is what leads Lacan to equate it with the term 'subject'. This equation is illustrated by the homophony between the German term *Es* and the letter S, which is Lacan's symbol for the subject (E, 129; see SCHEMA L).

One of Freud's most famous statements concerns the id and its relationship with psychoanalytic treatment; *Wo Es war, soll Ich werden* (which the *Standard Edition* renders 'Where id was, there ego shall be' Freud, 1933a: SE XXII, 80). One common reading of this cryptic statement has been to take it as meaning that the task of psychoanalytic treatment is to enlarge the field of consciousness; it is just such a reading that is crystallised in the original French translation of Freud's statement – *le moi doit déloger le ça* (the ego shall dislodge the id). Lacan is completely opposed to such a reading (S1, 195), arguing instead that the word *soll* is to be understood as an ethical injunction, so that the aim of analysis is for the ego to submit to the autonomy of the symbolic order. Thus Lacan prefers to translate Freud's statement as 'There where it was, or there where one was . . . it is my duty that I should come into being [*Là où c'était, peut-on dire, là où s'était . . . c'est mon devoir que je vienne à être*]' (E, 129, translation modified; Ec, 417–18; see also E, 299–300; S11, 44). The end of analysis, according to this view, is thus a kind of 'existential recognition' of the symbolic determinants of one's being, a recognition of the fact that 'You are this' (You are this symbolic chain, and no more) (S1, 3).

identification (*identification*) In Freud's work the term 'identification' denotes a process whereby one subject adopts as his own one or more attributes of another subject. In his later work, as Freud developed the idea that the ego and the superego are constructed on the basis of a series of identifications, the concept of identification eventually came to denote 'the operation itself whereby the human subject is constituted' (Laplanche and Pontalis, 1967: 206). It is thus a concept of central importance in psychoanalytic theory. However, it is also a concept which raises important theoretical problems. One of the most important of these problems, which Freud himself struggled with, is the difficulty of establishing the precise relationship between identification and object-love.

The concept of identification occupies an equally important position in Lacan's work. Lacan places a special emphasis on the role of the image, defining identification as 'the transformation that takes place in the subject when he assumes an image' (E, 2). To 'assume' an image is to recognise oneself in the image, and to appropriate the image as oneself.

From early on in his work, Lacan distinguishes between imaginary identification and symbolic identification.

1. Imaginary identification is the mechanism by which the ego is created in the MIRROR STAGE; it belongs absolutely to the imaginary order. When the human infant sees its reflection in the mirror, it identifies with that image. The constitution of the ego by identification with something which is outside (and even against) the subject is what 'structures the subject as a rival with himself' (E, 22) and thus involves aggressivity and alienation. The mirror stage constitutes the 'primary identification', and gives birth to the IDEAL EGO.

2. Symbolic identification is the identification with the father in the final stage of the OEDIPUS COMPLEX which gives rise to the formation of the EGO-IDEAL. It is by means of this secondary identification that the subject transcends the aggressivity inherent in primary identification (E, 23), and thus can be said to represent a certain 'libidinal normalisation' (E, 2). Although this identification is called 'symbolic', it is still a 'secondary identification' (E, 22) modelled on primary identification and thus, like all identification, partakes of the imaginary; it is only called 'symbolic' because it represents the completion of the subject's passage into the symbolic order.

Lacan's ideas on the nature of symbolic identification undergo complex changes during the course of his work. In 1948 he sees it in terms of the 'introjection of the *imago* of the parent of the same sex' (E, 22), whereas by 1958 he has moved on to seeing it in terms of the identification with the real father in the third time of the Oedipus complex.

In 1961, Lacan goes on to describe symbolic identification as an identification with the signifier. He finds support for this idea in the catalogue of three types of identification which Freud presents in chapter seven of *Group Psychology and the Analysis of the Ego* (Freud, 1921c). In the first two types of identification (with a love object or with a rival), the subject may often express the identification purely and simply by developing a symptom identical to the symptom suffered by the person with whom he identifies. In such cases, 'the identification is a partial and extremely limited one and only borrows a single trait [*nur einen einzigen Zug*] from the person who is its object' (Freud, 1921c: SE XVIII, 107). This 'single trait' (in French, *trait unaire* – which English translations of Lacan render variously as 'unbroken line', 'single-stroke' or 'unitary trait') is taken by Lacan to be a primordial symbolic term which is introjected to produce the ego-ideal. Though this trait may originate as a sign, it becomes a signifier when incorporated into a signifying system (S8, 413–14). In 1964, Lacan links the single trait to the first signifier (S$_1$), and compares it to the notch that primitive man made on a stick to signify that he had killed one animal (S11, 141, 256).

Lacan is firmly opposed to those writers (e.g. Balint) who claim that identification with the analyst is the END OF ANALYSIS; on the contrary, Lacan insists not only that 'the crossing of the plane of identification is possible' (S11, 273), but also that this is a necessary condition of true psychoanalysis. Thus the end of analysis is conceived of by Lacan as the destitution of the subject, a moment when the subject's identifications are placed under question in such a way that these identifications can no longer be maintained in the same way as before. However, while the end of analysis is precisely not a question of identification with the analyst, Lacan argues that it is possible to speak about identification at the end of analysis in a different sense: identification with the symptom (see SINTHOME).

imaginary (*imaginaire*) Lacan's use of the term 'imaginary' as a substantive dates back to 1936 (Ec, 81). From the beginning, the term has connotations of illusion, fascination and seduction, and relates specifically to the DUAL RELATION between the EGO and the SPECULAR IMAGE. It is important to note, however, that while the imaginary always retains connotations of illusion and lure, it is not simply synonymous with 'the illusory' insofar as the latter term implies something unnecessary and inconsequential (Ec, 723). The imaginary is far from inconsequential; it has powerful effects in the real, and is not simply something that can be dispensed with or 'overcome'.

From 1953 on, the imaginary becomes one of the three ORDERS which constitute the tripartite scheme at the centre of Lacanian thought, being opposed to the symbolic and the real. The basis of the imaginary order continues to be the formation of the ego in the MIRROR STAGE. Since the ego is formed by identifying with the counterpart or specular image, IDENTIFICATION is an important aspect of the imaginary order. The ego and the counterpart form the prototypical dual relationship, and are interchangeable. This relationship whereby the ego is constituted by identification with the little other means that the ego, and the imaginary order itself, are both sites of a radical ALIENATION; 'alienation is constitutive of the imaginary order' (S3, 146). The dual relationship between the ego and the counterpart is fundamentally narcissistic, and NARCISSISM is another characteristic of the imaginary order. Narcissism is always accompanied by a certain AGGRESSIVITY. The imaginary is the realm of image and imagination, deception and lure. The principal illusions of the imaginary are those of wholeness, synthesis, autonomy, duality and, above all, similarity. The imaginary is thus the order of surface appearances which are deceptive, observable phenomena which hide underlying structure; the affects are such phenomena.

However, the opposition between the imaginary and the symbolic does not mean that the imaginary is lacking in structure. On the contrary, the imaginary is always already structured by the symbolic order. For example in his discussion of the mirror stage in 1949, Lacan speaks of the relations in imaginary space, which imply a symbolic structuring of that space (E, 1). The expression 'imaginary matrix' also implies an imaginary which is structured by the symbolic (Ec, 221), and in 1964 Lacan discusses how the visual field is structured by symbolic laws (S11, 91–2).

The imaginary also involves a linguistic dimension. Whereas the signifier is the foundation of the symbolic order, the SIGNIFIED and SIGNIFICATION are part of the imaginary order. Thus language has both symbolic and imaginary aspects; in its imaginary aspect, language is the 'wall of language' which inverts and distorts the discourse of the Other (see SCHEMA L).

The imaginary exerts a captivating power over the subject, founded in the almost hypnotic effect of the specular image. The imaginary is thus rooted in the subject's relationship to his own body (or rather to the image of his body). This captivating/capturing power is both seductive (the imaginary is manifested above all on the sexual plane, in such forms as sexual display and courtship rituals; Lacan, 1956b: 272) and disabling: it imprisons the subject in a series of static fixations (see CAPTATION).

The imaginary is the dimension of the human subject which is most closely linked to ethology and animal psychology (S3, 253). All attempts to explain human subjectivity in terms of animal psychology are thus limited to the imaginary (see NATURE). Although the imaginary represents the closest point of contact between human subjectivity and animal ethology (S2, 166), it is not simply identical; the imaginary order in human beings is structured by the symbolic, and this means that 'in man, the imaginary relation has deviated [from the realm of nature]' (S2, 210).

Lacan has a Cartesian mistrust of the imagination as a cognitive tool. He insists, like Descartes, on the supremacy of pure intellection, without dependence on images, as the only way of arriving at certain knowledge. It is this that lies behind Lacan's use of topological figures, which cannot be represented in the imagination, to explore the structure of the unconscious (see TOPOLOGY). This mistrust of the imagination and the senses puts Lacan firmly on the side of rationalism rather than empiricism (see SCIENCE).

Lacan accused the major psychoanalytic schools of his day of reducing psychoanalysis to the imaginary order: these psychoanalysts made identification with the analyst into the goal of analysis, and reduced analysis to a dual relationship (E, 246–7). Lacan sees this as a complete betrayal of psychoanalysis, a deviation which can only ever succeed in increasing the alienation of the subject. Against such imaginary reductionism, Lacan argues that the essence of psychoanalysis consists in its use of the symbolic. This use of the symbolic is the only way to dislodge the disabling fixations of the imaginary. Thus the only way for the analyst to gain any purchase on the imaginary is by transforming the images into words, just as Freud treats the dream as a rebus: 'The imaginary is decipherable only if it is rendered into symbols' (Lacan,

1956b: 269). This use of the symbolic is the only way for the analytic process 'to cross the plane of identification' (S11, 273).

imago Originally introduced into psychoanalytic theory by Jung in 1911, the Latin term *imago* had already become standard in psychoanalytic terminology by the time Lacan began training as a psychoanalyst in the 1930s. The term is clearly related to the term 'image', but it is meant to emphasise the subjective determination of the image; in other words, it includes feelings as well as a visual representation. Imagos are specifically images of other people (Jung mentions paternal, maternal and fraternal imagos); however, they are not the product of purely personal experience but universal prototypes which may be actualised in anyone's psyche. Imagos act as stereotypes influencing the way the subject relates to other people, who are perceived through the lens of these various imagos.

The term 'imago' occupies a central role in Lacan's pre-1950 writings, where it is closely related to the term COMPLEX. In 1938, Lacan links each of the three family complexes to a specific imago: the weaning complex is linked to the imago of the maternal breast, the intrusion complex to the imago of the counterpart, and the Oedipus complex to the imago of the father (Lacan, 1938). In 1946, Lacan argues that in formulating the concept of the imago, psychoanalysis has provided PSYCHOLOGY with a proper object of study and thus set psychology on a truly scientific footing: 'it is possible . . . to designate in the imago the proper object of psychology, exactly to the same extent that Galileo's notion of the inert material point formed the basis of physics' (Ec, 188).

Whereas for Jung and Klein imagos have equally positive and negative effects, in Lacan's work they are weighted firmly towards the negative, being fundamentally deceptive and disruptive elements. Lacan speaks of the imago of the FRAGMENTED BODY, and even unified imagos such as the specular image are mere *illusions* of wholeness which introduce an underlying aggressivity. 'The first effect of the imago which appears in the human being is an effect of subjective *alienation*' (Ec, 181, emphasis in original).

After 1950, the term 'imago' disappears almost entirely from Lacan's theoretical vocabulary. However, the basic ideas developed around the term in Lacan's pre-1950 writings continue to play an important part in his thinking, being articulated around other terms, principally the term 'image'.

index (*indice*) In the typology of SIGNS devised by Charles S. Peirce, the North American semiotician, the index is a sign which has an 'existential relationship' to the object it represents (i.e. the index is always spatially or temporally contiguous with the object). Peirce contrasts the index with the *symbol*, which, like Saussure's concept of the sign, is characterised by the absence of all necessary connections between the sign and its object. For example, smoke is an index of fire, and red blotches are an index of various diseases such as measles (Peirce, 1932).

In Lacan's discourse, the term 'index' functions in opposition to the term 'SIGNIFIER' (and not, as in Peirce's philosophy, in opposition to the term symbol). Lacan thus conceives the index as a 'natural sign', one in which there is a fixed, bi-univocal correspondence between sign and object (unlike the signifier, which has no fixed link with any one signified). This opposition between index and signifier underpins the following distinctions in Lacan's work:

● **The psychoanalytic and medical concepts of the** SYMPTOM Whereas in medicine, the symptom is regarded as an index of the disease, in psychoanalysis the symptom is not an index but a signifier (E, 129). Hence in psychoanalysis there is no one-to-one fixed link between pathological phenomena and the underlying structure.

● CODES **(animal) and language (human)** Codes are composed of indices, whereas language is composed of signifiers. This explains why codes lack the most important feature of language: its potential for ambiguity and equivocation.

The opposition between signifier and index is complicated by the existence of certain signifiers which also function as indices; these are called SHIFTERS.

instinct (*instinct*) Lacan follows Freud in distinguishing the instincts from the DRIVES, and criticises those who, following Strachey, obscure this distinction by using the same English word ('instinct') to translate both Freud's terms (*Instinkt* and *Trieb*) (E, 301).

'Instinct' is a purely biological concept (see BIOLOGY) and belongs to the study of animal ethology. Whereas animals are driven by instincts, which are relatively rigid and invariable, and imply a direct relation to an object, human sexuality is a matter of drives, which are very variable and never attain their object. Although Lacan uses the term 'instinct' frequently in his early work, after 1950 he uses the word less frequently, preferring instead to reconceptualise the concept of instinct in terms of NEED.

From his earliest works, Lacan criticises those who attempt to understand human behaviour purely in terms of instincts, arguing that this is to suppose a harmonious relation between man and the world, which does not in fact exist (Ec, 88). The concept of instinct supposes some kind of direct innate knowledge of the object which is of an almost moral character (Ec, 851). Against such ideas, Lacan insists that there is something inadequate about human biology, a feature which he indicates in the phrases 'vital insufficiency' (*insuffisance vitale*) (Ec, 90) and 'congenital insufficiency'. This inadequacy, evident in the helplessness of the human baby, is compensated for by means of COMPLEXES. The fact that human psychology is dominated by complexes (which are determined entirely by cultural and social factors) rather than by instincts, means that any explanation of human behaviour that does not take social factors into account is useless.

International Psycho-Analytical Association   The International Psycho-Analytical Association (IPA) was founded by Freud in 1910 as an umbrella group for the various psychoanalytic societies that were springing up around the world at that time. The first headquarters were in Zurich, and later moved to London, but the Association has been dominated by its American members ever since the 1930s, when most of the Viennese analysts emigrated to the United States.

After resigning from the IPA-affiliated Société Psychanalytique de Paris (SPP) in 1953, to join the newly founded Société Française de Psychanalyse (SFP), Lacan was informed by letter that this also meant that he was no longer a member of the IPA. From that moment on until his death, Lacan and the IPA were at loggerheads. During the SFP's subsequent campaign for IPA membership (which Lacan seems to have supported) Lacan was regarded by the IPA as the principal obstacle blocking negotiations. The main bone of contention was Lacan's use of sessions of variable duration, which he continued to practise despite repeated IPA admonitions. Eventually, in 1963, the IPA agreed to grant membership to the SFP on condition that Lacan be stripped of his status as a training analyst. Many of the leading analysts in the SFP agreed, but to many others (including Lacan) this was unacceptable. Lacan resigned from the SFP and, followed by a number of other analysts and trainees, founded his own SCHOOL in 1964. From this point on, Lacan became much more vocal in his criticism of the IPA, accusing it of being a kind of church and comparing his own fate to Spinoza's 'excommunication' from the synagogue (S11, 3–4).

Lacan criticised both the institutional structure and the dominant theoretical tendencies of the IPA. As regards the institutional structure, he accused its bureaucratic procedures of producing nothing but mediocrities, and mocked its stuffy hierarchies (Ec, 474–86). Lacan argued that Freud had organised the IPA in such a way because this was the only way of assuring that his theories, misunderstood by all his first followers, would remain intact for someone else (Lacan) to disinter and resuscitate later on. The IPA, in other words, was like a tomb whose only function was to preserve Freud's doctrine despite the ignorance of the members of the association, the implication being that once Lacan had breathed new life into the doctrine, the IPA no longer had any valid function at all (see Lacan, 1956a). Even more important than this were Lacan's criticisms of the IPA TRAINING programme, which he accused of ignoring Freud's emphasis on the need for instruction in literary and cultural studies (Ec, 473), and for reducing the training analysis to a mere ritual. The specific organisational structures on which Lacan organised his own school, such as the cartel and the pass, were aimed at ensuring that this school did not repeat these errors of the IPA.

On a theoretical level, Lacan levelled various criticisms at all the main theoretical tendencies in the IPA, including Kleinian psychoanalysis and object-relations theory, but his most sustained and profound criticisms were reserved for the school of EGO-PSYCHOLOGY which had achieved a dominant position in the IPA by the 1950s. He accused the IPA of having betrayed Freud's most fundamental insights, renaming it the SAMCDA (*société d'assistance mutuelle contre le discours analytique*, or society for mutual assistance against analytic discourse – Lacan, 1973a: 27), and attributed this betrayal largely to the fact that the IPA was dominated by the USA (see FACTOR C). Lacan regarded his own teaching as a return to the insights that the IPA had betrayed (see FREUD, RETURN TO).

interpretation (*interprétation*) The role of the analyst in the treatment is twofold. First and foremost, he must listen to the analysand, but he must also intervene by speaking to the analysand. Although the analyst's speech is characterised by many different kinds of speech act (asking questions, giving instructions, etc.), it is the offering of interpretations which plays the most crucial and distinctive role in the treatment. Broadly speaking, the analyst can be said to offer an interpretation when he says something that subverts the analysand's conscious 'everyday' way of looking at something.

Freud first began offering interpretations to his patients in order to help them remember an idea that had been repressed from memory. These interpretations were educated guesses about what the patients had omitted from their account of the events which led up to the formation of their symptoms. For example, in one of the earliest interpretations he recorded, Freud told one patient that she had not revealed all her motives for the intense affection she showed towards her employer's children, and went on to say; 'I believe that really you are in love with your employer, the Director, though perhaps without being aware of it yourself' (Freud, 1895d: SE II, 117). The purpose of the interpretation was to help the patient become conscious of unconscious thoughts.

The model of interpretation was set down by Freud in *The Interpretation of Dreams* (Freud, 1900a); though only concerned explicitly with dreams, Freud's comments on interpretation in this work apply equally to all the other formations of the unconscious (parapraxes, jokes, symptoms, etc.). In the second chapter of this work the psychoanalytic method of interpretation is distinguished from the 'decoding' method of interpretation by the use of the method of free association: a psychoanalytic interpretation does not consist in attributing a meaning to a dream by referring to a pre-existing system of equivalences but by referring to the associations of the dreamer himself. It follows that the same image will mean very different things if dreamed by different people. Even when Freud later came to recognise the existence of 'symbolism' in dreams (i.e. the fact that there are some images which have fixed universal meanings in addition to their unique meaning for the individual dreamer), he always maintained that interpretation should focus primarily on the particular meaning and warned against 'overestimating the importance of symbols in dream interpretation' (Freud, 1900a: SE V, 359–60).

Early on in the history of the psychoanalytic movement, interpretation rapidly came to be the most important tool of the analyst, his primary means for achieving therapeutic effects in the patient. Since symptoms were held to be the expression of a repressed idea, the interpretation was seen to cure the symptom by helping the patient become conscious of the idea. However, after the initial period in which the offering of interpretations seemed to achieve remarkable effects, in the decade 1910–20 analysts began to notice that their interpretations were becoming less effective. In particular, the symptom would persist even after the analyst had offered exhaustive interpretations of it.

In order to explain this, analysts turned to the concept of RESISTANCE, arguing that it is not sufficient simply to offer an interpretation of the unconscious meaning of the symptom but that it is also necessary to get rid of the patient's resistance to becoming fully conscious of this meaning (see Strachey, 1934). Lacan, however, proposes a different explanation. He argues that the decreasing efficacy of interpretations after 1920 was due to a 'closure' of the unconscious which the analysts themselves had provoked (S2, 10–11; S8, 390). Among other things, Lacan blames the increasing tendency of the first generation of analysts to base their interpretations more on symbolism (despite Freud's warnings to the contrary), thereby returning to the pre-psychoanalytic 'decoding' method of interpretation. Not only did this reduce interpretations to set formulas, but the patients soon came to be able to predict exactly what the analyst would say about any particular symptom or association they produced (which, as Lacan wryly comments 'is surely the most annoying trick which can be played on a fortune-teller'; Ec, 462). Interpretations thus lacked both relevance and shock-value.

Other analysts before Lacan had recognised the problems caused by the fact that patients were increasingly knowledgeable of psychoanalytic theory. However, the solution which they proposed for this problem was that 'too much knowledge on the part of the patient should be replaced by more knowledge on the part of the analyst' (Ferenczi and Rank, 1925: 61). In other words, they urged the analyst to elaborate even more complex theories in order to stay one step ahead of the patient. Lacan, however, proposes a different solution. What is needed, he argues, is not interpretations of ever-increasing complexity, but a different way of approaching interpretation altogether. Hence Lacan calls for a 'renewed technique of interpretation' (E, 82), one that challenges the basic assumptions underlying the classical psychoanalytic model of interpretation.

Classical interpretations generally took the form of attributing to a dream, a symptom, a parapraxis, or an association, a meaning not given to it by the patient. For example the interpretation may be of the form 'What you really mean by this symptom is that you desire x'. The fundamental assumption was that the interpretation unmasks a hidden meaning, the truth of which could be confirmed by the patient producing more associations. It is this assumption that

Lacan challenges, arguing that analytic interpretations should no longer aim at discovering a hidden meaning, but rather at disrupting meaning; 'Interpretation is directed not so much at "making sense" as towards reducing the signifiers to their "non-sense" in order thereby to find the determinants of all the subject's conduct' (S11, 212, my translation). Interpretation thus inverts the relationship between signifier and signified: instead of the normal production of meaning (signifier produces signified), interpretation works at the level of s to generate S: interpretation causes 'irreducible signifiers' to arise, which are 'non-sensical' (S11, 250). Hence it is not a question, for Lacan, of fitting the analysand's discourse into a preconceived interpretive matrix or theory (as in the 'decoding' method), but of disrupting all such theories. Far from offering the analysand a new message, the interpretation should serve merely to enable the analysand to hear the message he is unconsciously addressing to himself. The analysand's speech always has other meanings apart from that which he consciously intends to convey. The analyst plays on the ambiguity of the analysand's speech, bringing out its multiple meanings. Often the most effective way for the interpretation to achieve this is for it too to be ambiguous. By interpreting in this way, the analyst sends the analysand's message back to the analysand in its true, inverted form (see COMMUNICATION).

An interpretation is therefore not offered to gain the analysand's assent, but is simply a tactical device aimed at enabling the analysand to continue speaking when the flow of assocations has become blocked. The value of an interpretation does not lie in its correspondence with reality, but simply in its power to produce certain effects; an interpretation may therefore be inexact, in the sense of not corresponding to 'the facts', but nevertheless true, in the sense of having powerful symbolic effects (see E, 237).

Lacan argues that in order to interpret in this way, the analyst must take the analysand's speech absolutely literally (*à la lettre*). That is, the task of the analyst is not to achieve some imaginary intuitive grasp of the analysand's 'hidden message', but simply to read the analysand's discourse as if it were a text, attending to the formal features of this discourse, the signifiers that repeat themselves (S2, 153). Hence Lacan's frequent warnings of the dangers of 'understanding'; 'the less you understand, the better you listen' (S2, 141). Understanding (*comprendre*) has negative connotations for Lacan, implying a kind of listening that seeks only to fit the other's speech into a preformed theory (see E, 270; S2, 103; S8, 229-30). In order to do avoid this, the analyst, must 'forget what he knows' when listening (Ec, 349) and when offering interpretations must do so 'exactly as if we were completely ignorant of theory' (Lacan, 1953b: 227).

On the complex question of Lacan's approach to 'interpreting the transference', see TRANSFERENCE.

intersubjectivity (*intersubjectivité*) When Lacan first begins (in 1953) to analyse in detail the function of SPEECH in psychoanalysis, he emphasises that speech is essentially an intersubjective process; 'the allocution of the subject entails an allocutor' and therefore 'the locutor is constituted in it as intersubjectivity' (E, 49). The term 'intersubjectivity' thus possesses, at this point in Lacan's work, a positive value, since it draws attention to the importance of language in psychoanalysis and emphasises the fact that the unconscious is 'transindividual'. Psychoanalysis is thus to be conceived in intersubjective rather than intrasubjective terms.

However, by 1960 the term has come to acquire negative connotations for Lacan. It is now associated, not with speech as such, but with the notions of reciprocity and symmetry that characterise the DUAL RELATIONSHIP (S8, 11); that is, with the imaginary rather than with the symbolic. Psychoanalysis is no longer to be conceived of in terms of intersubjectivity (S8, 20); indeed, the experience of the transference is precisely what undermines the notion of intersubjectivity (see Lacan, 1967).

introjection (*introjection*) The term 'introjection' was coined by Sándor Ferenczi in 1909, in order to denote the opposite of projection (Ferenczi, 1909). Freud took up the term soon afterwards, arguing that the 'purified pleasure-ego' is constituted by the introjection of everything that is a source of pleasure (Freud, 1915c). Melanie Klein uses the term a great deal, but restricts the term to the introjection of *objects*.

Lacan criticises the way psychoanalysts have tended to adopt 'magical' views of introjection, which confuse it with incorporation, thus mixing up the orders of fantasy and structure (S1, 169). Thus Lacan rejects the Kleinian imagery in which introjects are internal objects which pass into the analyst by some kind of fantastic incorporation. Instead he argues that what is introjected is always a signifier; 'introjection is always the introjection of the speech of the other' (S1, 83). Introjection thus refers to the process of symbolic identification, the process by which the EGO-IDEAL is constituted at the end of the Oedipus complex (see E, 22).

Lacan is also opposed to the view that introjection is the opposite of PROJECTION. Thus whereas in the Kleinian account an object can be introjected and then re-projected *ad infinitum*, Lacan argues that these two processes are located in entirely different registers and so cannot be conceived of as part of a single process. He argues that projection is an imaginary phenomenon which relates to images, whereas introjection is a symbolic process which relates to signifiers (Ec, 655).

inversion (*inversion*) Freud uses the term 'inversion' to designate homosexuality, the idea being that homosexuality is the inverse of heterosexuality. Lacan uses the term in this sense too in his early works (Lacan, 1938: 109).

However, in Lacan's post-war works the term is used in quite a different sense. Inversion then usually refers to a characteristic of the SPECULAR IMAGE;

what appears on one side of the real body appears on the other side of the image of the body reflected in the mirror (see Lacan, 1951b: 15). By extension, inversion becomes a quality of all imaginary phenomena, such as TRANSITIVISM. Thus in schema L, the imaginary is represented as a barrier blocking the discourse of the Other, causing this discourse to arrive at the subject *in an inverted form*. Hence Lacan's definition of analytic communication in which the sender receives his own message in an inverted form.

In 1957, both senses of the term are brought together in Lacan's discussion of Leonardo da Vinci. Taking up Freud's argument about Leonardo's homosexuality (Freud, 1910c), Lacan goes on to argue that Leonardo's specular identification was highly unusual in that it resulted in an inversion of the positions (on schema L) of the ego and the little other (S4, 433–4).

J

jouissance   The French word *jouissance* means basically 'enjoyment', but it has a sexual connotation (i.e. 'orgasm') lacking in the English word 'enjoyment', and is therefore left untranslated in most English editions of Lacan (though it has since been pointed out that the word 'jouissance' does actually figure in the *Shorter Oxford English Dictionary*; cf. Macey, 1988: 288, n.129). As Jane Gallop observes, whereas orgasm is a countable noun, the term *jouissance* is always used in the singular by Lacan, and is always preceded by a definite article (Gallop, 1982: 30).

The term does not appear in Lacan's work until 1953, but even then it is not particularly salient (E, 42, 87). In the seminars of 1953–4 and 1954–5 Lacan uses the term occasionally, usually in the context of the Hegelian dialectic of the MASTER and the slave: the slave is forced to work to provide objects for the master's enjoyment (*jouissance*) (S1, 223; S2, 269). Up to 1957, then, the term seems to mean no more than the enjoyable sensation that accompanies the satisfaction of a biological need such as hunger (S4, 125). Soon after, the sexual connotations become more apparent; in 1957, Lacan uses the term to refer to the enjoyment of a sexual object (Ec, 453) and to the pleasures of masturbation (S4, 241), and in 1958 he makes explicit the sense of *jouissance* as orgasm (Ec, 727). (For a fuller description of the development of this term in Lacan's work, see Macey, 1988: 200–5).

It is only in 1960 that Lacan develops his classic opposition between *jouissance* and pleasure, an opposition which alludes to the Hegelian/Kojevian distinction between *Genuß* (enjoyment) and *Lust* (pleasure) (cf. Kojève, 1947: 46). The pleasure principle functions as a limit to enjoyment; it is a law which commands the subject to 'enjoy as little as possible'. At the same time, the subject constantly attempts to transgress the prohibitions imposed on his enjoyment, to go 'beyond the pleasure principle'. However, the result of transgressing the pleasure principle is not more pleasure, but pain, since there is only a certain amount of pleasure that the subject can bear. Beyond this limit, pleasure becomes pain, and this 'painful pleasure' is what Lacan calls *jouissance*; '*jouissance* is suffering' (S7, 184). The term *jouissance* thus nicely expresses the paradoxical satisfaction that the subject derives from his symptom, or, to put it another way, the suffering that he derives from his own satisfaction (Freud's 'primary gain from illness').

The prohibition of *jouissance* (the pleasure principle) is inherent in the symbolic structure of language, which is why '*jouissance* is forbidden to him who speaks, as such' (E, 319). The subject's entry into the symbolic is conditional upon a certain initial renunciation of *jouissance* in the castration complex, when the subject gives up his attempts to be the imaginary phallus for the mother; 'Castration means that *jouissance* must be refused so that it can be reached on the inverted ladder (*l'échelle renversée*) of the Law of desire' (E, 324). The symbolic prohibition of enjoyment in the Oedipus complex (the incest taboo) is thus, paradoxically, the prohibition of something which is already impossible; its function is therefore to sustain the neurotic illusion that enjoyment would be attainable if it were not forbidden. The very prohibition creates the desire to transgress it, and *jouissance* is therefore fundamentally transgressive (see S7, ch.15).

The DEATH DRIVE is the name given to that constant desire in the subject to break through the pleasure principle towards the THING and a certain excess *jouissance*; thus *jouissance* is 'the path towards death' (S17, 17). Insofar as the drives are attempts to break through the pleasure principle in search of *jouissance*, every drive is a death drive.

There are strong affinities between Lacan's concept of *jouissance* and Freud's concept of the LIBIDO, as is clear from Lacan's description of jouissance as a 'bodily substance' (S20, 26). In keeping with Freud's assertion that there is only one libido, which is masculine, Lacan states that *jouissance* is essentially phallic; '*Jouissance*, insofar as it is sexual, is phallic, which means that it does not relate to the Other as such' (S20, 14). However, in 1973 Lacan admits that there is a specifically feminine *jouissance*, a 'supplementary *jouissance*' (S20, 58) which is 'beyond the phallus' (S20, 69), a *jouissance* of the Other. This feminine *jouissance* is ineffable, for women experience it but know nothing about it (S20, 71). In order to differentiate between these two forms of *jouissance*, Lacan introduces different algebraic symbols for each; Jφ designates phallic *jouissance*, whereas JA designates the *jouissance* of the Other.

Kleinian psychoanalysis

Kleinian psychoanalysis Kleinian psychoanalysis is the name given to the school of psychoanalytic theory that has grown up around the pioneering work of the Austrian psychoanalyst Melanie Klein (1882–1960). Born in Vienna, Klein settled in England in 1926 and remained there for the rest of her life. Kleinian psychoanalysis first began to emerge as a distinctive school of psychoanalytic theory during the 1940s in opposition to the group which gathered around Anna Freud after the latter's move to London. However, it was not until after the war that other analysts began to become known as 'Kleinians' and to develop a substantial body of Kleinian thought. These analysts included Hanna Segal, Herbert Rosenfeld, Wilfred Bion and (later) Donald Meltzer.

Along with the two other major non-Lacanian schools of psychoanalytic theory (EGO-PSYCHOLOGY and OBJECT-RELATIONS THEORY) Kleinian psychoanalysis forms a major point of reference for Lacan against which he puts forward his own particular reading of Freud. Lacan's criticisms of Klein are therefore important to understanding the originality of his position. While it is impossible to mention all of these criticisms here, some of the most important of them may be summarised as follows:

1. Lacan criticises Klein for placing too much emphasis on the mother and neglecting the role of the father (e.g. Ec, 728–9).

2. Lacan criticises Klein for theorising FANTASY entirely in the imaginary order. Such an approach is a misconception, argues Lacan, since it fails to take into account the symbolic structure that underpins all imaginary formations.

3. Lacan disagrees with Klein's views on the early development of the Oedipus complex. For Lacan, all debate on the precise dating of the Oedipus complex is futile, since it is not primarily a stage of development but a permanent structure of subjectivity. (Insofar as the Oedipus complex *can* be located in time, Lacan would not locate it as early as Klein does. Thus while Klein seems almost to deny the existence of a preoedipal phase, Lacan argues that there is one.)

4. Closely connected to the preceding point are Lacan's differences with respect to 'Melanie Klein's encroachments into the pre-verbal areas of the unconscious' (Lacan, 1951: 11). For Lacan, there are no pre-verbal areas of the unconscious, since the unconscious *is* a linguistic structure.

5. Lacan criticises Klein's interpretative style as being particulary brutal. In reference to the young patient ('Dick') whom Klein discusses in her paper on symbol formation (Klein, 1930), Lacan remarks that 'she slams the symbolism on him with complete brutality' (S1, 68).

However, to portray Lacan as entirely critical of Klein would be to oversimplify the matter. For while Lacan's disagreements with Kleinian psychoanalysis are at least as great as his disagreements with ego-psychology and object-relations theory, his comments on Klein are not characterised by the same dismissive tone which is evident in his acerbic criticisms of analysts from these other two schools. He certainly regards it as superior to ego-psychology, and praises Ernest Jones for taking sides with Melanie Klein against Anna Freud (Ec, 721–2). He also states that Melanie Klein is certainly more faithful to Freud than Anna Freud regarding the theory of transference (S8, 369).

In his pre-1950 writings, there are many allusions to Klein's work on the mother–child relationship and the various imagos that operate in fantasy. After 1950, Lacan praises Klein for emphasising the importance of the death drive in psychoanalytic theory (though his own way of conceiving the death drive differs markedly from Klein's) and for developing the concept of the PART-OBJECT (though once again Lacan's formulations on this concept differ greatly from Klein's).

knowledge (*connaissance/savoir*)

Lacan distinguishes between two kinds of knowledge: imaginary knowledge (*connaissance*) which is knowledge of the ego, and symbolic knowledge (*savoir*), which is knowledge of the subject. Since both of these French terms are translated by the single English word 'knowledge', it is important, when reading Lacan in translation, to be aware of which French word Lacan uses in the original text.

1. *Savoir* is the kind of knowledge which psychoanalytic treatment aims at. It is both knowledge of the subject's relation to the symbolic order, and also that relation itself. This knowledge is simply the articulation of signifiers in the subject's symbolic universe, the signifying chain (S_2). The unconscious is simply another name for symbolic knowledge insofar as it is an 'unknown knowledge', a knowledge which the subject does not know he knows. Psychoanalytic treatment aims at a progressive revelation of this knowledge to the subject, and is based on the premise that the only means of access to this knowledge is via a particular form of speech called free association. However, psychoanalytic treatment does not aim at a Hegelian 'absolute knowledge', because the unconscious is irreducible; there is an inescapable division between the subject and knowledge. Symbolic knowledge is knowledge of the truth about one's unconscious desire. Knowledge in this sense is a form of *jouissance*: 'knowledge is the *jouissance* of the Other' (S17, 13). Symbolic knowledge does not reside in any particular subject, nor in the Other (which is not a subject but a locus), but is intersubjective. However, this does not prevent one supposing that somewhere there is a subject who possesses this symbolic knowledge (see SUBJECT SUPPOSED TO KNOW).

2. *Connaissance* (and its necessary correlate, *méconnaissance*) is the kind of self-knowledge that belongs to the imaginary register. It is by misunderstanding and misrecognition (*méconnaissance*) that the subject comes to the imaginary knowledge of himself (*me-connaissance*) which is constitutive of the ego (E, 306). The ego is thus an illusory kind of self-knowledge based on a

fantasy of self-mastery and unity. There is also a co-birth (*co-naissance*) of the ego and the other (a reference to Claudel's formula, '*Toute naissance est une co-naissance*'). Imaginary knowledge is called 'paranoiac knowledge' by Lacan (E, 2) because it has the same structure as paranoia (both involve a delusion of absolute knowledge and mastery), and because one of the preconditions of all human knowledge is the 'paranoiac alienation of the ego' (Lacan, 1951b: 12). Imaginary knowledge is an obstacle which hinders the subject's access to symbolic knowledge. Psychoanalytic treatment must therefore continually subvert the subject's imaginary self-knowledge in order to reveal the symbolic self-knowledge which it blocks.

L

lack (*manque*) The term 'lack' is always related, in Lacan's teaching, to DESIRE. It is a lack which causes desire to arise (see S8, 139). However, the precise nature of what is lacking varies over the course of Lacan's work.

When the term first appears, in 1955, lack designates first and foremost a lack of BEING (there are close parallels with Sartre here; see Sartre, 1943). What is desired is being itself. 'Desire is a relation of being to lack. The lack is the lack of being properly speaking. It isn't the lack of this or that, but lack of being whereby the being exists' (S2, 223). Lacan returns to this theme in 1958, when he argues that desire is the metonymy of the lack of being (*manque à être*; translated by Sheridan as 'want-to-be' and by Schneiderman as 'want of being'; see E, 259). The subject's lack of being is 'the heart of the analytic experience' and 'the very field in which the neurotic's passion is deployed' (E, 251). Lacan contrasts the lack of being, which relates to desire, with the lack of having (*manque à avoir*), which relates to demand (Ec, 730).

AGENT	LACK	OBJECT
Real father	Symbolic castration	Imaginary phallus
Symbolic mother	Imaginary frustration	Real breast
Imaginary father	Real privation	Symbolic phallus

Figure 7 Table of three types of lack of object
Source: Jacques Lacan, *Le Séminaire. Livre IV. La relation d'objet*, ed. Jacques-Alain Miller, Paris: Seuil, 1994.

In 1956, lack comes to designate the lack of an object. Lacan distinguishes between three kinds of lack, according to the nature of the object which is lacking, as shown in Figure 7 (taken from S4, 269).

Of these three forms of lack, castration is the most important from the point of view of analytic experience, and the term 'lack' tends to become synonymous with castration (see CASTRATION COMPLEX).

In 1957, when Lacan introduces the algebraic symbol for the barred Other (Ⱥ), lack comes to designate the lack of a signifier in the Other. Lacan introduces the symbol S(Ⱥ) to designate 'the signifier of a lack in the Other'. No matter how many signifiers one adds to the signifying chain, the chain is always incomplete; it always lacks the signifier that could complete it. This 'missing signifier' (written -1 in Lacanian algebra) is constitutive of the subject.

language (*langue, langage*)   It is important to note that the English word 'language' corresponds to two French words: *langue* and *langage*. These two words have quite different meanings in Lacan's work; *langue* usually refers to a specific language, such as French or English, whereas *langage* refers to the system of language in general, abstracting from all particular languages. It is fundamentally the general structure of language (*langage*), rather than the differences between particular languages (*langues*) that interests Lacan. When reading Lacan in English it is therefore essential to be aware of which term is used in the original French; most of the time the French term will be *langage*.

Lacan's interest in linguistic phenomena can be traced back to his early interest in surrealist poetry and to his fascination with the psychotic language of Aimée, a paranoiac woman whose writings Lacan analyses in his doctoral dissertation (Lacan, 1932). After this, Lacan's thinking on the nature of language goes through a long process of development, in which four broad phases can be discerned (see Macey, 1988: 121–76):

1. Between 1936 and 1949 references to language are sparse, but they are significant; already in 1936, for example, Lacan emphasises that language is constitutive of the psychoanalytic experience (Ec, 82), and in 1946 he argues that it is impossible to understand madness without addressing the problem of language (Ec, 166). Lacan's comments on language at this time do not contain any references to a specific linguistic theory, and instead are dominated by philosophical allusions, mainly in terms derived from Hegel. Thus language is seen primarily as a mediating element which permits the subject to attain recognition from the other (see E, 9). Above and beyond its use for conveying information, language is first and foremost an appeal to an interlocutor; in Jakobson's terms, Lacan stresses the connative function above the referential. Thus he insists that language is not a nomenclature (Ec, 166).

2. From 1950 to 1954 language begins to occupy the central position that it will hold in Lacan's work thereafter. In this period, Lacan's discussion of language is dominated by references to Heideggerian phenomenology and,

more importantly, to the anthropology of language (Mauss, Malinowski and Lévi-Strauss). Language is thus seen as structuring the social laws of exchange, as a symbolic pact, etc. There are also occasional references to rhetoric, but these are not elaborated (e.g. E, 169). There are a few allusions to Saussure (e.g. S1, 248), but in his famous 'Rome discourse' Lacan establishes an opposition between *parole* and *langage* (and not, as Saussure does, between *parole* and *langue*; see Lacan, 1953a) (see SPEECH).

3. Between 1955 and 1970 language takes centre stage and Lacan develops his classic thesis that 'the unconscious is structured like a language' (S11, 20). It is in this period that the names of Ferdinand de Saussure and Roman Jakobson come to the fore in Lacan's work.

Lacan takes up Saussure's theory that language is a structure composed of differential elements, but whereas Saussure had stated this of *langue*, Lacan states it of *langage*. *Langage* becomes, for Lacan, the single paradigm of all structures. Lacan then proceeds to criticise the Saussurean concept of language, arguing that the basic unit of language is not the sign but the SIGNIFIER. Lacan then argues that the UNCONSCIOUS is, like language, a structure of signifiers, which also allows Lacan to formulate the category of the symbolic with greater precision. In 1969 Lacan develops a concept of DISCOURSE as a kind of social bond.

4. From 1971 on, the shift from LINGUISTICS to mathematics as the paradigm of scientificity is accompanied by a tendency to emphasise the poetry and ambiguity of language, as is evident in Lacan's increasing interest in the 'psychotic language' of James Joyce (see Lacan, 1975a; 1975–6). Lacan's own style reflects this change as it becomes ever more densely populated with puns and neologisms. Lacan coins the term *lalangue* (from the definite article *la* and the noun *langue*) to refer to these non-communicative aspects of language which, by playing on ambiguity and homophony, give rise to a kind of *jouissance* (S20, 126). The term 'language' now becomes opposed to *lalangue*. *Lalangue* is like the primary chaotic substrate of polysemy out of which language is constructed, almost as if language is some ordered superstructure sitting on top of this substrate: 'language is without doubt made of *lalangue*. It is an elucubration of knowledge [*savoir*] about *lalangue*' (S20, 127).

It is the emphasis placed by Lacanian psychoanalysis on language that is usually regarded as its most distinctive feature. Lacan criticises the way that other forms of psychoanalysis, such as Kleinian psychoanalysis and object-relations theory, tend to play down the importance of language and emphasise the 'non-verbal communication' of the analysand (his 'body language', etc.) at the expense of the analysand's speech. This is a fundamental error, according to Lacan, for three main reasons.

Firstly, all human communication is inscribed in a linguistic structure; even 'body language' is, as the term implies, fundamentally a form of *language*, with the same structural features.

Secondly, the whole aim of psychoanalytic treatment is to articulate the truth of one's desire in speech rather than in any other medium; the fundamental rule of psychoanalysis is based on the principle that speech is the only way to this truth.

And thirdly, speech is the only tool which the analyst has; therefore, any analyst who does not understand the way speech and language work does not understand psychoanalysis itself (see E, 40).

One consequence of Lacan's emphasis on language is his recommendation that the analyst must attend to the formal features of the analysand's speech (the signifiers), and not be sidetracked into an empathic attitude based on an imaginary understanding of the content (the signified).

One common misconception of Lacan is that language is synonymous with the symbolic order. This is, however, not correct; Lacan argues that language has both a symbolic and an imaginary dimension: 'there is something in the symbolic function of human discourse that cannot be eliminated, and that is the role played in it by the imaginary' (S2, 306). The symbolic dimension of language is that of the signifier and true speech. The imaginary dimension of language is that of the signified, signification, and empty speech. SCHEMA L represents these two dimensions of language by means of two axes which intersect. The axis A–S is language in its symbolic dimension, the discourse of the Other, the unconscious. The imaginary axis a'–a is language in its imaginary dimension, the wall of language which interrupts, distorts and inverts the discourse of the Other. In Lacan's words, 'language is as much there to found us in the Other as to drastically prevent us from understanding him' (S2, 244).

Lacan distinguishes between languages and CODES; unlike codes, in language there is no stable one-to-one correspondence between sign and referent, nor between signified and signifier. It is this property of language which gives rise to the inherent ambiguity of all discourse. This ambiguity is evident in the formations of the unconscious, which can only be interpreted by playing on homophony and other forms of equivocation (*l'équivoque*) (see INTERPRETATION).

law (*loi*)   Lacan's discussions of 'the Law' (which Lacan often writes with a capital 'L') owe much to the work of Claude Lévi-Strauss (see especially Lévi-Strauss, 1951). As in the work of Lévi-Strauss, the Law in Lacan's work refers not to a particular piece of legislation, but to the fundamental principles which underlie all social relations. The law is the set of universal principles which make social existence possible, the structures that govern all forms of social exchange, whether gift-giving, kinship relations or the formation of pacts. Since the most basic form of exchange is communication itself, the law is fundamentally a linguistic entity – it is the law of the signifier:

this law, then, is revealed clearly enough as identical with an order of language. For without kinship nominations, no power is capable of instituting the order of preferences and taboos that bind and weave the yarn of lineage through succeeding generations.

(E, 66)

This legal–linguistic structure is in fact no more and no less than the symbolic order itself.

Following Lévi-Strauss, Lacan argues that the law is essentially human; it is the law which separates man from the other animals, by regulating sexual relations that are, among animals, unregulated; human law is 'the primordial Law . . . which in regulating marriage ties superimposes the kingdom of culture on that of a nature abandoned to the law of mating. The prohibition of incest is merely its subjective pivot' (E, 66).

It is the FATHER who imposes this law on the subject in the OEDIPUS COMPLEX; the paternal agency (or paternal function) is no more than the name for this prohibitive and legislative role. In the second time of the Oedipus complex the father appears as the omnipotent 'father of the primal horde' of *Totem and Taboo* (Freud, 1912–13); this is the lawgiver who is not included in his own law because he *is* the Law, denying others access to the women of the tribe while he himself has access to them all. In the third time of the Oedipus complex the father is included in his own law, the law is revealed as a pact rather than an imperative. The Oedipus complex represents the regulation of desire by the law. It is the law of the PLEASURE PRINCIPLE, which commands the subject to 'Enjoy as little as possible!', and thus maintains the subject at a safe distance from the Thing.

The relationship between the law and desire is, however, a dialectical one; 'desire is the reverse of the law' (Ec, 787). If, on the one hand, law imposes limits on desire, it is also true that the law creates desire in the first place by creating interdiction. Desire is essentially the desire to transgress, and for there to be transgression it is first necessary for there to be prohibition (S7, 83–4). Thus it is not the case that there is a pregiven desire which the law then regulates, but that desire is born out of the process of regulation; 'what we see here is the tight bond between desire and the Law' (S7, 177).

If the law is closely connected to the father, this is not only because the father is the one who imposes the law, but also because the law is born out of the murder of the father. This is clearly illustrated in the myth of the father of the primal horde which Freud recounts in *Totem and Taboo*. In this myth, the murder of the father, far from freeing the sons from the law, only reinforces the law which prohibits incest.

letter (*lettre*) Lacan's frequent references to 'the letter' must be seen within the context of Saussure's discussion of LANGUAGE. In his *Course in General Linguistics*, Saussure privileges spoken language above written language, on the grounds that the former appears before the latter both in the history of humanity and in the life of the individual. Writing is conceived of as a mere secondhand representation of spoken language, and the SIGNIFIER is conceived of as purely an acoustic image and not as a graphic one (Saussure, 1916).

When Lacan takes up Saussure's work in the 1950s, he adapts it freely to his own purposes. He thus conceives of the letter, not as a mere graphic representation of a sound, but as the material basis of language itself; 'By *letter* I designate that material support that concrete discourse borrows from language' (E, 147). The letter is thus connected with the real, a material substrate that underpins the symbolic order. The concept of materiality implies, for Lacan, both the idea of indivisibility and the idea of locality; the letter is therefore 'the essentially localised structure of the signifier' (E, 153; see S20, 30) (see MATERIALISM).

As an element of the real, the letter is meaningless in itself. Lacan illustrates this by referring (as did Freud – see Freud, 1913b: SE XIII, 177) to ancient Egyptian hieroglyphics, which were indecipherable to Europeans for so long. Until Champollion was able to decipher them on the basis of the Rosetta Stone, no one knew how to understand these enigmatic inscriptions, but it was nevertheless clear that they were organised into a signifying system (S1, 244–5; see E, 160). In the same way, the signifier persists as a meaningless letter which marks the destiny of the subject and which he must decipher. A good example of this is the case of the Wolf Man, in which Freud noted that the meaningless letter V reappeared under many guises in the Wolf Man's life (Freud, 1918b).

As the example of the Wolf Man demonstrates, the letter is essentially that which returns and repeats itself; it constantly insists in inscribing itself in the subject's life. Lacan illustrates this REPETITION by reference to Edgar Allan Poe's story *The Purloined Letter* (Poe, 1844). Playing on the double-meaning of the term 'letter', Lacan presents Poe's account of a written document (a letter) which passes through various hands as a metaphor for the signifier which circulates between various subjects, assigning a peculiar position to whoever is possessed by it (Lacan, 1955a). It is in this paper that Lacan proposes that 'a letter always arrives at its destination' (Ec, 41).

It is because of the role of the letter in the unconscious that the analyst must focus not on the meaning or the signification of the analysand's discourse, but purely on its formal properties; the analyst must read the analysand's speech as if it were a text, 'taking it literally' (*prendre à la lettre*). There is thus a close connection between the letter and writing, a connection which Lacan explores in his seminar of 1972–3 (S20, 29–38). Although both the letter and writing are located in the order of the real, and hence partake of a meaningless quality, Lacan argues that the letter is that which one reads, as opposed to writing, which is not to be read (S20, 29). Writing is also connected with the idea of formalisation and the mathemes; Lacan thus speaks of his algebraic symbols as 'letters' (S20, 30).

Lacan's concept of the letter is the subject of a critique by Jacques Derrida (1975) and by two of Derrida's followers (Lacoue-Labarthe and Nancy, 1973). Lacan refers to the latter work in his 1972–3 seminar (S20, 62–6).

libido (*libido*)   Freud conceived of the libido as a quantitative (or 'economic') concept: it is an energy which can increase or decrease, and which can be displaced (see Freud, 1921c: SE XVIII, 90). Freud insisted on the sexual nature of this energy, and throughout his work he maintained a dualism in which the libido is opposed to another (non-sexual) form of energy. Jung opposed this dualism, positing a single form of life-energy which is neutral in character, and proposed that this energy be denoted by the term 'libido'.

Lacan rejects Jung's monism and reaffirms Freud's dualism (S1, 119–20). He argues, with Freud, that the libido is exclusively sexual. Lacan also follows Freud in affirming that the libido is exclusively masculine (E, 291). In the 1950s Lacan locates the libido in the imaginary order; 'Libido and the ego are on the same side. Narcissism is libidinal' (S2, 326). From 1964 on, however, there is a shift to articulating the libido more with the real (see Ec, 848–9). However, in general Lacan does not use the term 'libido' anywhere near as frequently as Freud, preferring to reconceptualise sexual energy in terms of *JOUISSANCE*.

linguistics (*linguistique*)   While Lacan's interest in LANGUAGE can be traced back to the early 1930s, when he analysed the writings of a psychotic woman in his doctoral dissertation (Lacan, 1932), it is only in the early 1950s that he begins to articulate his views on language in terms derived from a specific linguistic theory, and not until 1957 that he begins to engage with linguistics in any detail.

Lacan's 'linguistic turn' was inspired by the anthropological work of Claude Lévi-Strauss who, in the 1940s, had begun to apply the methods of structural linguistics to non-linguistic cultural data (myth, kinship relations, etc.), thus giving birth to 'structural anthropology'. In so doing, Lévi-Strauss announced an ambitious programme, in which linguistics would provide a paradigm of scientificity for all the social SCIENCES; 'Structural linguistics will certainly play the same renovating role with respect to the social sciences that nuclear physics, for example, has played for the physical sciences' (Lévi-Strauss, 1945: 33).

Following the indications of Lévi-Strauss, Lacan turns to linguistics to provide psychoanalytic theory with a conceptual rigour that it previously lacked. The reason for this lack of conceptual rigour was simply due, Lacan argues, to the fact that structural linguistics appeared too late for Freud to make use of it; '"Geneva 1910" and "Petrograd 1920" suffice to explain why Freud lacked this particular tool' (E, 298). However, Lacan argues that when Freud is reread in the light of linguistic theory, a coherent logic is revealed which is not otherwise apparent; indeed, Freud can even be seen to have anticipated certain elements of modern linguistic theory (E, 162).

As the references cited above indicate ('Geneva 1910' and 'Petrograd 1920'), Lacan's engagement with linguistics revolves almost entirely around the work of Ferdinand de Saussure (1857–1913) and Roman Jakobson (1896–1982). References to the work of other influential linguists such as Noam Chomsky, Leonard Bloomfield and Edward Sapir are almost completely absent from Lacan's work. There is a corresponding focus on the sign, rhetorical tropes, and phoneme analysis, at the expense of an almost complete neglect of other areas of linguistics such as syntax, semantics, pragmatics, sociolinguistics and language acquisition (though see DEVELOPMENT) (see Macey, 1988: 121–2).

Saussure was the founder of 'structural linguistics'. In contrast to the study of language in the nineteenth century, which had been exclusively *diachronic* (i.e. focusing exclusively on the ways that languages change over time), Saussure argued that linguistics should also be *synchronic* (i.e. focus on the state of a language at a given point in time). This led him to develop his famous distinction between *langue* and *parole*, and his concept of the SIGN as composed of two elements: signifier and signified. All these ideas are developed in Saussure's most famous work, the *Course in General Linguistics*, which was constructed by his students from notes they had taken at Saussure's lectures at the University of Geneva and published three years after his death (Saussure, 1916). Jakobson further developed the lines laid down by Saussure, pioneering the development of phonology, as well as making important contributions to the fields of grammatical semantics, pragmatics and poetics (see Caton, 1987).

From Saussure, Lacan borrows the concepts of language as a STRUCTURE, although whereas Saussure had conceived it as a system of signs, Lacan conceives it as a system of signifiers. From Jakobson, Lacan borrows the concepts of METAPHOR and METONYMY as the two axes (synchronic and diachronic) along which all linguistic phenomena are aligned, using these terms to understand Freud's concepts of condensation and displacement. Other concepts which Lacan takes from linguistics are those of the SHIFTER, and the distinction between the statement and the ENUNCIATION.

In his borrowing of linguistic concepts, Lacan has been accused of grossly distorting them. Lacan responds to such criticisms by arguing that he is not doing linguistics but psychoanalysis, and this requires a certain modification of the concepts borrowed from linguistics. In the end, Lacan is not really interested in linguistic theory in itself, but only in the ways it can be used to develop psychoanalytic theory (see Lacan, 1970–1; seminar of 27 January 1971). It was this that led Lacan to coin the neologism *linguistérie* (from the words *linguistique* and *hystérie*) to refer to his psychoanalytic use of linguistic concepts (S20, 20).

love (*amour*) Lacan argues that it is impossible to say anything meaningful or sensible about love (S8, 57). Indeed, the moment one starts to speak about love, one descends into imbecility (S20, 17). Given these views, it might seem surprising that Lacan himself dedicates a great deal of his seminar precisely to speaking about love. However, in doing so, Lacan is merely demonstrating what the analysand does in psychoanalytic treatment, for 'the only thing that we do in the analytic discourse is speak about love' (S20, 77).

Love arises in analytic treatment as an effect of TRANSFERENCE, and the problem of how an artificial situation can produce such an effect is one that fascinates Lacan throughout his work. This relationship between love and transference is proof, Lacan argues, of the essential role of artifice in all love. Lacan also lays great emphasis on the intimate connection between love and AGGRESSIVITY; the presence of one necessarily implies the presence of the other. This phenomenon, which Freud labels 'ambivalence', is seen by Lacan as one of the great discoveries of psychoanalysis.

Love is located by Lacan as a purely imaginary phenomenon, although it has effects in the symbolic order (one of those effects being to produce 'a veritable subduction of the symbolic' – S1, 142). Love is autoerotic, and has a fundamentally narcissistic structure (S11, 186) since 'it's one's own ego that one loves in love, one's own ego made real on the imaginary level' (S1, 142; see NARCISSISM). The imaginary nature of love leads Lacan to oppose all those analysts (such as Balint) who posit love as an ideal in psychoanalytic treatment (S7, 8; see GENITAL).

Love involves an imaginary reciprocity, since 'to love is, essentially, to wish to be loved' (S11, 253). It is this reciprocity between 'loving' and 'being loved' that constitutes the illusion of love, and this is what distinguishes it from the order of the drives, in which there is no reciprocity, only pure activity (S11, 200).

Love is is an illusory fantasy of fusion with the beloved which makes up for the absence of any SEXUAL RELATIONSHIP (S20, 44); this is especially clear in the asexual concept of courtly love (S20, 65).

Love is deceptive; 'As a specular mirage, love is essentially deception' (S11, 268). It is deceptive because it involves giving what one does not have (i.e. the phallus); to love is 'to give what one does not have' (S8, 147). Love is directed not at what the love-object has, but at what he lacks, at the nothing beyond him. The object is valued insofar as it comes in the place of that lack (see the schema of the veil in S4, 156).

One of the most complex areas of Lacan's work concerns the relationship between love and DESIRE. On the one hand, the two terms are diametrically opposed. On the other hand, this opposition is problematised by certain similarities between the two:

1. As an imaginary phenomenon which belongs to the field of the ego, love is clearly opposed to desire, which is inscribed in the symbolic order, the field of the Other (S11, 189–91). Love is a metaphor (S8, 53), whereas desire is

metonymy. It can even be said that love kills desire, since love is based on a fantasy of oneness with the beloved (S20, 46) and this abolishes the difference which gives rise to desire.

2. On the other hand, there are elements in Lacan's work which destabilise the neat opposition between love and desire. Firstly, they are both similar in that neither can ever be satisfied. Secondly, the structure of love as 'the wish to be loved' is identical to the structure of desire, in which the subject desires to become the object of the Other's desire (indeed, in Kojève's reading of Hegel, on which this account of desire is based, there is a degree of semantic ambiguity between 'love' and 'desire'; see Kojève, 1947: 6). Thirdly, in the dialectic of need/demand/desire, desire is born precisely from the unsatisfied part of DEMAND, which is the demand for love. Lacan's own discourse on love is thus often complicated by the same substitution of 'desire' for 'love' which he himself highlights in the text of Plato's *Symposium* (S8, 141).

lure (*leurre*) As Alan Sheridan points out in the short glossary he provides to his translation of *Écrits*, 'the French word translates variously "lure" (for hawks, fish), "decoy" (for birds), "bait" (for fish), and the notion of "allurement" and "enticement"' (Sheridan, 1977: xi).

Lures are part of the imaginary order. Thus the seductive manœuvres of the child in the preoedipal triangle (when the child tries to be the phallus for the mother) are described as lures (S4, 201). With respect to psychoanalytic treatment, the RESISTANCES encountered in analytic treatment are lures which the analyst must use all his cunning to avoid being ensnared by (see E, 168).

Human beings are not the only animals who are capable of setting lures, and this fact is sometimes used to argue in favour of the existence of 'animal consciousness'. However, Lacan argues that it is important to distinguish between animal lures and human lures:

● **Animal lures** Animals can deceive by their camouflage or by 'the feint by which an apparent straggler leads a predator away from the flock', but 'there is nothing even there that transcends the function of lure in the service of need' (E, 172). Animal lures are extremely important in mating ceremonies where an animal must entice another into copulation, and this is also what lends human sexuality its strong imaginary element; 'sexual behaviour is quite especially prone to the lure' (S1, 123).

● **Human lures** Whereas animal lures are straightforward, the human being is unique in being capable of a special kind of lure which involves a 'double deception'. This is a kind of lure which involves deceiving by pretending to deceive (i.e. telling a truth that one expects to be taken for a lie) (see E, 305). The classic example of the properly human lure is the joke quoted by Freud (and often cited by Lacan) about the two Polish Jews: 'Why do you tell me you are going to Cracow so I'll believe you are going to Lvov, when you are really going to Cracow?' (E, 173). Other animals are incapable of this special kind of lure owing to the fact that they do not possess language.

M

madness (*folie*)   When Lacan uses the term 'madness', or refers to someone as being 'mad', he is referring to PSYCHOSIS: 'The psychoses . . . correspond to what has always been called and legitimately continues to be called *madness*' (S3, 4). Lacan adds that 'there is no reason to deny oneself the luxury of this word' (S3, 4). Thus far from seeing it as a derogatory term, Lacan values it for its poetic resonances, and approves of its use, on condition that it is used in the precise sense of psychosis. So, for example, in 1946 Lacan congratulates the French psychiatrist Henri Ey for 'obstinately preserving the term' (Ec, 154).

master (*maître*)   In his work during the 1950s Lacan often refers to 'the dialectic of the master and the slave', which Hegel introduces in *Phenomenology of Spirit* (1807). As in all his other Hegelian references, Lacan is indebted to Alexandre Kojève's reading of Hegel, which Lacan encountered when attending Kojève's lectures on Hegel in the 1930s (see Kojève, 1947).

According to Kojève, the DIALECTIC of the master and the slave is the inevitable result of the fact that human DESIRE is the desire for recognition. In order to achieve recognition, the subject must impose the idea that he has of himself on an other. However, since this other also desires recognition, he also must do the same, and hence the subject is forced to engage in combat with the other. This fight for recognition, for 'pure prestige' (Kojève, 1947: 7; see S1, 223) must be a 'fight to the death', since it is only by risking his life for the sake of recognition that one can prove that he is truly human. However, the combat must in fact stop short of the death of either combatant, since recognition can only be granted by a living being. Thus the struggle ends when one of the two gives up his desire for recognition and surrenders to the other; the vanquished one recognises the victor as his 'master' and becomes his 'slave'. In fact, human society is only possible because some human beings accept being slaves instead of fighting to the death; a community of masters would be impossible.

After achieving victory, the master sets the slave to work for him. The slave works by transforming nature in order that the master may consume it and enjoy it. However, the victory is not as absolute as it seems; the relation between the master and the slave is dialectical because it leads to the negation of their respective positions. On the one hand, the recognition achieved by the master is unsatisfactory because it is not another man who grants him this recognition but only a slave, who is for the master a mere animal or thing; thus 'the man who behaves as a Master will never be satisfied' (Kojève, 1947: 20). On the other hand, the slave is partly compensated for his defeat by the fact that, by working, he raises himself above nature by making it other than it was. In the process of changing the world the slave changes himself and becomes the author of his own destiny, unlike the master who changes only through the mediation of the slave's work. Historical progress is now 'the product of the working slave and not of the warlike Master' (Kojève, 1947: 52). The outcome of the dialectic is therefore paradoxical: the master ends up in a dissatisfying 'existential impasse', while the slave retains the possibility of achieving true satisfaction by means of 'dialectically overcoming' his slavery.

Lacan draws on the dialectic of the master and the slave to illustrate a wide range of points. For example the struggle for pure prestige illustrates the intersubjective nature of desire, in which the important thing is for desire to be recognised by an other. The fight to the death also illustrates the AGGRESSIVITY inherent in the dual relationship between the ego and the counterpart (E, 142). Furthermore, the slave who resignedly 'waits for the master's death' (E, 99) offers a good analogy of the obsessional neurotic, who is characterised by hesitation and procrastination (see S1, 286).

Lacan also takes up the dialectic of the master and the slave in his theorisation of the DISCOURSE of the master. In the formulation of this discourse, the master is the master signifier (S_1) who puts the slave (S_2) to work to produce a surplus (*a*) which he can appropriate for himself. The master signifier is that which represents a subject for all other signifiers; the discourse of the master is thus an attempt at totalisation (which is why Lacan links the discourse of the master with philosophy and ontology, playing on the homophony between *maître* and *m'être*; S20, 33). However, this attempt always fails because the master signifier can never represent the subject completely; there is always some surplus which escapes representation.

materialism (*matérialisme*) By addressing the issues of psychogenesis, the mind/body problem, etc., psychoanalysis necessarily raises ontological questions. The question of whether Freud's views can be considered materialistic or not is difficult to answer. On the one hand, he insisted on the importance of the physical substratum of all mental events, in keeping with the materialist axioms of the scientists whom he had most respected during his studies (principally Hermann Helmholtz and Ernst Brücke). On the other hand, he opposed Charcot's attempts to explain all hysterical symptoms by reference to lesions in the brain, distinguished psychical reality from material reality, and constantly emphasised the role of experience rather than heredity in the aetiology of nervous illness. These two trends often converge in his writings in an uneasy alliance, as in the following sentence: 'Analysts are at bottom incorrigible mechanists and materialists, even though they seek to avoid robbing the mind and spirit of their still unrecognized characteristics' (Freud, 1941d [1921]: SE XVIII, 179).

Lacan too presents himself as a materialist; in 1936 he criticises associationist psychology for not living up to its purported materialism, and in 1964 he argues that psychoanalysis is opposed to any form of philosophical idealism (S11, 221).

However, as with Freud, Lacan's declarations of materialism are highly complex. Thus it is clear even in Lacan's earliest statements on the subject that he conceives of materialism in a very particular way. In 1936, for example, he argues that materialism does not imply a rejection of the categories of intentionality and meaning (Ec, 76–8), and rejects the simplistic idea of 'matter' as 'a naive form which has been left behind by authentic materialism' (Ec, 90). In 1946 he repeatedly criticises the crude form of materialism which regards thought as a mere 'epiphenomenon' (Ec, 159). And in 1956 he distinguishes between a 'naturalist materialism' and a 'Freudian materialism' (Ec, 465–6). It is clear, then, that Lacan does not subscribe to that kind of materialism which reduces all causation to a crude economic determinism, and which regards all cultural phenomena (including LANGUAGE) as a mere superstructure determined by the economic infrastructure. In opposition to this, Lacan cites Stalin's famous pronouncement that 'language is not a superstructure' (E, 125), and argues that language 'is something material' (S2, 82). On these grounds he declares that the importance he attributes to language is perfectly compatible with historical materialism (Ec, 875–6).

Lacan's materialism is thus a materialism of the SIGNIFIER: 'the point of view I am trying to maintain before you involves a certain materialism of the elements in question, in the sense that the signifiers are well and truly embodied, materialized' (S3, 289). However, the materiality of the signifier does not refer to a tangible inscription but to its indivisibility; 'But if we have insisted firstly on the materiality of the signifier, this materiality is singular in many ways, the first of which is that the signifier does not withstand partition' (Ec, 24). The signifier in its material dimension, the real aspect of the signifier, is the LETTER. It is Lacan's 'materialism of the signifier' which leads him to give 'a materialist definition of the phenomenon of consciousness' (S2, 40–52).

Lacan's claims that his theory of the signifier is a materialist theory are disputed by Derrida, who argues that Lacan's concept of the letter betrays an implicit idealism (Derrida, 1975).

mathematics (*mathématiques*)   In his attempt to theorise the category of the SYMBOLIC, Lacan adopts two basic approaches. The first approach is to describe it in terms borrowed from LINGUISTICS, using a Saussurean-inspired model of language as a system of signifiers. The second approach is to describe it in terms borrowed from mathematics. The two approaches are complementary, since both are attempts to describe formal systems with precise rules, and both demonstrate the power of the signifier. Although there is a general shift in

Lacan's work from the linguistic approach which predominates in the 1950s to a mathematical approach which predominates in the 1970s, there are traces of the mathematical approach as early as the 1940s (such as Lacan's analysis of a logical puzzle in Lacan, 1945; see his 1956 claim that 'the laws of inter-subjectivity are mathematical' in Ec, 472). The branches of mathematics which Lacan uses most are ALGEBRA and TOPOLOGY, although there are also incursions into set theory and number theory (e.g. E, 316–18).

Lacan's use of mathematics represents an attempt to formalise psychoanalytic theory, in keeping with his view that psychoanalytic theory should aspire to the formalisation proper to science; 'mathematical formalisation is our goal, our ideal' (S20, 108). Mathematics serves Lacan as a paradigm of modern scientific discourse, which 'emerged from the little letters of mathematics' (S7, 236).

However, this use of mathematics is not an attempt to produce a META-LANGUAGE, since 'no metalanguage can be spoken' (E, 311). 'The root of the difficulty is that you can only introduce symbols, mathematical or otherwise, by using everyday language, since you have, after all, to explain what you are going to do with them' (S1, 2). Thus Lacan's use of mathematics is not an attempt to escape from the ambiguity of language, but, on the contrary, to produce a way of formalising psychoanalysis which produces multiple effects of sense without being reducible to a univocal signification. Also, by using mathematics Lacan attempts to prevent all attempts at imaginary intuitive understanding of psychoanalysis.

matheme (*mathème*)   The term *mathème* is a neologism which Lacan derives from the word 'mathematics', presumably by analogy with the term *mytheme* (a term coined by Claude Lévi-Strauss to denote the basic constituents of mythological systems; see Lévi-Strauss, 1955). The mathemes are part of Lacanian ALGEBRA.

Although the term matheme is not introduced by Lacan until the early 1970s, the two formulae which are most often referred to as mathemes date from 1957. These formulae, which were both created to designate points in the GRAPH OF DESIRE, are the matheme for the drive, $(\$ \Diamond D)$, and the matheme for fantasy, $(\$ \Diamond a)$. The structural parallel between the two mathemes is clear; they are both composed of two algebraic symbols conjoined by a rhomboid (the symbol $\Diamond$, which Lacan calls the *poinçon*) and enclosed by brackets. The rhomboid symbolises a relation between the two symbols, which includes the relations of 'envelopment–development–conjunction–disjunction' (E, 280, n. 26).

Lacan argues that the mathemes 'are not transcendent signifiers; they are the indices of an absolute signification' (E, 314). They are 'created to allow a hundred and one different readings, a multiplicity that is admissible as long as the spoken remains caught in their algebra' (E, 313). They are constructed to resist any attempt to reduce them to one univocal signification, and to prevent the reader from an intuitive or imaginary understanding of psychoanalytic concepts; the mathemes are not to be understood but to be used. In this way, they constitute a formal core of psychoanalytic theory which may be transmitted integrally; 'one certainly doesn't know what they mean, but they are transmitted' (S20, 100).

méconnaissance   The French term *méconnaissance* corresponds roughly to the English words 'misunderstanding' and 'misrecognition'. However, the French term is usually left untranslated when translating Lacan into English in order to show its close relationship with the term *connaissance* (KNOWLEDGE). Thus, in the imaginary order, self-knowledge (*me-connaissance*) is synonymous with misunderstanding (*méconnaissance*), because the process by which the EGO is formed in the mirror stage is at the same time the institution of alienation from the symbolic determination of being.

As well as being the structure of ordinary neurotic self-knowledge, *méconnaissance* is also the structure of paranoiac DELUSIONS, which are described in terms of a *méconnaissance systématique de la réalité* (Lacan, 1951b: 12). This structural homology between the ordinary constitution of the ego and paranoiac delusions is what leads Lacan to describe all knowledge (*connaissance*), in both neurosis and psychosis, as 'paranoiac knowledge'.

Méconnaissance is to be distinguished from ignorance, which is one of the three passions (see AFFECT). Whereas ignorance is a passion for the absence of knowledge, *méconnaissance* is an imaginary misrecognition of a symbolic knowledge (*savoir*) that the subject does possess somewhere.

> Misrecognition is not ignorance. Misrecognition represents a certain organisation of affirmations and negations, to which the subject is attached. Hence it cannot be conceived without correlate knowledge. . . . There must surely be, behind his misrecognition, a kind of knowledge of what there is to misrecognise.
>
> (S1, 167)

Again, this applies both in the ordinary construction of the ego and in paranoia. In the former case, the ego is basically a misrecognition of the symbolic determinants of subjectivity (the discourse of the Other, the unconscious). In the latter case, paranoiac delusions always imply an obscure realisation of the truth; 'To misunderstand [*méconnaître*] implies a recognition [*reconnaissance*], as is evident in systematic misunderstanding [*méconnaissance systématique*], where it must clearly be admitted that that which is denied is in some way recognised [*reconnu*]' (Ec, 165).

memory (*mémoire*)   The term 'memory' is used in two very different ways in Lacan's work.

1. In the 1950s, memory is understood as a phenomenon of the symbolic

order, related to the SIGNIFYING CHAIN. It is related to the concepts of remember-ing and RECOLLECTION, and opposed to imaginary reminiscence.

Lacan makes it clear that his concept of memory is not a biological or psychological one; 'the memory which interests psychoanalysis is quite distinct from what psychologists speak of when they display its mechanism to us in an animate being in an experiment' (S3, 152). For psychoanalysis, memory is the symbolic history of the subject, a chain of signifiers linked up together, a 'signifying articulation' (S7, 223). Something is memorable and memorised only when it is 'registered in the signifying chain' (S7, 212). In this sense, the unconscious is a sort of memory (S3, 155), since 'what we teach the subject to recognise as his unconscious is his history' (E, 52).

The phenomena associated with memory which most interest the analyst are those moments when something goes wrong with memory, when the subject cannot recall a part of his history. It is the fact that he can forget, that a signifier can be elided from the signifying chain, that makes the psychoanalytic subject distinctive (S7, 224).

2. In the 1960s Lacan reserves the term 'memory' for the biological or physiological concept of memory as an organic property (Ec, 42). It thus no longer designates the symbolic history of the subject which is the concern of psychoanalysis, but something which lies outside psychoanalysis alto-gether.

metalanguage (*métalangage*)   Metalanguage is the technical term in linguistics for any form of language which is used to describe the properties of language. Roman Jakobson includes the metalingual function in his list of the functions of language (Jakobson, 1960: 25).

Lacan's first reference to metalanguage comes in 1956, when he echoes Jakobson's view on the metalingual function of all language: 'all language implies a metalanguage, it's already a metalanguage of its own register' (S3, 226).

A few years later, in 1960, he says precisely the opposite, arguing that 'no metalanguage can be spoken' (E, 311). What Lacan appears to mean by this remark is that, since every attempt to fix the meaning of language must be done in language, there can be no escape from language, no 'outside'. This is reminiscent of Heidegger's views on the impossibility of exiting 'the house of language'. This also appears similar to the structuralist theme of *il n'y a rien hors du texte* ('there is nothing outside the text'), but it is not the same; Lacan does not deny that there is a beyond of language (this beyond is the real), but he does argue that this beyond is not of a kind that could finally anchor meaning. There is, in other words, no transcendental signified, no way that language could 'tell the truth about truth' (Ec, 867–8). The same point is also expressed in the phrase; 'there is no Other of the Other' (E, 311); if the Other is the guarantee of the coherence of the subject's discourse, then the falsity of this guarantee is revealed by the fact that the guarantor himself lacks such a guarantee. In a clinical context, this means that there is no metalanguage of the transference, no point outside the transference from which it could be finally interpreted and 'liquidated'.

metaphor (*métaphore*)   Metaphor is usually defined as a trope in which one thing is described by comparing it to another, but without directly asserting a comparison. A classic example is the phrase 'Juliet is the sun', in which Shakespeare describes Juliet's radiant beauty by comparing her to the sun, yet does not indicate this comparison by the use of the word 'like'.

However, Lacan's use of the term owes little to this definition and much to the work of Roman Jakobson, who, in a major article published in 1956, established an opposition between metaphor and METONYMY. On the basis of a distinction between two kinds of aphasia, Jakobson distinguished two fundamentally opposed axes of language: the metaphorical axis which deals with the selection of linguistic items and allows for their substitution, and the metonymic axis which deals with the combination of linguistic items (both sequentially and simultaneously). Metaphor thus corresponds to Saussure's paradigmatic relations (which hold *in absentia*) and metonymy to syntagmatic relationships (which hold *in praesentia*) (Jakobson, 1956).

Lacan, like many other French intellectuals of the time (such as Claude Lévi-Strauss and Roland Barthes), was quick to take up Jakobson's reinterpretation of metaphor and metonymy. In the very same year that Jakobson's seminal article was published, Lacan refers to it in his seminar and begins to incorporate the opposition into his linguistic rereading of Freud (see S3, 218–20, 222–30). A year later he dedicates a whole paper to a more detailed analysis of the opposition (Lacan, 1957b).

Following Jakobson's identification of metaphor with the substitutive axis of language, Lacan defines metaphor as the substitution of one signifier for another (E, 164), and provides the first formula of metaphor (E, 164; Figure 8).

This formula is to be read as follows. On the lefthand side of the equation, outside the brackets, Lacan writes f S, the signifying function, which is to say the effect of SIGNIFICATION. Inside the brackets, he writes S'/S, which means 'the substitution of one signifier for another'. On the righthand side of the equation there is S, the signifier, and s, the signified. Between these two symbols there is the symbol (+) which represents the crossing of the BAR (−) of the Saussurean algorithm, and which represents 'the emergence of signification'. The sign ≅ is

$$f\left(\frac{S'}{S}\right) \; S \cong S\,(+)\,s$$

Figure 8 First formula of metaphor
Source: Jacques Lacan, *Ecrits*, Paris: Seuil, 1966.

$$\frac{S}{\cancel{S'}} \cdot \frac{\cancel{S'}}{x} \rightarrow S\left(\frac{1}{s}\right)$$

Figure 9   Second formula of metaphor
Source: Jacques Lacan, *Écrits*, Paris: Seuil, 1966.

to be read: 'is congruent with'. Thus the whole formula reads: the signifying function of the substitution of one signifier for another is congruent with the crossing of the bar.

The idea behind this rather obscure formulation is that there is an inherent resistance to signification in language (a resistance which is symbolised by the bar in the Saussurean algorithm). Meaning does not simply appear spontaneously, but is the product of a specific operation which crosses over the bar. The formula is meant to illustrate Lacan's thesis that this operation, the production of meaning, which Lacan calls 'signification', is only made possible by metaphor. Metaphor is thus the passage of the signifier into the signified, the creation of a new signified.

Lacan presents another formula for metaphor in a paper written a few months later (E, 200; Figure 9).

Lacan's own explanation of this second formula is as follows:

> the capital Ss are signifiers, x the unknown signification and s the signified induced by the metaphor, which consists in substitution in the signifying chain of S for S'. The elision of S', represented here by the bar through it, is the condition of the success of the metaphor.

(E, 200)

Lacan puts his concept of metaphor to use in a variety of contexts.

● **The Oedipus complex**   Lacan analyses the Oedipus complex in terms of a metaphor because it involves the crucial concept of substitution; in this case, the substitution of the Name-of-the-Father for the desire of the mother. This fundamental metaphor, which founds the possibility of all other metaphors, is designated by Lacan as the PATERNAL METAPHOR.

● REPRESSION **and neurotic symptoms**   Lacan argues that repression (secondary repression) has the structure of a metaphor. The 'metonymic object' (the signifier which is elided, S' in the previous formula) is repressed, but returns in the surplus meaning (+) produced in the metaphor. The return of the repressed (the symptom) therefore also has the structure of a metaphor; indeed, Lacan asserts that 'the symptom *is* a metaphor' (E, 175, emphasis in original).

● **Condensation**   Lacan also follows Jakobson in linking the metaphor–metonymy distinction to the fundamental mechanisms of the dream work described by Freud. However, he differs from Jakobson over the precise nature of this parallel. Whereas for Jakobson, metonymy is linked to both displacement and condensation, and metaphor to identification and symbolism, Lacan links metaphor to condensation and metonymy to displacement (see Jakobson, 1956: 258). Lacan then argues that just as displacement is logically prior to condensation, so metonymy is the condition for metaphor.

● **The anal drive** In his paper, 'On transformations of instinct as exemplified in anal eroticism', Freud shows how anal eroticism is closely connected with the possibility of substitution – for example the substitution of faeces for money (Freud, 1917c). Lacan takes this as grounds for linking anal eroticism to metaphor; 'The anal level is the locus of metaphor – one object for another, give the faeces in place of the phallus' (S11, 104).

● IDENTIFICATION Metaphor is also the structure of identification, since the latter consists in substituting oneself for another (see S3, 218).

● LOVE Love is structured like a metaphor since it involves the operation of substitution. 'It is insofar as the function of the *érastès*, of the lover, who is the subject of lack, comes in the place of, substitutes himself for, the function of the *érôménos*, the loved object, that the signification of love is produced' (S8, 53).

metonymy (*métonymie*)
Metonymy is usually defined as a trope in which a term is used to denote an object which it does not literally refer to, but with which it is closely linked. This link may be one of physical contiguity (such as when 'thirty sails' means 'thirty boats'), but not necessarily (such as when 'I haven't read Shakespeare' means 'I haven't read anything written by Shakespeare').

However, Lacan's use of the term owes little to this definition apart from the notion of contiguity, since it is inspired by the work of Roman Jakobson, who established an opposition between metonymy and METAPHOR (Jakobson, 1956). Following Jakobson, Lacan links metonymy to the combinatorial axis of language, as opposed to the substitutive axis. For example, in the sentence 'I am happy', the relation between the words 'I' and 'am' is a metonymic relation, whereas the possibility of substituting 'sad' for 'happy' depends on the metaphoric relation between these two terms.

In his most detailed work on the subject (Lacan, 1957b), Lacan defines metonymy as the diachronic relation between one signifier and another in the SIGNIFYING CHAIN. Metonymy thus concerns the ways in which signifiers can be combined/linked in a single signifying chain ('horizontal' relations), whereas metaphor concerns the ways in which a signifier in one signifying chain may be substituted for a signifier in another chain ('vertical' relations). Together, metaphor and metonymy constitute the way in which signification is produced.

Lacan provides a formula for metonymy (E, 164; Figure 10).

$$f \; (S \ldots S') \quad S \; \cong \; S \; (-) \; s$$

Figure 10 Formula of metonymy
Source: Jacques Lacan, *Écrits*, Paris: Seuil, 1966.

This formula is to be read as follows. On the lefthand side of the equation, outside the brackets, Lacan writes f S, the signifying function, which is to say the effect of signification. Inside the brackets he writes S . . . S', the link between one signifier and another in a signifying chain. On the righthand side of the equation there is S, the signifier, s, the signified, and $(-)$, the BAR of the Saussurean algorithm. The sign $\cong$ is to be read 'is congruent with'. Thus the whole formula reads: 'the signifying function of the connection of the signifier with the signifier is congruent with maintenance of the bar'. The formula is meant to illustrate Lacan's thesis that in metonymy the resistance of signification is maintained, the bar is not crossed, no new signified is produced.

Lacan puts his concept of metonymy to use in a variety of contexts.

● DESIRE Lacan presents metonymy as a diachronic movement from one signifier to another along the signifying chain, as one signifier constantly refers to another in a perpetual deferral of meaning. Desire is also characterised by exactly the same never-ending process of continual deferral; since desire is always 'desire for something else' (E, 167), as soon as the object of desire is attained, it is no longer desirable, and the subject's desire fixes on another object. Thus Lacan writes that 'desire *is* a metonymy' (E, 175, emphasis in original).

● **Displacement** Lacan also follows Jakobson in linking the metaphor–metonymy distinction to the mechanisms of the dream work described by Freud. However, he differs from Jakobson over the precise nature of this link (see METAPHOR). Just as displacement is logically prior to condensation, so metonymy is the condition for metaphor, because 'the coordination of signifiers has to be possible before transferences of the signified are able to take place' (S3, 229).

mirror stage (*stade du miroir*) The mirror stage (also translated in English as 'the looking-glass phase') was the subject of Lacan's first official contribution to psychoanalytic theory, when he propounded the concept to the Fourteenth International Psychoanalytical Congress at Marienbad in 1936 (the original 1936 paper was never published, but a rewritten version appeared in 1949). From this point on, the mirror stage forms a constant point of reference throughout Lacan's entire work. While apparently quite simple, the concept of the mirror stage takes on an ever-increasing complexity during the course of Lacan's work, as he takes it up and reworks it in various different contexts.

The 'mirror test' was first described by the French psychologist and friend of Lacan, Henri Wallon, in 1931, although Lacan attributes its discovery to Baldwin (E, 1). It refers to a particular experiment which can differentiate the human infant from his closest animal relative, the chimpanzee. The six-month-old child differs from the chimpanzee of the same age in that the former becomes fascinated with its reflection in the mirror and jubilantly assumes it as its own image, whereas the chimpanzee quickly realises that the image is illusory and loses interest in it.

Lacan's concept of the mirror *stage* (as opposed to Wallon's 'mirror *test*') is far more than a mere experiment: the mirror stage represents a fundamental aspect of the structure of subjectivity. Whereas in 1936–49, Lacan seems to see it is a stage which can be located at a specific time in the development of the child with a beginning (six months) and an end (eighteen months) (see E, 5), by the end of this period there are already signs that he is broadening the concept. By the early 1950s Lacan no longer regards it simply as a moment in the life of the infant, but sees it as also representing a permanent structure of subjectivity, the paradigm of the IMAGINARY order; it is a stadium (*stade*) in which the subject is permanently caught and captivated by his own image;

> [the mirror stage is] a phenomenon to which I assign a twofold value. In the first place, it has historical value as it marks a decisive turning-point in the mental development of the child. In the second place, it typifies an essential libidinal relationship with the body-image.
>
> (Lacan, 1951b: 14)

As Lacan further develops the concept of the mirror stage, the stress falls less on its 'historical value' and ever more on its structural value. Thus by 1956 Lacan can say: 'The mirror stage is far from a mere phenomenon which occurs in the development of the child. It illustrates the conflictual nature of the dual relationship' (S4, 17).

The mirror stage describes the formation of the EGO via the process of identification; the ego is the result of identifying with one's own SPECULAR IMAGE. The key to this phenomenon lies in the prematurity of the human baby: at six months, the baby still lacks coordination. However, its visual system is relatively advanced, which means that it can recognise itself in the mirror before attaining control over its bodily movements. The baby sees its own image as whole (see GESTALT), and the synthesis of this image produces a sense of contrast with the uncoordination of the body, which is experienced as a FRAGMENTED BODY; this contrast is first felt by the infant as a rivalry with its own image, because the wholeness of the image threatens the subject with fragmentation, and the mirror stage thereby gives rise to an aggressive tension between the subject and the image (see AGGRESSIVITY). In order to resolve this aggressive tension, the subject identifies with the image; this primary identification with the counterpart is what forms the ego. The moment of identification, when the subject assumes its image as its own, is described by Lacan as a moment of jubilation (E, 1), since it leads to an imaginary sense of mastery; '[the child's] joy is due to his imaginary triumph in anticipating a degree of muscular co-ordination which he has not yet actually achieved' (Lacan, 1951b: 15; see S1, 79). However, this jubilation may also be accompanied by a depressive reaction, when the child compares his own precarious sense of mastery with the omnipotence of the mother (Ec, 345; S4, 186). This identification also involves the ideal ego which functions as a promise of future wholeness which sustains the ego in anticipation.

The mirror stage shows that the ego is the product of misunderstanding (*méconnaissance*) and the site where the subject becomes alienated from himself. It represents the introduction of the subject into the imaginary order. However, the mirror stage also has an important symbolic dimension. The symbolic order is present in the figure of the adult who is carrying or supporting the infant. The moment after the subject has jubilantly assumed his image as his own, he turns his head round towards this adult, who represents the big Other, as if to call on him to ratify this image (Lacan, 1962–3: seminar of 28 November 1962).

The mirror stage is also closely related to narcissism, as the story of Narcissus clearly shows (in the Greek myth, Narcissus falls in love with his own reflection).

moebius strip (*bande de moebius*)   The moebius strip is one of the figures studied by Lacan in his use of TOPOLOGY. It is a three-dimensional figure that can be formed by taking a long rectangle of paper and twisting it once before joining its ends together (see Figure 11). The result is a figure which subverts our normal (Euclidean) way of representing space, for it seems to have two sides but in fact has only one (and only one edge). Locally, at any one point, two sides can be clearly distinguished, but when the whole strip is traversed it becomes clear that they are in fact continuous. The two sides are only distinguished by the dimension of time, the time it takes to traverse the whole strip.

The figure illustrates the way that psychoanalysis problematises various binary oppositions, such as inside/outside, love/hate, signifier/signified, truth/appearance. While the two terms in such oppositions are often presented as radically distinct, Lacan prefers to understand these oppositions in terms of the topology of the moebius strip. The opposed terms are thus seen to be not discrete but continuous with each other. Likewise, the discourse of the master is continuous with the discourse of the analyst.

The moebius strip also helps one to understand how it is possible to 'traverse the fantasy' (S11, 273). It is only because the two sides are continuous that it is possible to cross over from inside to outside. Yet, when one passes a finger round the surface of the moebius strip, it is impossible to say at which precise point one has crossed over from inside to outside (or vice versa).

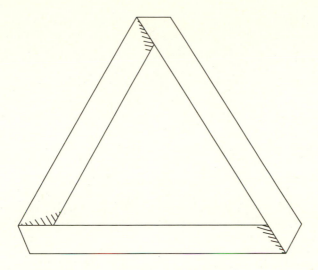

Figure 11   The moebius strip

mother (*mère*)   In Freud's account of the OEDIPUS COMPLEX, the mother is the first love object of the child; it is only the intervention of the FATHER, via the threat of castration, which forces the child to give up his desire for the mother. In the work of Melanie Klein, the emphasis shifted from the role of the father to the pregenital mother–child relation; the latter was described as a sadistic relation in which the child makes (in fantasy) vicious attacks on the mother's body and then fears retaliation from her.

In his pre-war writings, Lacan alludes several times to Melanie Klein's work, and describes the cannibalistic fantasies of devouring, and being devoured by, the mother. Lacan argues that the first of the family complexes is the weaning complex, in which the interruption of the symbiotic relation with the mother leaves a permanent trace in the child's psyche. He also describes the death drive as a nostalgic yearning to return to this relation of fusion with the mother's breast (Lacan, 1938: 35).

This view of the mother as an engulfing force which threatens to devour the child is a constant theme in Lacan's work thereafer (see S4, 195; S17, 118). Lacan argues that the child must detach himself from the imaginary relation with the mother in order to enter the social world; failure to do so can result in any one of various peculiarities ranging from phobia to perversion. Since the agent who helps the child to overcome the primary attachment to the mother is the father, these peculiarities may also be said to result from a failure of the paternal function. Hence much of Lacan's work is aimed at shifting the emphasis in analytic theory from the mother–child relation (the preoedipal,

117

the prototype of the imaginary) back onto the role of the father (the Oedipus complex, the prototype of the symbolic).

● **The desire of the mother**   According to Freud, a woman's desire to have a child is rooted in her envy of the man's penis. When the girl first realises that she does not possess a penis, she feels deprived of something valuable, and seeks to compensate for this by obtaining a child as a symbolic substitute for the penis she has been denied (Freud, 1924d). Lacan follows Freud, arguing that the child always represents for the mother a substitute for the symbolic phallus which she lacks (see PRIVATION). However, Lacan emphasises that this substitute never really satisfies the mother; her desire for the phallus persists even after she has had a child. The child soon realises that he does not completely satisfy the mother's desire, that her desire aims at something beyond him, and thus attempts to decipher this enigmatic desire; he must work out an answer to the question *Che vuoi?* ('What do you want from me?'). The answer the child comes up with is that what the mother desires is the imaginary phallus. The child then seeks to satisfy the mother's desire by identifying with the imaginary phallus (or by identifying with the phallic mother, the mother imagined as possessing the phallus). In this game of 'to be or not to be the phallus', the child is completely at the mercy of the capricious desire of the mother, helpless in the face of her omnipotence (S4, 69, 187). However, this sense of powerlessness may not give rise to much anxiety at first; for a time, the child experiences his attempts at being the phallus as a relatively satisfying game of seduction. It is only when the child's sexual drives begin to stir (e.g. in infantile masturbation), and an element of the real is thus introduced into the imaginary game, that the omnipotence of the mother begins to provoke greater anxiety in the child. This anxiety is manifested in images of being devoured by the mother, and is only resolved by the intervention of the real father who castrates the child in the third time of the Oedipus complex.

● **The mother: real, symbolic and imaginary**   Lacan argues that it is important to distinguish between the real mother, the symbolic mother and the imaginary mother.

The mother manifests herself in the real as the primary caretaker of the infant. The infant is incapable of satisfying its own needs and so depends absolutely on an Other to care for him (see HELPLESSNESS). The mother is first of all symbolic; she only becomes real by frustrating the subject's demand (see FRUSTRATION).

When the mother ministers to the infant, bringing him the objects that will satisfy his needs, these objects soon take on a symbolic function that completely eclipses their real function; the objects are seen as gifts, symbolic tokens of the mother's love. Finally, it is the mother's presence which testifies to this love, even if she does not bring any real object with her. Consequently, the mother's absence is experienced as a traumatic rejection, as loss of her

118

love. Freud showed how the child attempts to cope with this loss by symbolising the mother's presence and absence in games and language (Freud, 1920g). Lacan regards this primary symbolisation as the child's first steps into the symbolic order (S4, 67–8). The mother which interests psychoanalytic theory is thus above all the symbolic mother, the mother in her role as the primordial Other. It is she who introduces the child into language by interpreting the child's screams and thereby retroactively determining their meaning (see PUNCTUATION).

The mother is manifested in the imaginary order in a number of images. One important image that has already been mentioned is that of the devouring mother which is at the root of anxiety. Another important maternal image is that of the phallic mother, the mother imagined as possessing the imaginary phallus.

N

Name-of-the-Father (*Nom-du-Père*)

When the expression 'the name of the father' first appears in Lacan's work, in the early 1950s, it is without capital letters and refers generally to the prohibitive role of the FATHER as the one who lays down the incest taboo in the Oedipus complex (i.e. to the symbolic father); 'It is in the *name of the father* that we must recognise the support of the symbolic function which, from the dawn of history, has identified his person with the figure of the law' (E, 67).

From the beginning Lacan plays on the homophony of *le nom du père* (the name of the father) and *le 'non' du père* (the 'no' of the father), to emphasise the legislative and prohibitive function of the symbolic father.

A few years later, in the seminar on the psychoses (Lacan, 1955–6), the expression becomes capitalised and hyphenated and takes on a more precise meaning; the Name-of-the-Father is now the fundamental signifier which permits signification to proceed normally. This fundamental signifier both confers identity on the subject (it names him, positions him within the symbolic order) and signifies the Oedipal prohibition, the 'no' of the incest taboo. If this signifier is foreclosed (not included in the symbolic order), the result is PSYCHOSIS.

In another work on psychosis (Lacan, 1957–8b), Lacan represents of the Oedipus complex as a metaphor (the PATERNAL METAPHOR), in which one signifier (the Name-of-the-Father) substitutes another (the desire of the mother).

narcissism (*narcissisme*)

The term 'narcissism' first appears in Freud's work in 1910, but it is not until his work 'On narcissism: an introduction' (Freud, 1914c) that the concept begins to play a central role in psychoanalytic theory. From this point on, Freud defines narcissism as the investment of libido in the EGO, and opposes it to object-love, in which libido is invested in objects. Lacan attributes great importance to this phase in Freud's work, since it clearly inscribes the ego as an object of the libidinal economy, and links the birth of the ego to the narcissistic stage of development. Narcissism is different from the prior stage of autoeroticism (in which the ego does not exist as a unity), and only comes about when 'a new psychical action' gives birth to the ego.

Lacan develops Freud's concept by linking it more explicitly with its namesake, the myth of Narcissus. Lacan thus defines narcissism as the erotic attraction to the SPECULAR IMAGE; this erotic relation underlies the primary identification by which the ego is formed in the mirror stage. Narcissism has both an erotic character and an aggressive character (see AGGRESSIVITY). It is erotic, as the myth of Narcissus shows, since the subject is strongly attracted to the gestalt that is his image. It is aggressive, since the wholeness of the specular image contrasts with the uncoordinated disunity of the subject's real body, and thus seems to threaten the subject with disintegration. In 'Remarks on psychic causality' (Lacan, 1946), Lacan coins the term 'narcissistic suicidal aggression' (*agression suicidaire narcissique*) to express the fact that the erotic-aggressive character of the narcissistic infatuation with the specular image can lead the subject to self-destruction (as the myth of Narcissus also illustrates) (Ec, 187; Ec, 174). The narcissistic relation constitutes the imaginary dimension of human relationships (S3, 92).

nature (*nature*)   A constant theme running throughout Lacan's work is the distinction he draws between human beings and other animals, or, as Lacan puts it, between 'human society' and 'animal society' (S1, 223). The basis of this distinction is LANGUAGE; humans have language, whereas animals merely have CODES (but see S1, 240 for an interesting caveat). The consequence of this fundamental difference is that animal psychology is entirely dominated by the imaginary, whereas human psychology is complicated by the additional dimension of the symbolic.

Within the context of this binary opposition between human beings and other animals, Lacan uses the term 'nature' in a complex double sense. On the one hand, he uses it to designate one term in the opposition, namely the animal world. In this sense, Lacan adopts the traditional anthropological opposition between nature and culture (*culture* being, in Lacanian terms, the symbolic order). Like Claude Lévi-Strauss and other anthropologists, Lacan points to the prohibition of incest as the the kernel of the legal structure which differentiates culture from nature; 'The primordial Law is therefore that which in regulating marriage superimposes the kingdom of culture on that of a nature abandoned to the law of mating' (E, 66) (see LAW).

The regulation of kinship relations by the incest taboo, points to the fact that the paternal function is at the heart of the rift between humans and animals. By inscribing a line of descent from male to male and thus ordering a series of generations, the Father marks the difference between the symbolic and the imaginary. In other words, what is unique about human beings is not that they lack the imaginary dimension of animal psychology, but that in human beings this imaginary order is distorted by the added dimension of the symbolic. The imaginary is what animals and human beings have in common, except that in human beings it is no longer a natural imaginary. Hence Lacan repudiates 'the doctrine of a discontinuity between animal psychology and human psychology which is far away from our thought' (Ec, 484).

On the other hand, Lacan also uses the term 'nature' to denote the idea that there is a 'natural order' in human existence, an idea which Lacan calls 'the great fantasy of *natura mater*, the very idea of nature' (S1, 149). This great fantasy of nature, which is such a persistent theme in Romanticism (e.g. Rousseau's idea of the noble savage), underlies modern psychology, which attempts to explain human behaviour by reference to ethological categories such as instinct and adaptation.

Lacan is highly critical of all such attempts to explain human phenomena in terms of nature. He argues that they are based on a failure to recognise the importance of the symbolic order, which radically alienates human beings from natural givens. In the human world, even 'those significations that are the closest to need, significations that are relative to the most purely biological insertion into a nutritive and captivating environment, primordial significations, are, in their sequence and in their very foundation, subject to the laws of the signifier' (S3, 198).

Lacan thus argues that 'the Freudian discovery teaches us that all natural harmony in man is profoundly disconcerted' (S3, 83). There is not even a pure natural state at the beginning in which the human subject might exist before being caught up in the symbolic order: 'the Law is there *ab origine*' (S3, 83). Need is never present in a pure pre-linguistic state in the human being: such a 'mythical' pre-linguistic need can only be hypothesised after it has been articulated in demand.

The absence of a natural order in human existence can be seen most clearly in human sexuality. Freud and Lacan both argue that even sexuality, which might seem to be the signification closest to nature in the human being, is completely caught up in the cultural order; there is no such thing, for the human being, as a natural sexual relationship. One consequence of this is that perversion cannot be defined by reference to a supposed natural or biological norm governing sexuality. Whereas animal instincts are relatively invariable, human sexuality is governed by drives which are extremely variable and do not aim at a biological function (see BIOLOGY).

need (*besoin*) Around 1958, Lacan develops an important distinction between three terms: need, DEMAND and DESIRE. In the context of this distinction, 'need' comes close to what Freud referred to as INSTINCT (*Instinkt*); that is, a purely biological concept opposed to the realm of the drive (*Trieb*).

Lacan bases this distinction on the fact that in order to satisfy his needs the infant must articulate them in language; in other words, the infant must articulate his needs in a 'demand'. However, in so doing, something else is introduced which causes a split between need and demand; this is the fact that every demand is not only an articulation of need but also an (unconditional) demand for love. Now, although the other to whom the demand is addressed (in the first instance, the mother) can and may supply the object which satisfies the infant's need, she is never in a position to answer the demand for love unconditionally, because she too is divided. The result of this split between need and demand is an insatiable leftover, which is desire itself. Need is thus an intermittent tension which arises for purely organic reasons and which is discharged entirely by the specific action corresponding to the particular need in question. Desire, on the other hand, is a constant force which can never be satisfied, the constant 'pressure' which underlies the drives.

This account presents in chronological terms what is in fact a question of structure. In truth, it is not the case that there first exists a subject of pure need which then attempts to articulate that need in language, since the distinction between pure need and its articulation in demand only exists from the moment of its articulation, by which time it is impossible to determine what that pure need could have been. The concept of a pre-linguistic need is thus merely a hypothesis, and the subject of this pure need is a mythical subject; even the paradigmatic need of hunger never exists as a pure biological given, but is marked by the structure of desire. Nevertheless, this hypothesis is useful to Lacan for maintaining his theses about the radical divergence between human desire and all natural or biological categories (see NATURE).

negation (*dénégation*) For Freud the term negation (*Verneinung*) meant both logical negation and the action of denial (see Freud, 1925h). Lacan takes up Freud's concept of negation in his seminar of 1953–4 (see also Lacan, 1954a and 1954b) and in his seminar of 1955–6. Lacan argues that negation is a neurotic process that can only occur after a fundamental act of affirmation called BEJAHUNG. Negation must be distinguished from FORECLOSURE which is a kind of primitive negation prior to any possible *Verneinung* (S3, 46), a refusal of *Bejahung* itself.

neurosis (*névrose*) 'Neurosis' is originally a psychiatric term which came to denote, in the nineteenth century, a whole range of nervous disorders defined by a wide variety of symptoms. Freud uses the term in a number of ways, sometimes as a general term for all mental disorders in his early work, and sometimes to denote a specific class of mental disorders (i.e. in opposition to PSYCHOSIS).

In Lacan's work, the term neurosis always figures in opposition to psychosis and PERVERSION, and refers not to a set of symptoms but to a particular clinical STRUCTURE. This use of the term to designate a structure problematises Freud's distinction between neurosis and normality. Freud bases this distinction purely on quantitive factors ('psychoanalytic research finds no fundamental but only quantitative distinctions between normal and neurotic life', Freud 1900a: SE V, 373), which is not a structural distinction. In structural terms, therefore, there is no distinction between the normal subject and the neurotic. Thus Lacanian nosology identifies three clinical structures: neurosis, psychosis and perversion, in which there is no position of 'mental health' which could be called normal (S8, 374–5; but see E, 163). The normal structure, in the sense of that which is found in the statistical majority of the population, is neurosis, and 'mental health' is an illusory ideal of wholeness which can never be attained because the subject is essentially split. Thus whereas Freud sees neurosis as an illness that can be cured, Lacan sees neurosis as a structure that cannot be altered. The aim of psychoanalytic treatment is therefore not the eradication of the neurosis but the modification of the subject's position vis-à-vis the neurosis (see END OF ANALYSIS).

According to Lacan, 'the structure of a neurosis is essentially a question' (S3, 174). Neurosis 'is a question that being poses for the subject' (E, 168). The two forms of neurosis (HYSTERIA and OBSESSIONAL NEUROSIS) are distinguished by the content of the question. The question of the hysteric ('Am I a man or a woman?') relates to one's sex, whereas the question of the obsessional neurotic ('To be or not to be?') relates to the contingency of one's own existence. These two questions (the hysterical question about sexual identity, and the obsessional question about death/existence) 'are as it happens the two ultimate questions that have precisely no solution in the signifier. This is what gives neurotics their existential value' (S3, 190).

At times Lacan lists PHOBIA as a neurosis alongside hysteria and obsessional neurosis, thus raising the question of whether there are not two but three forms of neurosis (e.g. E, 168).

O

object-relations theory (*théorie du relation d'objet*) Freud defined the object as that in which and through which the drive attains its aim. In the years following Freud's death, the twin concepts of the 'object' and the 'object relation' attained a growing importance in psychoanalytic theory, and eventually a whole school of psychoanalytic theory came to be known as 'object-relations theory'. The main proponents of object-relations theory were Ronald Fairbairn, D. W. Winnicott and Michael Balint, all of whom were members of the Middle Group of the British Psycho-Analytical Society. These analysts differed on many points, and hence object-relations theory covers a wide range of theoretical points of view. However, despite its lack of precise definition, object-relations theory can be contrasted with EGO-PSYCHOLOGY on account of its focus on objects rather than on the drives in themselves. This focus on objects means that object-relations theory pays more attention to the intersubjective constitution of the psyche, in contrast to the more atomistic approach of ego-psychology. The distinction between these two approaches has been blurred by more recent analysts, such as Otto Kernberg, who have attempted to integrate object-relations theory within an ego-psychology framework.

Although Lacanian psychoanalysis has been compared with object-relations theory in that both schools of thought place more emphasis on INTERSUB-JECTIVITY, Lacan himself criticises object-relations theory repeatedly. His criticisms focus most on the way in which object-relations theory envisions the possibility of a complete and perfectly satisfying relation between the subject and the object. Lacan is opposed to such a view, arguing that for human beings there is no such thing as a 'pre-established harmony' between 'a need and an object that satisfies it' (S1, 209). The root of the error is, argues Lacan, that in object-relations theory, 'the object is first and foremost an object of satisfaction' (S1, 209). In other words, by locating the object in the register of satisfaction and NEED, object-relations theory confuses the object of psychoanalysis with the object of biology and neglects the symbolic dimension of desire. One dire consequence that follows from this is that the specific difficulties which arise from the symbolic constitution of desire are neglected, with the result that 'mature object relations' and ideals of 'genital love' are proposed as the goal of treatment. Thus object-relations theory becomes the site of a 'delirious moralism' (Ec, 716; see also GENITAL).

A closely related aspect of object-relations theory which Lacan also criticises is its shift of emphasis from the Oedipal triangle onto the mother–child relation, with the latter conceived of as a perfectly symmetrical, reciprocal relation. One of Lacan's fundamental concerns is to restore the centrality of the Oedipal triangle to psychoanalysis by re-emphasising the importance of the father in contrast to the object-relations emphasis on the mother. This concern can be seen in Lacan's criticism of the object relation as a symmetrical DUAL RELATION, and his view that the object relation is an intersubjective relation which involves not two but three terms.

Lacan's criticism of British object-relations theory, as summarised above, is one of the main themes of the first year of his public seminar (1953–4). In the fourth year of the seminar, entitled 'Object relations' (Lacan, 1956–7), Lacan discusses not the British school of object-relations theory (Balint, Fairbairn, Guntrip, etc.), but the French school of object-relations theory (Maurice Bouvet).*a*

objet (petit) *a* This term has sometimes been translated into English as 'object (little) *a*', but Lacan insisted that it should remain untranslated, 'thus acquiring, as it were, the status of an algebraic sign' (Sheridan, 1977: xi; see ALGEBRA).

The symbol *a* (the first letter of the word *autre*, or 'other') is one of the first algebraic signs which appears in Lacan's work, and is first introduced in 1955 in connection with SCHEMA L. It is always lower case and italicised to show that it denotes the little other, in opposition to the capital 'A' of the big Other. Unlike the big Other, which represents a radical and irreducible alterity, the little other is 'the other which isn't another at all, since it is essentially coupled with the ego, in a relationship which is always reflexive, interchangeable' (S2, 321). In schema L, then, *a* and *a'* designate indiscriminately the EGO and the COUNTERPART/SPECULAR IMAGE, and clearly belong to the imaginary order.

In 1957, when Lacan introduces the matheme of fantasy ($\$ \Diamond a$), *a* begins to be conceived as the object of desire. This is the imaginary PART-OBJECT, an element which is imagined as separable from the rest of the body. Lacan now begins to distinguish between *a*, the object of desire, and the specular image, which he now symbolises *i(a)*.

In the seminar of 1960–1, Lacan articulates the *objet petit a* with the term *agalma* (a Greek term meaning a glory, an ornament, an offering to the gods, or a little statue of a god) which he extracts from Plato's *Symposium*. Just as the *agalma* is a precious object hidden inside a relatively worthless box, so the *objet petit a* is the object of desire which we seek in the other (S8, 177).

From 1963 onwards, *a* comes increasingly to acquire connotations of the real, although it never loses its imaginary status; in 1973 Lacan can still say that it is imaginary (S20, 77). From this point on, *a* denotes the object which can never be attained, which is really the CAUSE of desire rather than that towards which desire tends; this is why Lacan now calls it 'the object-cause' of desire. *Objet petit a* is any object which sets desire in motion, especially the partial objects which define the drives. The drives do not seek to attain the *objet petit a*, but rather circle round it (S11, 179). *Objet petit a* is both the object of anxiety, and the final irreducible reserve of libido (Lacan, 1962–3: seminar of 16 January 1963). It plays an increasingly important part in Lacan's concept of the treatment, in which the analyst must situate himself as the semblance of *objet petit a*, the cause of the analysand's desire.

In the seminars of 1962–3 and of 1964, *objet petit a* is defined as the leftover, the remainder (Fr. *reste*), the remnant left behind by the introduction of the symbolic in the real. This is developed further in the seminar of 1969–70, in which Lacan elaborates his formulae of the four DISCOURSES. In the discourse of the master, one signifier attempts to represent the subject for all other signifiers, but inevitably a surplus is always produced; this surplus is *objet petit a*, a surplus meaning, and a surplus enjoyment (Fr. *plus-de-jouir*). This concept is inspired by Marx's concept of surplus value; *a* is the excess of *jouissance* which has no 'use value', but persists for the mere sake of enjoyment.

In 1973, Lacan links *objet petit a* to the concept of SEMBLANCE, asserting that *a* is a 'semblance of being' (S20: 87). In 1974 he places it at the centre of the

Borromean knot, at the place where the three orders (real, symbolic and imaginary) all intersect.

obsessional neurosis (*névrose obsessionnelle*) Obsessional neurosis was first isolated as a specific diagnostic category by Freud in 1894. In doing so, Freud grouped together as one condition a series of symptoms which had been described long before but which had been linked with a variety of different diagnostic categories (Laplanche and Pontalis, 1967: 281–2). These symptoms include obsessions (recurrent ideas), impulses to perform actions which seem absurd and/or abhorrent to the subject, and 'rituals' (compulsively repeated actions such as checking or washing). While Lacan also sees these symptoms as typical of obsessional neurosis, he argues that obsessional neurosis designates not a set of symptoms but an underlying STRUCTURE which may or may not manifest itself in the symptoms typically associated with it. Thus the subject may well exhibit none of the typical obsessional symptoms and yet still be diagnosed as an obsessional neurotic by a Lacanian analyst.

Following Freud, Lacan classes obsessional neurosis as one of the main forms of NEUROSIS. In 1956, Lacan develops the idea that, like HYSTERIA (of which Freud said it is a 'dialect'), obsessional neurosis is essentially a question which being poses for the subject (S3, 174). The question which constitutes obsessional neurosis concerns the contingency of one's existence, the question about DEATH, which may be phrased 'To be or not to be?', 'Am I dead or alive?', or 'Why do I exist?' (S3, 179–80). The response of the obsessional is to work feverishly to justify his existence (which also testifies to the special burden of guilt felt by the obsessional); the obsessional performs some compulsive ritual because he thinks that this will enable him to escape the lack in the Other, the castration of the Other, which is often represented in fantasy as some terrible disaster. For example, in the case of one of Freud's obsessional neurotic patients, whom Freud nicknamed the Rat Man, the patient had developed elaborate rituals which he performed to ward off the fear of a terrible punishment being inflicted on his father or on his beloved (Freud, 1909d). These rituals, both in their form and content, led Freud to draw parallels between the structure of obsessional neurosis and the structure of religion, parallels which Lacan also notes.

Whereas the hysterical question concerns the subject's sexual position ('Am I a man or a woman?'), the obsessional neurotic repudiates this question, refusing both sexes, calling himself neither male nor female: 'The obsessional is precisely neither one [sex] nor the other – one may also say that he is both at once' (S3, 249).

Lacan also draws attention to the way that the obsessional neurotic's question about existence and death has consequences for his attitude to time. This attitude can be one of perpetual hesitation and procrastination while waiting for death (E, 99), or of considering oneself immortal because one is already dead (S3, 180).

Other features of obsessional neurosis which Lacan comments on are the sense of guilt, and the close connection with anal erotism. In respect of the latter, Lacan remarks that the obsessional neurotic does not only transform his shit into gifts and his gifts into shit, but also transforms himself into shit (S8, 243).

Oedipus complex (*complexe d'Oedipe*) The Oedipus complex was defined by Freud as an unconscious set of loving and hostile desires which the subject experiences in relation to its parents; the subject desires one parent, and thus enters into rivalry with the other parent. In the 'positive' form of the Oedipus complex, the desired parent is the parent of the opposite sex to the subject, and the parent of the same sex is the rival. The Oedipus complex emerges in the third year of life and then declines in the fifth year, when the child renounces sexual desire for its parents and identifies with the rival. Freud argued that all psychopathological structures could be traced to a malfunction in the Oedipus complex, which was thus dubbed 'the nuclear complex of the neuroses'. Although the term does not appear in Freud's writings until 1910, traces of its origins can be found much earlier in his work, and by 1910 it was already showing signs of the central importance that it was to acquire in all psychoanalytic theory thereafter.

Lacan first addresses the Oedipus complex in his 1938 article on the family, where he argues that it is the last and most important of the three 'family complexes' (see COMPLEX). At this point his account of the Oedipus complex does not differ from Freud's, his only originality being to emphasise its historical and cultural relativity, taking his cue from the anthropological studies by Malinowski and others (Lacan, 1938: 66).

It is in the 1950s that Lacan begins to develop his own distinctive conception of the Oedipus complex. Though he always follows Freud in regarding the Oedipus complex as the central complex in the unconscious, he now begins to differ from Freud on a number of important points. The most important of these is that in Lacan's view, the subject always desires the mother, and the father is always the rival, irrespective of whether the subject is male or female. Consequently, in Lacan's account the male subject experiences the Oedipus complex in a radically asymmetrical way to the female subject (see SEXUAL DIFFERENCE).

The Oedipus complex is, for Lacan, the paradigmatic triangular structure, which contrasts with all dual relations (though see the final paragraph below). The key function in the Oedipus complex is thus that of the FATHER, the third term which transforms the dual relation between mother and child into a triadic structure. The Oedipus complex is thus nothing less than the passage from the imaginary order to the symbolic order, 'the conquest of the symbolic relation as such' (S3, 199). The fact that the passage to the symbolic passes via a complex sexual dialectic means that the subject cannot have access to the symbolic order without confronting the problem of sexual difference.

OEDIPUS COMPLEX

In *The Seminar, Book V*, Lacan analyses this passage from the imaginary to the symbolic by identifying three 'times' of the Oedipus complex, the sequence being one of logical rather than chronological priority (Lacan, 1957–8: seminar of 22 January 1958).

The first time of the Oedipus complex is characterised by the imaginary triangle of mother, child and phallus. In the previous seminar of 1956–7, Lacan calls this the preoedipal triangle (see PREOEDIPAL PHASE). However, whether this triangle is regarded as preoedipal or as a moment in the Oedipus complex itself, the main point is the same: namely, that prior to the invention of the father there is never a purely dual relation between the mother and the child but always a third term, the phallus, an imaginary object which the mother desires beyond the child himself (S4, 240–1). Lacan hints that the presence of the imaginary phallus as a third term in the imaginary triangle indicates that the symbolic father is already functioning at this time (Lacan, 1957–8: seminar of 22 January 1958).

In the first time of the Oedipus complex, then, the child realises that both he and the mother are marked by a lack. The mother is marked by lack, since she is seen to be incomplete; otherwise, she would not desire. The subject is also marked by a lack, since he does not completely satisfy the mother's desire. The lacking element in both cases is the imaginary PHALLUS. The mother desires the phallus she lacks, and (in conformity with Hegel's theory of DESIRE) the subject seeks to become the object of her desire; he seeks to be the phallus for the mother and fill out her lack. At this point, the mother is omnipotent and her desire is the law. Although this omnipotence may be seen as threatening from the very beginning, the sense of threat is intensified when the child's own sexual drives begin to manifest themselves (for example in infantile masturbation). This emergence of the real of the drive introduces a discordant note of anxiety into the previously seductive imaginary triangle (S4, 225–6). The child is now confronted with the realisation that he cannot simply fool the mother's desire with the imaginary semblance of a phallus – he must present something in the real. Yet the child's real organ (whether boy or girl) is hopelessly inadequate. This sense of inadequacy and impotence in the face of an omnipotent maternal desire that cannot be placated gives rise to anxiety. Only the intervention of the father in the subsequent times of the Oedipus complex can provide a real solution to this anxiety.

The second 'time' of the Oedipus complex is characterised by the intervention of the imaginary father. The father imposes the law on the mother's desire by denying her access to the phallic object and forbidding the subject access to the mother. Lacan often refers to this intervention as the 'castration' of the mother, even though he states that, properly speaking, the operation is not one of castration but of privation. This intervention is mediated by the discourse of the mother; in other words, what is important is not that the real father step in and impose the law, but that this law be respected by the mother herself in both her words and her actions. The subject now sees the father as a rival for the mother's desire.

The third 'time' of the Oedipus complex is marked by the intervention of the real father. By showing that he has the phallus, and neither exchanges it nor gives it (S3, 319), the real father castrates the child, in the sense of making it impossible for the child to persist in trying to be the phallus for the mother; it is no use competing with the real father, because he always wins (S4, 208–9, 227). The subject is freed from the impossible and anxiety-provoking task of having to *be* the phallus by realising that the father *has* it. This allows the subject to identify with the father. In this secondary (symbolic) identification the subject transcends the aggressivity inherent in primary (imaginary) identification. Lacan follows Freud in arguing that the superego is formed out of this Oedipal identification with the father (S4, 415).

Since the symbolic is the realm of the LAW, and since the Oedipus complex is the conquest of the symbolic order, it has a normative and normalising function: 'the Oedipus complex is essential for the human being to be able to accede to a humanized structure of the real' (S3, 198). This normative function is to be understood in reference to both clinical structures and the question of sexuality.

● **The Oedipus complex and clinical structures** In accordance with Freud's view of the Oedipus complex as the root of all psychopathology, Lacan relates all the clinical structures to difficulties in this complex. Since it is impossible to resolve the complex completely, a completely non-pathological position does not exist. The closest thing is a neurotic structure; the neurotic has come through all three times of the Oedipus complex, and there is no such thing as a neurosis without Oedipus. On the other hand, psychosis, perversion and phobia result when 'something is essentially incomplete in the Oedipus complex' (S2, 201). In psychosis, there is a fundamental blockage even before the first time of the Oedipus complex. In perversion, the complex is carried through to the third time, but instead of identifying with the father, the subject identifies with the mother and/or the imaginary phallus, thus harking back to the imaginary preoedipal triangle. A phobia arises when the subject cannot make the transition from the second time of the Oedipus complex to the third time because the real father does not intervene; the phobia then functions as a substitute for the intervention of the real father, thus permitting the subject to make the passage to the third time of the Oedipus complex (though often in an atypical way).

● **The Oedipus complex and sexuality** It is the particular way the subject navigates his passage through the Oedipus complex that determines both his assumption of a sexual position and his choice of a sexual object (on the question of object choice, see S4, 201).

In his seminar of 1969–70, Lacan re-examines the Oedipus complex, and analyses the myth of Oedipus as one of Freud's dreams (S17, ch. 8). In this seminar (though not for the first time, see S7) Lacan compares the myth of Oedipus with the other Freudian myths (the myth of the father of the horde in *Totem and Taboo*, and the myth of the murder of Moses; see Freud, 1912–13 and 1939a) and argues that the myth of *Totem and Taboo* is structurally opposite to the myth of Oedipus. In the myth of Oedipus, the murder of the father allows Oedipus to enjoy sexual relations with his mother, whereas in the myth of *Totem and Taboo* the murder of the father, far from allowing access to the father's women, only reinforces the Law which forbids incest (see S7, 176). Lacan argues that in this respect the myth of *Totem and Taboo* is more accurate than the myth of Oedipus; the former shows that enjoyment of the mother is impossible, whereas the latter presents enjoyment of the mother as forbidden but not impossible. In the Oedipus complex a prohibition of *jouissance* thus serves to hide the impossibility of this *jouissance*; the subject can thus persist in the neurotic illusion that, were it not for the Law which forbids it, *jouissance* would be possible.

In his reference to fourfold models, Lacan makes an implicit criticism of all triangular models of the Oedipus complex. Thus, though the Oedipus complex can be seen as the transition from a dual relationship to a triangular structure, Lacan argues that it is more accurately represented as the transition from a preoedipal triangle (mother–child–phallus) to an Oedipal QUATERNARY (mother–child–father–phallus). Another possibility is to see the Oedipus complex as a transition from the preoedipal triangle (mother–child–phallus) to the Oedipal triangle (mother–child–father).

optical model (*modèle optique*) Freud compares the psyche with an optical apparatus such as a microscope or a camera in *The Interpretation of Dreams* (Freud, 1900a: SE V, 536). Lacan also uses optical apparatuses at several points in his work: for example he uses the camera to provide a 'materialist definition of the phenomenon of consciousness' (S2, ch. 4).

Lacan argues that optics is a useful way of approaching the structure of the psyche because images play an important role in psychic structure (S1, 76). However, like Freud, Lacan warns that such an approach can never provide more than rather crude analogies, since optical images are not the same as the kind of images which are the object of psychoanalytic research. For this reason, Lacan soon replaces optical images with topological figures which are intended to prevent imaginary capture (see TOPOLOGY). Nevertheless, as Freud said of his own optical models, 'we need the assistance of provisional ideas' (Freud, 1900: 536).

The optical model first appears in 1954 (which is the version reproduced in Figure 12, taken from S1, 124), and is taken up later in 'A remark on Daniel Lagache's report' (1958b), in the seminar on the transference (1960–1), and elsewhere. It is basically an optical experiment which is constructed by means of a plane mirror and a concave mirror. The concave mirror produces a real

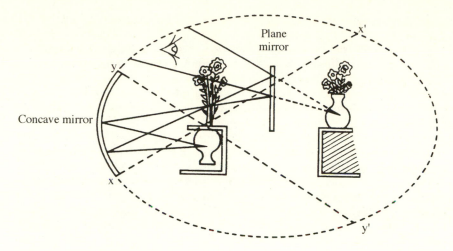

Figure 12 The optical model
Source: Jacques Lacan, *The Seminar, Book I. Freud's Papers on Technique*, trans. with notes by John Forrester, New York: Norton; Cambridge: Cambridge University Press, 1988.

image of an inverted flower-pot, hidden from view by a box, which is then reflected in the plane mirror to produce a virtual image. This virtual image is only visible to a subject who places himself within a particular area of vision.

Lacan uses the model to illustrate various points. Two of the most important points are the structuring role of the symbolic order and the function of the EGO-IDEAL.

1.   The optical model illustrates the way that the position of the subject in the symbolic order (represented by the angle of the plane mirror) determines the way in which the imaginary is articulated with the real. 'My position in the imaginary . . . is only conceivable insofar as one finds a guide beyond the imaginary, on the level of the symbolic plane' (S1, 141). The optical model thus illustrates the primary importance of the symbolic order in structuring the imaginary. The action of psychoanalytic treatment can be compared to the rotation of the plane mirror, which alters the position of the subject in the symbolic.

2.   The optical model also illustrates the function of the ideal ego, which is represented in the diagram as the real image, in opposition to the ego-ideal, which is the symbolic guide governing the angle of the mirror and hence the position of the subject (S1, 141).

order (*ordre*) Although Lacan uses the terms 'real', 'symbolic' and 'imaginary' from early on in his work, it is not until 1953 that he speaks of these as three 'orders' or three 'registers'. From that moment on they come to be the fundamental classification system around which all his theorising turns.

The IMAGINARY, the SYMBOLIC and the REAL thus comprise a basic classification system which allows important distinctions to be drawn between concepts which, according to Lacan, had previously been confused in psychoanalytic theory. For example Lacan argues that much misunderstanding has arisen in psychoanalytic theory due to a failure to distinguish between the imaginary father, the symbolic father and the real father. Thus Lacan claims that his tripartite classification system has shed invaluable light on Freud's work: 'Without these three systems to guide ourselves by, it would be impossible to understand anything of the Freudian technique and experience' (S1, 73).

The imaginary, the symbolic and the real are profoundly heterogeneous, each referring to quite distinct aspects of psychoanalytic experience. It is therefore difficult to see what they have in common, and yet, the fact that Lacan refers to all three as 'orders' implies that they share some common property. Lacan explores this question of what the three orders have in common by means of the topology of the BORROMEAN KNOT in his 1974–5 seminar. They are not mental forces like the three agencies in Freud's structural model. However, they are primarily concerned with mental functioning, and together they cover the whole field of psychoanalysis.

Although the three orders are profoundly heterogeneous, each order must be defined by reference to the other two. The structural interdependence of the three orders is illustrated by the Borromean knot, in which the severing of any one of the three rings causes the other two to become separated also.

other/Other (*autre/Autre*)

The 'other' is perhaps the most complex term in Lacan's work. When Lacan first begins to use the term, in the 1930s, it is not very salient, and refers simply to 'other people'. Although Freud does use the term 'other', speaking of both *der Andere* (the other person) and *das Andere* (otherness), Lacan seems to have borrowed the term from Hegel, to whose work Lacan was introduced in a series of lectures given by Alexandre Kojève at the École des Hautes Études in 1933–9 (see Kojève, 1947).

In 1955 Lacan draws a distinction between 'the little other' ('the other') and 'the big Other' ('the Other') (S2, ch. 19), a distinction which remains central throughout the rest of his work. Thereafter, in Lacanian algebra, the big Other is designated A (upper case, for French *Autre*) and the little other is designated *a* (lower case italicised, for French *autre*). Lacan asserts that an awareness of this distinction is fundamental to analytic practice: the analyst must be 'thoroughly imbued' with the difference between A and *a* (E, 140), so that he can situate himself in the place of Other, and not of the other (Ec, 454).

1.   The little other is the other who is not really other, but a reflection and

projection of the EGO (which is why the symbol *a* can represent the little other and the ego interchangeably in SCHEMA L). He is simultaneously the COUNTERPART and the SPECULAR IMAGE. The little other is thus entirely inscribed in the imaginary order. For a more detailed discussion of the development of the symbol *a* in Lacan's work, see OBJET PETIT A.

2. The big Other designates radical alterity, an other-ness which transcends the illusory otherness of the imaginary because it cannot be assimilated through identification. Lacan equates this radical alterity with language and the law, and hence the big Other is inscribed in the order of the symbolic. Indeed, the big Other *is* the symbolic insofar as it is particularised for each subject. The Other is thus both another subject, in his radical alterity and unassimilable uniqueness, and also the symbolic order which mediates the relationship with that other subject.

However, the meaning of 'the Other as another subject' is strictly secondary to the meaning of 'the Other as symbolic order'; 'the Other must first of all be considered a locus, the locus in which speech is constituted' (S3, 274). It is thus only possible to speak of the Other *as a subject* in a secondary sense, in the sense that a subject may occupy this position and thereby 'embody' the Other for another subject (S8, 202).

In arguing that speech originates not in the ego, nor even in the subject, but in the Other, Lacan is stressing that speech and language are beyond one's conscious control; they come from another place, outside consciousness, and hence 'the unconscious is the discourse of the Other' (Ec, 16). In conceiving of the Other as a place, Lacan alludes to Freud's concept of psychical locality, in which the unconscious is described as 'the other scene' (see SCENE).

It is the mother who first occupies the position of the big Other for the child, because it is she who receives the child's primitive cries and retroactively sanctions them as a particular message (see PUNCTUATION). The castration complex is formed when the child discovers that this Other is not complete, that there is a LACK in the Other. In other words, there is always a signifier missing from the treasury of signifiers constituted by the Other. The mythical complete Other (written A in Lacanian algebra) does not exist. In 1957 Lacan illustrates this incomplete Other graphically by striking a BAR through the symbol A, to produce Ⱥ; hence another name for the castrated, incomplete Other is the *barred Other*.

The Other is also 'the Other sex' (S20, 40). The Other sex is always WOMAN, for both male and female subjects; 'Man here acts as the relay whereby the woman becomes this Other for herself as she is this Other for him' (Ec, 732).

P

paranoia (*paranoïa*) Paranoia is a form of PSYCHOSIS characterised principally by DELUSIONS. Freud's experience of treating paranoiacs was limited, and his most extensive work on the subject is not the record of a course of treatment, but the analysis of the written memoirs of a paranoiac man (a judge by the name of Daniel Paul Schreber) (Freud, 1911c). It is in this work that Freud puts forward his theory that paranoia is a defence against homosexuality, arguing that the different forms of paranoiac delusion are based on different ways of negating the phrase 'I (a man) love him'.

Lacan's interest in paranoia predates his interest in psychoanalysis; it is the subject of his first major work, his doctoral dissertation (Lacan, 1932). In this work, Lacan discusses a psychotic woman whom he calls 'Aimée', whom he diagnoses as suffering from 'self-punishment paranoia' (*paranoïa d'autopunition*) – a new clinical category proposed by Lacan himself. Lacan returns to the subject of paranoia in his seminar of 1955–6, which he devotes to a sustained commentary on the Schreber case. Lacan finds Freud's theory about the homosexual roots of paranoia inadequate and proposes instead his own theory of FORECLOSURE as the specific mechanism of psychosis.

Like all clinical structures, paranoia reveals in a particularly vivid way certain basic features of the psyche. The ego has a paranoiac structure (E, 20) because it is the site of a paranoiac alienation (E, 5). Knowledge (*connaissance*) itself is paranoiac (E, 2, 3, 17). The process of psychoanalytic treatment induces controlled paranoia into the human subject (E, 15).

part-object (*objet partiel*) According to Melanie Klein, the infant's underdeveloped capacity for perception, together with the fact that he is only concerned with his immediate gratifications, means that the subject begins by relating only to a part of a person rather than the whole. The primordial part-object is, according to Klein, the mother's breast. As the child's visual apparatus develops, so also does his capacity to perceive people as whole objects rather than collections of separate parts (see Hinshelwood, 1989: 378–80).

While the term 'part-object' was first introduced by the Kleinian school of psychoanalysis, the origins of the concept can be traced back to Karl Abraham's work and ultimately to Freud. For example, when Freud states that partial drives are directed towards objects such as the breast or faeces, these are clearly part-objects. Freud also implies that the penis is a part-object in his discussion of the CASTRATION COMPLEX (in which the penis is imagined as a separable organ) and in his discussion of fetishism (see Laplanche and Pontalis, 1967: 301).

The concept of the part-object plays an important part in Lacan's work from early on. Lacan finds the concept of the part-object particularly useful in his criticism of object-relations theory, which he attacks for attributing a false sense of completeness to the object. In opposition to this tendency, Lacan argues that just as all DRIVES are partial drives, so all objects are necessarily partial objects.

Lacan's focus on the part-object is clear evidence of the important Kleinian influences in his work. However, whereas Klein defines these objects as partial because they are only part of a whole object, Lacan takes a different view. They are partial, he argues, 'not because these objects are part of a total object, the body, but because they represent only partially the function that produces them' (E, 315). In other words, in the unconscious only the pleasure-giving function of these objects is represented, while their biological function is not represented. Furthermore, Lacan argues that what isolates certain parts of the body as a part-object is not any biological given but the signifying system of language.

In addition to the partial objects already discovered by psychoanalytic theory before Lacan (the breast, the faeces, the PHALLUS as imaginary object, and the urinary flow), Lacan adds (in 1960) several more: the phoneme, the GAZE, the voice and the nothing (E, 315). These objects all have one feature in common: 'they have no specular image' (E, 315). In other words, they are precisely that which cannot be assimilated into the subject's narcissistic illusion of completeness.

Lacan's conceptualisation of the part-object is modified with the development around 1963–4 of the concept of *OBJET PETIT A* as the cause of desire. Now each partial object becomes an object by virtue of the fact that the subject takes it for the object of desire, *objet petit a* (S11, 104). From this point on in his work, Lacan usually restricts his discussion of part-objects to only four: the voice, the gaze, the breast and faeces.

pass (*passe*) In 1967, three years after founding his SCHOOL of psychoanalysis (the École Freudienne de Paris, or EFP), Lacan instituted a new kind of procedure in the School (Lacan, 1967). The procedure was called 'the pass' and was essentially an institutional framework designed to allow people to testify to the end of their analysis. The main idea behind this was Lacan's argument that the END OF ANALYSIS is not a quasi-mystical, ineffable experience, but must be (in accordance with the basic principle of psychoanalysis) articulated in language.

The procedure was as follows: the person seeking the pass (*le passant*) tells two witnesses (*les passeurs*), who must be in analysis at the time, about his own analysis and its conclusion, and these two witnesses then relay this account (separately) to a jury of seven (some of whom have succesfully been through the pass themselves). The jury then decides, on the basis of the two accounts, whether to award the pass to the candidate. There were no pre-established criteria to guide the jury, since the pass was based on the principle that each person's analysis is unique. If the the candidate was successful, he was accorded the title of A.E. (*Analyste de L'École*). Unsuccessful candidates were not to be prevented from seeking the pass again if they wished to do so.

The pass was designed to be the means by which a person might seek recognition by the School of the end of his analysis. The pass was not an obligatory process; whether or not an analyst decided to seek it was entirely up to him. It was not a qualification to practise analysis, since 'the authorisation of an analyst can only come from himself' (Lacan, 1967: 14) (see TRAINING). Nor was it a recognition by the School of the member's status as an analyst; this recognition was granted by another, wholly independent means in Lacan's School, and corresponded to the title of A.M.E. (*Analyste Membre de L'École*). It was solely the recognition that a person's analysis had reached its logical conclusion, and that this person could extract an articulated knowledge (*savoir*) from this experience. The pass thus concerns not a clinical function but a teaching function; it is supposed to testify to the capacity of the *passant* to theorise his own experience of psychoanalytic treatment, and thereby to contribute to psychoanalytic knowledge.

Jacques-Alain Miller comments that it is important to distinguish between (i) the pass as an institutional procedure (as described above) and (ii) the pass as the personal experience of the end of one's analysis, the passage from being an analysand to being an analyst, which may be testified to by 'the pass' in the first sense of the term (Miller, 1977).

In the 1970s the institution of the pass became the focus of intense controversy within the EFP. While some supported Lacan's own views that the pass would yield important contributions to knowledge of the end of analysis, others criticised it for being divisive and unworkable. These debates became even more heated in the final years of the EFP, before Lacan dissolved his School in 1980 (see Roudinesco, 1986). Of the various Lacanian organisations which exist today, some have abandoned Lacan's proposal, while many others retain the institution of the pass as a central part of their structure.

passage to the act (*passage à l'acte*) The phrase 'passage to the act' comes from French clinical psychiatry, which uses it to designate those impulsive acts, of a violent or criminal nature, which sometimes mark the onset of an acute psychotic episode. As the phrase itself indicates, these acts are supposed to mark the point when the subject proceeds from a violent idea or intention to the corresponding act (see Laplanche and Pontalis, 1967: 5). Because these acts are attributed to the action of the psychosis, French law absolves the perpetrator of civil responsibility for them (Chemama, 1993: 4).

As psychoanalytic ideas gained wider circulation in France in the first half of the twentieth century, it became common for French analysts to use the term *passage à l'acte* to translate the term *Agieren* used by Freud: i.e. as a synonym for ACTING OUT. However, in his seminar of 1962–3, Lacan establishes a distinction between these terms. While both are last resorts against anxiety, the subject who acts something out still remains in the SCENE, whereas a passage to the act involves an exit from the scene altogether. Acting out is a symbolic message addressed to the big Other, whereas a passage to the act is a flight from the Other into the dimension of the real. The passage to the act is thus an exit from the symbolic network, a dissolution of the social bond. Although the passage to the act does not, according to Lacan, necessarily imply an underlying psychosis, it does entail a dissolution of the subject; for a moment, the subject becomes a pure object.

In order to illustrate what he means, Lacan refers to the case of the young homosexual woman treated by Freud (Freud, 1920a). Freud reports that the young woman was walking in the street with the woman she loved when she was spotted by her father, who cast an angry glance at her. Immediately afterwards, she rushed off and threw herself over a wall down the side of a cutting onto a railway line. Lacan argues that this suicide attempt was a passage to the act; it was not a message addressed to anyone, since symbolisation had become impossible for the young woman. Confronted with her father's desire, she was consumed with an uncontrollable anxiety and reacted in an impulsive way by identifying with the object. Thus she fell down (Ger. *niederkommt*) like the *objet petit a*, the leftover of signification (Lacan, 1962–3: seminar of 16 January 1963).

paternal metaphor (*métaphore paternelle*) When, in 1956, Lacan first begins to discuss the tropes of METAPHOR and metonymy in detail, the example he takes to illustrate the structure of metaphor is a line from Victor Hugo's poem, *Booz endormi* (Hugo, 1859–83: 97–9). This poem retells the biblical story of Ruth and Boaz; while Ruth sleeps at his feet, Boaz dreams that a tree grows out of his stomach, a revelation that he is to be the founder of a race. In the line which Lacan quotes – 'His sheaf' was neither miserly nor spiteful' – the metaphoric substitution of 'sheaf' for 'Boaz' produces a poetic effect of SIGNIFICATION (S3, 218–25; see S4, 377–8; E, 156–8; S8, 158–9). Paternity is thus both the theme of the poem (its content) and also inherent in the structure of metaphor itself. All paternity involves metaphoric substitution, and vice versa.

The phrase 'paternal metaphor' is introduced by Lacan in 1957 (S4, 379). In 1958, he goes on to elaborate the structure of this metaphor; it involves the substitution of one signifier (the Name-of-the-Father) for another (the desire of the mother) (see Figure 13; E, 200).

The paternal metaphor thus designates the metaphorical (i.e. substitutive) character of the OEDIPUS COMPLEX itself. It is the fundamental metaphor on which all signification depends: for this reason, all signification is phallic. If the Name-of-the-Father is foreclosed (i.e. in psychosis), there can be no paternal metaphor, and hence no phallic signification.

$$\frac{\text{Name-of-the-Father}}{\text{Desire of the Mother}} \cdot \frac{\text{Desire of the Mother}}{\text{Signified to the subject}} \rightarrow \text{Name-of-the-Father}\left(\frac{A}{\text{Phallus}}\right)$$

Figure 13 The paternal metaphor
Source: Jacques Lacan, *Écrits*, Paris: Seuil, 1966.

perversion (*perversion*) Perversion was defined by Freud as any form of sexual behaviour which deviates from the norm of heterosexual genital intercourse (Freud, 1905d). However, this definition is problematised by Freud's own notions of the polymorphous perversity of all human sexuality, which is characterised by the absence of any pregiven natural order.

Lacan overcomes this impasse in Freudian theory by defining perversion not as a form of behaviour but as a clinical STRUCTURE.

> What is perversion? It is not simply an aberration in relation to social criteria, an anomaly contrary to good morals, although this register is not absent, nor is it an atypicality according to natural criteria, namely that it more or less derogates from the reproductive finality of the sexual union. It is something else in its very structure.
>
> (S1, 221)

The distinction between perverse acts and the perverse structure implies that, while there are certain sexual acts which are closely associated with perverse structures, it is also possible that such acts may be engaged in by non-perverse subjects, and equally possible that a perverse subject may never actually engage in such acts. It also implies a universalist position; while social disapproval and the infraction of 'good morals' may be what determines whether a particular act is perverse or not, this is not the essence of the perverse structure. A perverse structure remains perverse even when the acts associated with it are socially approved. Hence Lacan regards homosexuality as a perversion even when practised in Ancient Greece, where it was widely tolerated (S8, 43). (This is not because homosexuality or any other form of sexuality is *naturally* perverse; on the contrary, the perverse nature of homosexuality is entirely a question of its infringement of the normative requirements of the Oedipus complex (S4, 201). Thus Lacan criticises Freud for forgetting at times that the importance of heterosexuality in the Oedipal myth is a question of norms and not of nature (Ec, 223). The analyst's neutrality forbids him from taking sides with these norms; rather than defending such norms or attacking them, the analyst seeks merely to expose their incidence in the subject's history.)

There are two main ways in which Lacan characterises the perverse structure.

● **The PHALLUS and DISAVOWAL** Perversion is distinguished from the other clinical structures by the operation of disavowal. The pervert disavows castration; he perceives that the mother lacks the phallus, and at the same time refuses to accept the reality of this traumatic perception. This is most evident in FETISHISM (the 'perversion of perversions'; S4, 194), where the fetish is a symbolic substitute for the mother's missing phallus. However, this problematic relation to the phallus is not exclusive to fetishism but extends to all the perversions (S4, 192–3). 'The whole problem of the perversions consists in conceiving how the child, in his relation to the mother . . . identifies himself with the imaginary object of [her] desire [i.e. the phallus]' (E, 197–8). This is why the preoedipal imaginary triangle plays such an important role in the perverse structure. In the perversions, the phallus can only function as veiled (see Lacan's discussion of the role of the veil in fetishism, transvestism, homosexuality and exhibitionism; S4, 159–63).

● **The DRIVE** Perversion is also a particular way in which the subject situates himself in relation to the drive. In perversion, the subject locates himself as object of the drive, as the means of the other's *jouissance* (S11, 185). This is to invert the structure of FANTASY, which is why the formula for perversion appears as $a \Diamond S$ in the first schema in 'Kant with Sade' (Ec, 774), the inversion of the matheme of fantasy. The pervert assumes the position of the object–instrument of the 'will-to-enjoy' (*volonté-de-jouissance*), which is not his own will but that of the big Other. The pervert does not pursue his activity for his own pleasure, but for the enjoyment of the big Other. He finds enjoyment precisely in this instrumentalisation, in working for the enjoyment of the Other; 'the subject here makes himself the instrument of the Other's *jouissance*' (E, 320). Thus in scopophilia (also spelled *scoptophilia*), which comprises exhibitionism and voyeurism, the pervert locates himself as the object of the scopic drive. In SADISM/MASOCHISM, the subject locates himself as the object of the invocatory drive (S11, 182–5). The pervert is the person in whom the structure of the drive is most clearly revealed, and also the person who carries the attempt to go beyond the pleasure principle to the limit, 'he who goes as far as he can along the path of *jouissance*' (E, 323).

Freud's remark that 'the neuroses are the negative of the perversions' has sometimes been interpreted as meaning that perversion is simply the direct expression of a natural instinct which is repressed in NEUROSIS (Freud, 1905d: SE VII, 165). However, Lacan rejects this interpretation entirely (S4, 113, 250). Firstly, the drive is not to be conceived of as a natural instinct which could be discharged in a direct way; it has no zero degree of satisfaction. Secondly, as is clear from the above remarks, the pervert's relation to the drive is just as complex and elaborated as that of the neurotic. From the point of view of genetic development, perversion is at the same level as neurosis; both have reached the third 'time' of the Oedipus complex (S4, 251). Perversion therefore 'presents the same dimensional richness as [a neurosis], the same abundance, the same rhythms, the same stages' (S4, 113). It is therefore necessary to interpret Freud's remark in another way: perversion is structured in an inverse way to neurosis, but is equally structured (S4, 251).

While neurosis is characterised by a question, perversion is characterised by the lack of a question; the pervert does not doubt that his acts serve the *jouissance* of the Other. Thus it is extremely rare for a perverse subject to demand analysis, and in the rare cases when he does, it is not because he seeks to change his mode of *jouissance*. This perhaps explains why many psychoanalysts have argued that psychoanalytic treatment is not appropriate for perverse subjects, a line which even some Lacanian analysts have taken, comparing the certainty of the pervert with that of the psychotic, and arguing that perverts cannot take the position of 'one who does not know' before a 'subject supposed to know' (Clavreul, 1967). However, most Lacanian analysts do not take this view, since it is a view completely at odds with Lacan's own position. In the seminar of 1956–7, for example, Lacan points to the dream of the young homosexual woman whom Freud treated as a clear manifestation of transference in a perverse subject (S4, 106–7; see Freud, 1920a). Also, in the 1960–1 seminar, Lacan's principal example of transference is that shown by Alcibiades, whom he clearly regards as a pervert (see E, 323; 'Alcibiades is certainly not a neurotic'). Thus Lacan argues that perverse subjects can be treated at the same level as neurotics, although there will of course be different problems in the direction of the treatment. One important implication of this is that the psychoanalytic treatment of a perverse subject does not set as its objective the elimination of his perverse behaviour.

phallus (*phallus*) Freud's work abounds in references to the penis. Freud argues that children of both sexes set great value on the penis, and that their discovery that some human beings do not possess a penis leads to important psychical consequences (see CASTRATION COMPLEX). However, the term 'phallus' rarely appears in Freud's work, and when it does it is used as a synonym of 'penis'. Freud does use the adjective 'phallic' more frequently, such as in the expression 'the phallic phase', but again this implies no rigorous distinction between the terms 'phallus' and 'penis', since the phallic phase denotes a stage in development in which the child (boy or girl) knows only one genital organ – the penis.

Lacan generally prefers to use the term 'phallus' rather than 'penis' in order to emphasise the fact that what concerns psychoanalytic theory is not the male genital organ in its biological reality but the role that this organ plays in fantasy. Hence Lacan usually reserves the term 'penis' for the biological organ, and the term 'phallus' for the imaginary and symbolic functions of this organ.

While this terminological distinction is not found in Freud's work, it responds to the logic implicit in Freud's formulations on the penis. For example, when Freud speaks of a symbolic equation between the penis and the baby which allows the girl to appease her penis envy by having a child, it is clear that he is not talking about the real organ (Freud, 1917c). It can be argued, then, that Lacan's terminological innovation simply clarifies certain distinctions that were already implicit in Freud's work.

Although not prominent in Lacan's work before the mid-1950s, the term 'phallus' occupies an ever more important place in his discourse thereafter. The phallus plays a central role in both the OEDIPUS COMPLEX and in the theory of SEXUAL DIFFERENCE.

• **The phallus and the Oedipus complex**   The phallus is one of the three elements in the imaginary triangle that constitutes the PREOEDIPAL PHASE. It is an imaginary object which circulates between the other two elements, the mother and the child (S3, 319). The mother desires this object and the child seeks to satisfy her desire by identifying with the phallus or with the phallic mother. In the Oedipus complex the father intervenes as a fourth term in this imaginary triangle by castrating the child; that is, he makes it impossible for the child to identify with the imaginary phallus. The child is then faced with the choice of accepting his castration (accepting that he cannot be the mother's phallus) or rejecting it.

• **The phallus and sexual difference**   Lacan argues that both boys and girls must assume their castration, in the sense that every child must renounce the possibility of being the phallus for the mother; this 'relationship to the phallus . . . is established without regard to the anatomical difference of the sexes' (E, 282). The renunciation by both sexes of identification with the imaginary phallus paves the way for a relationship with the symbolic phallus which is different for the sexes; the man has the symbolic phallus (or, more precisely, 'he is not without having it' [*il n'est pas sans l'avoir*]), but the woman does not. This is complicated by the fact that the man can only lay claim to the symbolic phallus on condition that he has assumed his own castration (has given up being the imaginary phallus), and by the fact that the woman's lack of the symbolic phallus is also a kind of possession (S4, 153).

The status of the phallus: real, imaginary or symbolic? Lacan speaks of the real phallus, the imaginary phallus and the symbolic phallus:

• **The real phallus**   As has already been observed, Lacan usually uses the term 'penis' to denote the real biological organ and reserves the term 'phallus' to denote the imaginary and symbolic functions of this organ. However, he does not always maintain this usage, occasionally using the term 'real phallus' to denote the biological organ, or using the terms 'symbolic phallus' and 'symbolic penis' as if they were synonymous (S4, 153). This apparent confusion and semantic slippage has led some commentators to argue that the supposed distinction between the phallus and the penis is in fact highly unstable and that 'the phallus concept is the site of a regression towards the biological organ' (Macey, 1988: 191).

While the imaginary phallus and the symbolic phallus are discussed more extensively by Lacan than the real phallus, he does not entirely ignore the latter. On the contrary, the real penis has an important role to play in the Oedipus complex of the little boy, for it is precisely via this organ that his sexuality makes itself felt in infantile masturbation; this intrusion of the real in the imaginary preoedipal triangle is what transforms the triangle from something pleasurable to something which provokes anxiety (S4, 225–6; S4, 341). The question posed in the Oedipus complex is that of where the real phallus is located; the answer required for the resolution of this complex is that it is located in the real father (S4, 281). The real phallus is written Π in Lacanian algebra.

● **The imaginary phallus** When Lacan first introduces the distinction between penis and phallus, the phallus refers to an imaginary object (S4, 31). This is the 'image of the penis' (E, 319), the penis imagined as a part-object which may be detached from the body by castration (E, 315), the 'phallic image' (E, 320). The imaginary phallus is perceived by the child in the preoedipal phase as the object of the mother's desire, as that which she desires beyond the child; the child thus seeks to identify with this object. The Oedipus complex and the castration complex involve the renunciation of this attempt to be the imaginary phallus. The imaginary phallus is written φ (lower-case phi) in Lacanian algebra, which also represents phallic signification. Castration is written $-\phi$ (minus lower-case phi).

● **The symbolic phallus** The imaginary phallus which circulates between mother and child serves to institute the first dialectic in the child's life, which, although it is an imaginary dialectic, already paves the way towards the symbolic, since an imaginary element is circulated in much the same way as a signifier (the phallus becomes an 'imaginary signifier'). Thus Lacan's formulations on the imaginary phallus in the seminar of 1956–7 are accompanied by statements that the phallus is also a symbolic object (S4, 152) and that the phallus is a signifier (S4, 191). The idea that the phallus is a signifier is taken up again and further developed in the 1957–8 seminar and becomes the principle element of Lacan's theory of the phallus thereafter; the phallus is described as 'the signifier of the desire of the Other' (E, 290), and the signifier of *jouissance* (E, 320).

These arguments are stated in their most definitive form in Lacan's paper on 'The signification of the phallus' (Lacan, 1958c):

> The phallus is not a fantasy, if by that we mean an imaginary effect. Nor is it as such an object (part-, internal, good, bad, etc.). It is even less the organ, penis or clitoris, that it symbolises. . . . The phallus is a signifier. . . . It is the signifier intended to designate as a whole the effects of the signified.
>
> (E, 285)

Whereas the castration complex and the Oedipus complex revolve around the imaginary phallus, the question of sexual difference revolves around the symbolic phallus. The phallus has no corresponding female signifier; 'the phallus is a symbol to which there is no correspondent, no equivalent. It's a matter of a dissymmetry in the signifier' (S3, 176). Both male and female subjects assume their sex via the symbolic phallus.

Unlike the imaginary phallus, the symbolic phallus cannot be negated, for on the symbolic plane an absence is just as much a positive entity as a presence (see E, 320). Thus even the woman, who lacks the symbolic phallus in one way, can also be said to possess it, since not having it the symbolic is itself a form of having (S4, 153). Conversely, the assumption of the symbolic phallus by the man is only possible on the basis of the prior assumption of his own castration.

Lacan goes on in 1961 to state that the symbolic phallus is that which appears in the place of the lack of the signifier in the Other (S8, 278–81). It is no ordinary signifier but the real presence of desire itself (S8, 290). In 1973 he states that the symbolic phallus is 'the signifier which does not have a signified' (S20, 75).

The symbolic phallus is written Φ in Lacanian algebra. However, Lacan warns his students that the complexity of this symbol might be missed if they simply identify it with the symbolic phallus (S8, 296). The symbol is more correctly understood as designating 'the phallic function' (S8, 298). In the early 1970s Lacan incorporates this symbol of the phallic function in his formulae of sexuation. Using predicate logic to articulate the problems of sexual difference, Lacan devises two formulae for the masculine position and two formulae for the feminine position. All four formulae revolve around the phallic function, which is here equivalent with the function of castration.

● **Criticisms of Lacan** Of all Lacan's ideas, his concept of the phallus is perhaps the one which has given rise to most controversy. Objections to Lacan's concept fall into two main groups.

Firstly, some feminist writers have argued that the privileged position Lacan accords to the phallus means that he merely repeats the patriarchal gestures of Freud (e.g. Grosz, 1990). Other feminists have defended Lacan, arguing that his distinction between the phallus and the penis provides a way of accounting for sexual difference which is irreducible to biology (e.g. Mitchell and Rose, 1982).

The second main objection to Lacan's concept of the phallus is that put forward by Jacques Derrida (Derrida, 1975) and echoed by others. Derrida argues that, despite Lacan's protestations of anti-transcendentalism, the phallus operates as a transcendental element which acts as an ideal guarantee of meaning. How can there be such a thing as a 'privileged signifier', asks Derrida, given that every signifier is defined only by its differences from other signifiers? The phallus, in other words, reintroduces the metaphysics of presence which Derrida denominates as logocentrism, and thus Derrida concludes that, by articulating this with phallocentrism, Lacan has created a phallogocentric system of thought.

philosophy (*philosophie*)   Freud regarded philosophy as one of the great cultural institutions, alongside art and religion – the mark of a highly developed state of civilisation. However, he viewed the relationship between philosophy and psychoanalysis in ambiguous terms. On the one hand, he credited certain philosophers (such as Empedocles and Nietzsche) with having anticipated purely by intuition what psychoanalysts discovered only by laborious investigation (Freud, 1914d: SE XIV, 15–16). On the other hand, he repeatedly criticised philosophers for equating the psyche with consciousness and thus excluding the unconscious on purely *a priori* grounds (Freud, 1925e [1924]: SE XIX, 216–17), and likened philosophical systems to paranoiac delusions (Freud, 1912–13: SE XIII, 73).

In Lacan's work too there is an ambivalent relationship between psychoanalysis and philosophy. On the one hand, Lacan opposes psychoanalysis to the totalising explanations of philosophical systems (S1, 118–19; S11, 77), and links philosophy with the discourse of the MASTER, the reverse of psychoanalysis (S20, 33). On the other hand, Lacan's work is full of philosophical references; indeed, this is often regarded as one of the features that distinguishes Lacan from other psychoanalytic thinkers. The philosophers most frequently referred to by Lacan are the following:

- **Plato**   Lacan often compares the psychoanalytic method to the Socratic dialogue (see DIALECTIC). He also refers specifically to a number of Plato's works, especially *The Symposium*, to which he dedicates a large part of his 1960–1 seminar.

- **Aristotle**   Lacan discusses Aristotle's typology of causation in the 1964 seminar (see CHANCE), and Aristotelian logic in the seminar of 1970–1.

- **Descartes**   References to Descartes abound in Lacan's work, since he sees the philosophy of the *COGITO* as summing up the very heart of the psychology of modern man (S2, 6). The Lacanian concept of the subject is both the cartesian subject (in its quest to move from doubt to certainty) and the subversion of the cartesian subject.

- **Kant**   It is Kant's moral philosophy (the *Critique of Practical Reason*) which most interests Lacan, and he discusses this at length both in his seminar on ethics (1959–60) and his essay on 'Kant with Sade' (1962). Lacan uses Kant's categorical imperative to throw light on the Freudian concept of the superego.

- **Hegel**   Lacan attended a series of lectures on Hegel given by Alexandre Kojève in 1933–9 at the École des Hautes Études (these lectures were later collected and published by Raymond Queneau; see Kojève, 1947). The influence of these lectures on his work, especially his earlier work, is immense, and whenever Lacan refers to Hegel it is Kojève's reading of Hegel that he has in mind. From Hegel Lacan takes (among other things) an emphasis on dialectical modes of thought, the concept of the BEAUTIFUL SOUL, the dialectic of the MASTER and the slave, and a distinction between animal and human DESIRE.

● **Heidegger** Lacan established a personal friendship with Heidegger, visiting him and translating some of his works. Heidegger's influence on Lacan's work can be seen in Lacan's metaphysical discussions of BEING, and in the distinction between full SPEECH and empty speech.

These are only the philosophers to whom Lacan refers most frequently; he also discusses the work of many other philosophers such as St Augustine, Spinoza, Sartre, and others.

Lacan's work engages with many philosophical schools and areas of enquiry. In his early work he shows a bent towards phenomenology, even presenting a 'phenomenological description of the psychoanalytic experience' in 1936 (Ec, 82–5), but he later becomes quite opposed to phenomenology, and in 1964 presents a critique of Merleau-Ponty's *Phenomenology of Perception* (S11, 71–6). Insofar as psychoanalysis engages with ontological questions, Lacan aligns psychoanalysis with MATERIALISM, against all forms of idealism. Lacan also engages with epistemology and the philosophy of SCIENCE, where his constant approach is rationalist rather than empiricist.

Further information on Lacan's relationship with philosophy is provided in Juranville (1984), Macey (1988: ch. 4), Ragland-Sullivan (1986) and Samuels (1993).

phobia (*phobie*) A phobia is usually defined in psychiatry as an extreme fear of a particular object (such as an animal) or a particular situation (such as leaving the home). Those who suffer from a phobia experience ANXIETY if they encounter the phobic object or are placed in the feared situation, and develop 'avoidance strategies' so as to prevent this from happening. These avoidance strategies may become so elaborate that the subject's life is severely restricted.

Freud's most important contribution to the study of phobias concerned a young boy whom he dubbed Little Hans. Shortly before his fifth birthday, Hans developed a violent fear of horses and became unwilling to go outdoors lest he encounter one in the street. In his case study of Hans, Freud distinguished between the initial onset of anxiety (which was not attached to any object) and the ensuing fear which was focused specifically on horses; only the latter constituted the phobia proper. Freud argued that the anxiety was the transformation of sexual excitement generated in Hans by his relationship with his mother, and that the horses represented his father who Hans feared would punish him (Freud, 1909b).

Lacan, in his seminar of 1956–7, offers a detailed reading of the case of

Little Hans, and proposes his own view of phobia. Following Freud, he stresses the difference between phobia and anxiety: anxiety appears first, and the phobia is a defensive formation which turns the anxiety into fear by focusing it on a specific object (S4, 207, 400). However, rather than identifying the phobic object as a representative of the father, as Freud does, Lacan argues that the fundamental characteristic of the phobic object is that it does not simply represent one person but represents different people in turn (S4, 283–8). Lacan points out the extremely diverse ways in which Hans describes the feared horse at different moments of his phobia; for example, at one point Hans is afraid that a horse will bite him and at another moment that a horse will fall down (S4, 305–6). At each of these different moments, Lacan argues, the horse represents a different person in Hans's life (S4, 307). The horse thus functions not as the equivalent of a sole signified but as a signifier which has no univocal sense and is displaced onto different signifieds in turn (S4, 288).

Lacan argues that Hans develops the horse phobia because his real father fails to intervene as the agent of castration, which is his proper role in the OEDIPUS COMPLEX (S4, 212). When his sexuality begins to make itself felt in infantile masturbation, the preoedipal triangle (mother–child–imaginary phallus) is transformed from being Hans's source of enjoyment into something that provokes anxiety in him. The intervention of the real father would have saved Hans from this anxiety by symbolically castrating him, but in the absence of this intervention Hans is forced to find a substitute in the phobia. The phobia functions by using an imaginary object (the horse) to reorganise the symbolic world of Hans and thus help him to make the passage from the imaginary to the symbolic order (S4, 230, 245–6, 284). Far from being a purely negative phenomenon, then, a phobia makes a traumatic situation thinkable, livable, by introducing a symbolic dimension, even if it is only a provisional solution (S4, 82).

The phobic object is thus an imaginary element which is able to function as a signifier by being used to represent every possible element in the subject's world. For Hans, the horse represents at different moments his father, his mother, his little sister, his friends, himself, and many other things besides (S4, 307). In the process of developing all the permutations possible around 'the signifying crystal of his phobia', little Hans was able to exhaust all the impossibilities that blocked his passage from the imaginary to the symbolic and thus find a solution to the impossible by recourse to a signifying equation (E, 168). In other words, a phobia plays exactly the same role which Claude Lévi-Strauss assigns to myths, only on the level of the individual rather than of society. What is important in the myth, argues Lévi-Strauss, is not any 'natural' or 'archetypal' meaning of the isolated elements which make it up, but the way they are combined and re-combined in such a way that while the elements change position, the relations between the positions are immutable (Lévi-Strauss, 1955). This repeated re-combination of the same elements allows an impossible situation to be faced up to by articulating in turn all the different forms of its impossibility (S4, 330).

What are the practical consequences of Lacan's theory in the treatment of subjects who suffer from phobias? Rather than simply desensitising the subject (as in behavioural therapy), or simply providing an explanation of the phobic object (e.g. 'the horse is your father'), the treatment should aim at helping the subject to work through all the various permutations involving the phobic signifier. By helping the subject to develop the individual myth in accordance with its own laws, the treatment enables him finally to exhaust all the possible combinations of signifying elements and thus to dissolve the phobia (S4, 402). (It should be borne in mind that Lacan's discussion of the case of Little Hans only explicitly addresses the question of childhood phobias, and leaves open the question of whether these remarks also apply to adult phobias.)

As Freud himself noted in his case study of Little Hans, phobias had not previously been assigned any definite position in psychiatric nosographies. He attempted to remedy this uncertainty surrounding the classification of phobia, but his proposed solution is prey to a certain ambiguity. On the one hand, since phobic symptoms can be found among both neurotic and psychotic subjects, Freud argued that phobias could not be regarded as an 'independent patholo-gical process' (Freud, 1909b: SE X, 115). On the other hand, in the same work Freud did isolate a particular form of neurosis whose central symptom is a phobia. Freud called this new diagnostic category 'anxiety hysteria' in order to distinguish it from 'conversion hysteria' (which Freud had previously referred to simply as 'hysteria'). Freud's remarks are thus ambiguous, implying that phobia can be both a symptom *and* an underlying clinical entity.The same ambiguity is repeated in Lacan's works, where the question is rephrased in terms of whether phobia is a *symptom* or a STRUCTURE. Usually, Lacan distin-guishes only two neurotic structures (hysteria and obsessional neurosis), and describes phobia as a symptom rather than a structure (S4, 285). However, there are also points in Lacan's work where he lists phobia as a third form of neurosis in addition to hysteria and obsessional neurosis, thus implying that there is a phobic structure (e.g. E, 321); in 1961, for example, he describes phobia as 'the most radical form of neurosis' (S8, 425). The question is not resolved until the seminar of 1968–9, where Lacan states that

> One cannot see in it [phobia] a clinical entity but rather a revolving junction [*plaque tournante*], something that must be elucidated in its relations with that towards which it usually tends, namely the two great orders of neurosis, hysteria and obsessionality, and also the junction which it realises with perversion.
>
> (Lacan, 1968–9, quoted in Chemama, 1993: 210)

Thus phobia is not, according to Lacan, a clinical structure on the same level as hysteria and obsessional neurosis, but a gateway which can lead to either of them and which also has certain connections with the perverse structure. The link with perversion can be seen in the similarities between the fetish and the phobic object, both of which are symbolic substitutes for a missing element and both of which serve to structure the surrounding world. Furthermore, both phobia and perversion arise from difficulties in the passage from the imaginary preoedipal triangle to the symbolic Oedipal quaternary.

pleasure principle (*principe de plaisir*)

Even when Lacan uses the word 'pleasure' on its own, he is always referring to the pleasure *principle*, and never to a sensation.

The pleasure principle is one of the 'two principles of mental functioning' posited by Freud in his metapsychological writings (the other being the REALITY PRINCIPLE). The pleasure principle aims exclusively at avoiding unpleasure and obtaining pleasure.

Lacan's first extended discussion of the pleasure principle appears in the seminar of 1954–5. Here Lacan compares the pleasure principle to a homeostatic device that aims at maintaining excitation at the lowest functional level (S2, 79–80). This accords with Freud's thesis that unpleasure is related to the increase of quantities of excitation, and pleasure to their reduction. Lacan opposes the pleasure principle, which he dubs the 'restitutive tendency', to the death drive (the 'repetitive tendency'), in accordance with Freud's view that the death drive is 'beyond the pleasure principle' (S2, 79–80).

In 1960, Lacan develops what soon comes to be an important concept in his work; the idea of an opposition between pleasure and *JOUISSANCE*. *Jouissance* is now defined as an excessive quantity of excitation which the pleasure principle attempts to prevent. The pleasure principle is thus seen as a symbolic law, a commandment which can be phrased 'Enjoy as little as possible' (which is why Freud originally called it the *unpleasure* principle; see Freud, 1900a: SE V, 574). Pleasure is the safeguard of a state of homeostasis and constancy which *jouissance* constantly threatens to disrupt and traumatise.

> The function of the pleasure principle is, in effect, to lead the subject from signifier to signifier, by generating as many signifiers as are required to maintain at as low a level as possible the tension that regulates the whole functioning of the psychic apparatus.
>
> (S7, 119)

Put another way, the pleasure principle is the prohibition of incest, 'that which regulates the distance between the subject and *das Ding*' (S7, 69; see THING). When the subject transgresses this prohibition, gets too near to the Thing, then he suffers. Since it is the drives which permit the subject to transgress the pleasure principle, it follows that every drive is a DEATH DRIVE.

Since the pleasure principle is related to prohibition, to the law, and to regulation, it is clearly on the side of the symbolic, whereas *jouissance* is on the side of the real. The pleasure principle is thus 'nothing else than the dominance of the signifier' (S7, 134). This involves Lacan in a paradox, since the symbolic is also the realm of the REPETITION compulsion, which is, in Freud's terms, precisely that which goes *beyond* the pleasure principle. Indeed, some of Lacan's descriptions of the pleasure principle make it sound almost identical to the repetition compulsion: 'The function of the pleasure principle is to make man always search for what he has to find again, but which he will never attain' (S7, 68).

point de capiton The French term *point de capiton* is variously translated in English editions of Lacan's work as 'quilting point' or 'anchoring point'. To avoid the confusion resulting from this variety of translation, the term has here been left in the original French. It literally designates an upholstery button, the analogy being that just as upholstery buttons are places where 'the mattress-maker's needle has worked hard to prevent a shapeless mass of stuffing from moving too freely about' (Bowie, 1991: 74), so the *points de capiton* are points at which 'signified and signifier are knotted together' (S3, 268). Lacan introduces the term in his 1955–6 seminar on the psychoses to account for the fact that despite the continual slippage of the signified under the signifier (see SLIP), there are nevertheless in the normal (neurotic) subject certain fundamental 'attachment points' between the signified and the signifier where this slippage is temporarily halted. A certain minimum number of these points are 'necessary for a person to be called normal', and 'when they are not established, or when they give way' the result is PSYCHOSIS (S3, 268–9). This helps to explain how it is that in the psychotic experience, 'the signifier and the signified present themselves in a completely divided form' (S3, 268).

The *point de capiton* is thus the point in the signifying chain at which 'the signifier stops the otherwise endless movement of the signification' (E, 303) and produces the necessary illusion of a fixed meaning. Since the signifying chain has both a diachronic and a synchronic dimension, so also does the *point de capiton*:

1. The diachronic dimension of the *point de capiton* lies in the fact that communication is always a retroactive effect of PUNCTUATION. It is only when the sentence is completed that the sense of the first words is determined retroactively. This function is illustrated in the elementary cell of the GRAPH OF DESIRE, in which the *point de capiton* is the leftmost point of intersection between the vector S–S' and the vector Δ–$\mathcal{S}$.

2. The synchronic aspect is METAPHOR, by which the signifier crosses the bar into the signified. 'The synchronic structure [of the *point de capiton*] is more hidden, and it is this structure that takes us to the source. It is metaphor' (E, 303).

preoedipal phase (*stade préœdipien*) The preoedipal phase is the period of psychosexual development prior to the formation of the OEDIPUS COMPLEX. The term emerges very late in Freud's work, in the context of his discussion of female sexuality (Freud, 1931b).

149

Before Lacan, the preoedipal phase was usually represented as a DUAL RELATION between mother and child existing prior to any third term which could mediate it. However, Lacan argues that such an approach has the disadvantage of rendering the concept unthinkable in psychoanalytic theory. Psychoanalysis deals exclusively with structure, which requires a minimum of three terms, and thus a preoedipal phase which is represented as a purely dual relation 'cannot be conceived of in analytic terms' (E, 197). The child is never completely alone with the mother, since there is always a third term (S4, 240–1).

Hence when Lacan speaks of a preoedipal phase, he presents it not as a dual relation but as a triangle (S4, 81). The third element in the preoedipal triangle, which mediates the dual relation between the mother and the child, is the PHALLUS, an imaginary object which circulates between them in a series of exchanges. In the seminar of 1957–8 Lacan speaks of this imaginary triangle not as a preoedipal phase but as the first 'time' of the Oedipus complex.

Whether described as preoedipal, or as a moment in the Oedipus complex itself, the imaginary triangle of mother, child and phallus arises when the infant perceives a lack in the mother. The infant realises that the mother is not completely satisfied with him alone, but desires something else (the phallus). The child then seeks to be the phallus for the mother, which involves him in a seductive game of lures in which the child 'is never really there at the place where he is, and is never completely absent from the place where he is not' (S4, 193; see also S4, 223–4). In the seminar of 1956–7, where Lacan analyses the case of Little Hans (Freud, 1909b), he shows how, for a while, this game is satisfying for Hans, and argues that there is nothing inherent in it that would put an end to this preoedipal paradise (S4, 226). However, at some point something else intervenes which introduces a discordant note of anxiety into the game. This 'something else' is the first stirring of the drive, which manifests itself in infantile masturbation (S4, 225–6). The intervention of the real organ in this way transforms the imaginary triangle into a deadly game, an impossible task, in which the child is completely prey to the arbitrary desire of the omnipotent devouring mother (S4, 69, 195). The child is only saved from this deadly game by the intervention of the father as a fourth term, the father who rightfully claims possession of the phallus on the basis of a symbolic law.

The interest of the preoedipal phase for Lacan does not only lie in its function in paving the way for the Oedipus complex, but also in the fact that all the perversions have their origin in this phase (S4, 193). PERVERSION always involves some kind of identification with another term in the preoedipal triangle, whether it be the mother, or the imaginary phallus (or both, as in fetishism).

privation (*privation*) In his seminar of 1956–7, Lacan distinguishes between three types of 'lack of object': privation, frustration and castration (see LACK). Each of these types of lack is located in a different order, each is brought about by a different kind of agent, and each involves a different kind of object. Privation is defined as a lack in the real of a symbolic object (the symbolic phallus). The agent who brings about this lack is the imaginary father.

Privation is Lacan's attempt to theorise more rigorously Freud's concept of female castration and penis envy. According to Freud, when children realise that some people (women) do not have a penis, this is a traumatic moment which produces different effects in the boy and in the girl (see CASTRATION COMPLEX). Whereas the boy develops a fear of having his penis cut off, the girl envies the boy his possession of the penis, which she sees as a highly desirable organ. The girl blames the mother for depriving her of a penis, and redirects her affections to the father in the hope that he will provide her with a child as a symbolic substitute for the penis she lacks (Freud, 1924d).

Privation, then, refers to the female's lack of a penis, which is clearly a lack in the real. However, by definition, 'the real is full'; the real is never lacking in itself, and thus 'the notion of privation . . . implies the symbolisation of the object in the real' (S4, 218). In other words, when the child perceives the penis (a real organ) as *absent*, it is only because he has a notion that it somehow should be there, which is to introduce the symbolic into the real. Thus what is lacking is not the real organ, for, biologically speaking, the vagina is not incomplete without one; what is lacking is a symbolic object, the symbolic phallus. Its symbolic nature is confirmed by the fact that it can be substituted by a child in the girl's unconscious; in appeasing her penis envy by desiring a child, Freud argues, the girl 'slips – along the lines of a symbolic equation, one might say – from the penis to a baby' (Freud, 1924d: SE XIX, 178–9).

Freud argues that the little girl blames her mother for depriving her of a penis. Lacan, however, argues that it is the imaginary father who is held to be the agent of privation. However, these two accounts are not necessarily incompatible. Even though the girl may at first resent the mother for depriving her of a penis and turn to the father in the hope that he will provide her with a symbolic substitute, she later turns her resentment against the father when he fails to provide her with the desired child.

Freud argues that penis envy persists into adulthood, manifesting itself both in the desire to enjoy the penis in sexual intercourse, and in the desire to have a child (since the father has failed to provide her with a child, the woman turns to another man instead). Lacan argues that even when the woman has a child, this does not spell the end of her sense of privation. Her desire for the phallus remains unsatisfied, no matter how many children she has. The mother's basic dissatisfaction (S4, 194) is perceived by the child from very early on; he realises that she has a desire that aims at something beyond her relationship with him – the imaginary phallus. The child then seeks to fulfil her desire by identifying with the imaginary phallus. In this way, the privation of the mother is responsible for introducing the dialectic of desire in the child's life for the first time.

progress (*progrès*) Lacan claims that the idea of progress, like other humanist concepts, is alien to his teaching: 'There is not the slightest idea of progress in anything I articulate, in the sense that this term would imply a happy solution' (S17, 122). In this respect, Lacan is a basically pessimistic thinker, and he finds support for such pessimism in the gloomier works of Freud such as *Civilization and its Discontents* (Freud, 1930a). These texts allow Lacan to argue that 'Freud was in no way a progressive' (S7, 183).

Lacan rejects the idea of progress because it is based on a linear unidirectional concept of TIME, and also because it implies the possibility of synthesis (see DIALECTIC). Along with the idea of progress, Lacan rejects other related concepts such as that of a unilinear sequence of phases of psychosexual DEVELOPMENT.

There is one sense, however, in which Lacan does speak of progress: the progress in psychoanalytic TREATMENT. Insofar as treatment is a process which has a beginning and an end, when this treatment is moving and not 'stuck', we may speak of progress. The treatment is progressing as long as new material is emerging. Indeed, psychoanalytic treatment may be described as 'a progress towards truth' (E, 253).

projection (*projection*) Projection is a defence mechanism in which an internal desire/thought/feeling is displaced and located outside the subject, in another subject. For example a person who has been (or who feels) unfaithful to his partner may defend himself against feelings of guilt by accusing the partner of being unfaithful.

Whereas Freud and many other psychoanalysts use the term 'projection' to describe a mechanism which is present (to differing degrees) in both psychosis and neurosis, Lacan understands the term 'projection' as a purely neurotic mechanism and distinguishes it clearly from the apparently similar phenomenon that occurs in psychosis (which Lacan calls FORECLOSURE). Whereas projection is rooted in the imaginary dual relationship between the ego and the counterpart (S3, 145), foreclosure goes beyond the imaginary and instead involves a signifier which is not incorporated in the symbolic.

Lacan also rejects the view that INTROJECTION is the inverse of projection, arguing that these two processes are located on quite different levels. Whereas projection is an imaginary mechanism, introjection is a symbolic process (Ec, 655).

psychoanalysis (*psychanalyse*) Psychoanalysis is the theory and practice initiated by Sigmund Freud (1856–1939) founded on the discovery of the unconscious. Freud distinguishes between psychoanalysis as (i) a method for investigating unconscious mental processes, (ii) a method for treating neurotic disorders, and (iii) a set of theories about the mental processes revealed by the psychoanalytic method of investigation and treatment (Freud, 1923a: SE XVIII, 235). The word 'psychoanalysis' on its own is therefore ambiguous, since it can refer to psychoanalysis as a practice, or to psychoanalysis as a theory, or to both. In this dictionary, when it is necessary to avoid this ambiguity, the term 'psychoanalytic treatment' is used to refer to psychoanalysis as a practice and the term 'psychoanalytic theory' is used to refer to psychoanalysis as a body of thought.

Lacan trained initially as a psychiatrist, and turned to psychoanalysis to help him with his psychiatric research. This then led Lacan to train as a psychoanalyst himself in the 1930s. From then on, until his death in 1981, he dedicated himself to practising as an analyst and developing psychoanalytic theory. In the process, Lacan constructed a highly original way of discussing psychoanalysis which both reflected and determined an original way of conducting the treatment; in this sense it is thus possible to speak of a specifically Lacanian form of psychoanalytic treatment. However, Lacan never admits that he has created a distinctive 'Lacanian' form of psychoanalysis. On the contrary, when he describes his own approach to psychoanalysis, he speaks only of 'psychoanalysis', thus implying that his own approach is the only authentic form of psychoanalysis, the only one which is truly in line with Freud's approach. Thus the three major non-Lacanian schools of psychoanalytic theory (KLEINIAN PSYCHOANALYSIS, EGO-PSYCHOLOGY, OBJECT-RELATIONS THEORY) are all, in Lacan's view, deviations from authentic psychoanalysis whose errors his own return to Freud is designed to correct. (See FREUD, RETURN TO.)

From the very beginning, Lacan argues that psychoanalytic theory is a scientific rather than a religious mode of discourse (see SCIENCE), with a specific object. Attempts to apply concepts developed in psychoanalytic theory to other objects cannot claim to be doing 'applied psychoanalysis', since psychoanalytic theory is not a general master discourse but the theory of a specific situation (Ec, 747). Psychoanalysis is an autonomous discipline; it may borrow concepts from many other disciplines, but this does not mean that it is dependent on any of them, since it reworks these concepts in a unique way. Thus psychoanalysis is not a branch of PSYCHOLOGY (S20, 77), nor of medicine, nor of PHILOSOPHY (S20, 42), nor of LINGUISTICS (S20, 20), and it is certainly not a form of psychotherapy (Ec, 324), since its aim is not to 'cure' but to articulate truth.

psychology (*psychologie*) In his pre-1950 writings, Lacan sees psychoanalysis and psychology as parallel disciplines which can cross-fertilise each other. Although he is very critical of the conceptual inadequacies of associationist psychology, Lacan argues that psychoanalysis can help to build an 'authentic psychology' free from such errors by providing it with truly scientific concepts such as the IMAGO and the COMPLEX (Lacan, 1936).

However, from 1950 on, there is a gradual but constant tendency to dissociate psychoanalysis from psychology. Lacan begins by arguing that psychology is confined to an understanding of animal psychology (ethology): 'The psychological is, if we try to grasp it as firmly as possible, the ethological, that is the whole of the biological individual's behaviour in relation to his natural environment' (S3, 7). This is not to say that it cannot say anything about human beings, for humans are also animals, but that it cannot say anything about that which is uniquely human (although at one point Lacan does state that the theory of the ego and of narcissism 'extend' modern ethological research; Ec, 472). Thus psychology is reduced to general laws of behaviour which apply to all animals, including human beings; Lacan rejects 'the doctrine of a discontinuity between animal psychology and human psychology which is far away from our thought' (Ec, 484). However, Lacan vigorously rejects the behaviourist theory according to which the same general laws of behaviour are sufficient to explain all human psychic phenomena. Only psychoanalysis, which uncovers the linguistic basis of human subjectivity, is adequate to explain those psychic phenomena which are specifically human.

In the 1960s the distance between psychoanalysis and psychology is emphasised further in Lacan's work. Lacan argues that psychology is essentially a tool of 'technocratic exploitation' (Ec, 851; see Ec, 832), and that it is dominated by the illusions of wholeness and synthesis, NATURE and instinct, autonomy and self-consciousness (Ec, 832). Psychoanalysis, on the other hand, subverts these illusions cherished by psychology, and in this sense 'the Freudian enunciation has nothing to do with psychology' (S17, 144). For example the most cherished illusion of psychology is 'the unity of the subject' (E, 294), and psychoanalysis subverts this notion by demonstrating that the subject is irremediably split or 'barred'.

psychosis (*psychose*) The term psychosis arose in psychiatry in the nineteenth century as a way of designating mental illness in general. During Freud's life, a basic distinction between psychosis and NEUROSIS came to be generally accepted, according to which psychosis designated extreme forms of mental illness and neurosis denoted less serious disorders. This basic distinction between neurosis and psychosis was taken up and developed by Freud himself in several papers (e.g. Freud, 1924b and 1924e).

Lacan's interest in psychosis predates his interest in psychoanalysis. Indeed it was his doctoral research, which concerned a psychotic woman whom Lacan calls 'Aimée', that first led Lacan to psychoanalytic theory (see Lacan, 1932). It has often been remarked that Lacan's debt to this patient is reminiscent of Freud's debt to his first neurotic patients (who were also female). In other words, whereas Freud's first approach to the unconscious is by way of neurosis, Lacan's first approach is via psychosis. It has also been common to compare Lacan's tortured and at times almost incomprehensible style of writing and speaking to the discourse of psychotic patients. Whatever one makes of such comparisons, it is clear that Lacan's discussions of psychosis are among the most significant and original aspects of his work.

Lacan's most detailed discussion of psychosis appears in his seminar of 1955–6, entitled simply *The Pychoses*. It is here that he expounds what come to be the main tenets of the Lacanian approach to MADNESS. Psychosis is defined as one of the three clinical STRUCTURES, one of which is defined by the operation of FORECLOSURE. In this operation, the NAME-OF-THE-FATHER is not integrated in the symbolic universe of the psychotic (it is 'foreclosed'), with the result that a hole is left in the symbolic order. To speak of a hole in the symbolic order is not to say that the psychotic does not have an unconscious: on the contrary, in psychosis 'the unconscious is present but not functioning' (S3, 208). The psychotic structure thus results from a certain malfunction of the Oedipus complex, a lack in the paternal function; more specifically, in psychosis the paternal function is reduced to the image of the father (the symbolic is reduced to the imaginary).

In Lacanian psychoanalysis it is important to distinguish between psychosis, which is a clinical structure, and psychotic phenomena such as DELUSIONS and HALLUCINATIONS. Two conditions are required for psychotic phenomena to emerge: the subject must have a psychotic structure, and the Name-of-the-Father must be 'called into symbolic opposition to the subject' (E, 217). In the absence of the first condition, no confrontation with the paternal signifier will ever lead to psychotic phenomena; a neurotic can never 'become psychotic' (see S3, 15). In the absence of the second condition, the psychotic structure will remain latent. It is thus conceivable that a subject may have a psychotic structure and yet never develop delusions or experience hallucinations. When both conditions are fulfilled, the psychosis is 'triggered off', the latent psychosis becomes manifest in hallucinations and/or delusions.

Lacan bases his arguments on a detailed reading of the Schreber case (Freud, 1911c). Daniel Paul Schreber was an Appeal Court judge in Dresden who wrote an account of his paranoid delusions; an analysis of these writings constitutes Freud's most important contribution to the study of psychosis. Lacan argues that Schreber's psychosis was triggered off by both his failure to produce a child and his election to an important position in the judiciary; both of these experiences confronted him with the question of paternity in the real, and thus called the Name-of-the-Father into symbolic opposition with the subject.

In the 1970s Lacan reformulates his approach to psychosis around the notion of the BORROMEAN KNOT. The three rings in the knot represent the three orders: the real, the symbolic and the imaginary. While in neurosis these three rings are linked together in a particular way, in psychosis they become disentangled. This psychotic dissociation may sometimes however be avoided by a sympto-matic formation which acts as a fourth ring holding the other three together (see *SINTHOME*).

Lacan follows Freud in arguing that while psychosis is of great interest for psychoanalytic theory, it is outside the field of the classical method of psycho-analytic treatment, which is only appropriate for neurosis; 'to use the technique that [Freud] established outside the experience to which it was applied [i.e. neurosis] is as stupid as to toil at the oars when the ship is on the sand' (E, 221). Not only is the classical method of psychoanalytic treatment inappropri-ate for psychotic subjects, but it is even contraindicated. For example Lacan points out that the technique of psychoanalysis, which involves the use of the couch and free association, can easily trigger off a latent psychosis (S3, 15). This is the reason why Lacanian analysts usually follow Freud's recommenda-tion to begin the treatment of a new patient with a series of face-to-face interviews (Freud, 1913c: SE XII, 123–4). Only when the analyst is reason-ably sure that the patient is not psychotic will the patient be asked to lie down on the couch and free associate.

This does not mean that Lacanian analysts do not work with psychotic patients. On the contrary, much work has been done by Lacanian analysts in the treatment of psychosis. However, the method of treatment differs substan-tially from that used with neurotic and perverse patients. Lacan himself worked with psychotic patients but left very few comments on the technique he employed; rather than setting out a technical procedure for working with psychosis, he limited himself to discussing the questions preliminary to any such work (Lacan, 1957–8b).

Lacan rejects the approach of those who limit their analysis of psychosis to the imaginary order; 'nothing is to be expected from the way psychosis is explored at the level of the imaginary, since the imaginary mechanism is what gives psychotic alienation its form, but not its dynamics' (S3, 146). It is only by focusing on the symbolic order that Lacan is able to point to the funda-mental determining element of psychosis, namely, the hole in the symbolic order caused by foreclosure and the consequent 'imprisonment' of the psy-chotic subject in the imaginary. It is also this emphasis on the symbolic order which leads Lacan to value above all the linguistic phenomena in psychosis: 'the importance given to language phenomena in psychosis is for us the most fruitful lesson of all' (S3, 144).

The language phenomena most notable in psychosis are *disorders* of language, and Lacan argues that the presence of such disorders is a necessary condition for a diagnosis of psychosis (S3, 92). Among the psychotic language disorders which Lacan draws attention to are holophrases and the extensive use of neologisms (which may be completely new words coined by the psychotic, or already existing words which the psychotic redefines) (Ec, 167). In 1956, Lacan attributes these language disorders to the psychotic's lack of a sufficient number of POINTS DE CAPITON. The lack of sufficient *points de capiton* means that the psychotic experience is characterised by a constant slippage of the signified under the signifier, which is a disaster for signification; there is a continual 'cascade of reshapings of the signifier from which the increasing disaster of the imaginary proceeds, until the level is reached at which signifier and signified are stabilized in the delusional metaphor' (E, 217). Another way of describing this is as 'a relationship between the subject and the signifier in its most formal dimension, in its dimension as a pure signifier' (S3, 250). This relationship of the subject to the signifier in its purely formal aspect constitutes 'the nucleus of psychosis' (S3, 250). 'If the neurotic inhabits language, the psychotic is inhabited, possessed, by language' (S3, 250).

Of all the various forms of psychosis, it is PARANOIA that most interests Lacan, while schizophrenia and manic-depressive psychosis are rarely discussed (see S3, 3–4). Lacan follows Freud in maintaining a structural distinction between paranoia and schizophrenia.

punctuation (*ponctuation*) To punctuate a SIGNIFYING CHAIN is to produce meaning. Before punctuation, there is simply a chain of discourse; it is the listener/receiver who punctuates this discourse and thereby sanctions retroactively one particular meaning of an utterance. The punctuation of the signifying chain is that which creates the illusion of a fixed meaning: 'the punctuation, once inserted, fixes the meaning' (E, 99; see POINT DE CAPITON). This is essential in the structure of COMMUNICATION, where 'the sender receives his own message from the receiver', and is illustrated in the 'elementary cell' of the GRAPH OF DESIRE.

The operation of punctuation may be illustrated by reference to two situations which are of fundamental importance to psychoanalysis: the mother–child relation, and the relation between analysand and analyst. In the first of these situations, the baby who has not yet acquired speech can only articulate his needs in a very primitive kind of DEMAND, namely by screaming. There is no way of knowing for sure whether a scream articulates hunger, pain, tiredness, fear, or something else, and yet the mother interprets it in one particular way, thus determining its meaning retroactively.

Punctuation is one of the forms which the intervention of the analyst may take; by punctuating the analysand's discourse in an unexpected way, the analyst can retroactively alter the intended meaning of the analysand's speech: 'changing the punctuation renews or upsets' the fixed meaning that the analysand had attributed to his own speech (E, 99). Such punctuation is a way of 'showing the subject that he is saying more than he thinks he is' (S1, 54). The analyst can punctuate the analysand's discourse simply by repeating part of the analysand's speech back to him (perhaps with a different intonation or in a different context). For example, if the analysand says *tu es ma mère* ('you are my mother'), the analyst may repeat it in such a way as to bring out the homophony of this phrase with *tuer ma mère* ('to kill my mother') (E, 269). Alternatively, the analyst can also punctuate the analysand's speech by a moment of silence, or by interrupting the analysand, or by terminating the session at an opportune moment (see E, 44).

This last form of punctuation has been a source of controversy throughout the history of Lacanian psychoanalysis, since it contravenes the traditional IPA practice of sessions of fixed duration. Lacan's practice of sessions of variable duration (Fr. *séances scandées* – wrongly dubbed 'short sessions' by his critics) came to be one of the main reasons that the IPA gave for excluding him when the SFP was negotiating for IPA recognition in the early 1960s. Today, the technique of punctuation, especially as expressed in the practice of sessions of variable duration, continues to be a distinctive feature of Lacanian psychoanalysis.

Q

quaternary (*quaternaire*) A quaternary is a structure which comprises four elements. Although Lacan's rejection of dualistic schemas in favour of an emphasis on the triangular structure of the symbolic involves a predominance of triadic schemes in his work (see DUAL RELATION), Lacan also insists on the importance of fourfold schemes: 'A quadripartite structure has, since the introduction of the unconscious, always been required in the construction of a subjective ordering' (Ec, 774).

The emphasis on the quaternary first comes to the fore in Lacan's work in the early 1950s, and is perhaps due to the influence of Claude Lévi-Strauss, whose work on the structure of the avunculate shows that the basic unit of kinship always involves a minimum of four terms (Lévi-Strauss, 1945). Thus, in a 1953 paper which deals with the neurotic's 'individual myth' (another reference to Lévi-Strauss), Lacan remarks that 'there is within the neurotic a quartet situation' (Lacan, 1953b: 231), and adds that this quartet can demonstrate the particularities of each case of neurosis more rigorously than the traditional triangular thematisation of the Oedipus complex (Lacan, 1953b: 232). He concludes that 'the whole oedipal schema needs to be re-examined' (Lacan, 1953b: 235). Thus, in addition to the three elements of the Oedipus complex (mother, child, father), Lacan often speaks of a fourth element; sometimes he argues that this fourth element is DEATH (Lacan, 1953b: 237; S4, 431), and at other times he argues that it is the PHALLUS (S3, 319).

In 1955, Lacan goes on to compare psychoanalytic treatment to bridge, 'a game for four players' (E, 139; see E, 229–30). In the same year, he describes a quaternary made up of a triadic structure plus a fourth element (the LETTER) which circulates among these three elements (Lacan, 1955a).

Other important quaternary structures which appear in Lacan's work are SCHEMA L (which has four nodes), the four partial drives and their four corresponding part-objects, and the four discourses (each of which has four symbols assigned to four places). Lacan also enumerates four 'fundamental concepts of psychoanalysis' (Lacan, 1964a), and speaks of the *sinthome* as a fourth ring which prevents the other three rings in the BORROMEAN KNOT (the three orders of the real, the symbolic and the imaginary) from becoming separated.

R

real (*réel*) Lacan's use of the term 'real' as a substantive dates back to an early paper, published in 1936. The term was popular among certain philosophers at the time, and is the focus of a work by Emile Meyerson (which Lacan refers to in the 1936 paper; Ec, 86). Meyerson defines the real as 'an ontological absolute, a true being-in-itself' (Meyerson, 1925: 79; quoted in Roustang, 1986: 61). In speaking of 'the real', then, Lacan is following a common practice in one strand of early twentieth-century philosophy. However, while this may be Lacan's starting point, the term undergoes many shifts in meaning and usage throughout his work.

At first the real is simply opposed to the realm of the image, which seems to locate it in the realm of being, beyond appearances (Ec, 85). However, the fact that even at this early point Lacan distinguishes between the real and 'the true' indicates that the real is already prey to a certain ambiguity (Ec, 75).

After appearing in 1936, the term disappears from Lacan's work until the early 1950s, when Lacan invokes Hegel's view that 'everything which is real is rational (and vice versa)' (Ec, 226). It is not until 1953 that Lacan elevates the real to the status of a fundamental category of psychoanalytic theory; the real is henceforth one of the three ORDERS according to which all psychoanalytic phenomena may be described, the other two being the symbolic order and and the imaginary order. The real is thus no longer simply opposed to the imaginary, but is also located beyond the symbolic. Unlike the symbolic, which is constituted in terms of oppositions such as that between presence and absence, 'there is no absence in the real' (S2, 313). Whereas the symbolic opposition between presence and absence implies the permanent possibility that something may be missing from the symbolic order, the real 'is always in its place: it carries it glued to its heel, ignorant of what might exile it from there' (Ec, 25; see S11, 49).

Whereas the symbolic is a set of differentiated, discrete elements called signifiers, the real is, in itself, undifferentiated; 'the real is absolutely without fissure' (S2, 97). It is the symbolic which introduces 'a cut in the real' in the process of signification: 'it is the world of words that creates the world of things – things originally confused in the *hic et nunc* of the all in the process of coming-into-being' (E, 65).

In these formulations of the period 1953–5, the real emerges as that which is outside language and inassimilable to symbolisation. It is 'that which resists symbolization absolutely' (S1, 66); or, again, the real is 'the domain of whatever subsists outside symbolisation' (Ec, 388). This theme remains a constant throughout the rest of Lacan's work, and leads Lacan to link the real with the concept of impossibility. The real is 'the impossible' (S11, 167) because it is impossible to imagine, impossible to integrate into the symbolic order, and impossible to attain in any way. It is this character of impossibility and of resistance to symbolisation which lends the real its essentially traumatic quality. Thus in his reading of the case of Little Hans (Freud, 1909b) in the seminar of 1956–7, Lacan distinguishes two real elements which intrude and disrupt the child's imaginary preoedipal harmony: the real penis which begins to make itself felt in infantile masturbation, and the newly born sister (S4, 308–9).

The real also has connotations of matter, implying a material substrate underlying the imaginary and the symbolic (see MATERIALISM). The connotations of matter also link the concept of the real to the realm of BIOLOGY and to the body in its brute physicality (as opposed to the imaginary and symbolic functions of the body). For example the real father is the biological father, and the real phallus is the physical penis as opposed to the symbolic and imaginary functions of this organ.

Throughout his work, Lacan uses the concept of the real to elucidate a number of clinical phenomena:

● ANXIETY **and trauma** The real is the object of anxiety; it lacks any possible mediation, and is thus 'the essential object which isn't an object any longer, but this something faced with which all words cease and all categories fail, the object of anxiety *par excellence*' (S2, 164). It is the missed encounter with this real object which presents itself in the form of trauma (S11, 55). It is the *tyche* which lies 'beyond the [symbolic] *automaton*' (S11, 53) (see CHANCE).

● HALLUCINATIONS When something cannot be integrated in the symbolic order, as in psychosis, it may return in the real in the form of a hallucination (S3, 321).

The preceding comments trace out some of the main uses to which Lacan puts the category of the real, but are far from covering all the complexities of this term. In fact, Lacan takes pains to ensure that the real remains the most elusive and mysterious of the three orders, by speaking of it less than of the other orders, and by making it the site of a radical indeterminacy. Thus it is never completely clear whether the real is external or internal, or whether it is unknowable or amenable to reason.

● **External/internal** On the one hand, the term 'the real' seems to imply a simplistic notion of an objective, external reality, a material substrate which exists in itself, independently of any observer. On the other hand, such a 'naive' ·view of the real is subverted by the fact that the real also includes such things as hallucinations and traumatic dreams. The real is thus both inside and outside (S7, 118; see EXTIMACY) (*extimité*). This ambiguity reflects the ambiguity inherent in Freud's own use of the two German terms for *reality* (*Wirklichkeit* and *Realität*) and the distinction Freud draws between *material* reality and *psychical* reality (Freud, 1900a: SE V, 620).

● **Unknowable/rational** On the one hand, the real cannot be known, since it goes beyond both the imaginary and the symbolic; it is, like the Kantian thing-in-itself, an unknowable *x*. On the other hand, Lacan quotes Hegel to the effect that the real is rational and the rational is real, thus implying that it is amenable to calculation and logic.

It is possible to discern in Lacan's work, from the early 1970s on, an attempt to resolve this indeterminacy, by reference to a distinction between the real and 'reality' (such as when Lacan defines reality as 'the grimace of the real' in Lacan, 1973a: 17; see also S17, 148). In this opposition, the real is placed firmly on the side of the unknowable and unassimilable, while 'reality' denotes subjective representations which are a product of symbolic and imaginary articulations (Freud's 'psychical reality'). However, after this opposition is introduced, Lacan does not maintain it in a consistent or systematic way, but oscillates between moments when the opposition is clearly maintained and moments when he reverts to his previous custom of using the terms 'real' and 'reality' interchangeably.

reality principle (*principe de réalité*) According to Freud, the psyche is at first regulated entirely by the PLEASURE PRINCIPLE, which seeks to experience satisfaction via a hallucinatory cathexis of a memory of prior satisfaction. However, the subject soon discovers that hallucinating does not relieve his needs, and is thus forced 'to form a conception of the real circumstances in the external world' (Freud, 1911b: SE XII, 219). A new 'principle of mental functioning' is thus introduced (the 'reality principle'), which modifies the pleasure principle and forces the subject to take more circuitous routes to satisfaction. Since, however, the ultimate aim of the reality principle is still the satisfaction of the drives, it can be said that 'the substitution of the reality principle for the pleasure principle implies no deposing of the pleasure principle, but only a safeguarding of it' (Freud, 1911b: SE XII, 223).

From early on, Lacan is opposed to what he calls 'a naive conception of the reality principle' (1951b: 11). That is, he rejects any account of human development based on an unproblematic notion of 'reality' as an objective and self-evident given. He emphasises Freud's position that the reality principle is still ultimately in the service of the pleasure principle; 'the reality principle is a delayed action pleasure principle' (S2, 60). Lacan thus challenges the idea that the subject has access to an infallible means of distinguishing between reality and FANTASY. '[R]eality isn't just there so that we bump our heads up against the false paths along which the functioning of the pleasure principle leads us. In truth, we make reality out of pleasure' (S7, 225).

recollection (*remémoration*) Recollection (*remémoration*) and remembering (*mémoration*) are symbolic processes which Lacan contrasts with reminiscence (Fr. *réminiscence*), which is an imaginary phenomenon. Whereas remembering is the act whereby some event or signifier is registered for the first time in the symbolic MEMORY, recollection is the act whereby such an event or signifier is recalled.

Reminiscence involves reliving past experience and feeling once again the emotions associated with that experience. Lacan stresses that the analytic process does not aim at reminiscence but at recollection. In this sense, it differs from the 'cathartic method' invented by Josef Breuer, in which the emphasis was placed on a discharge of pathogenic affects via the reliving of certain traumatic events. While it is true that intense memories may be evoked in psychoanalytic treatment, with accompanying emotional discharge, this is not the basis of the analytic process. Reminiscence is also linked by Lacan to the Platonic theory of knowledge.

Recollection in the treatment involves the patient tracing the master signifiers of his life, or, in other words, 'the realization by the subject of his history in his relation to a future' (E, 88). By means of recollection, the treatment aims at 'the complete reconstitution of the subject's history' (S1, 12) and the 'assumption of his history by the subject' (E, 48). What matters is not 'reliving' the formative events of the past in any intuitive or experiential way (which would be mere reminiscence, or – even worse – ACTING OUT); on the contrary, what matters is what the analysand reconstructs of his past (S1, 13), the key word being 'reconstruct'. 'It is less a matter of remembering than of rewriting history' (S1, 14).

regression (*régression*) Freud introduced the concept of regression in *The Interpretation of Dreams* in order to explain the visual nature of dreams. Basing himself on a topographical model in which the psyche is conceived of as a series of distinct systems, Freud argued that during sleep progressive access to motor activity is blocked, thus forcing thoughts to travel regressively through these systems towards the system of perception (Freud, 1900a: SE V, 538–55). He later added a passage to this section distinguishing between this *topographical* kind of regression and what he called *temporal* regression (when the subject reverts to previous phases of development) and *formal* regression (the use of modes of expression which are less complex than others) (Freud, 1900a: SE V, 548 [passage added in 1914]).

Lacan argues that the concept of regression has been one of the most misunderstood concepts in psychoanalytic theory. In particular, he criticises the 'magical' view of regression, according to which regression is seen as a real phenomenon, in which adults 'actually regress, return to the state of a small child, and start wailing'. In this sense of the term, 'regression does not exist' (S2, 103). In place of this misconception, Lacan argues that regression must be understood first and foremost in a topographical sense, which is the way Freud understood the term when he introduced it in 1900, and not in a temporal sense (see TIME). In other words, 'there is regression on the plane of signification and not on the plane of reality' (S2, 103). Thus regression is to be understood 'not in the instinctual sense, nor in the sense of the resurgence of something anterior', but in the sense of 'the reduction of the symbolic to the imaginary' (S4, 355).

Insofar as regression can be said to have a temporal sense, it does not involve the subject 'going back in time', but rather a rearticulation of certain DEMANDS: 'regression shows nothing other than a return to the present of signifiers used in demands for which there is a prescription' (E, 255). Regression to the oral stage, for example, is to be understood in terms of the articulation of oral demands (the demand to be fed, evident in the demand for the analyst to supply interpretations). When understood in this sense, Lacan reaffirms the importance of regression in psychoanalytic treatment, arguing that regression to the anal stage, for example, is so important that no analysis which has not encountered this can be called complete (S8, 242).

religion (*religion*) Freud renounced the Jewish religion of his parents (though not his Jewish identity) and considered himself an atheist. While he regarded monotheistic forms of religion as the sign of a highly developed state of civilisation, he nevertheless thought that all religions were barriers to cultural progress, and thus argued that they should be abandoned in favour of SCIENCE. Freud argued that religions were an attempt to protect oneself against suffering by 'a delusional remoulding of reality', and thus concluded that they 'must be classed among the mass-delusions' of humankind (Freud, 1930a: SE XXI, 81). He saw the idea of God as an expression of infantile longing for a protective father (Freud, 1927c: SE XXI, 22–4), and described religion as 'a universal obsessional neurosis' (Freud, 1907b: SE IX, 126–7).

Lacan too considers himself an atheist, having renounced the Catholic religion of his parents (Lacan's brother, however, spent most of his life as a Benedictine monk). Like Freud he opposes religion to science, and aligns psychoanalysis with the latter (S11, 265). Distinguishing religion from magic, science and psychoanalysis on the basis of their different relations to truth as cause, Lacan presents religion as a denial of the truth as cause of the subject (Ec, 872), and argues that the function of sacrificial rites is to seduce God, to arouse his desire (S11, 113). He states that the true formula of atheism is not *God is dead* but *God is unconscious* (S11, 59) and echoes Freud's remarks about similarities between religious practices and obsessional neurosis (S7, 130).

Beyond these remarks on the concept of religion, Lacan's discourse abounds in metaphors drawn from Christian theology. The most obvious example is surely the phrase the NAME-OF-THE-FATHER, which Lacan adopts to denote a fundamental signifier whose foreclosure leads to psychosis. However, this is far from the only example. Thus the changes wrought by the symbolic are described in creationist rather than evolutionary terms, although paradoxically Lacan argues that this creationism is actually the only perspective that 'allows one to glimpse the possibility of the radical elimination of God' (S7, 213). In the seminar of 1972–3 he uses the term 'God' as a metaphor for the big Other, and compares feminine *jouissance* to the ecstasy experienced by Christian mystics such as St Teresa of Avila (S20, 70–1).

repetition (*répétition*)   Freud's most important discussion of the repetition compulsion (*Wiederholungszwang*) occurs in *Beyond the Pleasure Principle* (1920g) where he links it to the concept of the DEATH DRIVE. Freud posited the existence of a basic compulsion to repeat in order to explain certain clinical data: namely, the tendency of the subject to expose himself again and again to distressing situations. It is a basic principle of psychoanalysis that a person is only condemned to repeat something when he has forgotten the origins of the compulsion, and that psychoanalytic treatment can therefore break the cycle of repetition by helping the patient remember (see ACTING OUT).

In Lacan's pre-1950s work, the concept of repetition is linked with that of the COMPLEX – an internalised social structure which the subject repeatedly and compulsively re-enacts. At this time Lacan often translates Freud's *Wiederholungszwang* as *automatisme de répétition*, a term borrowed from French psychiatry (Pierre Janet, Gaëtan Gatian de Clérambault).

While Lacan never completely abandons the term *automatisme de répétition*, in the 1950s he increasingly uses the term 'insistence' (Fr. *instance*) to refer to the repetition compulsion. Thus repetition is now defined as the insistence of the signifier, or the insistence of the signifying chain, or the insistence of the letter (*l'instance de la lettre*); 'repetition is fundamentally the insistence of speech' (S3, 242). Certain signifiers insist on returning in the life of the subject, despite the resistances which block them. In SCHEMA L, repetition/insistence is represented by the axis A–S, while the axis *a–a'* represents the resistance (or 'inertia') which opposes repetition.

In the 1960s, repetition is redefined as the return of *jouissance*, an excess of enjoyment which returns again and again to transgress the limits of the PLEASURE PRINCIPLE and seek death (S17, 51).

The repetition compulsion manifests itself in analytic treatment in the TRANSFERENCE, whereby the analysand repeats in his relationship to the analyst certain attitudes which characterised his earlier relationships with his parents and others. Lacan lays great emphasis on this symbolic aspect of transference, distinguishing it from the imaginary dimension of transference (the affects of love and hate) (S8, 204). However, Lacan points out that although the repetition compulsion manifests itself perhaps most clearly in the transference, it is not in itself limited to the transference; in itself, 'the concept of repetition has nothing to do with the concept of transference' (S11, 33). Repetition is the general characteristic of the signifying chain, the manifestation of the unconscious in every subject, and transference is only a very special form of repetition (i.e. it is repetition *within psychoanalytic treatment*), which cannot simply be equated with the repetition compulsion itself (S8, 208).

repression (*refoulement*) The concept of repression is one of the most basic concepts in psychoanalytic theory, and denotes the process by which certain thoughts or memories are expelled from consciousness and confined to the unconscious. Freud was first led to hypothesise the process of repression through his investigation into the amnesia of hysterical patients. He later distinguished between primal repression (a 'mythical' forgetting of something that was never conscious to begin with, an originary 'psychical act' by which the unconscious is first constituted) and secondary repression (concrete acts of repression whereby some idea or perception that was once conscious is expelled from the conscious). Since repression does not destroy the ideas or memories that are its target, but merely confines them to the unconscious, the repressed material is always liable to return in a distorted form, in symptoms, dreams, slips of the tongue, etc. (the return of the repressed).

For Lacan, repression is the fundamental operation which distinguishes neurosis from the other clinical structures. Whereas psychotics *foreclose*, and perverts *disavow*, only neurotics *repress*.

What is it that is repressed? At one point Lacan speaks of the signified as the object of repression (E, 55), but he soon abandons this view and argues instead that it is always a signifier that is repressed, never a signified (S11, 218). This latter view seems to correspond more closely to Freud's view that what is repressed is not the 'affect' (which can only be displaced or transformed) but the 'ideational representative' of the drive.

Lacan also takes up Freud's distinction between primal repression and secondary repression:

1. Primal repression (Ger. *Urverdrängung*) is the alienation of desire when need is articulated in demand (E, 286). It is also the unconscious signifying chain (E, 314). Primary repression is the repression of the first signifier. 'From the moment he speaks, from that precise moment and not before, I understand that there is repression' (S20, 53). Lacan does not see primary repression as a specific psychical act, localisable in time, but as a structural feature of language itself – namely, its necessary incompleteness, the impossibility of ever saying 'the truth about truth' (Ec, 868).

2. Secondary repression (Ger. *Verdrängung*) is a specific psychical act by which a signifier is elided from the signifying chain. Secondary repression is structured like a metaphor, and always involves 'the return of the repressed', whereby the repressed signifier reappears under the guise of the various formations of the unconscious (i.e. symptoms, dreams, parapraxes, jokes, etc.). In secondary repression, repression and the return of the repressed 'are the same thing'.

resistance (*résistance*)   Freud first used the term 'resistance' to designate the unwillingness to recall repressed memories to consciousness. Since psychoanalytic treatment involves precisely such recollection, the term soon came to denote all those obstacles that arise during the treatment and interrupt its progress: 'Whatever disturbs the progress of the work is a resistance' (Freud, 1900a: SE V, 517). Resistance manifests itself in all the ways in which the subject breaks the 'fundamental rule' of saying everything that comes into his mind.

Though present in Freud's work from the beginning, the concept of resistance began to play an increasingly important part in psychoanalytic theory as a result of the decreasing efficacy of analytic treatment in the decade 1910–20 (see INTERPRETATION). As a consequence of this, ego-psychology placed increasing importance on overcoming the patient's resistances. Lacan is very critical of this shift in emphasis, arguing that it easily leads to an 'inquisitorial' style of psychoanalysis which sees resistance as based on the 'fundamental ill will' (S1, 30) of the patient. Lacan argues that this overlooks the structural nature of resistance and reduces analysis to an imaginary dual relation (see E, 78; Ec, 333ff). Lacan does accept that psychoanalytic treatment involves 'analysis of resistances', but only on condition that this phrase is understood correctly, in the sense of 'knowing at what level the answer should be pitched' (S2, 43). In other words, the crucial thing is that the analyst should be able to distinguish between interventions that are primarily orientated towards the imaginary and those that are orientated towards the symbolic, and know which are appropriate at each moment of the treatment.

In Lacan's view, resistance is not a question of the ill will of the analysand; resistance is structural, and it is inherent in the analytic process. This is due, ultimately, to a structural 'incompatibility between desire and speech' (E, 275). Therefore there is a certain irreducible level of resistance which can never be 'overcome'; 'after the reduction of the resistances, there is a residue which may be what is essential' (S2, 321). This irreducible 'residue' of resistance is 'essential' because it is the respect for this residue that distinguishes psychoanalysis from SUGGESTION. Psychoanalysis respects the right of the patient to resist suggestion and indeed values that resistance; 'When the subject's resistance opposes suggestion, it is only a desire to maintain the subject's desire. As such it would have to be placed in the ranks of positive transference' (E, 271).

However, Lacan points out that while the analyst cannot, and should not try to, overcome all resistance (S2, 228), he can minimise it, or at least avoid exacerbating it. He can do this by recognising his own part in the analysand's resistance, for 'there is no other resistance to analysis than that of the analyst himself' (E, 235). This is to be understood in two ways:

1. The resistance of the analysand can only succeed in obstructing the treatment when it responds to and/or evokes a resistance on the part of the analyst, i.e. when the analyst is drawn into the lure of resistance (as Freud was

drawn into the lure of Dora's resistance). 'The patient's resistance is always your own, and when a resistance succeeds it is because you [the analyst] are in it up to your neck, because you understand' (S3, 48). Thus the analyst must follow the rule of neutrality and not be drawn into the lures set for him by the patient.

2. It is the analyst who provokes resistance by pushing the analysand: 'There is no resistance on the part of the subject' (S2 228). '[R]esistance is the present state of an interpretation of the subject. It is the manner in which, at the same time, the subject interprets the point he's got to. . . . It simply means that he [the patient] cannot move any faster' (S2 228). Psychoanalytic treatment works on the principle that by not forcing the patient, resistance is reduced to the irreducible minimum. Thus the analyst must avoid all forms of suggestion.

The source of resistance lies in the ego: 'In the strict sense, the subject's resistance is linked to the register of the ego, it is an effect of the ego' (S2, 127). Thus resistance belongs to the imaginary order, not to the level of the subject; 'on the side of what is repressed, on the unconscious side of things, there is no resistance, there is only a tendency to repeat' (S2, 321). This is illustrated in SCHEMA L; resistance is the imaginary axis *a–a'* which impedes the insistant speech of the Other (which is the axis A–S). The resistances of the ego are imaginary lures, which the analyst must be wary of being deceived by (see E, 168). Thus it can never be the aim of analysis to 'strengthen the ego', as ego-psychology claims, since this would only serve to increase resistance.

Lacan also criticises ego-psychology for confusing the concept of resistance with that of DEFENCE. However, the distinction which Lacan draws between these two concepts is rather different from the way in which they are distinguished in Anglo-American psychoanalysis. Lacan argues that defence is on the side of the subject, whereas resistance is on the side of the object. That is, whereas defences are relatively stable symbolic structures of subjectivity, resistances are more transitory forces which prevent the object from being absorbed in the signifying chain.

S

sadism/masochism (*sadisme/masochisme*) The terms 'sadism' and 'masochism' were coined by Krafft-Ebing in 1893, with reference to the Marquis de Sade and Baron Sacher von Masoch. Krafft-Ebing used the terms in a very specific sense, to refer to a sexual PERVERSION in which sexual satisfaction is dependent upon inflicting pain on others (sadism) or upon experiencing pain oneself (masochism). When Freud took up the terms in his *Three Essays on the Theory of Sexuality*, he used them in the same sense as Krafft-Ebing (Freud, 1905d). Following Krafft-Ebing, Freud posited an intrinsic connection between sadism and masochism, arguing that they are simply the active and passive aspects of a single perversion.

Lacan too argues that sadism and masochism are intimately related, both being related to the invocatory drive (which he also calls the 'sado-masochistic drive'; S11, 183). Both the masochist and the sadist locate themselves as the object of the invocatory drive, the voice. However, whereas Freud argues that sadism is primary, Lacan argues that masochism is primary, and sadism is derived from it: 'sadism is merely the disavowal of masochism' (S11, 186). Thus, whereas the masochist prefers to experience the pain of existence in his own body, the sadist rejects this pain and forces the Other to bear it (Ec, 778).

Masochism occupies a special place among the perversions, just as the invoking drive occupies a privileged place among the partial drives; it is the 'limit-experience' in the attempt to go beyond the pleasure principle.

scene (*scène*) Freud borrowed the expression 'another scene' (*eine andere Schauplatz*) from G. T. Fechner, and used it in *The Interpretation of Dreams*, stating that 'the scene of action of dreams is different from that of waking ideational life' (Freud, 1900a: SE V, 535–6). This led Freud to formulate the idea of 'psychical locality'. However, Freud emphasised that this concept of locality is not to be confused with physical locality or anatomical locality, and Lacan takes this as a justification for his own use of TOPOLOGY (see E, 285). Lacan makes repeated reference to Fechner's expression in his work (e.g. E, 193); the 'other scene' is, in Lacanian terms, the Other.

Lacan also uses the term 'scene' to designate the imaginary and symbolic theatre in which the subject plays out his FANTASY, which is built on the edifice of the real (the world). The scene of fantasy is a virtual space which is framed, in the same way that the scene of a play is framed by the proscenium arch in a theatre, whereas the world is a real space which lies beyond the frame (Lacan, 1962–3: seminar of 19 December 1962). The notion of scene is used by Lacan to distinguish between ACTING OUT and PASSAGE TO THE ACT. The former still remains inside the scene, for it is still inscribed in the symbolic order. The passage to the act, however, is an exit from the scene, is a crossing over from the symbolic to the real; there is a total identification with the object (*objet petit a*), and hence an abolition of the subject (Lacan, 1962–3: seminar of 16 January 1963). The fantasy scene is also an important aspect in PERVERSION. The pervert typically stages his enjoyment in terms of some highly stylised scene, and according to a stereotypical script.

schema L (*schéma L*) The various 'schemata' that begin to appear in Lacan's work in the 1950s are all attempts to formalise by means of diagrams certain aspects of psychoanalytic theory. The schemata all consist of a number of points connected by a number of vectors. Each point in a schema is designated by one of the symbols of Lacanian ALGEBRA, while the vectors

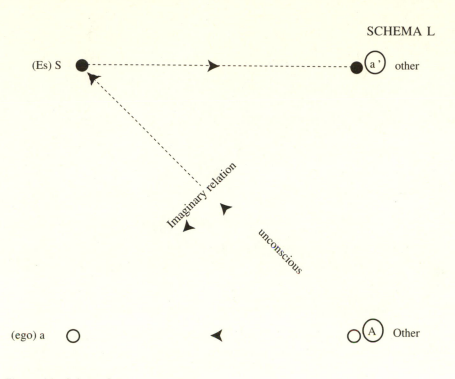

(Es) S ●- - - - - - - - - - - - -▶ - - - - - - - - - - - ●(a') other

Imaginary relation

unconscious

(ego) a ○   ◀   ○(A) Other

Figure 14   Schema L
Source: Jacques Lacan, *Écrits*, Paris: Seuil, 1966.

show the structural relations between these symbols. The schemata can be seen
as Lacan's first incursion into the field of TOPOLOGY.

The first schema to appear in Lacan's work is also the schema which he
makes the most use of. This schema is designated 'L' because it resembles the
upper-case Greek *lambda* (see Figure 14, taken from Ec, 53). Lacan first
introduces the schema in 1955 (S2, 243), and it occupies a central place in
his work for the next few years.

Two years later, Lacan replaces this version of the schema with a newer,
'simplified form' (Figure 15, taken from Ec, 548; see E, 193).

Although schema L allows many possible readings, the main point of the
schema is to demonstrate that the symbolic relation (between the Other and the
subject) is always blocked to a certain extent by the imaginary axis (between
the ego and the SPECULAR IMAGE). Because it has to pass through the imaginary
'wall of language', the discourse of the Other reaches the subject in an
interrupted and inverted form (see COMMUNICATION). The schema thus illustrates the opposition between the imaginary and the symbolic which is so
fundamental to Lacan's conception of psychoanalysis. This is of practical
importance in the treatment, since the analyst must usually intervene in the

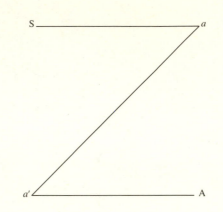

Figure 15   Schema L (simplified form)
Source: Jacques Lacan, *Écrits*, Paris: Seuil, 1966.

symbolic register rather than in the imaginary. Thus the schema also shows the position of the analyst in the treatment:

> If one wants to position the analyst within this schema of the subject's speech, one can say that he is somewhere in A. At least he should be. If he enters into the coupling of the resistance, which is just what he is taught not to do, then he speaks from *a'* and he will see himself in the subject.
>
> (S3, 161–2)

By positioning different elements in the four empty *loci* of the schema, schema L can be used to analyse various sets of relations encountered in psychoanalytic treatment. For example Lacan uses it to analyse the relations between Dora and the other people in her story (S4, 142–3; see Freud, 1905e), and also to analyse the relations between the various people in the case of the young homosexual woman (S4, 124–33; see Freud, 1920a).

In addition to providing a map of intersubjective relations, schema L also represents intrasubjective structure (insofar as the one can be distinguished from the other). Thus it illustrates the decentering of the subject, since the subject is not to be located only at the point marked S, but over the whole schema; 'he is stretched over the four corners of the schema' (E, 194).

In addition to schema L there are several other schemata that appear in Lacan's work (schema R – see E, 197; schema I – see E, 212; the two schemata of Sade – see Ec, 774 and Ec, 778). All of these schemata are transformations of the basic quaternary of schema L, on which they are based. However, unlike schema L, which serves as a constant point of reference for Lacan in the period 1954–7, each of these schemata only appears once in Lacan's work. By the time the last of these schemata (the schemata of Sade) appear, in 1962, the schemata have already ceased to play an important part in Lacan's discourse, although it can be argued that they lay the groundwork for Lacan's more rigorous topological work in the 1970s.

school (*école*)   When Lacan founded the École Freudienne de Paris (EFP) in 1964, after his resignation from the Société Française de Psychanalyse (SPP), he chose to call it a 'school' for precise reasons. Not only was it the first time that a psychoanalytic organisation had been called a 'school' rather than an 'association' or a 'society', but the term 'school' also highlighted the fact that the EFP was more a means of psychoanalytic formation centred around a doctrine than an institutional order centred around a group of important people. Thus the very use of the term 'school' in the name of the EFP indicated that it was an attempt to found a very different type of psycho-analytic institution from those which had been founded before. Lacan was particularly keen to avoid the dangers of the hierarchy dominating the institu-tion, which he saw in the INTERNATIONAL PSYCHO-ANALYTICAL ASSOCIATION (IPA), and which he blamed for the theoretical misunderstandings which had come to dominate the IPA; the IPA had become, he argued, a kind of church (S11, 4). However, it is also important to note that Lacan's criticisms of the IPA do not imply a criticism of the psychoanalytic institution *per se*; while Lacan is very critical of the dangers that beset all psychoanalytic institutions, the fact that he himself founded one is evidence that he thought that some kind of institutional framework was necessary for psychoanalysts. Thus Lacan is just as sceptical of those analysts who reject all institutions as he is of those who turn the institution into a kind of church.

Many of Lacan's ideas cannot be understood without some understanding of the history of the EFP (1964–80), especially those of Lacan's ideas which relate to the TRAINING of analysts. In this context it is important to note that the EFP was not merely a training institute, and that membership was not restricted to analysts/trainees, but was open to anyone with an interest in psychoanalysis. All members had equal voting rights, which meant that the EFP was the first truly democratic psychoanalytic organisation in history.

There were four categories of members in the EFP: M.E. (*Membre de l'École*, or simple member), A.P. (*Analyste Practiquant*), A.M.E. (*Analyste Membre de l'École*), and A.E. (*Analyste de l'École*). Members could, and often did, hold several titles simultaneously. Those who applied for membership of the school were interviewed by a committee called the *cardo* (a word meaning a hinge on which a door turns) before being admitted as an M.E.

Only the A.M.E. and the A.E. were recognised as analysts by the school, although other members were not forbidden to conduct analyses, and could award themselves the title of A.P. to indicate that they were practising analysts. The title of A.M.E. was granted to members of the school who satisfied a jury of senior members that they had conducted the analysis of two patients in a satisfactory manner; in this sense, the category of A.M.E, was similar to that of the titular members of other psychoanalytic societies. The title of A.E, was awarded on the basis of a very different procedure, which Lacan called the PASS. The pass was instituted by Lacan in 1967 as a means of verifying the end of analysis, and constitutes the most original feature of the EFP. Another original feature of the EFP was the promotion of research in small study groups known as CARTELS.

The final years of the EFP were dominated by intense controversy over the pass and other issues (see Roudinesco, 1986). In 1980, Lacan dissolved the EFP, and in 1981 he created a new institution in its stead, the École de la Cause Freudienne (ECF). Some of the original members of the EFP followed Lacan into the ECF, whereas others left to set up a variety of other groups. Some of these groups still exist today, as does the ECF.

science (*science*) Both Freud and Lacan use the term 'science' in the singular, thus implying that there is a specific unified, homogeneous kind of discourse that can be called 'scientific'. This discourse begins, according to Lacan, in the seventeenth century (Ec, 857), with the inauguration of modern physics (Ec, 855).

Freud regarded science (Ger. *Wissenschaft* – a term with markedly different connotations in German) as one of civilisation's highest achievements, and opposed it to the reactionary forces of RELIGION. Lacan's attitude to science is more ambiguous. On the one hand, he criticises modern science for ignoring the symbolic dimension of human existence and thus encouraging modern man 'to forget his subjectivity' (E, 70). He also compares modern science to a 'fully realised paranoia', in the sense that its totalising constructions resemble the architecture of a delusion (Ec, 874).

On the other hand, these criticisms are not levelled at science *per se*, but at the positivist model of science. Lacan implies that positivism is actually a deviation from 'true science', and his own model of science owes more to the rationalism of Koyré, Bachelard and Canguilhem than to empiricism. In other words, for Lacan, what marks a discourse as scientific is a high degree of mathematical formalisation. This is what lies behind Lacan's attempts to formalise psychoanalytic theory in terms of various mathematical formulae (see MATHEMATICS, ALGEBRA). These formulae also encapsulate a further characteristic of scientific discourse (perhaps the most fundamental one in Lacan's view), which is that it should be transmissible (Lacan, 1973a: 60).

Lacan argues that science is characterised by a particular relationship to TRUTH. On the one hand, it attempts (illegitimately, thinks Lacan) to monopolise truth as its exclusive property (Ec, 79); and, on the other hand (as Lacan later argues), science is in fact based on a foreclosure of the concept of truth as cause (Ec, 874).

Science is also characterised by a particular relationship to KNOWLEDGE (*savoir*), in that science is based on the exclusion of any access to knowledge by recourse to intuition and thus forces all the search for knowledge to follow only the path of reason (Ec, 831). The modern subject is the 'subject of science' in the sense that this exclusively rational route to knowledge is now a common presupposition. In stating that psychoanalysis operates only the subject of science (Ec, 858) Lacan is arguing that psychoanalysis is not based on any appeal to an ineffable experience or flash of intuition, but on a process of reasoned dialogue, even when reason confronts its limit in madness.

Although the distinction between the human sciences and the natural sciences had become quite well-established by the end of the nineteenth century (thanks to the work of Dilthey), it does not figure in Freud's work. Lacan, on the other hand, pays great attention to this distinction. However, rather than talking of the 'human sciences' (a term which Lacan dislikes intensely – see Ec, 859) and the 'natural sciences', Lacan prefers instead to talk of the 'conjectural sciences' (or sciences of subjectivity) and the 'exact sciences'. Whereas the exact sciences concern the field of phenomena in which there is no one who uses a signifier (S3, 186), the conjectural sciences are fundamentally different because they concern beings who inhabit the symbolic order. In 1965, however, Lacan problematises the distinction between conjectural and exact sciences:

> The opposition between the exact sciences and the conjectural sciences can no longer be sustained from the moment when conjecture is susceptible to an exact calculation (probability) and when exactitude is based only on a formalism which separates axioms and laws of grouping symbols.
>
> (Ec, 863)

Whereas in the last century physics provided a paradigm of exactitude for the exact sciences which made the conjectural sciences seem sloppy by comparison, the arrival on the scene of structural linguistics redressed the imbalance by providing an equally exact paradigm for the conjectural sciences. When Freud borrowed terms from other sciences, it was always from the natural sciences (principally BIOLOGY, medicine and thermodynamics) because these were the only sciences around in Freud's day that provided a model of rigorous investigation and thought. Lacan differs from Freud by importing concepts mainly from the 'sciences of subjectivity' (principally LINGUISTICS), and by aligning psychoanalytic theory with these rather than with the natural sciences. Lacan argues that this paradigm shift is in fact implicit in Freud's own reformulations of the concepts that he borrowed from the natural sciences. In other words, whenever Freud borrowed concepts from biology he reformulated those concepts so radically that he created a totally new paradigm which was quite alien to its biological origins. Thus, according to Lacan, Freud anticipated the findings of modern structural linguists such as Saussure, and his work can be better understood in the light of these linguistic concepts.

Is psychoanalysis a science? Freud was quite explicit in affirming the scientific status of psychoanalysis: 'While it was originally the name of a particular therapeutic method,' he wrote in 1924, 'it has now also become the name of a science – the science of unconscious mental processes' (Freud,

173

1925a: SE XX, 70). However, he also insisted on the unique character of psychoanalysis that sets it apart from the other sciences; 'Every science is based on observations and experiences arrived at through the medium of our psychical apparatus. But since our science has as its subject that apparatus itself, the analogy ends here' (Freud, 1940a: SE XXIII, 159).The question of the status of psychoanalysis and its relationship with other disciplines is also one to which Lacan devotes much attention. In his pre-war writings, psychoanalysis is seen unreservedly in scientific terms (e.g. Lacan, 1936). However, after 1950 Lacan's attitude to the question becomes much more complex.

In 1953, he states that in the opposition science versus ART, psychoanalysis can be located on the side of art, on condition that the term 'art' is understood in the sense in which it was used in the Middle Ages, when the 'liberal arts' included arithmetic, geometry, music and grammar (Lacan: 1953b: 224). However, in the opposition science versus religion, Lacan follows Freud in arguing that psychoanalysis has more in common with scientific discourse than religious discourse: 'psychoanalysis is not a religion. It proceeds from the same status as Science *itself*' (S11, 265).

If, as Lacan argues, a science is only constituted as such by isolating and defining its particular object of enquiry (see Lacan, 1946, where he argues that psychoanalysis has actually set psychology on a scientific footing by providing it with a proper object of enquiry – the imago – Ec, 188), then, when in 1965 he isolates the *objet petit a* as the object of psychoanalysis, he is in effect claiming a scientific status for psychoanalysis (Ec, 863).

However, from this point on Lacan comes increasingly to question this view of psychoanalysis as a science. In the same year he states that psychoanalysis is not a science but a 'practice' (*pratique*) with a 'scientific vocation' (Ec, 863), though in the same year he also speaks of 'the psychoanalytic science' (Ec, 876). By 1977 he has become more categorical:

> Psychoanalysis is not a science. It has no scientific status – it merely waits and hopes for it. Psychoanalysis is a delusion – a delusion which is expected to produce a science. . . . It is a scientific delusion, but this doesn't mean that analytic practice will ever produce a science.
>
> (Lacan, 1976–7; seminar of 11 January 1977; *Ornicar?*, 14: 4)

However, even when Lacan makes such statements, he never abandons the project of formalising psychoanalytic theory in linguistic and mathematical terms. Indeed, the tension between the scientific formalism of the MATHEME and the semantic profusion of *lalangue* constitutes one of the most interesting features of Lacan's later work.

semblance (*semblant*) Running throughout Lacan's work is the idea that appearances are deceptive, an idea that is closely connected to the classical philosophical opposition between appearance and essence (see S11, 103ff.). The very distinction between the imaginary and the symbolic implies this opposition between appearance and essence. The imaginary is the realm of observable phenomena which act as lures, while the symbolic is the realm of underlying structures which cannot be observed but which must be deduced.

This opposition informs all scientific enquiry, a basic presupposition of which is that the scientist must attempt to penetrate through false appearance into the hidden reality. Similarly, in psychoanalysis, as in science, 'only he who escapes from false appearances can achieve truth' (S7, 310). However, false appearance in psychoanalysis is different from false appearance in the natural sciences. For the natural scientist, the false appearance (e.g. a straight stick that appears to be bent when half submerged in water) lacks the dimension of deliberate deception, which is why Lacan states that the axiom of natural science is the belief in an honest, non-deceitful God (S3, 64). However, in the conjectural sciences, and in psychoanalysis, there is always the problem that the falsity of the appearance may be due to deception.

Lacan uses two terms to refer to false appearances. The term *apparence* is that used in philosophical discussions of the distinction between essence and appearance. The term *semblant* is less technical, but acquires a growing importance in Lacan's work over the years. It appears as early as 1957 (e.g. Ec, 435; S4, 207), and is used several times in the seminar of 1964 (S11, 107), but it is not until the early 1970s that the term comes to occupy an important place in Lacan's theoretical vocabulary. At first Lacan uses the term to refer to such issues as feminine sexuality, which is characterised by a dimension of masquerade (see Rivière, 1929). Later on, Lacan uses the term to characterise general features of the symbolic order and its relations to the imaginary and the real. Thus Lacan devotes his 1970–1 seminar to 'a discourse that would not be semblance', in which he argues that TRUTH is not simply the opposite of appearance, but is in fact continuous with it; truth and appearance are like the two sides of a moebius strip, which are in fact only one side. In the seminar of 1972–3, Lacan goes on to state that *objet petit a* is a 'semblance of being' (S20, 84), that love is addressed to a semblance (S20, 85), and that *jouissance* is only evoked or elaborated on the basis of a semblance (S20, 85).

seminar (*séminaire*)   In 1951, Lacan began to give private lectures in Sylvia Bataille's apartment at 3 rue de Lille. The lectures were attended by a small group of trainee psychoanalysts, and were based on readings of some of Freud's case histories: Dora, the Rat Man and the Wolf Man. In 1953, the venue of these lectures moved to the Hôpital Sainte-Anne, where a larger audience could be accommodated. Although Lacan sometimes refers to the private lectures of 1951–2 and 1952–3 as the first two years of his 'seminar', the term is now usually reserved for the public lectures which began in 1953. From that point on until his death in 1981, Lacan took a different theme each academic year and delivered a series of lectures on it. These twenty-seven annual series of lectures are usually referred to collectively as 'the seminar', in the singular.

After ten years at the Hôpital Sainte-Anne, the seminar moved to the École Normale Supérieure in 1964, and to the Faculté de Droit in 1973. These changes of venue were due to various reasons, not least of which was the need to accommodate the constantly growing audience as the seminar gradually became a focal point in the Parisian intellectual resurgence of the 1950s and 1960s.

Given Lacan's insistence that speech is the only medium of psychoanalysis (E, 40), it is perhaps appropriate that the original means by which Lacan developed and expounded his ideas should have been the spoken word. Indeed, as one commentator has remarked; 'It must be recalled that virtually all of Lacan's "writings" (*Écrits*) were originally oral presentations, that in many ways the open-ended Seminar was his preferred environment' (Macey, 1995: 77).

As Lacan's seminars became increasingly popular, demand grew for written transcripts of the seminar. However, apart from a few small articles that he wrote on the basis of some lectures delivered in the course of the seminar, Lacan never published any account of his own seminars. In 1956–9 Lacan authorised Jean-Bertrand Pontalis to publish a few summaries of sections of the seminar during those years, but this was not enough to satisfy the growing demand for written accounts of Lacan's teaching. Hence unauthorised transcripts of Lacan's seminar began increasingly to be circulated among his followers in an almost clandestine way. In 1973, Lacan allowed his son-in-law, Jacques-Alain Miller, to publish an edited transcript of the lectures given in 1964, the eleventh year of the seminar. Since then, Miller has continued to bring out edited versions of other years of the seminar, although the number published is still fewer than half. Miller's role in editing and publishing the seminar has led to some very heated arguments, with opponents claiming he has distorted Lacan's original. However, as Miller himself has pointed out, the transition from an oral to a written medium, and the editing required by this, means that these published versions of the seminar could never be simple transcripts of the lectures given by Lacan (see Miller, 1985). So far only nine of the yearly seminars have been published in book form, while authorised extracts from others have appeared in the journal *Ornicar?* Unauthorised transcripts of the unpublished years of the seminar continue to circulate today, both in France and abroad.

The titles of each year (or each 'book') of the seminar, are listed on p. 177. The original French titles and publication details are listed in the bibliography at the end of this dictionary.

Book	Year	Title
I	1953–4	Freud's papers on technique.
II	1954–5	The ego in Freud's theory and in the technique of psychoanalysis.
III	1955–6	The psychoses.
IV	1956–7	Object relations.
V	1957–8	The formations of the unconscious.
VI	1958–9	Desire and its interpretation.
VII	1959–60	The ethics of psychoanalysis.
VIII	1960–1	Transference.
IX	1961–2	Identification.
X	1962–3	Anxiety.
XI	1964	The four fundamental concepts of psychoanalysis.
XII	1964–5	Crucial problems for psychoanalysis.
XIII	1965–6	The object of psychoanalysis.
XIV	1966–7	The logic of fantasy.
XV	1967–8	The psychoanalytic act.
XVI	1968–9	From one other to the Other.
XVII	1969–70	The reverse of psychoanalysis.
XVIII	1970–1	On a discourse that would not be semblance.
XIX	1971–2	. . . Or worse.
XX	1972–3	*Encore*.
XXI	1973–4	The non-duped err/The names of the father.
XXII	1974–5	RSI.
XXIII	1975–6	The *sinthome*.
XXIV	1976–7	One knew that it was a mistaken moon on the wings of love.
XXV	1977–8	The moment of concluding.
XXVI	1978–9	Topology and time.
XVII	1980	Dissolution.

sexual difference   The phrase 'sexual difference', which has come into prominence in the debate between psychoanalysis and feminism, is not part of Freud's or Lacan's theoretical vocabulary. Freud speaks only of the anatomical *distinction* between the sexes and its psychical consequences (Freud, 1925d); Lacan speaks of sexual *position* and the sexual *relationship*, and occasionally of the *differentiation* of the sexes (S4, 153). However, both Freud and Lacan address the question of sexual difference, and an entry has been included for this term because it brings together an important set of related themes in Lacan's work, and because it constitutes an important focus for feminist approaches to Lacan's work (see Brennan, 1989; Gallop, 1982; Grosz, 1990; Mitchell and Rose, 1982).

One of the basic presuppositions underlying Freud's work is that just as there are certain physical differences between men and women, so also there are psychical differences. In other words, there are certain psychical characteristics that can be called 'masculine' and others that can be called 'feminine'. Rather than trying to give any formal definition of these terms (an impossible task – Freud, 1920a: SE XVIII, 171), Freud limits himself to describing how a human subject comes to acquire masculine or feminine psychical characteristics. This is not an instinctual or natural process, but a complex one in which anatomical differences interact with social and psychical factors. The whole process revolves around the CASTRATION COMPLEX, in which the boy fears being deprived of his penis and the girl, assuming that she has already been deprived of hers, develops penis envy.

Following Freud, Lacan also engages with the problem of how the human infant becomes a sexed subject. For Lacan, masculinity and femininity are not biological essences but symbolic positions, and the assumption of one of these two positions is fundamental to the construction of subjectivity; the subject is essentially a sexed subject. 'Man' and 'woman' are signifiers that stand for these two subjective positions (S20, 34).

For both Freud and Lacan, the child is at first ignorant of sexual difference and so cannot take up a sexual position. It is only when the child discovers sexual difference in the castration complex that he can begin to take up a sexual position. Both Freud and Lacan see this process of taking up a sexual position as closely connected with the OEDIPUS COMPLEX, but they differ on the precise nature of the connection. For Freud, the subject's sexual position is determined by the sex of the parent with whom the subject identifies in the Oedipus complex (if the subject identifies with the father, he takes up a masculine position; identification with the mother entails the assumption of a feminine position). For Lacan, however, the Oedipus complex always involves symbolic identification with the Father, and hence Oedipal identification cannot determine sexual position. According to Lacan, then, it is not identification but the subject's relationship with the PHALLUS which determines sexual position.

This relationship can either be one of 'having' or 'not having'; men have the symbolic phallus, and women don't (or, to be more precise, men are 'not

178

without having it' [*ils ne sont pas sans l'avoir*]). The assumption of a sexual position is fundamentally a symbolic act, and the difference between the sexes can only be conceived of on the symbolic plane (S4, 153):

> It is insofar as the function of man and woman is symbolized, it is insofar as it's literally uprooted from the domain of the imaginary and situated in the domain of the symbolic, that any normal, completed sexual position is realized.

(S3, 177)

However, there is no signifier of sexual difference as such which would permit the subject to fully symbolise the function of man and woman, and hence it is impossible to attain a fully 'normal, finished sexual position'. The subject's sexual identity is thus always a rather precarious matter, a source of perpetual self-questioning. The question of one's own sex ('Am I a man or a woman?') is the question which defines HYSTERIA. The mysterious 'other sex' is always the woman, for both men and women, and therefore the question of the hysteric ('What is a woman?') is the same for both male and female hysterics (S3, 178).

Although the anatomy/BIOLOGY of the subject plays a part in the question of which sexual position the subject will take up, it is a fundamental axiom in psychoanalytic theory that anatomy does not determine sexual position. There is a rupture between the biological aspect of sexual difference (for example at the level of the chromosomes) which is related to the reproductive function of sexuality, and the unconscious, in which this reproductive function is not represented. Given the non-representation of the reproductive function of sexuality in the unconscious, 'in the psyche there is nothing by which the subject may situate himself as a male or female being' (S11, 204). There is no signifier of sexual difference in the symbolic order. The only sexual signifier is the phallus, and there is no 'female' equivalent of this signifier: 'strictly speaking there is no symbolization of woman's sex as such . . . the phallus is a symbol to which there is no correspondent, no equivalent. It's a matter of a dissymmetry in the signifier' (S3, 176). Hence the phallus is 'the pivot which completes *in both sexes* the questioning of their sex by the castration complex' (E, 198).

It is this fundamental dissymmetry in the signifier which leads to the dissymmetry between the Oedipus complex in men and women. Whereas the male subject desires the parent of the other sex and identifies with the parent of the same sex, the female subject desires the parent of the same sex and 'is required to take the image of the other sex as the basis of its identification' (S3, 176). 'For a woman the realization of her sex is not accomplished in the Oedipus complex in a way symmetrical to that of the man's, not by identification with the mother, but on the contrary by identification with the paternal object, which assigns her an extra detour' (S3, 172). 'This signifying dissymmetry determines the paths down which the Oedipus complex will pass. The two paths make them both pass down the same trail – the trail of castration' (S3, 176).

If, then, there is no symbol for the opposition masculine–feminine as such, the only way to understand sexual difference is in terms of the opposition activity–passivity (S11, 192). This polarity is the only way in which the opposition male–female is represented in the psyche, since the biological function of sexuality (reproduction) is not represented (S11, 204). This is why the question of what one is to do as a man or a woman is a drama which is situated entirely in the field of the Other (S11, 204), which is to say that the subject can only realise his sexuality on the symbolic level (S3, 170).

In the seminar of 1970–1 Lacan tries to formalise his theory of sexual difference by means of formulae derived from symbolic logic. These reappear in the diagram of sexual difference which Lacan presents in the 1972–3 seminar (Figure16, taken from S20, 73). The diagram is divided into two sides: on the left, the male side, and on the right, the female side. The formulae of sexuation appear at the top of the diagram. Thus the formulae on the male side are $\exists x\overline{\Phi x}$ (= there is at least one x which is not submitted to the phallic function) and $\forall x\overline{\Phi x}$ (= for all x, the phallic function is valid). The formulae on the female side are $\overline{\exists x}\overline{\Phi x}$ (= there is not one x which is not submitted to the phallic function) and $\overline{\forall x}\Phi x$ (= for not all x, the phallic function is valid). The last formula illustrates the relationship of WOMAN to the logic of the not-all. What is most striking is that the two propositions on each side of the diagram seem to contradict each other: 'each side is defined by both an affirmation and a negation of the phallic function, an inclusion and exclusion of absolute (non-phallic) *jouissance*' (Copjec, 1994: 27). However, there is no symmetry between the two sides (no sexual relationship); each side

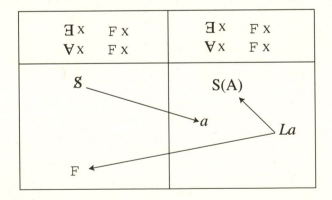

Figure 16 The diagram of sexual difference
Source: Jaques Lacan, *Le Séminaire. Livre XX. Encore*, ed. Jacques-Alain Miller, Paris: Seuil, 1975.

represents a radically different way in which the SEXUAL RELATIONSHIP can misfire (S20, 53–4).

sexual relationship (*rapport sexuel*) Lacan first proposes his famous formula: *il n'y a pas de rapport sexuel* in 1970 (see Lacan 1969–70: 134), and takes it up again in his seminar of 1972–3 (S20, 17). This formula is usually translated into English as 'There is no such thing as a sexual relationship', which is misleading since Lacan is certainly not denying that people have sex! The formula might be better rendered 'There is no relation between the sexes', thus emphasising that it is not primarily the act of sexual intercourse that Lacan is referring to but the question of the relation between the masculine sexual position and the feminine sexual position. The formula thus condenses a number of points in Lacan's approach to the question of SEXUAL DIFFERENCE:

1. There is no direct, unmediated relation between the male and female sexual position, because the Other of language stands between them as a third party (S20, 64). 'Between male and female human beings there is no such thing as an instinctive relationship' because all sexuality is marked by the signifier (Lacan, 1975b). One consequence of this is that it is not possible to define perversion by reference to a supposedly natural form of the sexual relationship (as Freud did). Heterosexuality is thus not natural but normative (Ec, 223).

2. There is no reciprocity or symmetry between the male and female positions because the symbolic order is fundamentally asymmetrical; there is no corresponding signifier which could signify woman in the same way that the male sex is symbolised. There is only one signifier, the PHALLUS, which governs the relations between the sexes (E, 289). There is thus no symbol for a symmetrical sexual relationship: 'the sexual relationship cannot be written' (S20, 35).

3. Relations between men and women can never be harmonious; 'The most naked rivalry between men and women is eternal' (S2, 263). Love is no more than an illusion designed to make up for the absence of harmonious relations between the sexes (whether presented in mythical terms, as in Plato's *Symposium*, or in psychoanalytic terms, as in Balint's concept of GENITAL love).

4. The sexual drives are directed not towards a 'whole person' but towards PART-OBJECTS. There is therefore no such thing as a sexual relationship between two subjects, only between a subject and a (partial) object. For the man, the object *a* occupies the place of the missing partner, which produces the matheme of fantasy ($\$ \Diamond a$); in other words, the woman does not exist for the man as a real subject, but only as a fantasy object, the cause of his desire (S20, 58).

5. Woman cannot function sexually *qua* woman but only *qua* mother; 'Woman begins to function in the sexual relationship only as mother' (S20, 36).

6. As something rooted in the real, sex is opposed to meaning; and 'sex, in

opposing itself to sense, is also, by definition, opposed to relation, to communication' (Copjec, 1994: 21).

shifter   The term 'shifter' was introduced into linguistics by Otto Jespersen in 1923 to refer to those elements in language whose general meaning cannot be defined without reference to the message. For example the pronouns 'I' and 'you', as well as words like 'here' and 'now', and the tenses, can only be understood by reference to the context in which they are uttered. Roman Jakobson developed the concept in an article published in 1957. Before this article, 'the peculiarity of the personal pronoun and other shifters was often believed to consist in the lack of a single, constant, general meaning' (Jakobson, 1957: 132). In terms of Peirce's typology of SIGNS, shifters were treated as pure indices (see INDEX). However, following Peirce's own argument (Peirce, 1932: 156–73), Jakobson argues that shifters *do* have a single general meaning; for example the personal pronoun *I* always means 'the person uttering *I*'. This makes the shifter a 'symbol'. Jakobson concludes that shifters combine both symbolic and indexical functions and 'belong therefore to the class of INDEXICAL SYMBOLS' (Jakobson, 1957: 132). In this way, Jakobson questions the possibility of a context-free grammar, since the ENUNCIATION is encoded in the statement itself. Also, since grammar is implicated in *parole*, the *langue/parole* distinction is also put into question (see Caton, 1987: 234–7).

Following Jakobson, Lacan uses the term 'shifter' (in English), or 'index-term' as he also calls it (E, 186), to show the problematic and undecidable nature of the *I (Je)*. However, while Jakobson (following Peirce) defines the shifter as an indexical symbol, Lacan defines it as an indexical signifier. This problematises the distinction between enunciation and statement. On the one hand, as a signifier it is clearly part of the statement. On the other hand, as an index it is clearly part of the enunciation. This division of the *I* is not merely illustrative of the splitting of the subject; it *is* that split. 'Indeed, the I of the enunciation is not the same as the I of the statement, that is to say, the shifter which, in the statement, designates him' (S11, 139). Lacan also identifies the French particle *ne* as a shifter (E, 298).

sign (*signe*)   Lacan defines the sign as that which 'represents something for someone', in opposition to the SIGNIFIER, which is 'that which represents a subject for another signifier' (S11, 207). By engaging with the concept of the sign, Lacan sets his work in close relation to the science of semiotics, which has grown rapidly in the twentieth century. Two main lines of development can be discerned within semiotics: the European line associated with Ferdinand de Saussure (which Saussure himself baptised with the name of 'semiology'), and the North American line associated with Charles S. Peirce.

1. According to Saussure, the sign is the basic unit of LANGUAGE (*langue*). The sign is constituted by two elements: a conceptual element (which Saussure

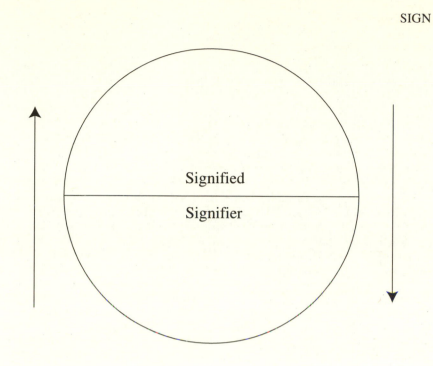

Figure 17   The Saussurean sign
Source: Ferdinand de Saussure, *Cours de linguistique générale*, 1916.

calls *the signified*), and a phonological element (called *the signifier*). The two elements are linked by an arbitrary but unbreakable bond. Saussure represented the sign by means of a diagram (Figure 17; see Saussure, 1916: 114).

In this diagram, the arrows represent the reciprocal implication inherent in signification, and the line between the signified and the signifier represents union.

Lacan takes up the Saussurean concept of the sign in his 'linguistic turn' in psychoanalysis during the 1950s, but subjects it to several modifications. Firstly, whereas Saussure posited the reciprocal implication between the signifier and the signified (they are as mutually interdependent as two sides of a sheet of paper), Lacan argues that the relation between signifier and signified is extremely unstable (see SLIP). Secondly, Lacan asserts the existence of an order of 'pure signifiers', where signifiers exist prior to signifieds; this order of purely logical structure is the unconscious. This amounts to a destruction of Saussure's concept of the sign; for Lacan, a language is not composed of signs but of signifiers.

To illustrate the contrast between his own views and those of Saussure,

SIGNIFICATION

$$\frac{S}{s}$$

Figure 18   The Saussurean algorithm
Source: Jacques Lacan, *Écrits*, Paris: Seuil, 1966.

Lacan replaces Saussure's diagram of the sign with an algorithm (Figure18) which, Lacan argues, should be attributed to Saussure (and is thus now sometimes referred to as the 'Saussurean algorithm' – see E, 149).

The S in Figure 18 stands for the signifier, and the *s* for the signified; the position of the signified and the signifier is thus inverted, showing the primacy of the signifier (which is capitalised, whereas the signifier is reduced to mere lower-case italic). The arrows and the circle are abolished, representing the absence of a stable or fixed relation between signifier and signified. The BAR between the signifier and the signified no longer represents union but the resistance inherent in signification. For Lacan, this algorithm defines 'the topography of the unconscious' (E, 163).

2. According to Peirce, the sign is something which represents an object to some interpretant (the term 'object' can mean, for Peirce, a physical thing, an event, an idea, or another sign). Peirce divides signs into three classes: 'symbols', 'indices' and 'icons', which differ in the way they relate to the object. The symbol has no 'natural' or necessary relationship to the object it refers to, but is related to the object by a purely conventional rule. The INDEX has an 'existential relation' to the object it represents (i.e. the index is always spatially or temporally contiguous to the object). The icon represents an object by exhibiting its form via similarity. Peirce's distinctions between icons, indices and symbols are analytical and not intended to be mutually exclusive. Hence a sign will almost always function in a variety of modes; personal pronouns, for example, are signs which function both symbolically and indexically (see Peirce, 1932: 156–73; Burks, 1949).

Lacan takes up Peirce's concept of the index in order to distinguish between the psychoanalytic and medical concepts of the symptom, and to distinguish between (animal) codes and (human) languages. Lacan also develops the concept of the index along the lines set down by Roman Jakobson in the concept of the SHIFTER, to distinguish between the subject of the statement and the subject of the enunciation.

signification (*signification*)   In Lacan's pre-1950 writings, the term 'signification' is used in a general way to connote both meaningfulness and importance (e.g. Ec, 81). In 1946, for example, Lacan criticises organicist psychiatry for ignoring 'the significations of madness' (Ec, 167; see Ec, 153–4). In the period 1953–7 the term retains these vague associations with the realm of meaning and language, and is thus located in the symbolic order (S4, 121).

184

It is from 1957 on that Lacan's use of the term takes on a direct reference to the Saussurean concept, and shifts from the symbolic to the imaginary order. Saussure reserves the term 'signification' for the relation between the SIGNIFIER and the SIGNIFIED; each sound-image is said to 'signify' a concept (Saussure, 1916: 114–17). Signification is, for Saussure, an unbreakable bond; the signifier and the signified are as inseparable as the two sides of a sheet of paper.

Lacan argues that the relationship between signifier and signified is far more precarious; he sees the BAR between them in the Saussurean algorithm (see Figure 18, p.184) as representing not a bond but a rupture, a 'resistance' to signification (E, 164). Firstly, the signifier is logically prior to the signified, which is merely an effect of the play of signifiers. Secondly, even when signifieds are produced, they constantly SLIP and slide underneath the signifier; the only things that detain this movement temporarily, pinning the signifier to the signified for a brief moment and creating the illusion of a stable meaning, are the *POINTS DE CAPITON*. Signification is, in Lacan's work, not a stable bond between signifier and signified, but a process – the process by which the play of signifiers produces the illusion of the signified via the two tropes of metonymy and metaphor.

Signification is metonymic because 'signification always refers to another signification' (S3, 33). In other words, meaning is not found in any one signifier, but in the play between signifiers along the signifying chain and is therefore unstable; 'it is in the chain of the signifier that the meaning insists, but none of its elements consists in the signification of which it is at the moment capable' (E, 153).

Signification is metaphoric because it involves the crossing of the bar, the 'passage of the signifier into the signified' (E, 164). The fundamental metaphor on which all signification depends is the paternal metaphor, and all signification is therefore phallic.

Signification is designated by the symbol s in Lacanian algebra (as in the notation $s(A)$ which labels one of the main nodes in the graph of desire). The notation for the signified is also s, which suggests that for Lacan the term 'signification' (the process by which the effect of meaning is produced) and the term 'signified' (the effect of meaning itself) tend to overlap.

In the late 1950s, Lacan establishes an opposition between signification and meaning (Fr. *sens*). The variety of ways in which these terms have been translated into English provides difficulty for the English reader of Lacan. This dictionary follows the practice of rendering the French *signification* by the English term 'signification', and reserves the English word 'meaning' to translate the French term *sens*.

Signification is imaginary and is the province of empty SPEECH; meaning is symbolic and is the province of full speech. (Later, in the 1970s, Lacan locates meaning not in the symbolic order but at the junction of the symbolic and the imaginary; see Figure 1.) Psychoanalytic interpretations go against signification and bear on meaning and its correlate, non-meaning (*non-sens*). Although signification and meaning are opposed, they are both related to the production of *jouissance*. Lacan indicates this by coining two neologisms: *signifiance* (from the words signification and *jouissance* – see E, 259; S20, 23), and *jouis-sens* (from *jouissance* and *sens*).

signified (*signifié*) According to Saussure, the signified is the conceptual element of the SIGN. It is not the real object denoted by a sign (the referent), but a psychological entity corresponding to such an object (Saussure, 1916: 66–7).

For Saussure, the signified has the same status as the SIGNIFIER; both form equal sides of the sign. Lacan, on the other hand, asserts the supremacy of the signifier, and argues that the signified is a mere effect of the play of signifiers, an effect of the process of signification produced by metaphor. In other words, the signified is not given, but produced.

Lacan's view is thus opposed to an expressionist view of language, according to which concepts exist in some pre-verbal state before being expressed in the material medium of language. In contrast to such a view, Lacan asserts the priority (logical rather than chronological) of the material element of language.

signifier (*signifiant*) Lacan takes the term 'signifier' from the work of the Swiss linguist, Ferdinand de Saussure. The term was not used by Freud, who was unaware of Saussure's work. According to Saussure, the signifier is the phonological element of the SIGN; not the actual sound itself, but the mental image of such a sound. In Saussure's terms, the signifier is the 'acoustic image' which signifies a SIGNIFIED (Saussure, 1916: 66–7).

Whereas Saussure argues that the signifier and the signified are mutually interdependent, Lacan states that the signifier is primary and produces the signified. The signifier is first of all a meaningless material element in a closed differential system; this 'signifier without the signified' is called by Lacan the 'pure signifier', though this is a question of logical rather than chronological precedence. 'Every real signifier is, as such, a signifier that signifies nothing. The more the signifier signifies nothing, the more indestructible it is' (S3, 185). It is these meaningless indestructible signifiers which determine the subject; the effects of the signifier on the subject constitute the unconscious, and hence also constitute the whole of the field of psychoanalysis.

Thus for Lacan language is not a system of signs (as it was for Saussure) but a system of signifiers. Signifiers are the basic units of language, and they are 'subjected to the double condition of being reducible to ultimate differential elements and of combining according to the laws of a closed order' (E, 152).

By the phrase 'reducible to ultimate differential elements', Lacan follows Saussure in asserting the fundamentally differential character of the signifier. Saussure states that in language there are no positive terms, only differences (Saussure, 1916: 120).

By the phrase 'combining according to the laws of a closed order', Lacan asserts that signifiers are combined in signifying chains according to the laws of metonymy.

The signifier is the constitutive unit of the symbolic order because it is integrally related with the concept of STRUCTURE; 'the notion of structure and that of signifier appear inseparable' (S3, 184). The field of the signifier is the field of the Other, which Lacan calls 'the battery of signifiers'.

Lacan defines a signifier as 'that which represents a subject for another signifier', in opposition to the sign, which 'represents something for someone'. (S11, 207). To be more precise, one signifier (called the master signifier, and written S_1) represents the subject for *all other signifiers* (written S_2). However, no signifier can *signify* the subject.

Although the term 'signifier' is absent from Freud's work, Lacan's use of the term focuses attention on a recurrent theme in Freud's writings. Freud's examples of psychoanalytic interpretations constantly focus on purely formal linguistic features. For example, he analyses his own failure to remember the name 'Signorelli' by dividing the word into formal segments and following the associative links with each segment (Freud, 1901: ch. 1). Thus Lacan's insistence that the analyst attend to the signifiers in the analysand's speech is not really an innovation in technique but an attempt to theorise Freud's own method in more rigorous terms.

While it is true that when Lacan talks about signifiers he is often referring to what others would call simply 'words', the two terms are not equivalent. Not only can units of language smaller than words (morphemes and phonemes) or larger than words (phrases and sentences) also function as signifiers, but so also can non-linguistic things such as objects, relationships and symptomatic acts (S4, 288). The single condition which characterises something as a signifier, for Lacan, is that it is inscribed in a system in which it takes on value purely by virtue of its difference from the other elements in the system. It is this differential nature of the signifier which means that it can never have a univocal or fixed meaning (S4, 289); on the contrary, its meaning varies according to the position which it occupies in the structure.

signifying chain (*chaîne signifiante, chaîne du signifiant*)

The term 'chain' is used increasingly by Lacan from the mid-1950s on, always in reference to the symbolic order. At first, in 1956, he speaks not of the signifying chain but of the *symbolic* chain, by which he denotes a line of descendence into which each subject is inscribed even before his birth and after his death, and which influences his destiny unconsciously (Ec, 468). In the same year he speaks of 'the chain of discourse' (S3, 261).

It is in 1957 that Lacan introduces the term 'signifying chain' to refer to a series of SIGNIFIERS which are linked together. A signifying chain can never be complete, since it is always possible to add another signifier to it, *ad infinitum*, in a way which expresses the eternal nature of desire; for this reason, desire is metonymic. The chain is also metonymic in the production of meaning; signification is not present at any one point in the chain, but rather meaning 'insists' in the movement from one signifier to another (see E, 153).

At times Lacan speaks of the signifying chain in linear metaphors, and at other times in circular metaphors;

● **Linearity** 'The linearity that Saussure holds to be constitutive of the chain of discourse applies to the chain of discourse only in the direction in which it is orientated in time' (E, 154).

● **Circularity** The signifying chain is compared to 'rings of a necklace that is a ring in another necklace made of rings' (E, 153).

On the one hand, the idea of linearity suggests that the signifying chain is the stream of speech, in which signifiers are combined in accordance with the laws of grammar (which Saussure calls 'syntagmatic' relationships, and Lacan, following Jakobson, locates on the metonymic axis of language). On the other hand, the idea of circularity suggests that the signifying chain is a series of signifiers linked by free associations, just one path through the network of signifiers which constitutes the symbolic world of the subject (which Saussure designates 'associative' relationships, and which Lacan, following Jakobson, locates on the metaphoric axis of language). In truth, the signifying chain is both of these things. In its diachronic dimension it is linear, syntagmatic, metonymic; in its synchronic dimension it is circular, associative, metaphoric. The two cross over: 'there is in effect no signifying chain [diachronic chain] that does not have, as if attached to the punctuation of each of its units, a whole articulation of relevant contexts [synchronic chains] suspended "vertically", as it were, from that point' (E, 154). Lacan thus combines in one concept the two types of relationship ('syntagmatic' and 'associative') which Saussure argued existed between signs, though for Lacan, the relationship is between signifiers, not signs.

sinthome The term *sinthome* is, as Lacan points out, an archaic way of writing what has more recently been spelt *symptôme*. Lacan introduces the term in 1975, as the title for the 1975–6 seminar, which is both a continuing elaboration of his topology, extending the previous seminar's focus on the BORROMEAN KNOT, and an exploration of the writings of James Joyce. Through this *coincidentia oppositorum* – bringing together mathematical theory and the intricate weave of the Joycean text – Lacan redefines the psychoanalytic symptom in terms of his final topology of the subject.

1. Before the appearance of *sinthome*, divergent currents in Lacan's thinking lead to different inflections of the concept of the SYMPTOM. As early as 1957, the symptom is said to be 'inscribed in a writing process' (Ec, 445), which already implies a different view to that which regards the symptom as a ciphered message. In 1963 Lacan goes on to state that the symptom, unlike

acting out, does not call for interpretation; in itself, it is not a call to the Other but a pure *jouissance* addressed to no one (Lacan, 1962–3: seminar of 23 January 1963; see Miller, 1987: 11). Such comments anticipate the radical transformation of Lacan's thought implicit in his shift from the linguistic definition of the symptom – as a signifier – to his statement, in the 1974–5 seminar, that 'the symptom can only be defined as the way in which each subject enjoys [*jouit*] the unconscious, in so far as the unconscious determines him' (Lacan, 1974–5: seminar of 18 February 1975).

This move from conceiving of the symptom as a message which can be deciphered by reference to the unconscious 'structured like a language', to seeing it as the trace of the particular modality of the subject's *jouissance*, culminates in the introduction of the term *sinthome*. The *sinthome* thus designates a signifying formulation beyond analysis, a kernel of enjoyment immune to the efficacy of the symbolic. Far from calling for some analytic 'dissolution', the *sinthome* is what 'allows one to live' by providing a unique organisation of *jouissance*. The task of analysis thus becomes, in one of Lacan's last definitions of the end of analysis, to identify with the *sinthome*.

2. The theoretical shift from linguistics to topology which marks the final period of Lacan's work constitutes the true status of the *sinthome* as unanalysable, and amounts to an exegetical problem beyond the familiar one of Lacan's dense rhetoric. The 1975–6 seminar extends the theory of the Borromean knot, which in the previous seminar had been proposed as the essential structure of the subject, by adding the *sinthome* as a fourth ring to the triad of the real, the symbolic and the imaginary, tying together a knot which constantly threatens to come undone. This knot is not offered as a model but as a rigorously non-metaphorical description of a topology 'before which the imagination fails' (Lacan, 1975–6: seminar of 9 December 1975). Since meaning (*sens*) is already figured within the knot, at the intersection of the symbolic and the imaginary (see Figure 1), it follows that the function of the *sinthome* – intervening to knot together real, symbolic and imaginary – is inevitably beyond meaning.

3. Lacan had been an enthusiastic reader of Joyce since his youth (see the references to Joyce in Ec, 25 and S20, 37). In the 1975–6 seminar, Joyce's writing is read as an extended *sinthome*, a fourth term whose addition to the Borromean knot of RSI allows the subject to cohere. Faced in his childhood by the radical non-function/absence (*carence*) of the Name-of-the-Father, Joyce managed to avoid psychosis by deploying his art as *suppléance*, as a supplementary cord in the subjective knot. Lacan focuses on Joyce's youthful 'epiphanies' (experiences of an almost hallucinatory intensity which were then recorded in enigmatic, fragmentary texts) as instances of 'radical foreclosure', in which 'the real forecloses meaning' (seminar of 16 March 1976). The Joycean text – from the epiphany to *Finnegan's Wake* – entailed a special relation to language; a 'destructive' refashioning of it as *sinthome*, the invasion

189

of the symbolic order by the subject's private *jouissance*. One of Lacan's puns, *synth-homme*, implies this kind of 'artificial' self-creation.

Lacan's engagement with Joyce's writing does not, he insists, entail 'applied psychoanalysis'. Topological theory is not conceived of as merely another kind of representational account, but as a form of writing, a praxis aiming to figure that which escapes the imaginary. To that extent, rather than a theoretical object or 'case', Joyce becomes an exemplary *saint homme* who, by refusing any imaginary solution, was able to invent a new way of using language to organise enjoyment.

(Author of this article: Luke Thurston)

slip (*glisser* [vb], *glissement* [n.])   Lacan uses the verb 'slip' (and its corresponding noun, 'slippage') to describe the unstable relationship between the signifier and the signified. The term thus emphasises the different ways in which Saussure and Lacan conceive of SIGNIFICATION; for Saussure, signification was a stable bond between signifier and signified, but for Lacan it is an unstable, fluid relationship. It is impossible to establish a stable one-to-one link between signifiers and signifieds, and Lacan symbolises this by inscribing a bar between them in the Saussurean algorithm (see Figure 18, p.184). The signified slips and slides under the bar of the Saussurean algorithm are in a continuous movement (E, 154), a movement which is only temporarily detained by the POINTS DE CAPITON. When there are not enough *points de capiton*, as is the case in PSYCHOSIS, the slippery movement of signification is endless, and stable meanings dissolve altogether.

specular image (*image spéculaire*)   When Lacan talks about *the* specular image, he is referring to the reflection of one's own body in the mirror, the image of oneself which is simultaneously oneself and OTHER (the 'little other'). It is by identifying with the specular image that the human baby first begins to construct his EGO in the MIRROR STAGE. Even when there is no real mirror, the baby sees its behaviour reflected in the imitative gestures of an adult or another child; these imitative gestures enable the other person to function as a specular image. The human being is completely captivated by the specular image: this is the basic reason for the power of the imaginary in the subject, and explains why man projects this image of his body onto all other objects in the world around him (see Lacan, 1975b; see CAPTATION).

There are certain things which have no specular image, which are not 'specularisable'. These are the phallus, the erogenous zones, and *objet petit a*.

speech (*parole*)   The French term *parole* presents considerable difficulty to the English translator because it does not correspond to any one English word. In some contexts it corresponds to the English term 'speech', and in others is best translated as 'word'.

Parole becomes one of the most important terms in Lacan's work from the early 1950s on. In his famous 'Rome discourse', Lacan denounces the way that the role of speech in psychoanalysis had come to be neglected by contemporary psychoanalytic theory, and argues for a renewed focus on speech and LANGUAGE (Lacan, 1953a). Lacan's use of the term *parole* owes little to Saussure (whose opposition between *parole* and *langue* is replaced in Lacan's work with the opposition between *parole* and *langage*), and is far more determined by references to anthropology, theology, and metaphysics.

● **Anthropology** Lacan's concept of speech as a 'symbolic exchange' which 'links human beings to each other' (S1, 142) is clearly influenced by the work of Mauss and Lévi-Strauss, especially their analysis of the exchange of gifts. Thus Freud's interpretations are described as 'a symbolic gift of speech, pregnant with a secret pact' (E, 79). The concept of speech as a pact which assigns roles to both the addressee and the addresser is formulated in Lacan's concept of FOUNDING SPEECH.

● **Theology** Speech also takes on religious and theological connotations in Lacan's work, in terms derived both from Eastern religions (E, 106–7) and the Judaeo–Christian tradition (E, 106). In 1954, Lacan discusses speech with reference to St Augustine's *De locutionis significatione* (S1, 247–60). Like the words uttered by God in *Genesis*, speech is a 'symbolic invocation' which creates, *ex nihilo*, 'a new order of being in the relations between men' (S1, 239).

● **Metaphysics** Lacan draws on Heidegger's distinction between *Rede* (discourse) and *Gerede* (chatter) to elaborate his own distinction between 'full speech' (*parole pleine*) and 'empty speech' (*parole vide*) (see E, 40ff.). Lacan first makes this distinction in 1953, and though it no longer plays an important part in his work after 1955, it never disappears completely. Full speech articulates the symbolic dimension of language, whereas empty speech articulates the imaginary dimension of language, the speech from the ego to the counterpart. 'Full speech is a speech full of meaning [*sens*]. Empty speech is a speech which has only signification' (Lacan, 1976–7; *Ornicar?*, nos 17/18: 11).

Full speech is also called 'true speech', since it is closer to the enigmatic truth of the subject's desire: 'Full speech is speech which aims at, which forms, the truth such as it becomes established in the recognition of one person by another. Full speech is speech which performs [*qui fait acte*]' (S1, 107). 'Full speech, in effect, is defined by its identity with that which it speaks about' (Ec, 381).

In empty speech, on the other hand, the subject is alienated from his desire; in empty speech 'the subject seems to be talking in vain about someone who . . . can never become one with the assumption of his desire' (E, 45).

One of the analyst's tasks when listening to the analysand is to discern the moments when full speech emerges. Full speech and empty speech are the extreme points on a continuum, and 'between these two extremes, a whole gamut of modes of realisation of speech is deployed' (S1, 50). The aim of psychoanalytic treatment is to articulate full speech, which is hard work; full speech can be quite laborious (*pénible*) to articulate (E, 253).

Empty speech is not the same as lying; on the contrary, lies often reveal the TRUTH about desire more fully than many honest statements (see S11, 139–40). It is never possible to articulate in speech the *whole* truth of one's desire, because of a fundamental 'incompatibility between desire and speech' (E, 275); 'I always tell the truth; not the whole truth, because we are not capable of telling it all. Telling it all is materially impossible' (Lacan, 1973a: 9). Full speech, then, is not the articulation in speech of the whole truth about the subject's desire, but the speech which articulates this truth as fully as possible at a particular time.

Speech is the only means of access to the truth about desire; 'speech alone is the key to that truth' (E, 172). Moreover, psychoanalytic theory claims that it is only a particular kind of speech that leads to this truth; a speech without conscious control, known as free association.

split (*refente*) Freud talks about the 'splitting of the ego' (Ger. *Ich-spaltung*, Fr. *clivage du moi*) as a process, observable in fetishism and psychosis, whereby two contradictory attitudes to reality come to exist side by side in the ego; those of acceptance and DISAVOWAL (see Freud, 1940b). Lacan amplifies the concept of *Spaltung* (which he prefers to translate by the term *refente*; see S8, 144) to designate not a process unique to fetishism or psychosis but a general characteristic of subjectity itself; the SUBJECT can never be anything other than divided, split, alienated from himself (see ALIENATION). The split is irreducible, can never be healed; there is no possibility of synthesis.

The split or divided subject is symbolised by the BAR which strikes through the S to produce the barred subject, $ (see E, 288). The split denotes the impossibility of the ideal of a fully present self-consciousness; the subject will never know himself completely, but will always be cut off from his own knowledge. It thus indicates the presence of the unconscious, and is an effect of the signifier. The subject is split by the very fact that he is a speaking being (E, 269), since speech divides the subject of the ENUNCIATION from the subject of the statement. In his seminar of 1964-5 Lacan theorises the split subject in terms of a division between truth and knowledge (*savoir*) (see Ec, 856).

structure (*structure*) When Lacan uses the term 'structure' in his early work of the 1930s, it is to refer to 'social structures', by which he means a specific set of affective relations between family members. The child perceives these relations much more profoundly than the adult, and internalises them in the COMPLEX (Ec, 89). The term serves as a peg upon which Lacan can hang his own views of the 'relational' nature of the psyche, in opposition to the atomistic theories then current in psychology (Lacan, 1936). From this point on, the term 'structure' retains this sense of something both intersubjective and intrasubjective, the internal representation of interpersonal relations. This remains a key point throughout Lacan's work, in which the emphasis on structure is a constant reminder that what determines the subject is not some supposed 'essence' but simply his position with respect to other subjects and other signifiers. Already in 1938, we find Lacan arguing that 'the most notable defect of analytic doctrine' at that time was that it tended 'to ignore structure in favour of a dynamic approach' (Lacan, 1938: 58). This anticipates his later emphasis on the symbolic order as the realm of structure which analysts have ignored in favour of the imaginary; 'social structures are symbolic' (Ec, 132).

In the mid-1950s, when Lacan begins to reformulate his ideas in terms borrowed from Saussurean structural linguistics, the term 'structure' comes to be increasingly associated with Saussure's model of LANGUAGE. Saussure analysed language (*la langue*) as a system in which there are no positive terms, only differences (Saussure, 1916: 120). It is this concept of a system in which each unit is constituted purely by virtue of its differences from the other units which comes to constitute the core meaning of the term 'structure' in Lacan's work from this point on. Language is the paradigmatic structure, and Lacan's famous dictum, 'the unconscious is structured like a language', is therefore tautologous, since 'to be structured' and 'to be like a language' mean the same thing.

Saussure's structural approach to linguistics was developed further by Roman Jakobson, who developed phoneme theory; Jakobson's work was then taken up by the French anthropologist, Claude Lévi-Strauss, who used the structural phonemic model to analyse non-linguistic cultural data such as kinship relations and myth. This application of structural analysis to anthropology launched the structuralist movement by showing how the Saussurean concept of structure could be applied to an object of enquiry other than language. Lacan was heavily influenced by all three of these thinkers, and in this sense he can be seen as part of the structuralist movement. However, Lacan prefers to dissociate himself from this movement, arguing that his approach differs in important ways from the structuralist approach (S20, 93).

Alongside the references to language, Lacan also refers the concept of structure to MATHEMATICS, principally to set theory and TOPOLOGY. In 1956, for example, he states that 'a structure is in the first place a group of elements forming a covariant set' (S3, 183). Two years later he again links the concept of structure with mathematical set theory, and adds a reference to topology (Ec, 648–9). By the 1970s, topology has replaced language as the principal paradigm of structure for Lacan. He now argues that topology is not a mere metaphor for structure; it is that structure itself (Lacan, 1973b).

The concept of structure is often taken to imply an opposition between surface and depth, between directly observable phenomena and 'deep structures' which are not the object of immediate experience. Such would seem to be the opposition implied in the distinction Lacan draws between SYMPTOMS (surface) and structures (depth). However, Lacan does not in fact agree that such an opposition is implicit in the concept of structure (Ec, 649). On the one hand, he rejects the concept of 'directly observable phenomena', arguing that observation is always already theoretical. On the other hand, he also rejects the idea that structures are somehow 'deep' or distant from experience, arguing that they are present in the field of experience itself; the unconscious is on the surface, and looking for it in 'the depths' is to miss it. As with many other binary oppositions, the model Lacan prefers is that of the moebius strip; just as the two sides of the strip are in fact continuous, so structure is continuous with phenomena.

The most important feature of structural analysis is not, then, any supposed distinction between surface and depth, but, as Lévi-Strauss shows in his structural analysis of myth, the discovery of fixed relations between *loci* which are themselves empty (Lévi-Strauss, 1955). In other words, whatever elements may be placed in the positions specified by a given structure, the relations between the positions themselves remain the same. Thus the elements interact not on the basis of any inherent or intrinsic properties they possess, but simply on the basis of the positions which they occupy in the structure.

In line with many other psychoanalysts, Lacan distinguishes three principal nosographic categories; NEUROSIS, PSYCHOSIS and PERVERSION. His originality lies in the fact that he regards these categories as structures rather than simply as collections of symptoms. (N.B. Lacan prefers to speak in terms of 'Freudian structures' rather than 'clinical structures', but the latter term is the one which predominates in the writings of Lacanian psychoanalysts today.)

Lacanian nosography is a categorical classification system based on a discrete series, rather than a dimensional system based on a continuum. The three major clinical structures are therefore mutually exclusive; a subject cannot be both neurotic *and* psychotic, for example. The three major clinical structures together constitute all the three possible positions of the subject in relation to the Other; every subject encountered in psychoanalytic treatment can therefore be diagnosed as either neurotic, or psychotic, or perverse. Each structure is distinguished by a different operation: neurosis by the operation of repression, perversion by the operation of disavowal, and psychosis by the operation of foreclosure. Lacan follows Freud in arguing that the classical method of psychoanalytic treatment (involving free association and the use of the couch) is only appropriate for neurotic subjects and perverse subjects, and not for psychotics. Thus when Lacanian analysts work with psychotic patients, they use a substantially modified method of treatment.

One of the most fundamental axioms of psychoanalysis is that the subject's clinical structure is determined by his experiences in the first years of life. In this sense, psychoanalysis is based on a 'critical period hypothesis'; the first years of life are the critical period in which the subject's structure is determined. Although it is not clear how long this critical period lasts, it is held that after this critical period the clinical structure is fixed for ever and cannot be changed. Neither psychoanalytic treatment nor anything else can, for example, turn a psychotic into a neurotic.Within each of the three major clinical structures Lacan distinguishes various subdivisions. For example within the clinical structure of neurosis, he distinguishes two kinds of neurosis (obsessional neurosis and hysteria), and within the clinical structure of psychosis he distinguishes between paranoia, schizophrenia and manic-depressive psychosis.

subject (*sujet*)   The term 'subject' is present from the very earliest of Lacan's psychoanalytic writings (see Lacan, 1932), and from 1945 on it occupies a central part in Lacan's work. This is a distinctive feature of Lacan's work, since the term does not constitute part of Freud's theoretical vocabulary, but is more associated with philosophical, legal and linguistic discourses.

In Lacan's pre-war papers, the term 'subject' seems to mean no more than 'human being' (see Ec, 75); the term is also used to refer to the analysand (Ec, 83).

In 1945, Lacan distinguishes between three kinds of subject. Firstly, there is the impersonal subject, independent of the other, the pure grammatical subject, the noetic subject, the 'it' of 'it is known that.' Secondly, there is the anonymous reciprocal subject who is completely equal to and substitutable for any other, and who recognises himself in equivalence with the other. Thirdly, there is the personal subject, whose uniqueness is constituted by an act of self-affirmation (Ec, 207–8). It is always this third sense of the subject, the subject in his uniqueness, that constitutes the focus of Lacan's work.

In 1953, Lacan establishes a distinction between the subject and the EGO which will remain one of the most fundamental distinctions throughout the rest of his work. Whereas the ego is part of the imaginary order, the subject is part of the symbolic. Thus the subject is not simply equivalent to a conscious sense of agency, which is a mere illusion produced by the ego, but to the unconscious; Lacan's 'subject' is the subject of the unconscious. Lacan argues that this distinction can be traced back to Freud: '[Freud] wrote *Das Ich und das Es* in order to maintain this fundamental distinction between the true subject of the unconscious and the ego as constituted in its nucleus by a series of alienating identifications' (E, 128). Although psychoanalytic treatment has powerful effects on the ego, it is the subject, and not the ego, on which psychoanalysis primarily operates.

Lacan plays on the various meanings of the term 'subject'. In linguistics and logic, the subject of a proposition is that about which something is predicated (see Lacan, 1967: 19), and is also opposed to the 'object'. Lacan plays on the philosophical nuances of the latter term to emphasise that his concept of the subject concerns those aspects of the human being that cannot (or must not) be objectified (reified, reduced to a thing), nor be studied in an 'objective' way.

'What do we call a subject? Quite precisely, what in the development of objectivation, is outside of the object' (S1, 194).

References to language come to dominate Lacan's concept of the subject from the mid-1950s on. He distinguishes the subject of the statement from the subject of the ENUNCIATION to show that because the subject is essentially a speaking being (*parlêtre*), he is inescapably divided, castrated, SPLIT. In the early 1960s Lacan defines the subject as that which is represented by a signifier for another signifier; in other words, the subject is an effect of language (Ec, 835).

Besides its place in linguistics and logic, the term 'subject' also has philosophical and legal connotations. In philosophical discourse, it denotes an individual self-consciousness, whereas in legal discourse, it denotes a person who is under the power of another (e.g. a person who is *subject to* the sovereign). The fact that the term possesses both these meanings means that it perfectly illustrates Lacan's thesis about the determination of consciousness by the symbolic order; 'the subject is a subject only by virtue of his subjection to the field of the Other' (S2, 188, translation modified). The term also functions in legal discourse to designate the support of action; the subject is one who can be held responsible for his ACTS.

The philosophical connotations of the term are particularly emphasised by Lacan, who links it with Descartes's philosophy of the COGITO:

> in the term *subject* . . . I am not designating the living substratum needed by this phenomenon of the subject, nor any sort of substance, nor any being possessing knowledge in his pathos . . . nor even some incarnated logos, but the Cartesian subject, who appears at the moment when doubt is recognised as certainty.
>
> (S11, 126)

The fact that the symbol of the subject, S, is a homophone of the Freud's term *Es* (see ID) illustrates that for Lacan, the true subject is the subject of the unconscious. In 1957 Lacan strikes through this symbol to produce the symbol $, the 'barred subject', thus illustrating the fact that the subject is essentially divided.

subject suppposed to know (*sujet supposé savoir*) The term *sujet supposé savoir* (often abbreviated to S.s.S.) is difficult to translate into English. Sheridan translates it as 'subject suppposed to know', and this is the translation adopted in most English works on Lacan. However, Schneiderman suggests the alternative translation 'supposed subject of knowledge', on the grounds that it is the subject, not just the knowledge, which is supposed (Schneiderman, 1980: vii).

The phrase is introduced by Lacan in 1961 in order to designate the illusion of a self-consciousness (Ger. *Selbstbewußtsein*) which is transparent to itself in its act of knowing (see CONSCIOUSNESS). This illusion, which is born in the mirror stage, is put into question by psychoanalysis. Psychoanalysis demonstrates that KNOWLEDGE (*savoir*) cannot be located in any particular subject but is, in fact, intersubjective (Lacan, 1961–2: seminar of 15 November 1961).

In 1964, Lacan takes up the phrase in his definition of TRANSFERENCE as the attribution of knowledge to a subject; 'As soon as the subject who is supposed to know exists somewhere there is transference' (S11, 232). This definition emphasises that it is the analysand's supposition of a subject who knows that initiates the analytic process, rather than the knowledge actually possessed by the analyst.

The term 'subject supposed to know' does not designate the analyst himself, but a function which the analyst may come to embody in the treatment. It is only when the analyst is perceived by the analysand to embody this function that the transference can be said to be established (S11, 233). When this occurs, what kind of knowledge is it that the analyst is presumed to possess? 'He is supposed to know that from which no one can escape, as soon as he formulates it – quite simply, signification' (S11, 253). In other words, the analyst is often thought to know the secret meaning of the analysand's words, the significations of speech of which even the speaker is unaware. This supposition alone (the supposition that the analyst is one who knows) causes otherwise insignificant details (chance gestures, ambiguous remarks) to acquire retroactively a special meaning for the patient who 'supposes'.

It may happen that the patient supposes the analyst to be a subject who knows from the very first moment of the treatment, or even before, but it often takes some time for the transference to become established. In the latter case, 'when the subject enters the analsysis, he is far from giving the analyst this place [of the subject supposed to know]' (S11, 233); the analysand may initially regard the analyst as a buffoon, or may withold information from him in order to maintain his ignorance (S11, 137). However, 'even the psychoanalyst put in question is credited at some point with a certain infallibility' (S11, 234); sooner or later some chance gesture of the analyst's is taken by the analysand as a sign of some secret intention, some hidden knowledge. At this point the analyst has come to embody the subject supposed to know; the transference is established.

The end of analysis comes when the analysand de-supposes the analyst of knowledge, so that the analyst falls from the position of the subject supposed to know.

The term 'subject supposed to know' also emphasises the fact that it is a particular relationship to knowledge that constitutes the unique position of the analyst; the analyst is aware that there is a split between him and the knowledge attributed to him. In other words, the analyst must realise that he only occupies the position of one who is presumed (by the analysand) to know, without fooling himself that he really does possess the knowledge attributed to him. The analyst must realise that, of the knowledge attributed to him by the analysand, he knows nothing (Lacan, 1967: 20). However, the fact that it is a supposed knowledge that is the mainstay of the analytic process, rather than the knowledge actually possessed by the analyst, does not mean that the analyst can therefore be content with knowing nothing; on the contrary, Lacan argues that analysts should emulate Freud in becoming experts in cultural, literary and linguistic matters.

Lacan also remarks that, for the analyst, the analysand is a subject supposed to know. When the analyst explains the fundamental rule of free association to the analysand, he is effectively saying; 'Come on, say anything, it will all be marvellous' (S17, 59). In other words, the analyst tells the analysand to behave as if he knew what it was all about, thereby instituting him as a subject supposed to know.

sublimation (*sublimation*)   In Freud's work, sublimation is a process in which the libido is channelled into apparently non-sexual activities such as artistic creation and intellectual work. Sublimation thus functions as a socially acceptable escape valve for excess sexual energy which would otherwise have to be discharged in socially unacceptable forms (perverse behaviour) or in neurotic symptoms. The logical conclusion of such a view is that complete sublimation would mean the end of all perversion and all neurosis. However, many points remain unclear in Freud's account of sublimation.

Lacan takes up the concept of sublimation in his seminar of 1959–60. He follows Freud in emphasising the fact that the element of social recognition is central to the concept, since it is only insofar as the drives are diverted towards socially valued objects that they can be said to be sublimated (S7, 107). It is this dimension of shared social values which allows Lacan to tie in the concept of sublimation with his discussion of ethics (see S7, 144). However, Lacan's account of sublimation also differs from Freud's on a number of points.

1. Freud's account implies that perverse sexuality as a form of direct satisfaction of the drive is possible, and that sublimation is only necessary because this direct form is prohibited by society. Lacan however rejects the concept of a zero degree of satisfaction (see Žižek, 1991: 83–4), arguing that perversion not simply a brute natural means of discharging the libido, but a highly structured relation to the drives which are already, in themselves, linguistic rather than biological forces.

2. Whereas Freud believed that complete sublimation might be possible for some particularly refined or cultured people, Lacan argues that 'complete sublimation is not possible for the individual' (S7, 91).

3. In Freud's account, sublimation involves the redirection of the drive to a different (non-sexual) object. In Lacan's account, however, what changes is not the object but its position in the structure of fantasy. In other words, sublimation does not involve directing the drive to a different object, but rather changing the nature of the object to which the drive was already directed, a 'change of object in itself', something which is made possible

198

because the drive is 'already deeply marked by the articulation of the signifier' (S7, 293). The sublime quality of an object is thus not due to any intrinsic property of the object itself, but simply an effect of the object's position in the symbolic structure of fantasy. To be more specific, sublimation relocates an object in the position of the THING. The Lacanian formula for sublimation is thus that 'it raises an object . . . to the dignity of the Thing' (S7, 112).

4. While Lacan follows Freud in linking sublimation with creativity and ART, he complicates this by also linking it with the DEATH DRIVE (S4, 431). Several reasons can be adduced to explain this. Firstly, the concept of the death drive is itself seen as a product of Freud's own sublimation (S7, 212). Secondly, the death drive is not only a 'destruction drive', but also 'a will to create from zero' (S7, 212–13). Thirdly, the sublime object, through being elevated to the dignity of the Thing, exerts a power of fascination which leads ultimately to death and destruction.

suggestion (*suggestion*)   In nineteenth-century French psychiatry, the term 'suggestion' referred to the use of hypnosis to remove neurotic symptoms; while the patient was in a state of hypnosis, the doctor would 'suggest' that the symptoms would disappear. Taking his cue from the French psychiatrists Charcot and Bernheim, Freud began using suggestion to treat neurotic patients in the 1880s. However, he became increasingly dissatisfied with suggestion, and thus came to abandon hypnosis and develop psycho-analysis. The reasons for Freud's dissatisfaction with hypnosis are hence fundamental for understanding the specific nature of psychoanalysis. How-ever, it is beyond the scope of this article to enter into a detailed discussion of these reasons. Suffice it to say that in Freud's later work the term 'suggestion' comes to represent a whole set of ideas which Freud associates with hypnosis and which is thus diametrically opposed to psychoanalysis.

Following Freud, Lacan uses the term 'suggestion' to designate a whole range of deviations from true psychoanalysis (deviations which Lacan also refers to as 'psychotherapy'), of which the following are perhaps the most salient:

1. Suggestion includes the idea of directing the patient towards some ideal or some moral value (see ETHICS). In opposition to this, Lacan reminds analysts that their task is to direct the treatment, not the patient (E, 227). Lacan is opposed to any conception of psychoanalysis as a normative process of social influence.

2. Suggestion also arises when the patient's RESISTANCE is seen as something that must be liquidated by the analyst. Such a view is completely foreign to psychoanalysis, argues Lacan, since the analyst recognises that a certain residue of resistance is inherent in the structure of the treatment.

3. In suggestion, the interpretations of the therapist are orientated around signification, whereas the analyst orientates his interpretations around meaning (*sens*) and its correlate, nonsense. Thus whereas in psychotherapy there is an

attempt to avoid the ambiguity and equivocation of discourse, it is precisely this ambiguity which psychoanalysis thrives on.

Suggestion has a close relation with TRANSFERENCE (E, 270). If transference involves the analysand attributing knowledge to the analyst, suggestion refers to a particular way of responding to this attribution. Lacan argues that the analyst must realise that he only occupies the position of one who is presumed (by the analysand) to know, without fooling himself that he really does possess the knowledge attributed to him. In this way, the analyst is able to transform the transference into 'an analysis of suggestion' (E, 271). Suggestion, on the other hand, arises when the analyst assumes the position of one who really *does* know.

Like Freud, Lacan sees hypnosis as the model of suggestion. In *Group Psychology and the Analysis of the Ego*, Freud shows how hypnotism makes the object converge with the ego-ideal (Freud, 1921). To put this in Lacanian terms, hypnotism involves the convergence of the object *a* and the I. Psychoanalysis involves exactly the opposite, since 'the fundamental mainspring of the analytic operation is the maintenance of the distance between I – identification – and the *a*' (S11, 273).

superego (*surmoi*)   The term 'superego' does not appear until quite late in Freud's work, being first introduced in *The Ego and the Id* (Freud, 1923b). It was in this work that Freud introduced his so-called 'structural model', in which the psyche is divided into three agencies; the EGO, the ID and the superego. However, the concept of a moral agency which judges and censures the ego can be found in Freud's work long before he locates these functions in the superego, such as in his concept of censorship.

Lacan's first discussion of the superego comes in his article on the family (Lacan, 1938). In this work he distinguishes clearly between the superego and the EGO-IDEAL, terms which Freud seems to use interchangeably in *The Ego and the Id*. He argues that the primary function of the superego is to repress sexual desire for the mother in the resolution of the Oedipus complex. Following Freud, he argues that the superego results from Oedipal identification with the father, but he also refers to Melanie Klein's thesis on the maternal origins of an archaic form of the superego (Lacan, 1938: 59–60).

When Lacan returns to the subject of the superego in his 1953–4 seminar, he locates it in the symbolic order, as opposed to the imaginary order of the ego: 'the superego is essentially located within the symbolic plane of speech' (S1, 102). The superego has a close relationship with the Law, but this relationship is a paradoxical one. On the one hand, the Law as such is a symbolic structure which regulates subjectivity and in this sense prevents disintegration. On the other hand, the law of the superego has a 'senseless, blind character, of pure imperativeness and simple tyranny' (S1, 102). Thus 'the superego is at one and the same time the law and its destruction' (S1, 102). The superego arises from the misunderstanding of the law, from the gaps in the symbolic chain, and fills out those gaps with an imaginary substitute that distorts the law (see E, 143; see Lacan's almost identical remarks on the censorship: 'Censorship is always related to whatever, in discourse, is linked to the law in so far as it is not understood' – S2, 127).

More specifically, in linguistic terms, 'the superego is an imperative' (S1, 102). In 1962, Lacan argues that this is none other than the Kantian categorical imperative. The specific imperative involved is the command 'Enjoy!'; the superego is the Other insofar as the Other commands the subject to enjoy. The superego is thus the expression of the will-to-enjoy (*volonté de jouissance*), which is not the subject's own will but the will of the Other, who assumes the form of Sade's 'Supreme Being-in-Evil' (Ec, 773). The superego is an 'obscene, ferocious Figure' (E, 256) which imposes 'a senseless, destructive, purely oppressive, almost always anti-legal morality' on the neurotic subject (S1, 102). The superego is related to the voice, and thus to the invoking drive and to SADISM/MASOCHISM.

symbolic (*symbolique*)   The term 'symbolic' appears in adjectival form in Lacan's earliest psychoanalytic writings (e.g. Lacan, 1936). In these early works the term implies references to symbolic logic and to the equations used in mathematical physics (Ec, 79). In 1948 symptoms are said to have a 'symbolic meaning' (E, 10). By 1950, the term has acquired anthropological overtones, as when Lacan praises Marcel Mauss for having shown that 'the structures of society are symbolic' (Ec, 132).

These different nuances are combined into a single category in 1953 when Lacan begins to use the term 'symbolic' as a noun. It now becomes one of the three ORDERS that remain central throughout the rest of Lacan's work. Of these three orders, the symbolic is the most crucial one for psychoanalysis; psychoanalysts are essentially 'practitioners of the symbolic function' (E, 72). In speaking of 'the symbolic function', Lacan makes it clear that his concept of the symbolic order owes much to the anthropological work of Claude Lévi-Strauss (from whom the phrase 'symbolic function' is taken; see Lévi-Strauss, 1949a: 203). In particular, Lacan takes from Lévi-Strauss the idea that the social world is structured by certain laws which regulate kinship relations and the exchange of gifts (see also Mauss, 1923). The concept of the gift, and that of a circuit of exchange, are thus fundamental to Lacan's concept of the symbolic (S4, 153–4, 182).

Since the most basic form of exchange is communication itself (the exchange of words, the gift of speech; S4, 189), and since the concepts of LAW and of STRUCTURE are unthinkable without LANGUAGE, the symbolic is essentially a linguistic dimension. Any aspect of the psychoanalytic experience which has a linguistic structure thus pertains to the symbolic order.

However, Lacan does not simply equate the symbolic order with language. On the contrary, language involves imaginary and real dimensions in addition to its symbolic dimension. The symbolic dimension of language is that of the

SIGNIFIER; a dimension in which elements have no positive existence but which are constituted purely by virtue of their mutual differences.

The symbolic is also the realm of radical alterity which Lacan refers to as the OTHER. The UNCONSCIOUS is the discourse of this Other, and thus belongs wholly to the symbolic order. The symbolic is the realm of the Law which regulates desire in the Oedipus complex. It is the realm of culture as opposed to the imaginary order of nature. Whereas the imaginary is characterised by dual relations, the symbolic is characterised by triadic structures, because the intersubjective relationship is always 'mediated' by a third term, the big Other. The symbolic order is also the realm of DEATH, of ABSENCE and of LACK. The symbolic is both the PLEASURE PRINCIPLE which regulates the distance from the Thing, and the DEATH DRIVE which goes 'beyond the pleasure principle' by means of repetition (S2, 210); in fact, 'the death drive is only the mask of the symbolic order' (S2, 326).

The symbolic order is completely autonomous: it is not a superstructure determined by biology or genetics. It is completely contingent with respect to the real: 'There is no biological reason, and in particular no genetic one, to account for exogamy. In the human order we are dealing with the complete emergence of a new function, encompassing the whole order in its entirety' (S2, 29). Thus while the symbolic may *seem* to 'spring from the real' as pre-given, this is an illusion, and 'one shouldn't think that symbols actually have come from the real' (S2, 238).

The totalising, all-encompassing effect of the symbolic order leads Lacan to speak of the symbolic as a universe: 'In the symbolic order the totality is called a universe. The symbolic order from the first takes on its universal character. It isn't constituted bit by bit. As soon as the symbol arrives, there is a universe of symbols' (S2, 29). There is therefore no question of a gradual continuous transition from the imaginary to the symbolic; they are completely heterogeneous domains. Once the symbolic order has arisen, it creates the sense that it has always been there, since 'we find it absolutely impossible to speculate on what preceded it other than by symbols' (S2, 5). For this reason it is strictly speaking impossible to conceive the origin of language, let alone what came before, which is why questions of development lie outside the field of psychoanalysis.

Lacan criticises the psychoanalysis of his day for forgetting the symbolic order and reducing everything to the imaginary. This is, for Lacan, nothing less than a betrayal of Freud's most basic insights; 'Freud's discovery is that of the field of the effects, in the nature of man, produced by his relation to the symbolic order. To ignore this symbolic order is condemn the discovery to oblivion' (E, 64).

Lacan argues that it is only by working in the symbolic order that the analyst can produce changes in the subjective position of the analysand; these changes will also produce imaginary effects, since the imaginary is structured by the symbolic. It is the symbolic order which is determinant of subjectivity, and the imaginary realm of images and appearances are merely effects of the symbolic. Psychoanalysis must therefore penetrate beyond the imaginary and work in the symbolic order.

Lacan's concept of the symbolic is diametrically opposed to Freud's 'symbolism'. For Freud, the symbol was a relatively fixed bi-univocal relation between meaning and form which corresponds more to the Lacanian concept of the INDEX (see Freud 1900a: SE V, ch. 6, sect. E, on symbolism in dreams). For Lacan, however, the symbolic is characterised precisely by the absence of any fixed relations between signifier and signified.

symptom (*symptôme*) In medicine, symptoms are the perceptible manifestations of an underlying illness that might otherwise remain undetected. The concept of the symptom is thus predicated on a basic distinction between surface and depth, between phenomena (objects which can be directly experienced) and the hidden causes of those phenomena which cannot be experienced but must be inferred. A similar distinction operates in Lacan's work, in which symptoms are always distinguished from STRUCTURES. This distinction has the advantage of transcending the opposition between surface and depth, since structures are held to be just as much 'on the surface' as the symptoms themselves. It is the clinical structure of the patient (neurosis, psychosis or perversion) which constitutes the real focus of psychoanalysis, and not his symptoms, and thus the END OF ANALYSIS must be conceived of in structural terms rather than in terms of curing symptoms.

In Lacan's work the term 'symptom' usually refers to *neurotic* symptoms, that is, to the perceptible manifestations of neurosis, and not to manifestations of the other clinical structures (but see E, 281 for an exception). Hence the manifestations of psychosis, such as hallucinations and delusions, are not usually referred to as symptoms but as *phenomena*, whereas perversion manifests itself in perverse *acts*. The aim of Lacanian psychoanalysis is not the removal of neurotic symptoms, since when one neurotic symptom disappears it is often simply replaced by another. This is what distinguishes psychoanalysis from any form of therapy.

Lacan follows Freud in affirming that neurotic symptoms are formations of the unconscious, and that they are always a compromise between two conflicting desires. Lacan's originality lies in his understanding of neurotic symptoms in linguistic terms: 'The symptom resolves itself entirely in an analysis of language, because the symptom is itself structured like a language' (E, 59).

Over the course of his work, Lacan identifies the symptom with different features of language:

1. In 1953 he argues that the symptom is a SIGNIFIER (E, 59). This distinguishes the psychoanalytic concept of the symptom from the medical

approach, in that the latter regards the symptom not as a signifier but as an INDEX (E, 129; see S2, 320). One consequence of this distinction is that, as far as psychoanalytic theory is concerned, there is no universal meaning for a neurotic symptom, since each symptom is a product of a particular subject's unique history. Despite their apparent similarities, all neurotic symptoms are unique. Another consequence is that there is no fixed one-to-one link between neurotic symptoms and the underlying neurotic structure; no neurotic symptom is in itself hysterical or obsessional. This means that whereas a doctor can arrive at a diagnosis on the basis of the symptoms presented by the patient, a Lacanian analyst cannot determine whether a neurotic patient is a hysteric or an obsessional simply on the basis of his symptoms. For example the analyst will not diagnose a patient as obsessional simply because the patient presents typical obsessional symptoms (ritual actions, compulsive behaviour, etc.). Conversely, the analyst may well attribute an obsessional structure to a patient who does not present any of the typical symptoms of obsessional neurosis. The Lacanian analyst can only arrive at a diagnosis of hysteria or obsessional neurosis by identifying the fundamental question that animates the neurotic's speech.

2. In 1955, Lacan identifies the symptom with SIGNIFICATION: 'The symptom is in itself, through and through, signification, that is to say, truth, truth taking shape' (S2, 320).

3. In 1957, the symptom is described as a METAPHOR, 'the symptom being a metaphor in which flesh or function is taken as a signifying element' (E, 166). Lacan means this description to be taken literally: 'if the symptom is a metaphor, it is not a metaphor to say so' (E, 175).

4. In the GRAPH OF DESIRE, which first appears in the seminar of 1957–8, the symptom is described as a message. In 1961, Lacan goes on to say that the symptom is an enigmatic message which the subject thinks is an opaque message from the real instead of recognising it as his own message (S8, 149).

From 1962 on, there is a gradual tendency in Lacan's work away from the linguistic conception of the symptom, and towards a view of the symptom as pure *jouissance* which cannot be interpreted. This conceptual shift culminates in 1975 with the introduction of the term SINTHOME.

T

Thing (*chose*)   Lacan's discussion of 'the Thing' constitutes one of the central themes in the seminar of 1959–60, where he uses the French term *la chose* interchangeably with the German term *das Ding*. There are two main contexts in which this term operates.

1. The context of Freud's distinction between 'word-presentations' (*Wortvorstellungen*) and 'thing-presentations' (*Sachvorstellungen*). This distinction is prominent in Freud's metapsychological writings, in which he argues that

the two types of presentation are bound together in the preconscious–conscious system, whereas in the unconscious system only thing-presentations are found (Freud, 1915e). This seemed to some of Lacan's contemporaries to offer an objection to Lacan's theories about the linguistic nature of the unconscious. Lacan counters such objections by pointing out that there are two words in German for 'thing': *das Ding* and *die Sache* (see S7, 62–3, 44–5). It is the latter term which Freud usually employs to refer to the thing-presentations in the unconscious, and Lacan argues that although on one level *Sachvorstellungen* and *Wortvorstellungen* are opposed, on the symbolic level 'they go together'. Thus *die Sache* is the representation of a thing in the symbolic order, as opposed to *das Ding*, which is the thing in its 'dumb reality' (S7, 55), the thing in the real, which is 'the beyond-of-the-signified' (S7, 54). The thing-presentations found in the unconscious are thus still linguistic phenomena, as opposed to *das Ding*, which is entirely outside language, and outside the unconscious. 'The Thing is characterised by the fact that it is impossible for us to imagine it' (S7, 125). Lacan's concept of the Thing as an unknowable *x*, beyond symbolisation, has clear affinities with the Kantian 'thing-in-itself'.

2. The context of JOUISSANCE. As well as the object of language, *das Ding* is the object of desire. It is the lost object which must be continually refound, it is the prehistoric, unforgettable Other (S7, 53) – in other words, the forbidden object of incestuous desire, the mother (S7, 67). The pleasure principle is the law which maintains the subject at a certain distance from the Thing (S7, 58, 63), making the subject circle round it without ever attaining it (S7, 95). The Thing is thus presented to the subject as his Sovereign Good, but if the subject transgresses the pleasure principle and attains this Good, it is experienced as suffering/evil (Lacan plays on the French term *mal*, which can mean both suffering and evil, see S7, 179), because the subject 'cannot stand the extreme good that *das Ding* may bring to him' (S7, 73). It is fortunate, then, that the Thing is usually inaccessible (S7, 159).

After the seminar of 1959–60, the term *das Ding* disappears almost entirely from Lacan's work. However, the ideas associated with it provide the essential features of the new developments in the concept of the *objet petit a* as Lacan develops it from 1963 onwards. For example the *objet petit a* is circled by the drive (S11, 168), and is seen as the cause of desire just as *das Ding* is seen as 'the cause of the most fundamental human passion' (S7, 97). Also, the fact that the Thing is not the imaginary object but firmly in the register of the real (S7, 112), and yet is 'that which in the real suffers from the signifier' (S7, 125), anticipates the transition in Lacan's thought towards locating *objet petit a* increasingly in the register of the real from 1963 on.

time (*temps*) One of the most distinctive features of Lacanian psycho-analysis is Lacan's approach to questions of time. Broadly speaking, Lacan's approach is characterised by two important innovations: the concept of logical time, and the stress on retroaction and anticipation.

● **Logical time** In his paper entitled 'Logical time' (1945), Lacan undermines the pretensions of logic to timelessness and eternity by showing how certain logical calculations include an inescapable reference to a temporality. However, the kind of temporality involved is not specificiable by reference to the clock, but is itself the product of certain logical articulations. This distinction between logical time and chronological time underpins Lacan's whole theory of temporality.

The fact that logical time is not objective does not mean that it is simply a question of subjective feeling; on the contrary, as the adjective 'logical' indicates, it is a precise dialectical structure which may be formulated rigorously in mathematical terms. In the 1945 paper, Lacan argues that logical time has a tripartite structure, the three moments of which are: (i) the instant of seeing; (ii) the time for understanding; (iii) the moment of concluding. By means of a sophism (the problem of the three prisoners) Lacan shows how these three moments are constructed not in terms of objective chronometric units but in terms of an intersubjective logic based on a tension between waiting and haste, between hesitation and urgency. Logical time is thus 'the intersubjective time that structures human action' (E, 75).

Lacan's notion of logical time is not just an exercise in logic; it also has practical consequences for psychoanalytic treatment. The most famous of these consequences, historically speaking, has been Lacan's use of sessions of variable duration (Fr. *séances scandées*), which was regarded by the International Psycho-Analytical Association (IPA) as sufficient grounds for excluding him from membership. However, to focus exclusively on this particular practice is to miss various other interesting clinical dimensions of the theory of logical time, such as the way in which Lacan's concept of 'the time for understanding' can throw light on the Freudian concept of working-through. (See Forrester, 1990: ch. 8.)

Lacan's concept of logical time anticipates his incursions into Saussurean linguistics, which is based on the distinction between the diachronic (or temporal) and the synchronic (atemporal) aspects of language. Hence Lacan's increasing stress, beginning in the 1950s, on synchronic or timeless STRUCTURES rather than on developmental 'stages'. Thus when Lacan uses the term 'time', it is usually to be understood not as a fleeting diachronic moment but as a structure, a relatively stable synchronic state. Similarly, when he speaks of 'the three times of the Oedipus complex', the ordering is one of logical priority rather than of a chronological sequence. Change is not seen as a gradual or smooth move along a continuum, but as an abrupt shift from one discrete structure to another.

Lacan's emphasis on synchronic or timeless structures can be seen as an attempt to explore Freud's statement about the non-existence of time in the unconscious. However, Lacan modifies this with his proposal, in 1964, that the unconscious be characterised in terms of a temporal movement of opening and closing (S11, 143, 204).

● **Retroaction and anticipation**   Other forms of psychoanalysis, such as ego-psychology, are based on a linear concept of time (as can be seen, for example, in their stress on a linear sequence of developmental stages through which the child naturally passes; see DEVELOPMENT). Lacan, however, completely abandons such a linear notion of time, since in the psyche time can equally well act in reverse, by retroaction and anticipation.

● **Retroaction (Fr. *après coup*)**   Lacan's term *après coup* is the term used by French analysts to translate Freud's *Nachträglichkeit* (which the *Standard Edition* renders 'deferred action'). These terms refer to the way that, in the psyche, present events affect past events *a posteriori*, since the past exists in the psyche only as a set of memories which are constantly being reworked and reinterpreted in the light of present experience. What concerns psychoanalysis is not the real past sequence of events in themselves, but the way that these events exist now in memory and the way that the patient reports them. Thus when Lacan argues that the aim of psychoanalytic treatment is 'the complete reconstitution of the subject's history' (S1, 12), he makes it clear that what he means by the term 'history' is not simply a real sequence of past events, but 'the present synthesis of the past' (S1, 36). 'History is not the past. History is the past in so far as it is historicised in the present' (S1, 12). Hence the pregenital stages are not to be seen as real events chronologically prior to the genital stage, but as forms of DEMAND which are projected retroactively onto the past (E, 197). Lacan also shows how discourse is structured by retroaction; only when the last word of the sentence is uttered do the initial words acquire their full meaning (E, 303) (see PUNCTUATION).

● **Anticipation**   If retroaction refers to the way the present affects the past, anticipation refers to the way the future affects the present. Like retroaction, anticipation marks the structure of speech; the first words of a sentence are ordered in anticipation of the words to come (E, 303). In the mirror stage, the ego is constructed on the basis of the anticipation of an imagined future wholeness (which never, in fact, arrives). The structure of anticipation is best illustrated linguistically by the future-perfect tense (E, 306). Anticipation also plays an important role in the tripartite structure of logical time; the 'moment of concluding' is arrived at in haste, in anticipation of future certainty (Ec, 209).

topology (*topologie*)   Topology (originally called *analysis situs* by Leibniz) is a branch of mathematics which deals with the properties of figures in space which are preserved under all continuous deformations. These properties are those of continuity, contiguity and delimitation. The notion of space in topology is one of *topological space*, which is not limited to Euclidean (two- and three-dimensional space), nor even to spaces which can be said to have a dimension at all. Topological space thus dispenses with all references to distance, size, area and angle, and is based only on a concept of closeness or neighbourhood.

Freud used spatial metaphors to describe the psyche in *The Interpretation of Dreams*, where he cites G. T. Fechner's idea that the scene of action of dreams is different from that of waking ideational life and proposes the concept of 'psychical locality'. Freud is careful to explain that this concept is a purely topographical one, and must not be confused with physical locality in any anatomical fashion (Freud, 1900a: SE V, 536). His 'first topography' (usually referred to in English as 'the topographic system') divided the psyche into three systems: the conscious (Cs), the preconscious (Pcs) and the unconscious (Ucs). The 'second topography' (usually referred to in English as 'the structural system') divided the psyche into the three agencies of the ego, the superego and the id.

Lacan criticises these models for not being topological enough. He argues that the diagram with which Freud had illustrated his second topology in *The Ego and the Id* (1923b) led the majority of Freud's readers to forget the analysis on which it was based because of the intuitive power of the image (see E, 214). Lacan's interest in topology arises, then, because he sees it as providing a non-intuitive, purely intellectual means of expressing the concept of STRUCTURE that is so important to his focus on the symbolic order. It is thus the task of Lacan's topological models 'to forbid imaginary capture' (E, 333). Unlike intuitive images, in which 'perception eclipses structure', in Lacan's topology 'there is no occultation of the symbolic' (E, 333).

Lacan argues that topology is not simply a metaphorical way of expressing the concept of structure; it is structure itself (Lacan, 1973b). He emphasises that topology privileges the function of the cut (*coupure*), since the cut is what distinguishes a discontinuous transformation from a continuous one. Both kinds of transformation play a role in psychoanalytic treatment. As an example of a continuous transformation, Lacan refers to the MOEBIUS STRIP; just as one passes from one side to the other by following the strip round continuously, so the subject can traverse the fantasy without making a mythical leap from inside to outside. As an example of a discontinous transformation, Lacan also refers to the moebius strip, which when cut down the middle is transformed into a single loop with very different topological properties; it now has two sides instead of one. Just as the cut operates a discontinuous transformation in the moebius strip, so an effective interpretation proferred by the analyst modifies the structure of the analysand's discourse in a radical way.

While SCHEMA L and the other schemata which are produced in the 1950s can be seen as Lacan's first incursion into topology, topological forms only come into prominence when, in the 1960s, he turns his attention to the figures of the TORUS, the moebius strip, Klein's bottle, and the cross-cap (see Lacan, 1961–2). Later on, in the 1970s, Lacan turns his attention to the more complex area of knot theory, especially the BORROMEAN KNOT. For an introduction to Lacan's use of topological figures, see Granon-Lafont (1985).

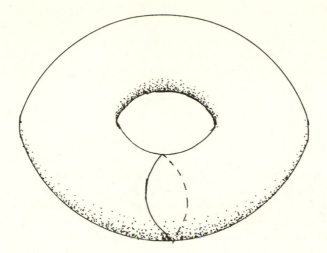

Figure 19   The torus

torus (*tore*)   The torus is one of the figures that Lacan analyses in his study of TOPOLOGY. In its simplest form, it is a ring, a three-dimensional object formed by taking a cylinder and joining the two ends together (Figure19).

Lacan's first reference to the torus dates from 1953 (see E, 105), but it is not until his work on topology in the 1970s that it begins to figure prominently in his work. The topology of the torus illustrates certain features of the structure of the subject:

One important feature of the torus is that its centre of gravity falls outside its volume, just as the centre of the subject is outside himself; he is decentred, ex-centric.

Another property of the torus is that 'its peripheral exteriority and its central exteriority constitute only one single region' (E, 105). This illustrates the way that psychoanalysis problematises the distinction between 'inside' and 'outside' (see *EXTIMITÉ*).

training (*formation, didactique*)   The English word 'training' is used to translate two French terms used by Lacan: *analyse didactique* ('training analysis') and *formation* ('professional training').

● **'Training analysis'** (Fr. *analyse didactique*)   By the time Lacan began training as an analyst, in the 1930s, it had become established practice in the International Psycho-Analytical Association (IPA) to make a distinction between 'therapeutic analysis' and 'training analysis' (this distinction is still maintained by the IPA today). In the context of this distinction, the term 'therapeutic analysis' refers to a course of analytic treatment entered into by the analysand for the purpose of treating certain symptoms, whereas the term 'training analysis' refers exclusively to a course of analytic treatment entered into by the analysand for the purpose of training as an analyst. According to the rules governing all the societies affiliated to the IPA, all members must first undergo a training analysis before being allowed to practise as analysts. However, an analysis is only recognised as a training analysis by these societies if it is conducted by one of the few senior analysts designated as a 'training analyst', and if it is embarked upon purely for the purpose of training.

This institutional distinction between training analysis and therapeutic analysis became one of the main objects of Lacan's criticism. While Lacan agrees with the IPA that it is absolutely necessary to undergo psychoanalytic treatment if one wants to become an analyst, he firmly disagrees with the artificial distinction drawn between therapeutic analysis and training analysis. For Lacan, there is only one form of the analytic process, irrespective of the reason for which the analysand embarks upon treatment, and the culmination of that process is not the removal of symptoms but the passage from analysand to analyst (see END OF ANALYSIS).

All analyses are thus capable of producing an analyst, and all claims by institutions to say which analyses count as training and which do not are bogus, for 'the authorisation of an analyst can only come from himself' (Lacan, 1967: 14). Lacan therefore abolishes the distinction between therapeutic analysis and training analysis; all analyses are training analyses, at least potentially. 'There is only one kind of psychoanalysis, the training analysis' (S11, 274). Today, many Lacanians have dispensed with both the term 'therapeutic analysis' and the term 'training analysis', preferring to use the term personal analysis (a term Lacan himself uses occasionally; see S8, 222) to designate any course of analytic treatment.

● **The training of analysts (Fr.** *formation des analystes***)** This refers to the process by which people learn how to conduct psychoanalytic treatment, i.e. how to be analysts. For Lacan, this is not simply a process that analysts go through at the beginning of their professional life, but an ongoing process. There are two sources from which analysts learn how to conduct psychoanalytic treatment: their own experience of treatment (first as patients, then as analysts), and the experience of others which is transmitted to them via psychoanalytic theory. Lacan insists that the most fundamental of these sources is the analyst's own experience of psychoanalytic treatment as a patient. However, this does not excuse the analyst from having to learn a lot more besides; Lacan's syllabus for the training of analysts is very extensive, and includes literature, linguistics, mathematics and history (E, 144–5). The analyst must seek to become, as Freud was, 'an encyclopedia of the arts and muses' (E, 169). This broad curriculum is evident in Lacan's public seminar which is filled with incursions into philosophy, topology, logic, literature and linguistics – all of which Lacan regards as essential to the training of analysts.

It is worth noting that the English term 'training' is nuanced rather differently to the French term *formation*. Whereas the English term carries connotations of a formal programme, or a bureaucratic structure, the French term (especially in Lacan's work) connotes a process which alters the subject in the very kernel of his being, and which cannot be regulated by set ritualistic procedures nor guaranteed by a printed qualification.

transference (*transfert*) The term 'transference' first emerged in Freud's work as simply another term for the displacement of affect from one idea to another (see Freud, 1900a: SE V, 562). Later on, however, it came to refer to the patient's relationship to the analyst as it develops in the treatment. This soon became the central meaning of the term, and is the sense in which it is usually understood in psychoanalytic theory today.

The use of a special term to denote the patient's relationship to the analyst is justified by the peculiar character of this relationship. Freud was first struck by the intensity of the patient's affective reactions to the doctor in Breuer's treatment of Anna O in 1882, which he argued was due to the patient transferring unconscious ideas onto the doctor (Freud, 1895d). As he developed the psychoanalytic method, Freud first regarded the transference exclusively as a RESISTANCE which impedes the recall of repressed memories, an obstacle to the treatment which must be 'destroyed' (Freud, 1905e: SE VII, 116). Gradually, however, he modified this view, coming to see the transference also as a positive factor which helps the treatment to progress. The positive value of transference lies in the fact that it provides a way for the analysand's history to be confronted in the immediacy of the present relationship with the analyst; in the way he relates to the analyst, the analysand inevitably repeats earlier relationships with other figures (especially those with the parents). This paradoxical nature of transference, as both an obstacle to the treatment and that which drives the treatment forward, perhaps helps to explain why there are so many different and opposing views of transference in psychoanalytic theory today.

Lacan's thinking about transference goes through several stages. His first work to deal with the subject in any detail is 'An Intervention on the Transference' (Lacan, 1951), in which he describes the transference in dialectical terms borrowed from Hegel. He criticises ego-psychology for defining the transference in terms of AFFECTS; 'Transference does not refer to any mysterious property of affect, and even when it reveals itself under the appearance of emotion, it only acquires meaning by virtue of the dialectical moment in which it is produced' (Ec, 225).

In other words, Lacan argues that although transference often manifests itself in the guise of particularly strong affects, such as LOVE and hate, it does not consist of such emotions but in the structure of an intersubjective relationship. This structural definition of transference remains a constant theme throughout the rest of Lacan's work; he consistently locates the essence of transference in the symbolic and not in the imaginary, although it clearly has powerful imaginary effects. Later on, Lacan will remark that if transference often manifests itself under the appearance of love, it is first and foremost the love of knowledge (*savoir*) that is concerned.

Lacan returns to the subject of the transference in the seminar of 1953–4. This time he conceives it not in terms borrowed from Hegelian dialectics but in terms borrowed from the anthropology of exchange (Mauss, Lévi-Strauss). Transference is implicit in the speech act, which involves an exchange of signs that transforms the speaker and listener:

> In its essence, the efficacious transference which we're considering is quite simply the speech act. Each time a man speaks to another in an authentic and full manner, there is, in the true sense, transference, symbolic transference – something which takes place which changes the nature of the two beings present.
>
> (S1, 109)

In the seminar of the following year, he continues to elaborate on the symbolic nature of transference, which he identifies with the compulsion to repeat, the insistence of the symbolic determinants of the subject (S2, 210–11). This is to be distinguished from the imaginary aspect of transference, namely, the affective reactions of love and aggressivity. In this distinction between the symbolic and imaginary aspects of transference, Lacan provides a useful way of understanding the paradoxical function of the transference in psychoanalytic treatment; in its symbolic aspect (REPETITION) it helps the treatment progress by revealing the signifiers of the subject's history, while in its imaginary aspect (love and hate) it acts as a resistance (see S4, 135; S8, 204).

Lacan's next approach to the subject of transference is in the eighth year of his seminar (Lacan, 1960–1), entitled simply 'The Transference'. Here he uses Plato's *Symposium* to illustrate the relationship between the analysand and the analyst. Alcibiades compares Socrates to a plain box which encloses a precious object (Grk *agalma*); just as Alcibiades attributes a hidden treasure to Socrates, so the analysand sees his object of desire in the analyst (see *OBJET PETIT A*).

In 1964, Lacan articulates the concept of transference with his concept of the SUBJECT SUPPOSED TO KNOW, which remains central to Lacan's view of the transference from then on; indeed, it is this view of the transference which has come to be seen as Lacan's most complete attempt to theorise the matter. According to this view, transference is the attribution of knowledge to the Other, the supposition that the Other is a subject who knows; 'As soon as the subject who is supposed to know exists somewhere . . . there is transference' (S11, 232).

Although the existence of the transference is a necessary condition of psychoanalytic treatment, it is not sufficient in itself; it is also necessary that the analyst deal with the transference in a unique way. It is this that differentiates psychoanalysis from SUGGESTION; although both are based on the transference, psychoanalysis differs from suggestion because the analyst refuses to use the power given to him by the transference (see E, 236).

From quite early on in the history of psychoanalysis it became common to distinguish between those aspects of the patient's relationship to the analyst which were 'adapted to reality' and those which were not. In the latter category fell all the patient's reactions which were caused by 'perceiving the analyst in a distorted way'. Some analysts used the term 'transference' to refer to all aspects of the analysand's relationship to the analyst, in which case they distinguished the distorted 'neurotic transference' or 'transference neurosis' from the 'unobjectionable part of the transference' or 'therapeutic alliance' (Edward Bibring, Elizabeth Zeztel). Other analysts argued that the term 'transference' should be restricted to the 'unrealistic' or 'irrational' reactions of the analysand (William Silverberg, Franz Alexander). However, the common assumption underlying both of these positions was that the analyst could tell when the patient was not reacting to him on the basis of who he really was but rather on the basis of previous relationships with other people. The analyst was credited with this ability because he was supposed to be better 'adapted to reality' than the patient. Informed by his own correct perception of reality, the analyst could offer 'transference interpretations'; that is, he could point out the discrepancy between the real situation and the irrational way that the patient was reacting to it. It was argued that such transference interpretations helped the analysand to gain 'insight' into his own neurotic transference and thereby resolve it or 'liquidate' it.

Some of Lacan's most incisive criticisms are directed at this way of representing psychoanalytic treatment. These criticisms are based on the following arguments:

1. The whole idea of adaptation to reality is based on a naive empiricist epistemology, involving an appeal to an unproblematic notion of 'reality' as an objective and self-evident given. This entirely neglects what psychoanalysis has discovered about the construction of reality by the ego on the basis of its own *méconnaissance*. Hence when the analyst assumes that he is better adapted to reality than the patient he has no other recourse than 'to fall back on his own ego' since this is the only 'bit of reality he knows' (E, 231). The healthy part of the patient's ego is then defined simply as 'the part that thinks as we do' (E, 232). This reduces psychoanalytic treatment to a form of suggestion in which the analyst simply 'imposes his own idea of reality' on the analysand (E, 232). Thus 'the inability [of the analyst] to sustain a praxis in an authentic manner results, as is usually the case with mankind, in the exercise of power' (E, 226).

2. The idea that the analysand's 'distorted perception of the analyst' could be liquidated by means of interpretations is a logical fallacy, since 'the transference is interpreted on the basis of, and with the instrument of, the transference itself' (S8, 206). In other words, there is no METALANGUAGE of the

transference, no vantage point outside the transference from which the analyst could offer an interpretation, since any interpretation he offers 'will be received as coming from the person that the transference imputes him to be' (E, 231). Thus it is contradictory to claim that the transference can be dissolved by means of an interpretation when it is the transference itself which conditions the analysand's acceptance of that interpretation; 'the emergence of the subject from the transference is thus postponed *ad infinitum*' (E, 231).

Does this mean that Lacanian analysts never interpret the transference? Certainly not; Lacan affirms that 'it is natural to interpret the transference' (E, 271), but at the same time he harbours no illusions about the power of such interpretations to dissolve the transference. Like any other interpretation, the analyst must use all his art in deciding if and when to interpret the transference, and above all must avoid gearing his interpretations exclusively to interpreting the transference. He must also know exactly what he is seeking to achieve by such an interpretation; not to rectify the patient's relationship to reality, but to maintain the analytic dialogue. 'What does it mean, to interpret the transference? Nothing else than to fill the void of this deadlock with a lure. But while it may be deceptive, this lure serves a purpose by setting off the whole process again' (Ec, 225).

When describing the transference as 'positive' or 'negative', Lacan takes two different approaches. Following Freud, Lacan sometimes uses these adjectives to refer to the nature of the affects, 'positive transference' referring to loving affects and 'negative transference' referring to aggressive affects (Ec, 222). Sometimes, however, Lacan takes the terms 'positive' and 'negative' to refer to the favourable or unfavourable effects of the transference on the treatment (see E, 271, where Lacan argues that when the analysand's resistance opposes suggestion, this resistance must be 'placed in the ranks of the positive transference' on the grounds that it maintains the direction of the analysis).

Although Lacan does speak occasionally of COUNTERTRANSFERENCE, he generally prefers not to use this term.

transitivism (*transitivisme*)   Transitivism, a phenomenon first discovered by Charlotte Bühler (see E, 5), refers to a special kind of IDENTIFICATION often observed in the behaviour of small children. For example a child can hit another child of the same age on the left side of his face, and then touch the right side of his own face and cry in imagined pain. For Lacan, transitivism illustrates the confusion of ego and other which is inherent in imaginary identification. The INVERSION (right to left) is further evidence of the function of the mirror.

Transitivism is also evident in paranoia, in which attack and counter-attack are bound together 'in an absolute equivalence' (Lacan, 1951b: 16).

treatment (*cure*)   The term 'treatment' designates the practice of PSYCHOANALYSIS as opposed to the theory of psychoanalysis. Although the term was inherited by psychoanalysis from medicine, it has acquired a specific meaning in Lacanian psychoanalytic theory which is quite different from the way it is understood in medicine. In particular, the aim of psychoanalytic treatment is not seen by Lacan as 'healing' or 'curing' people in the sense of producing a perfectly healthy psyche. The clinical structures of neurosis, psychosis and perversion are seen as essentially 'incurable', and the aim of analytic treatment is simply to lead the analysand to articulate his truth.

Lacan argues that the treatment is a process with a definite direction, a structural progression with a beginning, middle and end (see END OF ANALYSIS). The beginning, or 'point of entry into the analytic situation', is a contract, or 'pact', between analyst and analysand which includes the analysand's agreement to abide by the fundamental rule. Following the initial consultation, a series of face-to-face preliminary interviews take place. These preliminary interviews have several aims. Firstly, they enable a properly psychoanalytic symptom to be constituted in place of the vague collection of complaints often brought by the patient. Secondly, they allow time for the transference to develop. Thirdly, they permit the analyst to ascertain whether or not there is really a demand for psychoanalysis, and also to hypothesise about the clinical structure of the analysand.

After the preliminary interviews, the treatment is no longer conducted face to face, but with the analysand reclining on a couch while the analyst sits behind him, out of the analysand's field of vision (the couch is not used in the treatment of psychotic patients). As he free associates, the analysand works through the signifiers that have determined him in his history, and is driven by the very process of speech itself to articulate something of his desire. This is a dynamic process which involves a conflict between a force which drives the treatment on (see TRANSFERENCE, DESIRE OF THE ANALYST) and an opposing force which blocks the process (see RESISTANCE). The analyst's task is to direct this process (not to direct the patient), and to get the process going again when it gets stuck.

truth (*vérité*) Truth is one of the most central, and yet most complex terms in Lacan's discourse. A few basic points are clear and constant in Lacan's concept of truth; truth always refers to truth about desire, and the aim of psychoanalytic treatment is to lead the analysand to articulate this truth. Truth does not await, in some preformed state of fullness, to be revealed to the analysand by the analyst; on the contrary, it is gradually constructed in the dialectical movement of the treatment itself (Ec, 144). Lacan argues, in opposition to the traditions of classical philosophy, that truth is not beautiful (S7, 217) and that it is not necessarily beneficial to learn the truth (S17, 122). While Lacan always speaks about 'truth' in the singular, this is not a single universal truth, but an absolutely particular truth, unique to each subject (see S7, 24). However, beyond these few simple points, it is impossible to give a univocal definition of the way Lacan uses the term, since it functions in multiple contexts simultaneously, in opposition to a wide variety of terms. All that will be attempted here, therefore, is a general indication of some of the contexts in which it functions.

● **Truth versus exactitude** Exactitude is a question of 'introducing measurement into the real' (E, 74), and constitutes the aim of the exact sciences. Truth, however, concerns desire, which is not a matter for the exact sciences but for the sciences of subjectivity. Therefore truth is only a meaningful concept in the context of language: 'It is with the appearance of language that the dimension of truth emerges' (E, 172). Psychoanalytic treatment is based on the fundamental premise that speech is the only means of revealing the truth about desire. 'Truth hollows its way into the real thanks to the dimension of speech. There is neither true nor false prior to speech' (S1, 228).

● **Truth and SCIENCE** From Lacan's earliest writings, the term 'truth' has metaphysical, even mystical, nuances which problematise any attempt to articulate truth and science. It is not that Lacan denies that science aims to know the truth, but simply that science cannot claim to monopolise truth as its exclusive property (Ec, 79). Lacan later argues that science is in fact based on a foreclosure of the concept of truth as cause (Ec, 874). The concept of truth is essential for understanding madness, and modern science renders madness meaningless by ignoring the concept of truth (Ec, 153–4).

● **Truth, lies and deception** Truth is intimately connected with deception, since lies can often reveal the truth about desire more eloquently than honest statements. Deception and lies are not the opposite of truth: on the contrary, they are inscribed in the text of truth. The analyst's role is to reveal the truth inscribed in the deception of the analysand's speech. Although the analysand may in effect be saying to the analyst 'I am deceiving you', the analyst says to the analysand 'In this *I am deceiving to you*, what you are sending as message is what I express to you, and in doing so you are telling the truth' (S11, 139–40; see S4, 107–8).

● **Truth versus false appearances** The false appearances presented by the analysand are not merely obstacles that the analyst must expose and discard in order to discover the truth; on the contrary, the analyst must take them into account (see SEMBLANCE).

● **Truth, error and mistakes** Psychoanalysis has shown that the truth about desire is often revealed by mistakes (parapraxes; see ACT). The complex relations between truth, mistakes, error and deception are evoked by Lacan in a typically elusive phrase when he describes 'the structuration of speech in search of truth' as 'error taking flight in deception and recaptured by mistake' (S1, 273).

● **Truth and fiction** Lacan does not use the term 'fiction' in the sense of 'a falsehood', but in the sense of a scientific construct (Lacan takes his cue here from Bentham – see S7, 12). Thus Lacan's term 'fiction' corresponds to Freud's term *Konvention*, convention (see S11, 163), and has more in common with truth than falsehood. Indeed, Lacan states that truth is structured like a fiction (E, 306; Ec, 808).

• **Truth and the** REAL   The opposition which Lacan draws between truth and the real dates back to his pre-war writings (e.g. Ec, 75), and is taken up at various points; 'We are used to the real. The truth we repress' (E, 169). However, Lacan also points out that truth is similar to the real; it is impossible to articulate the whole truth, and '[p]recisely because of this impossibility, truth aspires to the real' (Lacan, 1973a: 83).

U

unconscious (*inconscient*)   Although the term 'unconscious' had been used by writers prior to Freud, it acquires a completely original meaning in his work, in which it constitutes the single most important concept.

Freud distinguished between two uses of the term 'unconscious' (Freud, 1915e). As an adjective, it simply refers to mental processes that are not the subject of conscious attention at a given moment. As a noun (the unconscious; *das Unbewußte*), it designates one of the psychical systems which Freud described in his first theory of mental structure (the 'topographical model'). According to this theory, the mind is divided into three systems or 'psychical localities'; the conscious (Cs), the preconscious (Pcs) and the unconscious (Ucs). The unconscious system is not merely that which is outside the field of consciousness at a given time, but that which has been radically separated from consciousness by repression and thus cannot enter the conscious–preconscious system without distortion.

In Freud's second theory of mental structure (the 'structural theory'), the mind is divided into the three 'agencies' of ego, superego and id. In this model, no one agency is identical to the unconscious, since even the ego and the superego have unconscious parts.

Lacan, before 1950, uses the term 'unconscious' principally in its adjectival form, making his early work seem particularly strange to those who are more familiar with Freud's writings. In the 1950s, however, as Lacan begins his 'return to Freud', the term appears more frequently as a noun, and Lacan increasingly emphasises the originality of Freud's concept of the unconscious, stressing that it is not merely the opposite of consciousness; 'a large number of psychical effects that are quite legitimately designated as unconscious, in the sense of excluding the characteristics of consciousness, are nonetheless without any relation whatever to the unconscious in the Freudian sense' (E, 163). He also insists that the unconscious cannot simply be equated with 'that which is repressed'.

Lacan argues that the concept of the unconscious was badly misunderstood by most of Freud's followers, who reduced it to being 'merely the seat of the instincts' (E, 147). Against this biologistic mode of thought, Lacan argues that 'the unconscious is neither primordial nor instinctual' (E, 170); it is primarily linguistic. This is summed up in Lacan's famous formula, 'the unconscious is structured like a language' (S3, 167; see LANGUAGE, STRUCTURE). Lacan's analysis of the unconscious in terms of synchronic structure is supplemented by his idea of the unconscious opening and closing in a temporal pulsation (S11, 143, 204).

Some psychoanalysts have objected to Lacan's linguistic approach to the unconscious on the grounds that it is overly restrictive, and on the grounds that Freud himself excluded word-presentations from the unconscious (S7, 44; for Lacan's refutation of these objections, see THING). Lacan himself qualifies his linguistic approach by arguing that the reason why the unconscious is structured like a language is that 'we only grasp the unconscious finally when it is explicated, in that part of it which is articulated by passing into words' (S7, 32).

Lacan also describes the unconscious as a discourse: 'The unconscious is the discourse of the Other' (Ec, 16; see OTHER). This enigmatic formula, which has become one of Lacan's most famous dictums, can be understood in many ways. Perhaps the most important meaning is that 'one should see in the unconscious the effects of speech on the subject' (S11, 126). More precisely, the unconscious is the effects of the SIGNIFIER on the subject, in that the signifier is what is repressed and what returns in the formations of the unconscious (symptoms, jokes, parapraxes, dreams, etc.).

All the references to language, speech, discourse and signifiers clearly locate the unconscious in the order of the SYMBOLIC. Indeed, 'the unconscious is structured as a function of the symbolic' (S7, 12). The unconscious is the determination of the subject by the symbolic order.

The unconscious is not interior: on the contrary, since speech and language are intersubjective phenomena, the unconscious is 'transindividual' (E, 49); the unconscious is, so to speak, 'outside'. 'This exteriority of the symbolic in relation to man is the very notion of the unconscious' (Ec, 469). If the unconscious seems interior, this is an effect of the imaginary, which blocks the relationship between the subject and the Other and which inverts the message of the Other.

Although the unconscious is especially visible in the formations of the unconscious, 'the unconscious leaves none of our actions outside its field' (E, 163). The laws of the unconscious, which are those of repetition and desire, are as ubiquitous as structure itself. The unconscious is irreducible, so the aim of analysis cannot be to make conscious the unconscious.

In addition to the various linguistic metaphors which Lacan draws on to conceptualise the unconscious (discourse, language, speech), he also conceives of the unconscious in other terms.

● MEMORY The unconscious is also a kind of memory, in the sense of a symbolic history of the signifiers that have determined the subject in the course of his life; 'what we teach the subject to recognize as his unconscious is his history' (E, p. 52).

● KNOWLEDGE Since it is an articulation of signifiers in a signifying chain, the unconscious is a kind of knowledge (symbolic knowledge, or *savoir*). More precisely, it is an 'unknown knowledge'.

W

woman (*femme*) Freud's account of SEXUAL DIFFERENCE is based on the view that there are certain psychical characteristics that can be called 'masculine' and others that can be called 'feminine', and that these differ from each other significantly. However, Freud constantly refuses to give any definition of the terms 'masculine' and 'feminine', arguing that they are foundational concepts which can be used but not elucidated by psychoanalytic theory (Freud, 1920a: SE XVIII, 171).

One feature of this opposition is that the two terms do not function in an exactly symmetrical way. Masculinity is taken by Freud as the paradigm; he asserts that there is only one libido, which is masculine, and that the psychical development of the girl is at first identical to that of the boy, only diverging at a later moment. Femininity is thus that which diverges from the masculine paradigm, and Freud regards it as a mysterious, unexplored region, a 'dark continent' (Freud, 1926e: SE XX, 212). The 'riddle of the nature of femininity' (Freud, 1933a: SE XXII, 113) comes to preoccupy Freud in his later writings, and drives him to ask the famous question, 'What does woman want?' (see Jones, 1953–7: vol. 2, 468). Masculinity is a self-evident given, femininity is a zone of mystery:

> Psychoanalysis does not try to describe what a woman is – that would be a task it could scarcely perform – but sets about enquiring how she comes into being, how a woman develops out of a child with a bisexual disposition.
> (Freud, 1933a: SE XXII, 116).

Apart from a few remarks on the function of the MOTHER in the family complexes (Lacan, 1938), Lacan's pre-war writings do not engage with the debate on femininity. The occasional statements on the subject which occur in Lacan's work in the early 1950s are couched in terms derived from Claude Lévi-Strauss; women are seen as objects of exchange which circulate like signs between kinship groups (see Lévi-Strauss, 1949b). 'Women in the real order serve . . . as objects for the exchanges required by the elementary structures of kinship' (E, 207). Lacan argues that it is precisely the fact that woman is pushed into the position of an exchange object that constitutes the difficulty of the feminine position:

> For her, there's something insurmountable, let us say unacceptable, in the fact of being placed in the position of an object in the symbolic order, to which, on the other hand, she is entirely subjected no less than the man.
>
> (S2, 262)

Lacan's analysis of the Dora case makes the same point: what is unacceptable for Dora is her position as object of exchange between her father and Herr K (see Lacan, 1951a). Being in this position of exchange object means that woman 'has a relation of the second degree to this symbolic order' (S2, 262; see S4, 95–6).

In 1956, Lacan takes up the traditional association of HYSTERIA with femininity, arguing that hysteria is in fact nothing other than the question of femininity itself, the question which may be phrased 'What is a woman?'. This is true for both male and female hysterics (S3, 178). The term 'woman' here refers not to some biological essence but to a position in the symbolic order; it is synonymous with the term 'feminine position'. Lacan also argues that 'there is no symbolisation of woman's sex as such', since there is no feminine equivalent to the 'highly prevalent symbol' provided by the phallus (S3, 176). This symbolic dissymmetry forces the woman to take the same route through the Oedipus complex as the boy, i.e. to identify with the father. However, this is more complex for the woman, since she is required to take the image of a member of the other sex as the basis for her identification (S3, 176).

Lacan returns to the question of femininity in 1958, in a paper entitled 'Guiding remarks for a congress on feminine sexuality' (Lacan, 1958d). In this paper he notes the impasses which have beset psychoanalytic discussions of feminine sexuality, and argues that woman is the Other for both men and women; 'Man here acts as the relay whereby the woman becomes this Other for herself as she is this Other for him' (Ec, 732).

Lacan's most important contributions to the debate on femininity come, like Freud's, late in his work. In the seminar of 1972–3, Lacan advances the concept of a specifically feminine JOUISSANCE which goes 'beyond the phallus' (S20, 69); this *jouissance* is 'of the order of the infinite', like mystical ecstasy (S20, 44). Women may experience this *jouissance*, but they know nothing about it (S20, 71). It is also in this seminar that Lacan takes up his controversial formula, first advanced in the seminar of 1970–1, 'Woman does not exist' (*la femme n'existe pas* – Lacan, 1973a: 60), which he here rephrases as 'there is no such thing as Woman' (*il n'y a pas* La *femme* – S20, 68). As is clear in the original French, what Lacan puts into question is not the noun 'woman', but the definite article which precedes it. In French the definite article indicates universality, and this is precisely the characteristic that women lack; women 'do not lend themselves to generalisation, even to phallocentric generalisation' (Lacan, 1975b). Hence Lacan strikes through the definite article whenever it precedes the term *femme* in much the same way as he strikes through the A to produce the symbol for the barred Other, for like woman, the Other does not exist (see BAR). To press home the point, Lacan speaks of woman as 'not-all' (*pas-toute*; S20, 13); unlike masculinity, which is a universal function founded upon the phallic exception (castration), woman is a non-universal which admits of no exception. Woman is compared to truth, since both partake of the logic of the not-all (there is no such thing as all women; it is impossible to say 'the whole truth') (Lacan, 1973a: 64).

Lacan goes on in 1975 to state that 'a woman is a symptom' (Lacan, 1974–5: seminar of 21 January 1975). More precisely, a woman is a symptom *of a man*, in the sense that a woman can only ever enter the psychic economy of men as a fantasy object (*a*), the cause of their desire.

Lacan's remarks on woman and on feminine sexuality have become the focus of controversy and debate in feminist theory. Feminists have divided over whether to see Lacan as an ally or an enemy of the feminist cause. Some have seen his theories as providing an incisive description of patriarchy and as a way of challenging fixed concepts of sexual identity (e.g. Mitchell and Rose, 1982). Others have argued that his concept of the symbolic order reinstates patriarchy as a transhistorical given, and that his privileging of the phallus simply repeats the alleged misogynies of Freud himself (e.g. Gallop, 1982; Grosz, 1990). For representative samples of the debate, see Adams and Cowie (1990) and Brennan (1989). For a Lacanian account of feminine sexuality, see Leader (1996).

Appendix: Page references to Lacan's Écrits

Page references to Lacan's *Écrits* refer to the English edition whenever possible (Jacques Lacan, *Écrits: A Selection*, trans. Alan Sheridan, London: Tavistock, 1977); these references are indicated by the abbreviation E. As this edition is only a partial translation of the original work, page references to untranslated sections of the *Écrits* refer to the French edition (Jacques Lacan, *Écrits*, Paris: Seuil, 1966); these references are indicated by the abbreviation Ec. In order to overcome the confusion which this referencing system might produce, the following table has been included to enable the reader to identify the source of all quotations from the *Écrits*.

Page references to the English edition

E, 1–7	The mirror stage as formative of the function of the I (1949).
E, 8–29	Aggressivity in psychoanalysis (1948).
E, 30–113	The function and field of speech and language in psychoanalysis (1953a).
E, 114–45	The Freudian thing (1955c).
E, 146–78	The agency of the letter in the unconscious or reason since Freud (1957b).
E, 179–225	On a question preliminary to any possible treatment of psychosis (1957–8b).
E, 226–80	The direction of the treatment and the principles of its power (1958a).
E, 281–91	The signification of the phallus (1958c).
E, 292–325	The subversion of the subject and the dialectic of desire in the Freudian unconscious (1960a).

Page references to the French edition

Ec, 9–10	Overture to this collection (1966b).
Ec, 11–61	Seminar on 'The Purloined Letter' (1955a).
Ec, 65–72	On our predecessors (1966c).
Ec, 73–92	Beyond the 'reality principle' (1936).
Ec, 125–49	A theoretical introduction to the functions of psycho-analysis in criminology (1950).
Ec, 151–93	Remarks on psychical causality (1946).

APPENDIX

Bibliography

In order to avoid the anachronisms created by the Harvard reference system, works by Jacques Lacan are referenced by date of composition. Works by other authors are referenced by date of first publication.

The volume numbers and page numbers in the references to Freud's works refer to *The Standard Edition of the Complete Psychological Works of Sigmund Freud*, edited by James Strachey, 24 vols, London: Hogarth Press and the Institute of Psycho-Analysis (here abbreviated to SE). The letters attached to the dates of Freud's works are in accordance with the bibliography included in vol. XXIV of the *Standard Edition*.

For a more complete bibliography of Lacan's works, the reader is referred to Dor (1983).

Adams, Parveen and Cowie, Elizabeth (1990) *The Woman in Question*, Cambridge, Mass: MIT Press.

American Psychiatric Association (1987) *Diagnostic and Statistical Manual of Mental Disorders* (3rd edn, revised), New York: American Psychiatric Association.

Balint, Michael (1947) 'On genital love', in *Primary Love and Psychoanalytic Technique*, London: Hogarth Press and the Institute of Psycho-Analysis, 1952.

Benvenuto, Bice and Kennedy, Roger (1986) *The Works of Jacques Lacan: An Introduction*, London: Free Association Books.

Blakemore, Diane (1992) *Understanding Utterances*, Oxford: Blackwell.

Borch-Jacobsen, Mikkel (1991) *Lacan: The Absolute Master*, trans. Douglas Brick, Stanford: Stanford University Press.

Bowie, Malcolm (1991) *Lacan*, London: Fontana.

Bracher, Mark, Alcorn, Marshall, Corthell, Ronald and Massardier-Kenney, Françoise (eds) (1994) *Lacanian Theory of Discourse. Subject, Structure and Society*, New York: New York University Press.

Brennan, Teresa (ed.) (1989) *Between Feminism and Psychoanalysis*, London and New York: Routledge.

Burks, Arthur W. (1949) 'Icon, index, and symbol', *Philosophy and Phenomenological Research*, vol. 9: 673–89.

Caton, Stephen C. (1987) 'Contributions of Roman Jakobson', *Ann. Rev. Anthropol.*, vol. 16: 223–60.

Chemama, Roland (ed.) (1993) *Dictionnaire de la Psychanalyse. Dictionnaire actuel des signifiants, concepts et mathèmes de la psychanalyse*, Paris: Larousse.

Clavreul, Jean (1967) 'The perverse couple', trans. Stuart Schneiderman, in Stuart Schneiderman (ed.), *Returning to Freud: Clinical Psychoanalysis in the School of Lacan*, New Haven and London: Yale University Press, 1980, pp. 215–33.

Clément, Cathérine (1981) *The Lives and Legends of Jacques Lacan*, trans. A. Goldhammer, New York: Columbia University Press, 1983.

Copjec, Joan (1989) 'The orthopsychic subject: film theory and the reception of Lacan', *October*, 49, reprinted in *Read My Desire: Lacan against the Historicists*, Cambridge, Mass. and London: MIT Press, 1994, pp. 15–38.

———(1994) 'Sex and the euthanasia of reason', in Joan Copjec (ed.), *Supposing the Subject*, London: Verso, pp. 16–44.

Davis, Robert Con (ed.) (1983) *Lacan and Narration. The Psychoanalytic Difference in Narrative Theory*, Baltimore and London: Johns Hopkins University Press.

Derrida, Jacques (1975) 'Le facteur de la vérité', in *The Post Card: From Socrates to Freud and Beyond*, trans. Alan Bass, Chicago and London: University of Chicago Press, 1987, pp. 413–96.

Descartes, René (1637) *Discourse on the Method of Properly Conducting One's Reason and of Seeking the Truth in the Sciences*, trans. F. E. Sutcliffe, Harmondsworth: Penguin, 1968.

Dor, Joël (1983) *Bibliographie des travaux de Jacques Lacan*, Paris: InterEditions.

Ducrot, Oswald and Todorov, Tzvetan (1972) *Dictionnaire encyclopédique des sciences du langage*, Paris: Seuil.

Feldstein, Richard, Fink, Bruce and Jaanus, Marie (eds) (1995) *Reading Seminar XI: Lacan's Four Fundamental Concepts of Psychoanalysis*, Albany: State University of New York.

Felman, Shoshana (1987) *Jacques Lacan and the Adventure of Insight. Psychoanalysis in Contemporary Culture*, Cambridge, Mass. and London: Harvard University Press.

Ferenczi, Sándor (1909) 'Introjection and transference', in *Sex in Psychoanalysis*, New York: Basic Books, pp. 35–57.

Ferenczi, Sándor and Rank, Otto (1925) 'The development of psychoanalysis', trans. Caroline Newton, *J. Nerv. Ment. Dis.*, Monograph no. 40.

Forrester, John (1990) *The Seductions of Psychoanalysis: On Freud, Lacan and Derrida*, Cambridge and New York: Cambridge University Press.

Freud, Anna (1936) *The Ego and the Mechanisms of Defence*, London: Hogarth, 1937.

Freud, Sigmund (1894a) 'The Neuro-Psychoses of Defence', SE III, 43.

———(1895d) with Josef Breuer *Studies on Hysteria*, SE II.

———(1900a) *The Interpretation of Dreams*, SE IV–V.

———(1901b) *The Psychopathology of Everyday Life*, SE VI.

———(1905c) *Jokes and their Relation to the Unconscious*, SE VIII.

———(1905d) *Three Essays on the Theory of Sexuality*, SE VII, 125.

———(1905e [1901]) 'Fragment of an Analysis of a Case of Hysteria', SE VII, 3.

————(1907b) 'Obsessive Actions and Religious Practices', SE IX, 116.

————(1908c) 'On the Sexual Theories of Children', SE IX, 207.

————(1908d) '"Civilized" Sexual Morality and Modern Nervous Illness', SE IX, 179.

————(1909b) 'Analysis of a Phobia in a Five-Year-Old Boy', SE X, 3.

————(1909c) 'Family Romanies', SE IX, 237.

————(1909d) 'Notes upon a Case of Obsessional Neurosis', SE X, 155.

————(1910c) *Leonardo da Vinci and a Memory of his Childhood*, SE XI, 59.

————(1911b) 'Formulations on the Two Principles of Mental Functioning', SE XII, 215.

————(1911c) 'Psycho-Analytic Notes on an Autobiographical Account of a Case of Paranoia (Dementia Paranoides)', SE XII, 3.

————(1912–13) *Totem and Taboo*, SE XIII, 1.

————(1913c) 'On Beginning the Treatment', SE XII, 122.

————(1913j) 'The Claims of Psycho-Analysis to Scientific Interest', SE XIII, 165.

————(1914b) 'The Moses of Michelangelo', SE XIII, 211.

————(1914c) 'On Narcissism: An Introduction', SE XIV, 69.

————(1914d) 'On the History of the Psycho-Analytic Movement', SE XIV, 3.

————(1915a) 'Observations on Transference Love', SE XII, 160.

————(1915e) 'The Unconscious', SE XIV, 161.

————(1915c) 'Instincts and their Vicissitudes', SE XIV, 111.

————(1917c) 'On the Transformations of Instinct, as Exemplified in Anal Erotism', SE XVII, 127.

————(1918b [1914]) 'From the History of an Infantile Neurosis', SE XVII, 3.

————(1919a [1918]) 'Lines of Advance in Psycho-Analytic Therapy', SE XVII, 159.

————(1919e) 'A Child Is Being Beaten', SE XVII, 177.

————(1919h) 'The Uncanny', SE XVII, 219.

————(1920a) 'The Psychogenesis of a Case of Female Homosexuality', SE XVIII, 147.

————(1920g) *Beyond the Pleasure Principle*, SE XVIII, 7.

————(1921c) *Group Psychology and the Analysis of the Ego*, SE XVIII, 69.

————(1923a) 'Two Encyclopaedia Articles', SE XVIII, 235.

————(1923b) *The Ego and the Id*, SE XIX, 3.

————(1923e) 'The Infantile Genital Organisation', SE XIX, 141.

————(1924b [1923]) 'Neurosis and Psychosis', SE XIX, 149.

————(1924d) 'The Dissolution of the Oedipus Complex', SE XIX, 173.

————(1924e) 'The Loss of Reality in Neurosis and Psychosis', SE XIX, 183.

————(1925d) *An Autobiographical Study*, SE XX, 3.

————(1925e [1924]) 'The Resistances to Psycho-Analysis', SE XIX, 213.

————(1925h) 'Negation', SE XIX, 235.

BIBLIOGRAPHY

————(1925j) 'Some Psychical Consequences of the Anatomical Distinction between the Sexes', SE XIX, 243.

————(1926e) *The Question of Lay-Analysis*, SE XX, 179.

————(1927c) *The Future of an Illusion*, SE XXI, 3.

————(1927e) 'Fetishism', SE XXI, 149.

————(1930a) *Civilization and Its Discontents*, SE XXI, 59.

————(1931b) 'Female Sexuality', SE XXI, 223.

————(1933a) *New Introductory Lectures on Psycho-Analysis*, SE XXII, 3.

————(1937c) 'Analysis Terminable and Interminable', SE XXIII, 211.

————(1939a [1937–9]) *Moses and Monotheism*, SE XXIII, 3.

————(1940a [1938]) *An Outline of Psycho-Analysis*, SE XXIII, 141.

————(1940e [1938]) 'Splitting of the Ego in the Process of Defence', SE XXIII, 273.

————(1941d [1921]) 'Psycho-Analysis and Telepathy', SE XVIII, 177.

Gallop, Jane (1982) *Feminism and Psychoanalysis: The Daughter's Seduction*, London: Macmillan.

————(1985) *Reading Lacan*, Ithaca and London: Cornell University Press.

Granon-Lafont, Jeanne (1985) *La topologie ordinaire de Jacques Lacan*, Paris: Point Hors Ligne.

Groddeck, Georg (1923) *The Book of the It*, London: Vision Press, 1949.

Grosz, Elizabeth (1990) *Jacques Lacan: A Feminist Introduction*, London and New York: Routledge.

Hartmann, Heinz (1939) *Ego Psychology and the Problem of Adaptation*, New York: International Universities Press, 1958.

Hegel, G. W. F. (1807) *Phenomenology of Spirit*, trans. A. V. Miller, with Analysis of the Text and Foreword by J. N. Findlay, Oxford: Clarendon Press, 1985.

Heidegger, Martin (1927) *Being and Time*, trans. J. Macquirrie and E. Robinson, London: SCM Press, 1962.

————(1956) *The Question of Being*, trans. William Kluback and Jean T. Wilde, London: Vision, 1959.

Heimann, Paula (1950) 'On counter-transference', *Int. J. Psycho-Anal.*, vol. 31: 81–4.

Hinshelwood, R. D. (1989) *A Dictionary of Kleinian Thought*, London: Free Association Books, 1991 (2nd edn, revised and enlarged).

Hughes, Jennifer (1981) *An Outline of Modern Psychiatry*, Chichester: Wiley, 1991 (3rd edn).

Hugo, Victor (1859–83) *La légende des siècles*, Paris: Garnier-Flammarion, 1979.

Jakobson, Roman (1956) 'Two aspects of language and two types of aphasic disturbances', in *Selected Writings*, vol. II, *Word and Language*, The Hague: Mouton, 1971, pp. 239–59.

————(1957) 'Shifters, verbal categories, and the Russian verb', in *Selected*

Writings, vol. II, *Word and Language*, The Hague: Mouton, 1971, pp. 130–47.

——(1960) 'Linguistics and poetics', in *Selected Writings*, vol. III, *Poetry of Grammar and Grammar of Poetry*, The Hague: Mouton, 1981, pp. 18–51.

Jay, Martin (1993) *Downcast Eyes: Denigration of Vision in Twentieth-Century French Thought*, Berkeley: University of California Press.

Jones, Ernest (1927) 'Early Development of Female Sexuality' in *Papers on Psychoanalysis* (5th edn), Baltimore: Williams & Wilkins, 1948.

——(1953–7) *Sigmund Freud: Life and Work*, 3 vols, London: Hogarth Press.

Juranville, Alain (1984) *Lacan et la philosophie*, Paris: Presses universitaires de France.

Kauftman, Phillipe (ed.) (1994) *L'apport freudien*, Paris: Bordas.

Klein, Melanie (1930) 'The importance of symbol-formation in the development of the ego', in Roger Money-Kyrle (ed.), *The Writings of Melanie Klein*, London: Hogarth Press and the Institute of Psycho-Analysis, 1975, vol. 1, pp. 219–32.

Kris, Ernst (1951) 'Ego-psychology and interpretation in psychoanalytic therapy', *Psychoanalytic Quarterly*, vol. 20: 15–30.

Kojève, Alexandre (1947 [1933–39]) *Introduction to the Reading of Hegel*, trans. James H. Nichols Jr., New York and London: Basic Books, 1969.

Lacan, Jacques (1932) *De la psychose paranoiaque dans ses rapports avec la personalité*, Paris: Seuil, 1975.

——(1936) 'Au-delà du "principe de realité"', in Jacques Lacan, *Écrits*, Paris: Seuil, 1966, pp. 73–92.

——(1938) *Les complexes familiaux dans la formation de l'individu. Essai d'analyse d'une fonction en psychologie*, Paris: Navarin, 1984.

——(1945) 'Le temps logique', in Jacques Lacan, *Écrits*, Paris: Seuil, 1966, pp. 197–213.

——(1946) 'Propos sur la causalité psychique', in Jacques Lacan, *Écrits*, Paris: Seuil, 1966, pp. 151–93.

——(1948) 'L'agressivité en psychanalyse', in Jacques Lacan, *Écrits*, Paris: Seuil, 1966, pp. 101–24 ['Aggressivity in psychoanalysis', trans. Alan Sheridan, in Jacques Lacan, *Écrits: A Selection*, London: Tavistock, 1977, pp. 8–29].

——(1949) 'Le stade du miroir comme formateur de la fonction du Je', in Jacques Lacan, *Écrits*, Paris: Seuil, 1966, pp. 93–100 ['The mirror stage as formative of the function of the I', trans. Alan Sheridan, in Jacques Lacan, *Ecrits: A Selection*, London: Tavistock, 1977, pp. 1–7].

——(1950) 'Introduction théorique aux fonctions de la psychanalyse en criminologie', in Jacques Lacan, *Écrits*, Paris: Seuil, 1966, pp. 125–49.

——(1951a) 'Intervention sur le transfert', in Jacques Lacan, *Écrits*, Paris: Seuil, 1966, pp. 215–26 ['Intervention on the transference', trans. Jacqueline Rose, in Juliet Mitchell and Jacqueline Rose (eds), *Feminine Sexuality:*

Jacques Lacan and the école freudienne, London: Macmillan, 1982, pp. 61–73].

———(1951b) 'Some reflections on the ego', *Int. J. Psycho-Anal.*, vol. 34, 1953: pp. 11–17.

———(1953a) 'Fonction et champ de la parole et du langage en psychanalyse', in Jacques Lacan, *Écrits*, Paris: Seuil, 1966, pp. 237–322 ['The function and field of speech and language in psychoanalysis', trans. Alan Sheridan, in Jacques Lacan, *Écrits: A Selection*, London: Tavistock, 1977, pp. 30–113].

———(1953b) 'The neurotic's individual myth', trans. Martha Evans, in L. Spurling (ed.), *Sigmund Freud: Critical Assessments*, vol. II, *The Theory and Practice of Psychoanalysis*, London and New York: Routledge, 1989, pp. 223–38. [Originally published in *Psychoanalytic Quarterly*, 48 (1979)].

———(1953–4) *Le Séminaire. Livre I. Les écrits techniques de Freud, 1953–4*, ed. Jacques-Alain Miller, Paris: Seuil, 1975 [*The Seminar. Book I. Freud's Papers on Technique. 1953–4*, trans. John Forrester, with notes by John Forrester, Cambridge: Cambridge University Press, 1987].

———(1954a) 'Introduction aux commentaire de Jean Hyppolite sur la "Verneinung" de Freud', in Jacques Lacan, *Écrits*, Paris: Seuil, 1966, pp. 369–80.

———(1954b) 'Réponse aux commentaire de Jean Hyppolite sur la "Verneinung" de Freud', in Jacques Lacan, *Écrits*, Paris: Seuil, 1966, pp. 381–99.

———(1954–5) *Le Séminaire. Livre II. Le moi dans la théorie de Freud et dans la technique de la psychanalyse, 1954–55*, ed. Jacques-Alain Miller, Paris: Seuil, 1978 [*The Seminar. Book II. The Ego in Freud's Theory and in the Technique of Psychoanalysis, 1954–55*, trans. Sylvana Tomaselli, notes by John Forrester, Cambridge: Cambridge University Press, 1988].

———(1955a) 'Le séminaire sur "La lettre volée"', in Jacques Lacan, *Écrits*, Paris: Seuil, 1966, pp. 11–61 ['Seminar on "The Purloined Letter"', trans. Jeffrey Mehlman, *Yale French Studies*, 48 (1972): 38–72, reprinted in John Muller and William Richardson (eds), *The Purloined Poe. Lacan, Derrida and Psychoanalytic Reading*, Baltimore: Johns Hopkins University Press, 1988, pp. 28–54].

———(1955b) 'Variantes de la cure-type', in Jacques Lacan, *Écrits*, Paris: Seuil, 1966, pp. 323–62.

———(1955c) 'La chose freudienne', in Jacques Lacan, *Écrits*, Paris: Seuil, 1966, pp. 401–36 ['The Freudian thing', trans. Alan Sheridan, in Jacques Lacan, *Ecrits: A Selection*, London: Tavistock, 1977, pp. 114–45].

———(1955–6) *Le Séminaire. Livre III. Les psychoses, 1955–56*, ed. Jacques-Alain Miller, Paris: Seuil, 1981 [*The Seminar. Book III. The Psychoses, 1955–56*, trans. Russell Grigg, with notes by Russell Grigg, London: Routledge, 1993].

————(1956a) 'Situation de la psychanalyse et formation du psychanalyste en 1956', in Jacques Lacan, *Écrits*, Paris: Seuil, 1966, pp. 459–91.

————(1956b) 'Fetishism: the symbolic, the imaginary and the real' (with W. Granoff), in M. Balint (ed.), *Perversions: Psychodynamics and Therapy*, New York: Random House, London: Tavistock, pp. 265–76.

————(1956–7) *Le Séminaire. Livre IV. La relation d'objet, 1956–57*, ed. Jacques-Alain Miller, Paris: Seuil, 1994.

————(1957a) 'La psychanalyse et son enseignement', in Jacques Lacan, *Écrits*, Paris: Seuil, 1966, pp. 437–58.

————(1957b) 'L'instance de la lettre dans l'inconscient ou la raison depuis Freud', in Jacques Lacan, *Écrits*, Paris: Seuil, 1966, pp. 493–528 ['The agency of the letter in the unconscious or reason since Freud', trans. Alan Sheridan, in Jacques Lacan, *Ecrits: A Selection*, London: Tavistock, 1977, pp. 146–78].

————(1957–8a) *Le Séminaire. Livre V. Les formations de l'inconscient, 1957–58*, unpublished [partial summary by Jean-Bertrand Pontalis in *Bulletin de Psychologie*, XII/2–3, November 1958, pp. 182–92 and XII/4, December 1958, pp. 250–6].

————(1957–8b) 'D'une question préliminaire à tout traitement possible de la psychose', in Jacques Lacan, *Écrits*, Paris: Seuil, 1966, pp. 531–83 ['On a question preliminary to any possible treatment of psychosis', trans. Alan Sheridan, in Jacques Lacan, *Ecrits: A Selection*, London: Tavistock, 1977, pp. 179–225].

————(1958a) 'La direction de la cure et les principes de son pouvoir', in Jacques Lacan, *Écrits*, Paris: Seuil, 1966, pp. 585–645 ['The direction of the treatment and the principles of its power', trans. Alan Sheridan, in Jacques Lacan, *Écrits: A Selection*, London: Tavistock, 1977, pp. 226–80].

————(1958b) 'Jeunesse de Gide ou la lettre et le désir', in Jacques Lacan, *Écrits*, Paris: Seuil, 1966, pp. 739–64.

————(1958c) 'La signification du phallus', in Jacques Lacan, *Écrits*, Paris: Seuil, 1966, pp. 685–95 ['The signification of the phallus', trans. Alan Sheridan, in Jacques Lacan, *Écrits: A Selection*, London: Tavistock, 1977, pp. 281–91].

————(1958d) 'Propos directifs pour un congrès sur la sexualité féminine', in Jacques Lacan, *Écrits*, Paris: Seuil, 1966, pp. 725–36 ['Guiding remarks for a congress on feminine sexuality', trans. Jacqueline Rose, in Juliet Mitchell and Jacqueline Rose (eds), *Feminine Sexuality: Jacques Lacan and the école freudienne*, London: Macmillan, 1982, pp. 86–98].

————(1958–9) *Le Séminaire. Livre VI. Le désir et son interprétation,1958–59*, published in part in *Ornicar?*, 24–27, 1981–83 ['Desire and the Interpretation of Desire in *Hamlet*', trans. James Hulbert, *Yale French Studies*, vol. 55/6, 1977: 11–52].

————(1959) 'A la mémoire d'Ernest Jones: sur sa théorie du symbolisme', in Jacques Lacan, *Écrits*, Paris: Seuil, 1966, pp. 697–717.

BIBLIOGRAPHY

————(1959–60) *Le Séminaire. Livre VII. L'éthique de la psychanalyse, 1959–60*, ed. Jacques-Alain Miller, Paris: Seuil, 1986 [*The Seminar. Book VII. The Ethics of Psychoanalysis, 1959–60*, trans. Dennis Porter, with notes by Dennis Porter, London: Routledge, 1992].

————(1960a) 'Subversion du sujet et dialectique du désir dans l'inconscient freudien', in Jacques Lacan, *Écrits*, Paris: Seuil, 1966, pp. 793–827 ['The subversion of the subject and the dialectic of desire in the Freudian unconscious', trans. Alan Sheridan, in Jacques Lacan, *Ecrits: A Selection*, London: Tavistock, 1977, pp. 292–325].

————(1960b) 'Remarque sur la rapport de Daniel Lagache: "Psychanalyse et structure de la personalité"', in Jacques Lacan, *Écrits*, Paris: Seuil, 1966, pp. 647–84.

————(1960–1) *Le Séminaire. Livre VIII. Le transfert, 1960–61*, ed. Jaques-Alain Miller, Paris: Seuil, 1991.

————(1961–2) *Le Séminaire. Livre IX. L'identification, 1961–62*, unpublished.

————(1962) 'Kant avec Sade', in Jacques Lacan, *Écrits*, Paris: Seuil, 1966, pp. 765–90 ['Kant with Sade', trans. James B. Swenson Jr, *October*, no. 51, winter 1989, pp. 55–75].

————(1962–3) *Le Séminaire. Livre X. L'angoisse, 1962–63*, unpublished.

————(1964a) *Le Séminaire. Livre XI. Les quatre concepts fondamentaux de la psychanalyse, 1964*, ed. Jacques-Alain Miller, Paris: Seuil, 1973 [*The Seminar. Book XI. The Four Fundamental Concepts of Psychoanalysis*, trans. Alan Sheridan, London: Hogarth Press and the Institute of Psycho-Analysis, 1977].

————(1964b) 'Acte de fondation', *Annuaire de l'École Freudienne de Paris*, Paris: Les presses artistiques, 1977.

————(1964c) 'Position de l'inconscient', in Jacques Lacan, *Écrits*, Paris: Seuil, 1966, pp. 829–50.

————(1964d) 'Du "Trieb" de Freud et du désir du psychanalyste', in Jacques Lacan, *Écrits*, Paris: Seuil, 1966, pp. 851–4.

————(1964–5) *Le Séminaire. Livre XII. Problèmes cruciaux pour la psychanalyse, 1964–65*, unpublished.

————(1965a) 'La science et la vérité', in Jacques Lacan, *Écrits*, Paris: Seuil, 1966, pp. 855–77.

————(1965b) 'Hommage fait à Marguérite Duras, du ravissement de Lol V. Stein', *Ornicar?*, no. 36, 1986.

————(1965–6) *Le Séminaire. Livre XIII. L'objet de la psychanalyse, 1965–66*, unpublished.

————(1966a) 'Of structure as an inmixing of an otherness prerequisite to any subject whatever', in Richard Macksey and Eugenio Donato (eds), *The Structuralist Controversy*, Baltimore and London: Johns Hopkins University Press, 1970: 186–200.

———(1966b) 'Ouverture de ce recueil', in Jacques Lacan, *Écrits*, Paris: Seuil, 1966, pp. 9–10.

———(1966c) 'De nos antécédents', in Jacques Lacan, *Écrits*, Paris: Seuil, 1966, pp. 65–72.

———(1966d) 'Du sujet enfin en question', in Jacques Lacan, *Écrits*, Paris: Seuil, 1966, pp. 229–36.

———(1966e) 'D'un dessein', in Jacques Lacan, *Écrits*, Paris: Seuil, 1966, pp. 363–7.

———(1966f) 'D'un syllabaire après coup', in Jacques Lacan, *Écrits*, Paris: Seuil, 1966, pp. 717–24.

———(1966–7) *Le Séminaire. Livre XIV. La logique du fantasme, 1966–67*, unpublished.

———(1967) 'Proposition du 9 octobre 1967 sur le psychanalyste de l'École', *Scilicet*, no. 1 (1968) pp. 14–30.

———(1967–8) *Le Séminaire. Livre XV. L'acte psychanalytique, 1967–68*, unpublished.

———(1968–9) *Le Séminaire. Livre XVI. D'un Autre à l'autre, 1968–69*, unpublished.

———(1969–70) *Le Séminaire. Livre XVII. L'envers de la psychanalyse, 1969–70*, ed. Jacques-Alain Miller, Paris: Seuil, 1991.

———(1970) 'Radiophonie', *Scilicet*, nos 2–3, 1970.

———(1970–1) *Le Séminaire. Livre XVIII. D'un discours qui ne serait pas du semblant, 1970–71*, unpublished.

———(1971) 'Lituraterre', *Littérature*, no. 3, p. 3.

———(1971–2a) *Le Séminaire. Livre XIX. . . . Ou pire, 1971–72*, unpublished.

———(1971–2b) *Le savoir du psychanalyste*, lectures given in the Hospital of Sainte Anne, 1971–72, unpublished.

———(1972–3) *Le Séminaire. Livre XX. Encore, 1962–63*, ed. Jacques-Alain Miller, Paris: Seuil, 1975.

———(1973a) *Télévision*, Paris: Seuil, 1973 [*Television: A Challenge to the Psychoanalytic Establishment*, ed. Joan Copjec, trans. Denis Hollier, Rosalind Krauss and Annette Michelson, New York: Norton, 1990].

———(1973b) 'L'Étourdit', *Scilicet*, no. 4, 1973, pp. 5–52.

———(1973–4) *Le Séminaire. Livre XXI. Les non-dupes errent/Les noms du père, 1973–74*, unpublished.

———(1974–5) *Le Séminaire. Livre XXII. RSI, 1974–75*, published in *Ornicar?*, nos. 2–5, 1975.

———(1975a) 'Joyce le symptôme', in Jacques Aubert (ed.), *Joyce avec Lacan*, Paris: Navarin, 1987.

———(1975b) 'Conférence à Genève sur le symptôme', *Les Block-Notes de la psychanalyse*, Brussels.

———(1975–6) *Le Séminaire. Livre XXIII. Le sinthome, 1975–76*, published in *Ornicar?*, nos 6–11, 1976–7.

————(1976) 'Conférences et entretiens dans des universités nord-américaines', *Scilicet*, nos 6–7, 1976.

————(1976–7) *Le Séminaire. Livre XXIV. L'insu que sait de l'une bévue s'aile à mourre, 1976–77*, published in *Ornicar?*, nos 12–18, 1977–9.

————(1977–8) *Le Séminaire. Livre XXV. Le moment de conclure, 1977–78*, published in part in *Ornicar?*, no. 19, 1979.

————(1978–9) *Le Séminaire. Livre XXVI. Le topologie et le temps, 1978–79*, unpublished.

————(1980a) *Le Séminaire. Livre XXVII. Dissolution, 1980*, published in *Ornicar?*, nos 20–23, 1980–1.

————(1980b) 'Séminaire de Caracas', *L'Ane*, no. 1, July 1981.

Lacoue-Labarthe, Philippe, and Nancy, Jean-Luc (1973) *Le Titre de la lettre*, Paris: Galilée.

Laplanche, Jean and Pontalis, Jean-Bertrand (1967) *The Language of Psycho-Analysis*, trans. Donald Nicholson-Smith, London: Hogarth Press and the Institute of Psycho-Analysis, 1973.

Leader, Darien (with Judith Groves) (1995) *Lacan for Beginners*, Cambridge: Icon.

————(1996) *Why Do Women Write More Letters than they Post?*, London: Faber & Faber.

Lemaire, Anika (1970) *Jacques Lacan*, trans. David Macey, London: Routledge & Kegan Paul, 1977.

Lévi-Strauss, Claude (1945) 'Structural analysis in linguistics and in anthropology', in *Structural Anthropology*, trans. Claire Jacobson and Brooke Grundfest Schoepf, New York: Basic Books, 1963, pp. 29–53.

————(1949a) 'The effectiveness of symbols', in *Structural Anthropology*, trans. Claire Jacobson and Brooke Grundfest Schoepf, New York: Basic Books, 1963, pp. 186–205.

————(1949b) *The Elementary Structures of Kinship*, Boston: Beacon Press, 1969.

————(1950) 'Introduction à l'œuvre de Marcel Mauss', in Marcel Mauss, *Sociologie et Anthropologie*, Paris: Presses Universitaires de France, 1966, pp. ix–lii.

————(1951) 'Language and the analysis of social laws', in *Structural Anthropology*, trans. Claire Jacobson and Brooke Grundfest Schoepf, New York: Basic Books, 1963, pp. 55–66.

————(1955) 'The structural study of myth', in *Structural Anthropology*, trans. Claire Jacobson and Brooke Grundfest Schoepf, New York: Basic Books, 1963, pp. 206–31.

MacCannell, Juliet Flower (1986) *Figuring Lacan. Criticism and the Cultural Unconscious*, London: Croom Helm.

Macey, David (1988) *Lacan in Contexts*, London and New York: Verso.

————(1995) 'On the subject of Lacan', in Anthony Elliott and Stephen Frosh (eds), *Psychoanalysis in Contexts: Paths between Theory and Modern Culture*, London and New York: Routledge, 1995, pp. 72–86.

Mauss, Marcel (1923) *The Form and Reason for Exchange in Archaic Societies*, trans. W. D. Halls, with foreword by Mary Douglas, London and New York: Routledge, 1990.

Metz, Christian (1975) *The Imaginary Signifier: Psychoanalysis and the Cinema*, trans. Annwyl Williams, Ben Brewster and Alfred Guzetti, Bloomington: Indiana University Press, 1977.

Meyerson, Émile (1925) *La déduction relativiste*, Paris: Payot.

Miller, Jacques-Alain (1977) 'Introduction aux paradoxes de la passé', *Ornicar?*, nos 12–13.

———(1981) 'Encyclopédie', *Ornicar?*, no. 21: 35–44.

———(1985) *Entretien sur le Séminaire*, avec François Ansermet, Paris: Navarin.

———(1987) 'Préface' in Jacques Aubert (ed.) *Joyce avec Lacan*, Paris, Navarin.

Mitchell, Juliet and Rose, Jacqueline (eds) (1982) *Feminine Sexuality: Jacques Lacan and the école freudienne*, London: Macmillan.

Muller, John and Richardson, William (1982) *Lacan and Language: A Reader's Guide to Écrits*, New York: International Universities Press.

———(eds) (1988) *The Purloined Poe. Lacan, Derrida and Psychoanalytic Reading*. Baltimore: Johns Hopkins University Press.

Mulvey, Laura (1975) 'Visual pleasure and narrative cinema', *Visual and Other Pleasures*, Bloomington: Indiana University Press, pp. 14–26.

Nietzsche, Friedrich (1886) *Beyond Good and Evil*, trans. R. J. Hollingdale, Harmondsworth: Penguin, 1990.

Peirce, Charles S. (1932) *Collected Papers of Charles Sanders Peirce*, vol. II, *Elements of Logic*, Cambridge, Mass: Harvard University Press.

Poe, Edgar Allan (1844) 'The Purloined Letter', in *Great Tales and Poems of Edgar Allan Poe*, New York: Pocket Library, 1951.

Ragland-Sullivan, Ellie (1986) *Jacques Lacan and the Philosophy of Psychoanalysis*, London and Chicago: Croom Helm and the University of Illinois Press.

Rivière, Joan (1929) 'Womanliness as mascarade', *Int. J. Psycho-Anal.*, 10: 303–13.

Rose, Jacqueline (1986) *Sexuality in the Field of Vision*, London: Verso.

Roudinesco, Elisabeth (1986) *Jacques Lacan & Co.: A History of Psychoanalysis in France, 1925–1985*, trans. Jeffrey Mehlman, London: Free Association Books, 1990.

———(1993) *Jacques Lacan, esquisse d'une vie, histoire d'un système de pensée*, Paris: Fayard.

Roustang, François (1986) *The Lacanian Delusion*, trans. Greg Sims, Oxford: Oxford University Press, 1990.

BIBLIOGRAPHY

Rycroft, Charles (1968) *A Critical Dictionary of Psychoanalysis*, Harmondsworth: Penguin, 1972.

Sade, Marquis de (1797) *Juliette*, trans. Austryn Wainhouse, New York: Grove Press, 1968.

Saint-Drôme, Oreste (1994) *Dictionnaire inespéré de 55 termes visités par Jacques Lacan*, Paris: Seuil.

Samuels, Andrew, Shorter, Bani and Plant, Fred (1986) *A Critical Dictionary of Jungian Analysis*, London and New York: Routledge.

Samuels, Robert (1993) *Between Philosophy and Psychoanalysis. Lacan's Reconstruction of Freud*, London and New York: Routledge.

Sartre, Jean-Paul (1943) *Being and Nothingness: An Essay on Phenomenological Ontology*, trans. Hazel E. Barnes, London: Methuen, 1958.

Sarup, Madan (1992) *Jacques Lacan*, Hemel Hempstead: Harvester Wheatsheaf.

Saussure, Ferdinand de (1916) *Course in General Linguistics*, ed. Charles Bally and Albert Sechehaye, trans. Wade Baskin, Glasgow: Collins Fontana.

Schneiderman, Stuart (1980) *Returning to Freud: Clinical Psychoanalysis in the School of Lacan*, New Haven and London: Yale University Press.

——(1983) *Jacques Lacan: The Death of an Intellectual Hero*, Cambridge, Mass. and London: Harvard University Press.

Sheridan, Alan (1977) 'Translator's note', in Jacques Lacan, *Écrits: A Selection*, trans. Alan Sheridan, London: Tavistock, pp. vii–xii.

Spinoza, Baruch (1677) *Ethics*, trans. A. Boyle, London: Dent, 1910.

Strachey, James (1934) 'The nature of the therapeutic action of psychoanalysis', *Int. J. Psycho-Anal.*, vol. 15: 126–59.

Turkle, Sherry (1978) *Psychoanalytic Politics: Freud's French Revolution*, New York: Basic Books.

Wilden, Anthony (ed.) (1968) *The Language of the Self: The Function of Language in Psychoanalysis*, Baltimore and London: Johns Hopkins University Press.

Wright, Elizabeth (1984) *Psychoanalytic Criticism: Theory in Practice*, London: Methuen.

——(ed.) (1992) *Feminism and Psychoanalysis: A Critical Dictionary*, Oxford: Blackwell.

Žižek, Slavoj (1991) *Looking Awry: An Introduction to Jacques Lacan through Popular Culture*, Cambridge, Mass: MIT Press.

Index of terms